HUDSON AREA ASSOCIATION LIBRARY
W9-BZB-106

THE
Brewmaster's Table

For Rich, Tim, and Ed,
Cheers!

THE Brewmaster's Table

Discovering the Pleasures of Real Beer with Real Food

Garrett Oliver

WITH PHOTOGRAPHS BY **Denton Tillman**

ecco

An Imprint of HarperCollins*Publishers*

 For information address HarperCollins Publishers Inc., 10 East 53rd Street, New York, NY 10022.

HarperCollins books may be purchased for educational, business, or sales promotional use. For information please write: Special Markets Department, HarperCollins Publishers Inc., 10 East 53rd Street, New York, NY 10022.

FIRST EDITION

Design by Douglas Riccardi and David Jacobson, Memo Productions, Inc.

Except as credited otherwise, photographs are ©2003 by Denton Tillman.

Library of Congress Cataloging-in-Publication Data

Oliver, Garrett.
The brewmaster's table: discovering the pleasures of real beer with real food / Garrett Oliver; photographs by Denton Tillman.
p. cm.
ISBN 0-06-000570-X
1. Beer. 2. Brewing. I. Title.
TP577 .055 2003
641.2′3—dc21 2002035245

03 04 05 06 07 ❖/QF 10 9 8 7 6 5 4 3 2 1

Contents

Acknowledgments

Since graduating from college nearly twenty years ago, I had forgotten how terrifying a blank page can be. In the past year I became reacquainted with that terror. A great many people have helped me banish my fears and turn an idea into a book.

I'd like to thank Steve Hindy, Tom Potter, Eric Ottaway, and all my other colleagues at the Brooklyn Brewery for encouraging and sharing my vision of brewing great beer. I feel fortunate to be working with such interesting, dynamic, smart, fun people. My unflappable brewhouse team, Andrew Ety, Tom Villa, and Seth Bruning, have held down the fort, brewing our beer while I've been hunched over my computer. If they ever stop making fun of me, I'll know I'm in trouble.

My first agent, Melissa Rosati, was instrumental in helping me collect my thoughts into a format that made sense. Her boundless enthusiasm made me believe that I could write this book. When Melissa left for Europe, she handed me off to Richard Curtis, and he took on her vision, encouraging and advising me through the whole publishing process. I met my editor, Dan Halpern, at a party and again a few weeks later at Gramercy Tavern. We were meant to work together. I've enjoyed his quick wit, his incisive analysis, and his innate sense of what this book should be. When people ask who my editor is and I tell them that it's Dan, they always tell me that I'm lucky. They're right. Thanks also to Patricia Fernandez and Gheña Glijansky, who did a lot of the heavy lifting to guide a neophyte author through production.

Thanks to my photographer, Denny Tillman, whose work has made this book beautiful. We spent weeks dashing across Europe, capturing wonderful images of great breweries. It's been a true adventure, and I promise him that I'll learn to drive a stick shift very soon.

The groundbreaking beer writer Michael Jackson has been a breeze in my sails for more than a decade, helping me in large ways and small. I would not presume to call him a mentor, but I'm glad to call him a friend. Larry Lustig gave me my first homebrewing kit. John Mided took me to the pub. Mark Witty taught me how to brew English ales and Mark Dorber taught me how to appreciate them. Roger Protz and his colleagues at the Campaign for Real Ale welcomed me into an international community of brewers. Charlie Papazian has built an American community of brewers. Every morning, I wake up happy to be a brewmaster; these people built the road that I'm traveling.

This book originally contained recipes from some of the best chefs in the country, but it was decided that the recipes would have to wait for a later book. My heartfelt thanks to Michael Romano, Mario Batali, Alice Waters, Waldy Malouf, Rick Moonen, Barbara Lynch, Floyd Cardoz, Fortunato Nicotra, Greg Higgins, Barbara Sibley, Rick Bayless, Vincent Sacré, and Norman Van Aken for their contributions to this project. Thanks also to Felidia Ristorante, La Palapa, and James Rodewald for helping me with my research. Danny Meyer and his merry band at Gramercy Tavern and Blue Smoke have been wonderful at every turn. The learned sommeliers Paul Grieco, Richard Luftig, and Kevin Mahan have taught me the wonders of wine while teaching their customers the wonders of beer.

Thanks to the people at the breweries Denny and I visited, especially Fuller's, Young's, Greene King, J. W. Lees, Harveys, Boon, Lindemans, Rodenbach, De Koninck, Chimay, Westmalle, Orval, Rochefort, Kaltenberg, Schneider, Ayinger, Heller-Trum, and the Weyermann Maltings. Thanks to *Gourmet* magazine, Briess Maltings, Cargill Maltings, HopUnion, Tuller Fine Foods, Wendy Littlefield, the Ägyptisches Museum in Berlin, John Larson, Merchant du Vin, and B. United International for helping with images and more.

Finally, my thanks to the worldwide community of artisan brewers who have shunned the path of easy commercialism to create small works of art that we can enjoy every day. It's a privilege to know them and to have their beers at my dinner table.

For

JOYCE THURSTON OLIVER

and for

ALEXANDER SIDNEY OLIVER (1931–2003)

who've given me everything I'll ever need

Introduction

It seems impossible to me now, but it's been twenty years since I discovered the joys of real beer. It was a discovery that completely changed my life. With college degree in one hand and duffel bag in the other, I was fresh off a plane to London from New York, and I was feeling a bit shaky. I'd been overseas only once before, and now I planned to live in London for an entire year. It was a cool September day, and despite the fact that it was still morning, my situation seemed to call for a beer. I made my way to a rundown, shaggy-looking place tucked behind Victoria Station, where I was sure a beer would be waiting for me. As far as I was concerned, the place had charm—carpeting, plush chairs, beer, and a barkeep with a British accent. What was not to like? I ordered a pint. With two long pulls of the tap, liquid flowed into the glass. The barkeep handed me something that looked like a dimpled fishbowl with a handle, brimming with maple syrup. I paid him with the Monopoly money I'd picked up at the airport and moved to stretch out on a couch.

The first sip was odd. This beer hardly had a head, just a loose lace of bubbles around the rim of the glass. As I started to drink it, I wondered, "What is this stuff?" The bitterness ran across my tongue, assisted by only the faintest prickle of carbonation. Then it exploded in layers of flavor—hay, earth, newly mowed grass, orange marmalade, and baking bread. It wasn't even cold—in fact, it was barely cool. Each sip seemed to reveal something new—a whiff of sea air, a different flower or fruit. Did I like it? I wasn't sure. But it was so interesting that I couldn't stop drinking it. Then my glass was empty. The beer was all gone, and I missed it already. With that, I stepped outside into the cool mist and went to look for someplace to live.

Little did I know that my beer odyssey had begun. As fall turned into winter, and winter into a foggy, damp spring, I sampled hundreds of pints of what the British call "real ale." Real ale and the homeyness of the pub were my personal windows into Britain and what made it a different place from the States. Beer was always the first topic of conversation in the pub, and we chose our pubs for how well they kept their casks. "The pint's spot-on tonight" meant we were staying for the evening, and a round of "tired pints" meant we were out the door. Bad music was one thing—bad pints were intolerable.

After my year in England, I bought a European rail pass. Through my travels I discovered people who really understood how to live. Pleasure wasn't just a reward for a job well done. Pleasure was nothing less than the goal of a life well lived. Wherever people were laughing and eating and drinking, I found great beer and great food together—it never occurred to me that anyone would want to separate them.

When I got to Paris, I imagined that the city would be full of wine snobs, but far from it. The Parisians were drinking earthy, spicy Jenlain farmhouse ale with their garlicky Toulouse sausages. The beer in England had been terrific, but the food—well, let's just say it had a long way to go. Those French sausages were the best food I'd had in months, exploding with hot garlic and the unmistakable flavor of great pork. The yeasty, anise-like flavor of the beer blended perfectly; it was impossible to imagine eating these sausages with anything else. As an added bonus for me, the French beers matched their great cheeses. Paris was expensive and I didn't have much money, but a baguette and a hunk of cheese made an affordable meal. Accompanied by farmhouse ale, these humble meals were rich in the simple pleasures of life in France.

In beautiful Bruges, the Belgian "Venice of the north," everyone I met cooked with beer. In Belgium, great beer is everywhere and in everything. Naturally, I fell in love with the place. Chicken waterzooi—a stewed chicken cooked in a beer-based stock—was as ubiquitous in Bruges as bagels are in New York. It was full of onions and bay leaves, shredded carrot and cabbage, a touch of cream, and the distinctive flavor of beer. Underneath it all, a whole chicken leg, the meat falling from the bone. The Belgian beer was an even bigger surprise. Gueuze beer, pale and hazy, was tart, acidic, and as funky as Roquefort cheese. Flavors of yeast and hay, lemon peels, and damp wool mingled with the sharpness of the onions and married the beer in the stock—the combination was wonderful. The locals nodded their approval and told me that this was the only beer in the world still brewed the way it had been thousands of years ago. No yeast was added, they said—the fermentation started by itself. In Pieter Brueghel the Elder's paintings, they said, everyone was drinking gueuze. Everywhere I looked, I could see the intense pride people had in this prehistoric throwback of a beer.

The people of Amsterdam were relaxed and breezy. At the same time, I detected a faint smugness; but then, if I lived on a beautiful canal and had a barge with a living room set on the deck, I would feel smug, too. Not only was the beer cloudy, it was the palest beer I'd ever seen. I ordered one at a canalside café. The beer was called witbier, meaning "white beer," and tasted like summer. It was bright and citrusy, with a spicy aroma and an amazingly refreshing, slightly tart spritz on the palate. My sandwich came to the table, an open-faced ciabatta roll topped with grilled salmon and Gouda cheese. The beer's bright acidity was like a squeeze of lemon on the salmon and sliced right through the cheese. The combination filled my senses—it was so magical that I was almost overwhelmed by the interplay of flavors. The beer, the salmon, and the sunshine bouncing off the water … I started to seriously consider moving to Amsterdam.

Instead, however, I came back to the States. And there was *nothing to drink*.

Store shelves had been stocked with only a few brands of identical mass-market American yellow fizz before I left for Europe, and they were still stocked with the same beers. But I had changed—I couldn't drink this stuff anymore. What was I going to do? I did the only thing I could think of—I started to brew real beer in my kitchen. It was the first step onto a long, slippery slope. Eventually, I lost my grip. My college degree said that I was a filmmaker, but I was now destined to become a brewmaster. I've never looked back.

My problem with returning to the United States wasn't just the beer, though—it was everything. Back then, our supermarket shelves were dominated by frozen vegetables, Wonder Bread, pasteurized processed "cheese food," and freeze-dried coffee. It was a pretty bleak scene for anyone who wanted to eat well.

Well, the dark ages are finally over. Salsa has eclipsed ketchup as America's favorite condiment, and those same supermarket shelves are packed with a beguiling variety of breads, olive oils, artisanal cheeses, aged hams, fresh vegetables and herbs, spices, real coffee, chili peppers, and flavorful traditionally brewed beers. When it comes to cuisine, the United States has quickly become the most exciting place in the world.

Traditional beer is the new star with the international cuisines that we are all eating today. Real beer can do amazing things with food, and it goes places where wine cannot go. Don't get me wrong—I love wine. I've spent some of the most pleasurable days of my life in Piemontese wine country, sipping terrific old Barolos over languorous four-hour lunches. I've marveled at magnificently aromatic German Rieslings. Wine is wonderful. But let's be honest—it can't do everything.

Real beer *can* do everything. Mexican, Thai, Japanese, Indian, Cajun, and Middle Eastern food, and barbecue, are far better with real beer than with wine.

Even with traditionally wine-friendly foods, beer often shows superior versatility and flavor compatibility. The range of flavors and aromas in beer is vast—it's deep and wide and tall, and it easily surpasses that of wine. Beer has bitterness to slice through fat, carbonation to refresh the palate, caramelized flavors to match those in your food, and sweetness to quench the fire of chilies.

If you've tasted only mass-market beer, I'm afraid that you haven't actually tasted beer at all. Real beer can be imperial stout, matching your dessert with flavors as bold, chocolaty, and roasty as espresso, or it can be Belgian witbier, matching your fish dish with flavors as light and citrusy as fresh lemonade. It can be American pale ale, full of bright grapefruit and pine needle aromatics; or framboise, as fruity and sharp as a great sorbet. It can be a ten-year-old British barley wine, as warming, complex, thick, and unctuous as vintage port; or German weissbier, light, spritzy, and redolent of cloves and bananas. When paired with food, these flavorful beers can make a meal really sing. No matter how complex or refined the dish, whether it's foie gras or a simple sausage, there is a terrific beer out there that will provide a perfect accompaniment. If you love food, but you know only wine, then you're trying to write a symphony using only half the notes and half the orchestra. At Brooklyn Brewery, we enjoy eating well, brewing well, and drinking well. My colleagues and I love to cook, and in our cellars the world's greatest beers sit next to the best wines we can get our hands on. I've been a brewmaster for fourteen years now, and every day is still exciting, because I spend my days thinking about texture, flavor, aroma—and food.

I intend for this book to change your life in small but important ways. That sounds boastful, but it's the truth. I've hosted hundreds of beer tastings and dinners over the years, and not a week goes by when someone doesn't stop me on the street and thank me for introducing him or her to real beer. I'd love to take the credit, but it's not me—it's the beer. Great beer from around the world is now available everywhere, and, unlike wine, it's an affordable luxury. You can enjoy it literally every day. Once you discover traditional beer, your "food life" will be transformed into something fascinating, fun, and infinitely more enjoyable.

The Brewmaster's Table is a guide to traditional beer and its relationship with our history, our lives, and—most important—our food. Even in everyday life there is an art to eating, and eating should be a symphony, conducted with gusto. Welcome to a whole new world of fantastic flavors. You're going to have a great time. I hope you're ready for a feast.

MALT
ED KINGDOM
BAIRDS MA
UNITED KING

PART ONE:
The Basics

1

WHAT IS BEER?

WHEN PEOPLE ASK ME WHAT I DO FOR A LIVING, I REPLY THAT I AM A BREWMASTER.

I have to admit that I get a kick out of their reactions. Often they take a step or two back and look me over carefully, perhaps inspecting me for horns or a cloven foot. Might I turn them into newts? One thing hasn't changed much over the past 4,000 years—brewing has always been considered mysterious. Old documents incorporating medieval brewers' guilds mention the "mystery and art of brewing." There is little mystery to winemaking—after all, many of us made crude wine as a science project in elementary school. We all know what wine is, even those of us who never drink it. Do you know what beer is? Most people haven't the slightest clue. Even people who drink beer every day rarely know anything about where it came from, a fact that makes it unique as a food product. Before we delve into history, styles, flavors, and food matches, we need to have some idea what beer is and where it comes from. I don't carry a wand, but there are parts of the brewing process that still strike me as magical, even after all these years.

Wine is a simple beverage to produce. In order to make wine, one needs only grapes. Crush the grapes, and the natural yeast on the grape skins will start the fermentation; and pretty soon—voilà!—you'll have wine. In fact, if you have enough grapes, they'll actually crush themselves by their own weight—the winemaker doesn't even need to do that! Beer is not nearly so simple, and brewing is a far more complicated art than winemaking. I can already hear the bleats of protest from the wine folks, but I'm afraid it's true. Brewing, at the very simplest, requires barley malt, yeast, hops, and water. True, the vintner must tend, prune, and choose his grapes carefully, and then oversee a long process of vinification. The brewmaster, however, must choose among a dizzying array of malts, roasted grains, unmalted grains, sugars, dozens of varieties of hops, and hundreds of strains of yeast, and then cause these ingredients to create exactly what he has in mind. In many ways, the brewmaster is more like a chef than he is like a winemaker. If the beer turns out poorly, he cannot shrug his shoulders and claim it was a bad year. A fine beer is not a discovery or simply a part of nature, but a work of art: a product of pure intention and imagination.

Brewing is also hard work. There are no easy sun-filled days of dancing in woven baskets—you can dance on the barley all you want, but it has no juice to yield up. The brewer must work to loosen its grip on the essential ingredient—sugar. Anyone who seeks to create an alcoholic beverage must have sugar to ferment. Grapes have their own sugar, but barley is packed with starch, which must be converted into sugar in order to make beer. This process starts with the mash, where starches are converted into a sweet liquid called the wort (pronounced "wert"). The wort is collected in a kettle, where the bitterness, flavor, and aroma of the hops are extracted into the wort by boiling. The hopped wort is then chilled and sent into a fermentation vessel where yeast is added and works its wonders, transforming homely sweet wort into beer. Sounds simple, doesn't it? In some ways, it is. But then, so is a soufflé.

There are many details along the way that will determine how the beer will turn out. Join me now on a journey from grain to glass as we unlock the mystery and art of brewing. First, let's have a look at the ingredients. Every journey must begin with a single step; and when it comes to beer, that first step is malting the barley.

Barley may look soft, but its seeds are as hard as pebbles. Malting will soften them and develop enzymes needed for brewing.

Courtesy Cargill Malts and Washington Barley Commission.

Barley (*Hordeum vulgare*) is a tall, tawny-colored grass with a seed head on top of its stalk. A field of barley looks a lot like a wheat field. For the brewer, barley has special gifts that other grains cannot offer. Its hard husk, low protein content, and high starch content all make it a more suitable candidate for brewing than for baking. Barley grows in temperate climates around the world. Like many grains, it comes in a number of strains and varieties. And like many other agricultural food products, barley varieties have become largely homogenized over the years. Growers have sought to maximize their yields per acre and also to produce barleys with little depth of flavors for use in mass-market beers. There are, however, still many barley varieties that command respect and high prices for their rare depth of flavor, such as the old British varieties Maris Otter and Golden Promise. "Maritime" varieties, grown near the sea in England and Germany, are favored by some brewers, while others prefer flavors developed in the sunshine on the plains of the United States. The sweet, toffeeish flavor of German barley varieties is unmistakable, and German brewers combine them with special mashing techniques to create beers with unique malt flavors. The distinct character of the barley variety will find its way through the brewing and fermentation process and show itself in the finished beer. At one time, all breweries malted their own barley, but these days the job is usually done by professional "maltsters." At Brooklyn Brewery, I buy malt from the United States, England, Scotland, Canada, Belgium, and Germany. Buying malt this way is more expensive, but each of these malts has distinctive qualities it lends to our beer.

Malted barley, also known simply as malt, is barley seed that has been steeped in water until it starts to sprout, then dried out in a kiln. Unmalted barley is as hard as stone—try to eat it, and you risk breaking a tooth. Malting turns the starch inside the seed soft, white, powdery, and ready for brewing. The germination is traditionally carried out by spreading the barley several feet deep over a large concrete floor specially built for the purpose. Water is sprayed onto the barley, and the dormant seed wakes up—germination begins. The maltster must keep the seedbed cool and aerated, and he does this by sending rakes through the germinating seeds. This also keeps the seeds separate—they would otherwise become a tangled mass as their rootlets braided together. The raking would once have been done by hand, but today this is rare; mechanized raking systems are now the norm.

A barley seed is essentially like a little egg—an egg with a plan. The plan calls for the seed to develop enzymes to break down its starch into sugars, burn the sugars for energy, use that energy to grow leaves, and then start photosynthesis when the sugars are used up. The maltster has far loftier plans for the barley seed.

He must wait for exactly the right moment to act, because the seed is rapidly changing. About three days into the sprouting process, the starch in the seed has become soft and packed with natural enzymes. The malting room now has a strong green aroma, reminiscent of bean or alfalfa sprouts. Eat the barley now, and the starch will squish out between your teeth—it's become a paste. The acrospire—the part that will become the barley shoot—is starting to form. The seed has already sprouted little roots, and it's ready for action. Before the seed can carry out its plan, the maltster drains all the water out of the grain bed and puts the grain into a roasting drum to dry. Once the grain is dried, it's ready for its new mission. Now it is malt and destined for beer or perhaps Scotch whisky, which is simply a distilled form of beer.

Ah, but not so fast. What kind of malt is it? From the beginning of the malting process, differences in moisture content, barley variety, and kilning temperatures and times are crucial and result in different varieties of malt. Each variety has a flavor, a color, an aroma, and a purpose. This is where the brewer starts to design the beer, choosing the color and flavor components. Will the beer be golden? Then pilsner malt may be called for. A low kilning temperature results in a malt that can give a pale golden color and a slightly bready flavor. Will the beer be biscuity? Pale ale malt, kilned at slightly higher temperatures, will give a deeper color along with

This barley has sprouted roots but will never use them. It's now "green malt," headed for the kiln and then the brewhouse.

slightly toasty biscuit notes, prized in English ales. Vienna and Munich malts are stewed and then lightly kilned. This converts some of the starches into sugars, giving the beer an orangey amber color and the classic toffeeish, nutty flavors of Oktoberfest beers and other Bavarian specialties. Caramel and crystal malts are stewed until all their starches are converted into sugars; then they are kilned until the sugar caramelizes, leaving a little nugget of barley caramel under the husk. This sweet, caramel-flavored malt imparts a reddish-amber color, rich flavors, and a fuller body. Just as with coffee beans, higher kilning temperatures result in higher gradations of roast, resulting in chocolate, coffee, and finally espresso-like flavors. Carbonized black malts look and taste just like miniature coffee beans. It is here, in the malt, that beer derives some of its superior power to match foods. Wine cannot deliver truly caramelized or roasted flavors, but beer can and does. When these flavors link up with similar flavors in our food, magic can result.

This is starting to get complicated, and we're still on the first ingredient. In fact, when it comes to putting our recipe together, we've barely gotten started. For instance, the brewer may have decided to use pale ale malt as the base of his beer, but now he must choose which variety. Each maltster makes a different malt, and each malt will have different flavors and properties and therefore make different beers. Some beers are brewed from just one malt, but many are brewed from a blend of malts, with each malt adding a different quality to the beer. The artful blending of these malt flavors and colors forms the basis of a beer's character, and often of its affinities for foods. The toffeeish character of Munich malt marries the earthy gaminess of venison; the caramel flavors in crystal malt match the caramelization on the skin of a roasted free-range chicken; the cocoa flavors of chocolate malt blend seamlessly with your chocolate dessert. Maris Otter malt is prized for its round, juicy, deeply bready flavors, which can meld wonderfully with the flavors of red meats. By the way, if you want to know what malt tastes like, get yourself a box of Grape Nuts breakfast cereal. The wine guys must have great marketing people—there are no grapes in Grape Nuts. This cereal is made from barley malt and yeast. It's practically beer in a box.

Most people seem to know that beer contains hops. In fact, many people seem to think that hops are the main ingredient in beer—and that perhaps hops are a grain. Actually, the hop is a flower—and quite a flower it is. Not only does it lend natural preservative qualities to the finished beer, but it also provides bitterness and a range of flavors and aromas. Essentially, it acts as a spice. The bitterness of the hop is the backbone of the beer, balancing out the natural sweetness of the malt. At one time brewers used a variety of herbs and spices to achieve a similar balance. Their beers, containing such ingredients as bog myrtle, yarrow, myrrh, rosemary, wormwood, woodruff, ginger, and licorice, would be difficult for us to recognize today because those ingredients left the beer suffused with powerful herbal aromatics. These days, we're used to the flavor of hops in our beer.

The hop plant (*Humulus lupulus*) is a vigorous perennial vine (technically, it's actually a "bine," a closely related form of plant). Botanically, it is in the order Cannabicea and is the nearest relative to *Cannabis sativa*, also known as marijuana. In the 1940s and 1950s, jazz musicians who succumbed to "reefer madness" were called hopheads, but the hop got a bum rap—it does not induce the same effects. Still, the hop flower has often been used as a folk sedative; the English used to stuff pillows with it, and it is still the major ingredient of some "natural" sleep aids on the market. And anyone who is an aficionado of highly hopped beers can tell you that they are rather relaxing.

The hop vine can grow to be twenty feet or taller during a spring and summer growing season, after which it dies back to a woody crown under the soil in the autumn. To accommodate their natural climbing tendencies, hop plants are grown trained to poles or on trellises with wire supports for the vine. Hop plants are generally grown not from seed but from transplanted rootstock. Only the female plant is commercially cultivated. In the late summer and early autumn the hop vine flowers, resulting in a green "hop cone," shaped like a little pinecone. Inside the hop cone, at the base of the petals, are glands that produce a resinous bright yellow powder called lupulin. The lupulin contains all the goods the brewer is after, and the hops must be handled gently to avoid losing this delicate powder.

Imagine red wine without its tannins or white wine without its acidity, and you'll understand why beer needs hops. Hops won out over other spices because of their clean, sharp bitterness, as well as their preservative qualities. Without hops, beer would be a sweet, cloying, and ultimately less satisfying drink. Hops also contain tannins, which help settle proteins in the kettle, promoting clarity in the finished beer. The bitterness of the hop gives beer its balance, its thirst-quenching qualities, and part of its affinity for foods. This bitterness has a cutting power, clearing the palate of strong flavors. Hop aromatics link up with food aromatics to create powerful, dynamic bonds that can thrill the senses.

Hops are varietal, like wine grapes. There are dozens of varieties for the brewer to choose from, and the choices are critically important to the flavor of the beer. Just as various chili peppers can have different qualities and intensities of spiciness, so it is with the bitterness of hop varieties. Some are more bitter than others or have different flavors and aromas. Over the centuries, hop growers have cultivated the finest native varieties and created hybrids with the qualities that brewers have sought. The native Czech Saaz variety, grown near Zatec, Bohemia, has long been prized for the fine bitterness and delicate floral aroma it lends to pilsner beers. The German Perle hop is snappy and up-front on the palate, while the fruity, woody English Golding gives a broad bitterness across the tongue. Hop aromatics run the gamut from the earthy hay and fennel character of the English Fuggle variety to the piney, grapefruity blast of the popular American Cascade and the catty, limey, Riesling-like Chinook. German Tettnang combines notes of earth and flowers. A brewer may use many different hops in a beer, each variety a different color in his aromatic palette.

In the United States, the Pacific Northwest is hop country, with production centered on the Willamette Valley of Oregon and the Yakima Valley of Washington. American hops are often disdained by European brewers, who find them too exuberantly bright, piney, and citric in their flavors and aromas. American craft brewers counter that while European hops are very fine, exuberance has its place. This reminds me of the differences between European and American culture as a

Courtesy Hop Union.

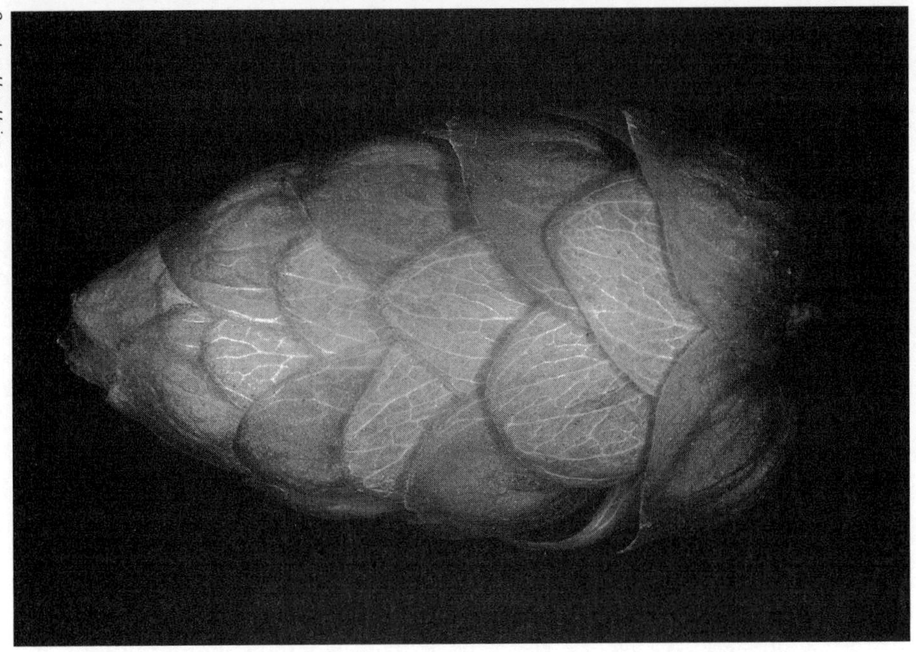

The hop flower provides bitterness, the backbone of a real beer's flavor. Beer without hops would be sweet and unsatisfying, like wine without acidity or tannin.

whole. Americans live loudly—we like loud music, spicy food, brightly hoppy beers, and big jammy blockbuster wines—and we don't want anyone complaining that we're laughing too loud.

The joke around the brewhouse is that in reality we work for the yeast. We're there only to feed it and keep it happy. Actually, I'm not quite sure this is a joke—there's a large element of truth in it. Unfortunately, yeast doesn't really care what kind of beer it makes or even whether the beer tastes good. The brewer's job is to anticipate the conditions under which the yeast will produce the desired beer and then maintain those conditions so the yeast will do what he wants. Yeast is an ornery creature, and all brewmasters are yeast wranglers. No sooner is the yeast finished fermenting one batch of beer than we gather it up and use it to ferment another. When we gather the yeast, it looks just like pancake batter, but it is very much alive.

Yeast is a single-celled organism in the fungi class of flora. Yeast is everywhere—in the air, in the soil, on your skin, on this page. There are many species of yeast, but for most brewing purposes we are principally concerned only with two: *Saccharomyces cerevisae*, the ale yeast; and *Saccharomyces uvarum*, the lager yeast. Within these species are hundreds of strains, and each strain has its own unique characteristics. It matters little what strain of wine yeast the vintner uses to make his wines, but in this respect beer is different. Especially for ales, the yeast strain often makes a major contribution to the flavor of the finished beer. For example, a weissbier yeast strain will produce aromas of bananas and cloves, while an English strain may give notes of orange marmalade. The yeasts are not interchangeable—orangey weissbier might not go down so well in Munich, and Londoners would be likely to reject a clovey pint of bitter. Belgian brewers are particularly attuned to the flavor and aroma contributions of specific yeast strains, which they use to brilliant effect to create some of the most complex beverages in the world.

The right yeast will produce the right flavors, but the brewer wants the yeast to have other attributes as well. Does it rise to the top of the fermenting vessel at the end of fermentation, or does it drop to the bottom? How long does it take to complete its fermentation? How much sugar will it consume? Will it ferment a strong beer, or might it fall asleep on the job? We may work for the yeast, but the yeast must satisfy dozens of our criteria before we choose it to make our beer. If this seems confusing, consider the dog. All dogs are the

same species, but you'd scarcely know it. I don't want a German lager strain fermenting my English bitter any more than I'd want a Chihuahua guarding my house. Each yeast strain has a different talent, and the brewer selects it for that talent.

Every brewer is a "yeast wrangler," trying to keep his yeast happy and productive. Here, brewmaster Hans Peter Drexler confers with his microscopic partners at the Schneider brewery in Kelheim, Germany.

In many respects, the yeast can be the single most important ingredient the brewer selects. Centuries ago, before brewers learned what yeast truly was, beer was allowed to ferment spontaneously. As soon as the wort cooled, wild yeasts in the air and in the fermentation vessel would invade the wort and start the fermentation. This ancient way of brewing lives on in the lambic beers of Belgium, but all other brewers now choose a specific strain or a blend of strains to produce the beer they desire. In other cultures, a stick would be placed into the fermenting beer and then removed and dried out. This stick, now covered with dried yeast, would then be tossed into the next batch of beer, where the yeast would awaken and start the fermentation. The stick was considered magical—no one knew how it worked.

The two species of yeast provide one of the great divides in the beer world—the divide between ales and lagers. Ale yeast is by far the older type of brewing yeast. Ale yeasts ferment at warm temperatures, typically between 62 and 75 degrees Fahrenheit. Ales ferment rapidly—an ale fermentation can take as little as a few days. During the fermentation, most ale yeasts will produce flavors and aromas that lend a unique stamp to the beer. The aromas tend toward fruitiness but may also be spicy and complex, and they can combine with other characteristics to produce a beer of great depth. Once the fermentation is over and the yeast has consumed its fill of sugars, ale yeasts tend to rise to the top of the fermentation vessel and float there in a cake-like mass. For that reason, ale yeasts are often described as "top-fermenting" yeasts. Traditionally, brewers gather these yeasts by skimming them from the surface of the beer in an open fermentation vessel. The yeast can then be used to ferment the next batch. Ale fermentations can be so quick that the beer is ready to drink within a week or so, though it is usually aged longer. If you prefer lagers, you will have to be more patient.

Lagers are relative newcomers to the beer world, but they have made a dramatic impact. Various forms of pilsner, properly a hoppy golden style of lager, are the world's most popular beers. The lager yeast was not discovered until the mid-1800s, but in Bavaria brewers had probably been using it for years. Before refrigeration, the Bavarian brewers carried out their fermentations in deep, cool caves and tunnels to protect them from the ravages of heat. Eventually, they ended up with yeast that preferred cool temperatures. Lager yeasts ferment best at temperatures between 45 and 56 degrees Fahrenheit, and the fermentation is slower and less tumultuous than an ale fermentation. When the lager fermentation is finished, though, the beer cannot be hurried unceremoniously into a glass. It needs some time to itself. The German word *lagerung* means "to store." Lager beers are stored cold and allowed to age for weeks or even months, at temperatures as low as 32 degrees Fahrenheit. Eventually, the flavors and aromas smooth and soften, leaving a beer of great finesse. Lager yeasts usually do not produce the fruity and spicy flavors that are produced by ale yeasts. Lager yeasts are less flashy and are content to stand aside and let the other ingredients do the talking. Lagers have clean, straightforward flavors of malt and hops. When combined with the right malt varieties and brewing techniques, lager yeasts can produce beers with spectacular malt depth and wonderfully refreshing aromatics.

Many people seem to think that ales are dark while lagers are pale, or that ales are strong while lagers are more moderate. There is no truth to this at all. The difference is entirely in the yeast, the fermentation temperature, and the aging time used to produce the beer. There are black ales that are weak in alcohol—Irish Stout is a good example—and golden lagers that rival wines in strength. Dark, strong lagers are much prized in Germany, while England's bitters are often pale and very light in alcohol. Broadly speaking, most ale brewing traditions have sprung from England, Belgium, and France, while lager brewing traditions come to us from Czech Bohemia and Germany. American craft brewers have tended toward ales but are now discovering the more subtle pleasures of lagers as well.

"Where does your water come from?" is one of the questions most frequently asked of brewers. The answer, frankly, is usually the municipal water source, or perhaps the brewery's own well. While this doesn't sound nearly as romantic as "our beer is brewed from melting glaciers" or some other advertising blather, the fact is that most municipalities have quite good water supplies. That said, water is important. Most beers are at least 90 percent water, so it should come as no surprise that water is a critical element in the flavor of beer. At the turn of the twentieth century, Brooklyn, New York, was home to forty-eight breweries, partly because of the quality of Brooklyn's water, derived from the nearby Catskill Mountains. I brew with that same water today.

In the past two centuries, various European cities became renowned for their unique brewing water and for the beer brewed with it. Burton-upon-Trent, for example, sits atop huge limestone deposits in the English Midlands. The amazingly hard water is suffused with calcium sulfate and other minerals. If you're trying to lather up your hair in the shower in Burton, you're pretty much out of luck, but if you're brewing, it's a different story. The minerals promote a vigorous fermentation, and in a finished beer they produce a dry, sharp-edged hop character that is the hallmark of Burton ales. Great brewing dynasties such as Bass & Company built their reputations and fortunes on the quality of Burton water and the resulting flinty India pale ales, beers that were brewed for shipping from England to Calcutta.

A thousand miles away, in the Czech Bohemian town of Pilsen (Plzeň), the water is known for its softness rather than its hardness. The water is so soft that it virtually tastes distilled. The almost complete lack of mineral salts in Pilsen's water supply helped give rise to the pilsner style of beer. Pilsners have a sharp crackle of bitterness, but this is followed by a soft, sweet, bready, delicate malt flavor prized by lager brewers and drinkers alike. Harder water would produce an entirely different beer.

Today, in an age of filters and blended water supplies, most brewers can adjust the mineral content of their brewing water to meet their needs. A pilsner brewer whose municipality has hard water may decide to soften it, while a brewer of pale ales might add "Burton salts" to his brewing water to bring out the dry edge in his beer. Once upon a time, the majority of brewers produced only one or two styles of beer, but these days it pays to be more flexible. I know that isn't terribly romantic, but it's true. The rest is advertising. Besides, if you can really taste the Rocky Mountains in a can of mass-market fizz, your taste buds are far better than mine.

While we refer to "brewing beer," technically speaking the brewer brews wort, which the yeast then ferments into beer. OK, let's get to work. First, we need our malt recipe, which is called the grist. We weigh out and blend the malts, preparing them for milling. Today's recipe is for Brooklyn Brown Ale, so we've got some English pale ale malt (full-bodied and toasty), crystal malt (for color and caramel flavors), chocolate malt (for chocolaty flavors), roasted barley (coffeeish flavors), Belgian aromatic malt (nice bready flavors), Belgian biscuit malt (biscuity flavors), and a dash of protein-rich wheat malt to help produce a nice, fluffy head. We're going to put this malt through our mill, which will crack each kernel into several pieces, exposing the white floury starch within. We send the grist into a vessel called the mash tun, where it is mixed with hot water to form a hot porridge called the mash. The brewhouse fills with the bready aroma of malt. The mash will unlock the sugars that we'll later ferment into beer. The natural enzymes developed by the barley seed during the malting process will be activated by the hot water, breaking down the starches into sugars. Let's keep an eye on our temperatures, because they are critically important—the malt enzymes work differently at different temperatures. A few degrees can make all the difference. A mash at 145 degrees Fahrenheit will turn

"Mashing" with hot water converts malt starches into fermentable sugars. At Brooklyn Brewery, our brewhouse fills with the bready aroma of hot cereal.

out different sugars—and therefore a different beer—than a mash at 150 degrees. Some brewers, particularly English ale brewers, use a single-temperature mash, holding it at one temperature for an hour or more. I'm not English, though, so I use a different technique, designed to help break down some of the less helpful proteins in the malt that I'm using. I start the mash lukewarm, then raise the temperature in steps to the point where the starch will convert into sugars.

When we come back an hour later, the mash looks very different. The white flecks of starch are all gone, and the mash looks darker and more viscous. Our once starchy porridge is now composed of barley husks and concentrated sweet wort, which has the consistency of a light syrup. Now it's time for the sugar extraction called the runoff or lauter. We pump the mash from the mash tun into another vessel called the lauter tun. The lauter tun is basically a sieve. It has a set of screens at the bottom that will hold the barley husks in place while we rinse the sugars away. The clear wort strains out through the screens and is pumped into the kettle. The undiluted wort that is sent into the kettle first is called the first runnings. It's very sweet and particularly delicious—it would be great on pancakes, and I once partnered with an ice cream company that used it to flavor some delicious malted ice cream.

If we were brewing a very strong beer, we might use only the first runnings of the mash. The highly concentrated sugars would produce a beer with over 10 percent alcohol by volume. Our Brooklyn Brown Ale is meant to be more moderate, so we'll start the process of rinsing the rest of the sugars out of the mash. We spray hot water down on top of the grain bed, gently and carefully, until all the malt sugars have been collected in the kettle. This is called sparging. We mustn't make the water too hot, or we'll extract unpleasant astringent tannins from the grain husk. And if the water is too cool, we won't be able to dissolve the malt sugars and send them into the kettle. In my brewery, we use rakes to slice through the grain bed, making sure that our sparging water moves smoothly through the grain bed. In a smaller brewery, this job is often done by hand, the brewer using a wooden oar to slice through the grain.

Now our kettle is full, and a quick check shows that we've done a fine job and we have exactly the sugar concentration we're looking for. The sugar concentration is referred to as the original gravity, expressed in a scale of "brewing degrees." The Plato scale roughly expresses a sugar percentage by weight and is similar to the Brix scale used in winemaking. The English Balling scale is an older system based on the specific gravity of the liquid. The grain husks, known as spent grain, would make a great bran muffin (if you believe there is such a thing); but in our case the spent grain is on its way to New Jersey, where it will be fed to some very lucky

Time for the boil? Once the kettle is full, a rolling boil will extract bitterness and aroma from the hops.

cows. I'd love to have a cow that I would feed exclusively on spent grain from our Brooklyn Brown Ale mash. I suspect that the milk would be particularly delicious—with a hint of chocolate and coffee?

Now we bring the kettle to a boil and add the hops. The hops that we add at the beginning of the boil are largely for bitterness, since their aromatic compounds will vaporize during the boil. In order to extract the bittering resins from the hops, we need a vigorous, rolling boil. The boil also sterilizes the wort, so that our yeast won't have any competition during the fermentation. As the boil continues, some malt proteins will coagulate; later they'll drop to the bottom of the kettle, and we'll remove them with the spent hops. Over an hour later, we toss in a last addition of hops. These are for aroma—we won't boil them long enough to vaporize their aromatic oils, which we want to capture in the wort. We cut off the heat, and the wort settles into a simmer and then finally lies still.

FERMENTATION

Now we've got a kettle full of bittersweet wort, coagulated proteins, and spent hops. The excess protein and spent hops have to be removed. Some breweries have a strainer, but we use a whirlpool, which gathers all the particulate matter into the center of the vessel so that we can extract clear wort from a pipe at the outer edge. At this point, our nascent beer still has an identity crisis. Will it be a lager or an ale? If we chilled the wort to 45 degrees Fahrenheit and added a lager yeast, it would be destined to become a lager. Instead, we've taken some ale yeast from our last batch of Brown Ale and poured it into a sterilized fermentation vessel—it's just waiting for our wort to arrive. As the clear wort leaves the kettle, we crash-cool it from over 200 degrees

Fahrenheit to about 60 degrees. It joins the waiting yeast, which immediately gets down to business.

Over the next few hours, the wort lies quiet, but there's plenty going on. The single-cell yeast are furiously dividing and building their numbers in preparation for the fermentation. Several hours later, their strength gathered, they begin their magical work. At first, only a small wisp of foam hints at any activity, but soon the entire surface of the wort is churned up into a frothy head. Ales put on the more impressive display—their higher fermentation temperatures and natural surface activity give rise to a thick yeasty meringue on top of the fermenting beer. The fermentation creates its own heat, but cooling jackets on the fermentation vessel keep the temperature in check. After the second day of fermentation, the activity reaches a crescendo and then begins to slow.

When the beer has reached the gravity (sugar content) we're looking for, we'll cool the beer down, causing the yeast to settle out. Yeast never consumes all the sugars in the wort, nor do we want it to; we want some residual sugars for both flavor and body. Now the beer needs to rest. Since it is an ale, its respite will be brief—only a few weeks. Most ales need no more than a month of aging, though some very strong ales might be aged for up to a year before being bottled. During the aging, flavors become more refined, and more yeast and protein sediment out. Some brewers will add additional raw hops at this stage, an old English technique

Is it beer yet? Tasting is paramount for brewers. Aging rounds out the beer's flavors.

called dry-hopping. The hops are left to steep in the beer like tea leaves, suffusing the beer with more of the aroma of fresh hops.

When a lager emerges from its long, cold fermentation, it still tends to have a lot of rough flavors. The lagering or cold-aging process is necessary to allow the beer to mellow and fine-tune its delicate flavors. Traditionally, a small amount of still-fermenting beer will be added to the lagering tank, restarting the fermentation. This process, called krausening, helps remove some leftover sulfur notes and adds some natural carbonation. Then the temperature of the lagering tank is dropped further, often to nearly freezing, and the beer settles down for a long, well-deserved sleep. A proper lager enjoys a slumber of at least a month or two, but the average mass-market American lager is lucky to get a two-week nap before it's kicked out into the fluorescent glare of the supermarket aisles.

FILTRATION AND PACKAGING

The packaging of the beer before it leaves the brewery may be very simple or quite complex. Traditional cask-conditioned English ales will be siphoned directly into casks, sometimes with a natural clarifier, a dose of priming sugar, a handful of hops, or all three. The priming sugar will ferment out, giving a light, natural carbonation to the beer. The finished beer will be ready to draw through hand pumps in the pub in only a few days.

Most types of beer are destined for bottles or kegs. Some beers are refermented in the bottle and are referred to as bottle-conditioned beers. Bottle-conditioned beers will usually have a dose of yeast and sugar added before bottling. The yeast consumes the sugar and produces a natural, pinpoint, spritzy carbonation similar to that of champagne. In fact, the technique is identical to the *méthode champagnoise* except that there is no *degorgement*; the yeast is left in the bottle, where it settles as a sediment. Bottle-conditioned beers can be served hazy or decanted off their yeast, according to the preference of the drinker. Many Belgian ales are bottle-conditioned, as are some English ales, American craft-brewed beers, Bavarian weissbiers, and the occasional German kellerbier. Bottle-conditioned beers can be particularly complex, with the yeast continuing to work slowly, adding layers of flavor over time.

Other beers will be filtered, removing unwanted yeast and proteins and leaving the beer clear. This filtered beer will be referred to as "bright" beer and will be stored in a bright beer tank, where it will await bottling or kegging. When done properly, filtration clears the beer and protects it while leaving its best qualities

Off to the pub—ale being "racked" into casks at J. W. Lees in Manchester, England.

relatively undisturbed. Like most refinements, however, filtration can be overdone, so we must be careful not to remove the flavors we've worked so hard to achieve. After filtration, the beer will have some natural carbonation, but in most cases carbonation is also added, resulting in a beer with exactly the amount of carbonation the brewer seeks.

By the way, you've seen the mass-market beer commercials extolling the virtues of the mega-brewery's "cold-filtered" beer, right? And I suppose you've seen the commercials for "mountain-grown" coffee too, yes? Well, perhaps the commercials are from the same ad agency—*all beer filtration is done cold*, at just about the freezing mark. The chill causes haze-forming proteins to coagulate so that they can be filtered out with the yeast. There's no such thing as warm filtration. And all coffee grows in the mountains. If you seek the pleasures of real beer, always pay attention to flavor, never to advertising.

2

A BRIEF HISTORY OF BEER

"The mouth of a perfectly contented man is filled with beer."

—Egyptian inscription, 2200 B.C.

In the beginning, there was beer. OK, I'm afraid that's probably not quite true. Mead, or honey wine, was almost certainly the first alcoholic beverage. After all, with a heavy downpour and a beehive with a bad roof, mead can pretty much make itself. Bears have been enjoying mead for at least 100,000 years, ever since there have been bears. We can scarcely doubt that early humans enjoyed it too, when the bears let them. While mead making has largely gone by the wayside, beer is now the world's most popular fermented beverage. Why? Well, although we're here to discover the combination of beer and food, it's important to remember that beer *is* food. In fact, it was an important part of the diet of early humans. Real beer is full of vitamins, minerals, protein, and antioxidants. In short, it's good for you, and people have known that for thousands of years. The people working in the surgeon general's office discovered the same thing only a few years ago. Mead lacks beer's nutrients, and in order to make any significant amount of mead, you had to gather a huge amount of honey. That was a big drawback, especially in the days before protective clothing for beekeepers.

Gathering enough grain to make a significant amount of beer was also difficult for early humans. Most anthropologists now believe that societies gave up the hunter-gatherer lifestyle and settled down to pursue agriculture in order to grow enough grain to make beer. The archaeological record shows that many of the first cereals to be farmed were barleys. It would have been difficult to make bread out of these barleys, but easy to make beer. Wheat varieties, suitable for making other foods, were available, but that is not what people usually decided to grow. Beer was considered magical, and it kept people happy and healthy. If people were to get enough beer, they had to grow the grain themselves. To a large extent, beer is responsible for civilization itself.

Beer, unlike wine and mead, does not make itself. The discovery of beer was a happy accident somewhere in Africa more than 10,000 years ago. Someone used damp, sprouted grain to make porridge, and when the porridge was heated, it became sweet. The enzymes in the sprouted grain, activated by the heat, had converted the starches into sugars. If the porridge was left out to ferment, beer would result—not very tasty beer, but beer nonetheless. All ancient brewing started with the making of porridge or bread. The words "brewing" and "bread" are linguistically related, growing out of the High German words *Briuwan*, meaning "cooking," and *Brot*, which originally meant not "bread," but "porridge" or "mash."

By now it should not surprise you that the oldest known recipe is for beer. Over 4,000 years ago, the Sumerians of Mesopotamia worshipped Ninkasi, the goddess of beer. A hymn to Ninkasi was inscribed on clay tablets in the eighteenth century B.C., and those tablets have survived for us to read. The hymn praises the goddess as it describes all the wonderful things she does—and all the wonderful things she does just happen to produce beer. The whole hymn is a recipe rendered as a poem or a song. Ninkasi bakes bread called *bappir*, seasoned with dates and

Courtesy University of Pennsylvania Museum.

All ancient societies brewed beer, which was often drunk out of clay jars through reed straws. This tablet shows beer drinking in ancient Sumeria.

spices, then soaks the bread and squeezes the liquid through a straw mat into a jar. Once the liquid had fermented into beer, it was drunk through reed straws.

This brewing method, essentially unchanged, is still practiced in parts of Africa, where indigenous traditional beers are widely enjoyed. Village elders can be found sitting around large clay pots, drinking home-brewed beer through long reeds and discussing the affairs of the day. The clay pots look exactly like those in ancient Sumerian drawings and stamps. The seal of Lady Pu-Abi, queen of the city of Ur around 2600 B.C., shows her drinking beer from a cup through a straw. She didn't have to stoop to using a reed—her beer straw was made of gold and lapis lazuli, and it now resides in the British Museum in London. By 1720 B.C., during the reign of King Hammurabi, Sumerian legal codes were steeped in beer, which played an important role in Mesopotamian rituals, myths, and medical treatments. Everyone, from king to pauper, drank beer, and tavern keepers were kept honest by harsh penalties—the penalty for overcharging, for example, was drowning. Clearly, the Sumerians took their beer very seriously indeed.

When it comes to brewing, the Egyptians were the ones who really got down to business—big business. Pharaoh Ramses II had massive breweries capable of producing 30,000 barrels of beer annually. His war chest and his cities were built with beer money. Up to 40 percent of the grain stores of ancient Egyptian cities was given over to barley for brewing. Beer, called *hekt*, was a staple food product in ancient Egypt. It was so important, in fact, that it was actually used as money. Many of the skilled workers who built the pyramids were paid in beer, which they were given three times a day. They had at least five varieties to choose from. Royalty and commoners alike enjoyed beers with brand names like "Joy Bringer," "The Beautiful," and "The Heavenly." The gods Osiris and Isis were held to have been the inventors of beer, and many other gods and goddesses conveniently demanded beer drinking as part of their worship. You had to be careful whom you drank with, though—if an Egyptian woman accepted a sip of a gentleman's beer, she was considered betrothed. In ancient Egypt, beer shows up everywhere—in writings, in medical prescriptions, on pottery, in paintings, in friezes, in storage pots buried with mummies. You certainly didn't want to head into the afterlife without an adequate supply of beer—what kind of paradise would that be?

From the beginning, brewing was the work not of men but of women. From ancient Egypt until medieval Europe, women ran the households, baked the bread, and brewed the beer. While women were by no means equal to men in European societies, several medieval laws held that the household brewing vessels remained the personal property of the housewife, who in England was often referred to as the alewife or brewster. In England, not only did women brew the beer; they also sold it and operated taverns. Some of these taverns were fairly rough places frequented by both men and women, and female tavern keepers could make enough money to be independent. Men were jealous of this commerce, and their laws placed restrictions on it. In the year 1284, the Brewers Guild of Berwick decreed that "it is enacted that no alewife is allowed to sell a bottle of beer from Easter to St. Michaels for more than two pennies, and from St. Michaels to Easter for more than one penny." Furthermore, they ruled that "no woman is allowed to buy more than one bushel of oats on the market to brew beer for sale from the same. If she buys more, she loses all she has bought, and one-third goes to the custodians, and two parts to the bailiff, for the brewing of beer which is [to be] consumed in his own house."

Clearly, men did not enjoy seeing women pursuing independent businesses, especially since the women seemed to be having such a good time at it. If fact, the men were so put off by the idea that they sang songs against it. Here's a classic from Scotland called, fetchingly, "The Ale-Wife and Her Barrel":

Bildarchiv Preussischer Kulturbesitz, Berlin.

The ancient Egyptians were prodigious and enthusiastic brewers. They even had their own brand names. Is this a batch of "Joy Bringer"?

My mind is vex'd and sair perplex'd,
I'll tell you a' that grieves me:
A drunken wife I hae at hame,
Her noisome din aye deaves me.

The alewife, the drunken wife,
The alewife she grieves me;
My wifie and her barrelie,
They'll ruin me and deave me.

She takes her barrel on her back,
Her pint-stoup in her hand,
And she is to the market gane,
For to set up a stand.

Can you imagine? The nerve of her.

When men decided on monastic lives, they gave up women, but they certainly didn't forsake their beer. In fact, the first commercial brewing operations in Europe were almost certainly monasteries. Throughout Europe, special beers were brewed for religious holidays—Advent ales, Easter ales, and Whitsun ales. In some cases, the situation was reversed, and rather than buying beer from the monks, churchgoers had an obligation to supply their church with a tithe of beer. "It is reported," writes St. Boniface in the eighth century, to the archbishop of Canterbury, "that in your diocese the vice of drunkenness is too frequent, so that not only certain bishops do not hinder it, but they themselves indulge in excess of beer and force others to drink until they are intoxicated." It can hardly be surprising that when in 1066 the Normans and the English clashed in the fateful battle of Hastings, a contemporary wrote that the English "were no better than drunk when they came to fight." Perhaps it is true that for a few pints of ale, the kingdom was lost.

When the Normans conquered England, they brought their language and their wine with them. Although the French language married Old English to create Modern English, the wine of the conquerors and the beer of the conquered did not mix very well. Four hundred years of French rule instilled into English-speaking people the idea that everything French was sophisticated, noble, and superior, an idea the French never quite lost. This bias is even hardwired into the English language, where Latin-based words are considered more sophisticated than Anglo-Saxon words. To "strike" is more elegant than to "hit," and why would one merely

"eat" when one could "dine"? When a Latin-based word and an Anglo-Saxon word have the same meaning, the Latin is preferred for elegance, while the Anglo-Saxon is reserved for blunter talk. This cultural inferiority complex followed through to the relationship between wine and beer, and English-speakers have been cursed with it ever since. Many European cultures, unaffected by this history, properly see beer and wine as equals, especially with food.

Medieval brewing was hard work, but skilled brewers could make a good living. Inevitably, the tax man was waiting around the corner.

Ironically, the Normans were quite impressed with English beer. The house of Plantagenet assumed the English throne in 1154 and planted vineyards in the south of England, but they praised English beer even more than the English themselves did. A twelfth-century Norman aristocrat opined that English ale "is wholesome, clear, of the color of wine, and of better taste." English beers were so well loved by the French that when Thomas à Becket went to France as ambassador in 1158, he brought casks of ale with him as a gift, even though the French had their own extensive brewing industry at the time.

Across Europe, the life of common people changed as they began to escape ancient bonds. As people moved to cities and opened businesses, taxes inevitably followed. People who were still bound by tenuous threads of serfdom were called the *Biergelden*, meaning "beer duty-bound." These people were required to pay taxes for the right to brew beer. The word *Gelden*, meaning a debt that one is obliged to pay, eventually became the English word "guilt." To protect their interests, free brewers established guilds, which were conveniently run by the taxing bishops. As long as the bishops got their beer, everyone could be made happy. To this day, though I consider myself quite free, I am apparently a member of the taxpaying *Biergelden*, though the bishops have been replaced by the Bureau of Alcohol, Tobacco, and Firearms. I don't feel guilty, though how I got lumped in with tobacco and firearms I'll never understand.

Even 700 years ago, it was a very bad idea to try to avoid paying your beer taxes, especially in the French city of Aix-la-Chapelle. On April 30, 1272, it was decreed that anyone attempting to evade the beer tax "*shall be punished by the chopping off of the right hand, and he shall remain outside of the city and jurisdiction of Aix-la-Chapelle for five years; the house in which the excess of beer was brewed or sold shall be destroyed, and also if beer which has been brought from outside the jurisdiction of Aix-la-Chapelle has been sold, the house in which such sales have been made shall be destroyed.*" No doubt the modern IRS looks on those days with considerable envy.

If evading the beer tax was inadvisable, making bad beer was also a pretty poor idea. In the year 1268 the brewers of Paris established industrywide corporate statutes regarding all aspects of beer sales, including penal statutes for those who adulterated their beer. As nasty as these punishments may have been, they seem lenient compared with what could befall a bad brewer in Germany. *Malam cerevisiam facieus in cathedram stercoris*—"Whoever makes a poor beer shall be tossed onto the town dung heap"—was an ordinance of the city of Danzig. To a certain extent, the brewers didn't mind these ordinances—which certainly discouraged any challenges to their business. Knowledge of brewing, such as it was, was tightly held by the brewers and their guilds, and any technical advances were shrouded in secrecy. The apprenticeship system ensured that the brewing arts were passed down within families as a form of inheritance. For rivals from outside the system, modern brewing knowledge was difficult to come by—the dung heap loomed for those who lacked it.

Despite the best efforts of governments, the quality of beer was still highly variable, and beer was subject to trickery and adulteration. The Bavarians took increasingly severe steps to protect the citizenry from bad beer. In 1516, Duke Wilhelm IV initiated the *Reinheitsgebot*, or "Beer Purity Law." This stated that beer could be made only from barley malt, hops, and water. The use of malted wheat was later approved for production of wheat beer, and the use of yeast was approved as well. The *Reinheitsgebot*, by banning raw grains and flavorings other than hops, set German brewing on its modern course. Gruit, the blend of herbs that had once flavored Bavarian beer, was now consigned to the forerunners of herbal concoctions like Jägermeister. Beer was to be made pure. The Bavarian Trade Statutes of 1539 forbade brewing during the summer—everyone knew that beer brewed in warm weather was likely to spoil quickly. From April 24 through September 29, brewing kettles were placed under seal. The duke's four beer inspectors enforced strict compliance.

Beer, an especially important provision, arrived on the ships of the first American colonists. The Pilgrims planned to land in the New York area, but they had to settle for Massachusetts because they "could not now take time for further search or consideration, our victuals being much spent, especially our Beere." Time and again, there is note of people dying for want of beer—the lack of it forced them to drink water, which was often impure and soon sickened them. Puritans may have been, well, puritanical, but they certainly had no objection to beer. They had a difficult time in America until the arrival in 1628 of a thousand well-provisioned emigrants, carrying 10,000 gallons of English beer on the ship *Arbella*.

New York, then New Amsterdam, was already a center of commerce, essentially run by the Dutch West India Company. New Amsterdam produced enough beer to supply itself and ship its beer to other colonies. The Dutch were even more partial to beer than the English. Peter Minuit, director-general of New Amsterdam, established the first public brewery in America in 1632 in lower Manhattan. By the mid-1630s, New Amsterdam already boasted a Brouwer Straat, or "Brewers' Street." The Dutch West India Company brewed beer, free landholders brewed beer, tavern keepers brewed beer, and many colonists brewed beer in their own houses. By 1638 it was estimated that one-quarter of New Amsterdam consisted of houses in which beer could be bought. There were apparently seventeen licensed taverns and at least seven illegal ones. It didn't take long for the tax man to show up—in 1644 the director-general of New Netherland imposed excise taxes on brewers and tavern keepers. Failure to pay taxes could result in the seizure of the beer, which would be distributed to New Netherland's soldiers, no doubt bolstering their loyalty. New Amsterdam's brewers fought back. They were among the city's most prominent citizens, and they eventually complained so bitterly that the director-general was recalled to Holland.

OPPOSITE: The *Reinheitsgebot*, or Beer Purity Law, of 1516 has protected the quality of German beer for centuries, though it may also have stifled creativity.

When the English took over and New Amsterdam became New York, the duke of York himself took care to see that only decent beer was brewed in the town. The "Duke's Laws" of 1664 declared "that no person whatsoever shall henceforth undertake the calling or work of brewing beer for sale, but only such as are known to have sufficient skill and knowledge in the art and mystery of a brewer." From

Wie das Pier summer vñ winter auf dem Land sol geschenckt vnd prawen werden

Item Wir ordnen/setzen/vnnd wöllen/ mit Rathe vnnser Lanndtschafft/ das füran allenthalben in dem Fürstenthumb Bayrn/auff dem lande/ auch in vnsern Stettñ vñ Märckthen/da deßhalb hieuor kain sonndere ordnung ist/ von Michaelis biß auff Georij/ ain mass oder kopffpiers über ainen pfenning Müncher werung/ vñ von sant Jorgen tag/biß auff Michaelis/ die mass über zwen pfenning derselben werung/ vnd derenden der kopff ist/ über drey haller/bey nachgesetzter Pene/nicht gegeben noch außgeschenckht sol werden. Wo auch ainer nit Mertzñ/ sonder annder Pier prawen/oder sonst haben würde/sol Er doch das/kains wegs höher/dann die maß vmb ainen pfenning schencken/vnd verkauffen. Wir wöllen auch sonderlichen/ das füran allenthalben in vnsern Stetten/Märckthen/vñ auff dem Lannde/zů kainem Pier/merer stückh/ dañ allain Gersten/Hopffen/vñ wasser/genomen vñ gepraucht sölle werdñ. Welher aber dise vnsere Ordnung wissentlich überfaren vnnd nit hallten wurde/ dem sol von seiner gerichtzöbrigkait/dasselbig vas Pier/zůstraff vnnachläßlich/ so offt es geschicht/ genommen werden. Yedoch wo ain Gäuwirt von ainem Pierprewen in vnnsern Stettñ/ Märckten/oder aufm lande/yezůzeitñ ainen Emer piers/ zwen oder drey/kauffen/ vnd wider vnnter den gemaynnen Pawrsuolck außschencken würde/dem selben allain/ aber sonnßt nyemandts/sol dye mass/ oder der kopffpiers/ vmb ainen haller höher dann oben gesetzt ist/zegeben/ vñ/ außzeschencken erlaubt vnnd vnuerpotñ.

Gegeben zu Ingolstadt
am Georgitag 1516

there, of course, the regulation goes on to describe the harsh penalties for brewing bad beer, but at least there is no mention of a dung heap.

While the mid-Atlantic colonies sprouted breweries left and right, the southern colonies were slower to establish them. Hotter weather hampered brewing operations, and businessmen saw better opportunities in growing and selling tobacco, rice, cotton, and trees. The northern colonies had the opposite problem—colder weather precluded good barley crops, so Massachusetts Bay Colony and other northern colonies concentrated on fishing and whaling, preferring to import beer from England, New York, Pennsylvania, or New Jersey. Harvard College, founded in 1636, was brewing beer for its students by 1639. Apparently the college didn't brew enough—the first president of Harvard, Nathaniel Eaton, was dismissed in disgrace for failing to supply the students with enough beer. The college later solved that problem—Harvard's first full-scale brewhouse was in operation by 1674. The arrangements were very convenient for all involved, as students often paid for their room and board in barley malt.

As the Revolutionary War began, all trade with England ceased. Most colonists had stopped drinking British beer, and American brewers took up the slack. During the war, home brewing was common and many small breweries were established. The founding fathers looked on beer as a wholesome, nutritious homegrown beverage and distinguished it from distilled liquor, which was then described as "ardent spirits." James Madison hoped and trusted "that the brewing industry would strike deep root in every State in the Union." Benjamin Rush, a prominent physician and later a signer of the Declaration of Independence, published a pamphlet in 1775 decrying the harmful effects of liquor. Beer, however, was another matter entirely. Rush wrote: "Beer is a wholesome liquor compared with spirits. It abounds with nourishment; hence we find many of the common people in Great Britain endure hard labor with no other food than a quart to three pints of this liquor, with a few pounds of bread a day."

George Washington was particularly fond of porter, especially that brewed by Robert Hare of Philadelphia. We still have many of Washington's letters requesting copious amounts of Hare's porter. On July 20, 1788, he wrote to the beer agent Clement Biddle, "I beg you will send me a gross of Mr. Hare's best bottled Porter if the price is not much enhanced by the copious droughts you took of it at the late Procession," referring to the Federal Festival celebrating the ratification of the Constitution. Ardent spirits were banned from the Federal Festival held in Philadelphia in 1788, while beer and cider were supplied to the participants.

Thomas Jefferson, while a great collector of French wine, often spoke publicly about the importance of beer to the populace. He himself brewed sporadically, and

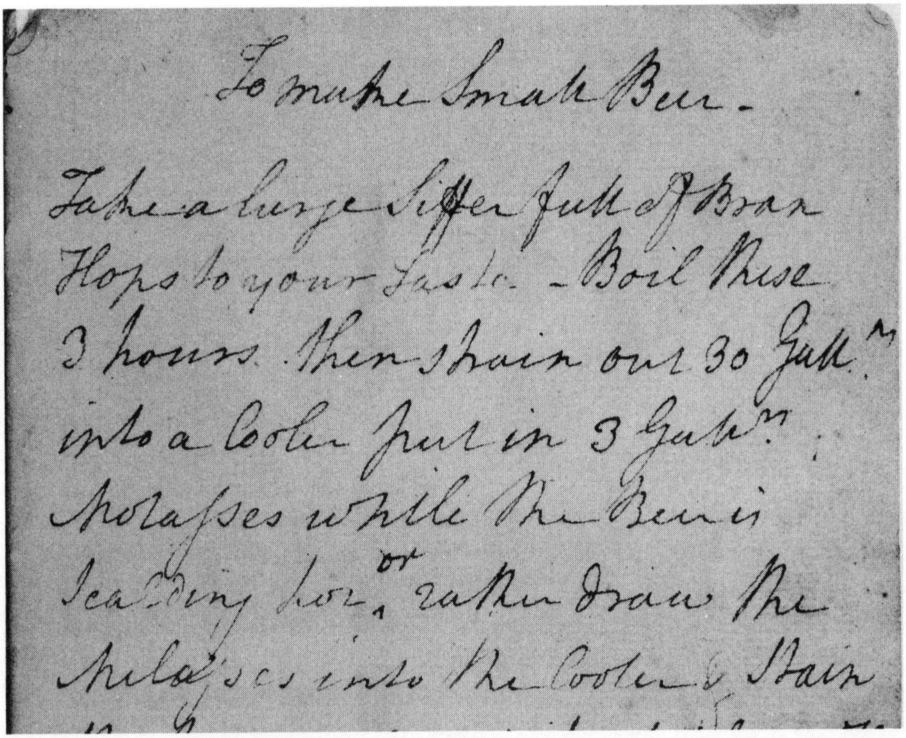

To make Small Beer.

Take a large Sifter full of Bran Hops to your Taste — Boil these 3 hours. Then strain out 30 Gall.ns into a Cooler put in 3 Gall.ns Molasses while the Beer is Scalding hot, or rather draw the Molasses into the Cooler & Strain

Manuscripts and Archives Division, the New York Public Library.

George Washington was famously fond of porter beer and brewed it for his own household. This is his original recipe for "small beer."

he began to take brewing seriously after he retired from the presidency and settled at Monticello. In 1813, he wrote a letter to one of his neighbors asking for the return of a borrowed book: "I lent you some time ago the 'London & Country Brewer' and Combrun's book on the same subject. We are this day beginning, under the direction of Capt. Millar, the business of brewing Malt liquors, and if these books are no longer useful to you I will thank you for them, as we may perhaps be able to derive some information from them." In Jefferson's letters we find many references to beer, and especially to his quest for useful books about brewing.

Jefferson's beer was apparently strong and tasty; we have flattering letters from his neighbors, including James Madison, asking for his advice about brewing and recipes for beer. Jefferson graciously encouraged them to send their brewers to Monticello for instruction.

Samuel Adams, a founder of the commonwealth of Massachusetts, was a prominent maltster, though he was not a brewer as is often claimed. He graduated from Harvard in 1740 and, after a brief stint as a lawyer, went into his father's malting business. He apparently wasn't very good at it, which is perhaps fortunate, since he later turned his attention to the pursuit of American independence.

By 1810, there were 140 breweries in the United States, producing 183,000 barrels of beer per year. Forty-eight of these were in Pennsylvania, forty-two in New York, and thirteen in Ohio, and the others were scattered throughout the rest of the country and its territories. In 1814, sitting over a few pints of ale at the Fountain Inn in Baltimore, Francis Scott Key put the finishing touches on his "Star Spangled Banner." Perhaps the beer inspired him—the melody he chose was that of "To Anacreon in Heaven," an old English beer-drinking song.

The 1830s brought a wave of German immigration into the United States. There were many German immigrants here already—they had fled religious persecution in Europe. In the 1830s many came because of economic distress in Germany or to evade military service, and in the 1840s many came for political reasons. No sooner had they set foot on American soil than the Germans started setting up breweries. So many Germans were arriving every day that the brewers did not have to worry about selling their beer to local Americans or to other immigrants—there were

Baltimore News-American.

German immigration throughout the 1800s brought a European flavor to American beer culture.

plenty of Germans to drink it. Like all new immigrants, they tended to keep to themselves and keep up the traditions of their homeland. Between 1840 and 1860, more than 1,350,000 Germans emigrated to the United States.

Lager brewing was already well established in Bavaria and was very quick to spread to America once the secret yeast was isolated. John Wagner brewed the first American lager in Philadelphia in 1840; he was followed by the firm of Engel & Wolf in 1844. According to Wolf, his brewery "was for many years the resort of the Germans of Philadelphia, who more than once drank the brewery dry. . . . Often we were compelled to display the placard that beer would again be dispensed after a certain date." David G. Yuengling was born in Germany and immigrated to America in 1828. By 1830, he was brewing in Pottsville, Pennsylvania. D. G. Yuengling & Sons, the oldest continuously operating brewery in the United States, is still in Pottsville and is run by his descendents.

New York state was a major beer producer, but New York City, hampered by a foul water supply, lagged far behind Philadelphia. By 1845, however, good water was finally supplied to New York City from reservoirs to the north, and it started brewing in earnest. Brooklyn, then a separate city, had a far better water supply than Manhattan. When it annexed the heavily German towns of Williamsburgh (the current home of the Brooklyn Brewery) and Bushwick, serious brewing began in Brooklyn. One twelve-square-block area of Bushwick, nicknamed "Brewer's Row," could boast eleven breweries in the period between 1850 and 1880. Brooklyn became a major brewing center, and by the end of the century it had forty-eight breweries. Several of these breweries produced nothing but weissbier, several more still produced ales, and more than twenty brewed only lagers. During this period one out of every ten beers consumed in the United States was brewed in Brooklyn. Milwaukee, often thought of as America's great brewing city, never held a candle to Brooklyn in its brewing heyday, which lasted from the mid-1800s until the dark days of Prohibition.

So many Germans were employed in the brewing industry in the United States that until World War I the Master Brewers Association of the Americas held its meetings and kept its records in German. The "German-ness" of the American brewing industry proved to be a factor in its eventual undoing as cultural storm clouds gathered against the brewers.

In 1893, the Prohibitionists started to organize in earnest. The Anti-Saloon League was formed as a local organization in Oberlin, Ohio, but by 1895 it had gone national. At first, the Prohibitionists preached the evils of the saloon, arguing that it kept men away from their wives and families and was therefore unchristian and contrary to the public good. Within a few years, they had moved the goalposts and sought to abolish alcohol altogether. Money poured in from churches and from Prohibitionist millionaires, including John D. Rockefeller and the department store magnate S. S. Kresge. Many owners of large breweries—the "beer barons"—had become rich and influential men who were respected in their communities. They simply couldn't believe that Prohibition would ever happen. Americans clearly loved their beer—they consumed 33.6 million barrels in 1895, a 530 percent increase over consumption in 1869. But the movement was gathering steam. As New York City's police commissioner, Teddy Roosevelt started to actually enforce the laws banning the sale of alcoholic beverages on Sundays, laws that had previously been ignored.

People had been made to believe that alcohol was causing all the ills of modern society. Get rid of alcohol, they reasoned, and all of America's social problems would evaporate. Entire counties started going "dry," and in 1907 Oklahoma joined the union as the first completely dry state. In late December of that year, the New State Brewing Association of Oklahoma City was forced to dump 230 barrels of beer into the gutters. A large crowd, outfitted with scoops, cups, and buckets, chased the stream of beer down the street, desperate for their last taste of the real thing.

By 1911, the United States was producing more beer than any other country in the world, 62.8 million barrels, or 21 gallons per capita. (The Bavarians, with a per capita beer consumption of 75 gallons, would not have been impressed.) After 1914, however, the Prohibitionists began to gain the upper hand, and one state after another passed dry laws; by 1916, eighteen states were dry. Anheuser-Busch, seeing that the brewers were losing the battle, released Bevo, a nearly alcohol-free beer. Then, on April 6, 1917, the United States declared war on Germany. The Prohibitionists quickly moved to exploit the rising tide of anti-German sentiment, pointing an accusing finger at brewers named Busch, Yuengling, Schlitz, Schmidt, Pabst, Blatz, and Schaeffer.

OPPOSITE: **At the end of the nineteenth century, Brooklyn, New York, was home to more than forty-five breweries. The Doelger family owned breweries in Brooklyn and Manhattan.**

It mattered little that many of these brewers had contributed significantly to the American war effort. The last nail had been hammered into the coffin of American brewing. On January 17, 1920, the Volstead Act, banning the sale, manufacture, consumption, or transportation of any beverage containing more than 0.5 percent alcohol, became the law of the land. On January 18, the speakeasies were open for business.

Many of the breweries in the country produced "near beer," a nearly alcohol-free malt-based concoction. Many others simply shut down. Still others struggled to find new products to make. The Adolph Coors Brewery began producing malted milk, supplying it to the Mars Candy Company—malt meant for beer production found its way into Milky Way and Snickers bars. Stroh and Yuengling produced

JOS. DOELGER'S SONS

ESTABLISHED 1846.

TRADE MARK.

LAGER BEER

Brewery 54th to 55th St. between 2nd & 3rd Ave.

NEW YORK.

ice cream, and Anheuser-Busch produced everything from baker's yeast to boats. Many brewers produced malt extracts and syrups, supposedly for use in cooking. The real use for these products was obvious—home brewing. Malt and hops shops became common, and even large grocery store chains unabashedly stacked cans of malt syrup in their windows. In 1926 and 1927, production of malt extracts reached 888 million pounds.

The Volstead Act was widely and flagrantly disregarded. The word "scofflaw" was coined by an entrant in a contest—to create a new word for people who disobeyed the dry laws. It was an epithet that many were proud to wear. American sailors coming back from Europe steamed into their home harbors flying flags proclaiming "We Want Our Beer!" People marched in the street demanding to have their beer back. They would have to wait more than thirteen years. Over those years, the complete failure of Prohibition became obvious even to its former proponents. The loss of vital commerce and the rise of organized crime slowly poisoned the economy of the country. By 1933, almost everyone had decided that it was time for the "noble experiment" to end.

On April 7, 1933, the *New York Times* ran a banner headline: BEER FLOWS IN 19 STATES AT MIDNIGHT. Everyone was thrilled, not least the brewers, who couldn't wait to be made legitimate again. But their world had changed, and they soon found that they had to change with it. It had been thirteen long years, and many people were not feeling terribly picky about the flavor qualities of the beer that was now offered. During Prohibition, soft drinks had become very popular, and they were new competition for the brewers. Millions of young people had grown to adulthood without ever tasting real beer. Now the brewers, facing new potential customers weaned on soft drinks, started to remove strong flavors from beer in order to make it appealing to everyone. New laws forced the alcohol content of beer to remain at or below 3.2 percent by weight, or about 4 percent by volume. This further watered down the flavor of beer. The brewers were desperate to rebuild the financial health of their companies, but the country was in the throes of the Great Depression; brewers were told that if they were truly patriotic, they'd keep the price of beer down to five cents a glass.

Fearful of a reversal and a return to Prohibition, they complied. If they were to manage to sell beer this cheaply and make a profit, brewers would have to use more adjuncts like rice and corn, which were less expensive than barley malt. Expensive aging would have to be reduced. American beer, now sold by huge advertising campaigns, moved swiftly away from its European roots. Many breweries struggled out of Prohibition only to close or be absorbed by larger breweries. By the end of World War II, the American brewing industry was transformed. It would be an industry of fewer and fewer breweries, which themselves grew to become national behemoths. The product, following the cultural norms of the day, would become innocuous and bland, to the extent that even brewers could barely tell the beers apart. Volume selling, driven by advertising, would take over as the number one goal of American brewers. The modern mass-market American lager beer, a watery, flavorless beverage unrecognizable to any visiting German, emerged into an American culinary landscape paved over by fast-food restaurants, processed cheese, and frozen vegetables. After 10,000 years of flavorful brewing around the world, the American brewers had finally reduced the progenitor of human civilization to a pallid ghost in a can. By 1974, there were only forty breweries left in the United States, all making essentially the same product. A few years later, just as these dark ages threatened to erase traditional beer from the American memory, dawn broke over California. A new age of American brewing was about to begin.

3

Principles of Matching Beer with Food

People have been enjoying beer with food for millennia, so it's fair to ask what the point is of trying to formalize an already happy relationship.

Beer by itself can be wonderful, even revelatory. Food, however, is where the rubber meets the road—it's where we live. Most of us can clearly remember some of the best meals we've ever had. Those meals may stand out as peak moments in our lives. Unfortunately, modern life, for most Americans, provides too few moments like these. Even those of us who cook seriously, and I count myself among them, go through times when all our meals seem rushed and our food is little more than fuel. Even when the meals are good, there's often something missing. This is where beer comes in.

If, to you, "beer" means the yellow fizzy stuff sitting in cans on supermarket shelves, I want you to clear your mind of the fact that those products even exist. We're not concerned with them—we're talking about the real thing here. And this is what real beer can do: it can make every single decent meal you have an interesting and memorable flavor experience. It can be something that will light up your senses and make you actually want to pay attention to what's happening on your palate. Paying that little bit of attention, both to your food and to your beer, is the difference between having an "OK" culinary life and having one filled with boundless riches of flavor. Learn a little bit about the amazing variety and complexity of flavor that traditional beer brings to the table, and in return I *promise* you a better life. I'm not kidding—it's that simple. You'll have to cook, buy, or order nice meals—traditional beer will not turn a Big Mac into a feast. But it can turn a quesadilla into a fireworks display or a simple roast chicken into a spectacular meal.

Gourmet

THE MAGAZINE OF GOOD LIVING

FRESH
LOBSTERS
EVERY DAY!

Can't wine do the same thing? Yes and no. I love wine and frequently enjoy it with my meals. But I've never enjoyed wine with all the types of food that I actually eat every day. A roast rack of lamb? Sure, I'd love to have a bottle of Burgundy (though I know beers that will match the lamb just as well). But how about Mexican, Chinese, Japanese, Thai, Middle Eastern, Indian, and Cajun cuisine, and American barbecue? I love this stuff too, and I don't want wine with it. Yes, I've had all the wines that will supposedly match these foods. Guess what? They are a poor substitute for traditional beer. Why? Because spices distort wine flavors, turning white wines hot and red wines bitter. Because wine doesn't refresh the palate the way beer does. Because wine has no caramelized or roasted flavors to match those in our favorite dishes. And because, even according to wine experts, there are many foods that are simply no good with wine.

For example, wine enthusiasts preface their selections with talk of "tricky ingredients." These tricksters include eggs, cheeses, chilies, smoked meats, smoked fish, tomatoes, ginger, curry, chocolate, avocados, garlic, vinaigrette dressings, spinach, artichokes, asparagus, cumin, and dozens of other tasty things. But beer, because it is so versatile, has no problem with any of these ingredients. Wheat beers are light, spritzy, and wonderful with eggs. Spicy Belgian farmhouse ales work wonders with chilies, cumin, ginger, and curries. Rich imperial stouts are full of coffee-like, chocolaty flavors—they match chocolate desserts perfectly. There are no tricks here, only natural affinities and terrific matches.

Still, no one wants a "beer belly." What about calories? Actually, beer has no more calories than wine, and so it is not more fattening; a glass of wine and a bottle of beer are roughly equivalent on that score. "Light" beer? Not only does that stuff taste like seltzer water, but it often has only 16 fewer calories per 12 ounces than the regular version. It's all about advertising, not calories. Want some "light" wine? I didn't think so. Neither do I. No matter what you eat or drink, moderation and balance are key to enjoying yourself.

And I have plenty of fun. Here's what the "food week" looked like at my place:

SUNDAY Free-range chicken. I covered the skin with sea salt and garlic; stuffed the chicken with a dressing of bread, onion, sage, and thyme; and roasted it. Next, I roasted some potatoes in a little duck fat, salt, pepper, and rosemary; then I blanched some sugar snap peas and tossed them with butter and fleur de sel. Castelain, a spicy golden farmhouse ale from France, has the herbal qualities to highlight the sage, rosemary, and thyme.

MONDAY I made soft corn tacos. I tossed some shrimp in a wok with olive oil, cumin, lime juice, and habanero sauce, and then stuffed the corn tortillas with shrimp, avocado, onion, chopped jalapeños, tomato, and sour cream. We drank my own Brooklyn Pilsner, which cut through the spiciness and refreshed the palate. Nice and snappy, if I do say so myself.

TUESDAY I slathered a well-marbled rib-eye steak with olive oil, salt, and cracked pepper; broiled it medium-rare; made some mashed potatoes with truffle butter; and had the steak and potatoes with a mesclun and tomato salad with a vinaigrette dressing. The perfect accompaniment was Saison Dupont, an earthy, spicy, peppery, explosively flavorful Belgian farmhouse ale.

WEDNESDAY I got lazy and ordered crispy duck and cold sesame noodles from a local Chinese restaurant. OK, so it was a bit greasy, but it sure was good with Schneider Weisse, a spritzy, refreshing, hazy Bavarian wheat beer full of the flavors of cloves, smoke, and bananas.

THURSDAY I repented and had a salad. Well, sort of: strips of spicy grilled chicken breast, tomatoes, avocado, cucumber, roasted peppers, goat cheese, and balsamic vinaigrette smothered the baby greens. We drank Blanche de Bruges, a Belgian wheat beer that is slightly tart, light in bitterness, and has a wonderfully spicy citrus nose from the use of Curaçao orange peel and coriander. There's nothing better with a hearty salad, even if it is hard to see the lettuce.

FRIDAY I went out to my favorite French restaurant, a little place that serves New York's best cassoulet, the classic stew of duck, white beans, and sausage. (My repentance didn't last long, I suppose.) This restaurant has a nice beer list, too. The Samuel Smith's Nut Brown Ale, with its warm, malty, slightly chocolaty, biscuitlike flavors, tasted great, and it had just enough bitterness to cut through the heaviness of those stock-soaked beans. I can never manage to finish the huge cassoulet—I take home a doggy bag every time. Believe it or not, cassoulet makes delicious omelettes. Trust me on this one.

SATURDAY It's Saturday now, and I'm planning to go out for dinner to my favorite Italian restaurant, Babbo. I've been dreaming about chef Mario Batali's beef cheek ravioli and risotto with porcini and foie gras. Fortunately, Mario likes Brooklyn Ale with his food, and so do I. The Scottish heirloom malt it's brewed with imparts a juicy toffeeish malt quality that just melts into these earthy dishes. Babbo, of course, has a brilliant wine list. It also, like many great restaurants, has a serious beer list, picked to match the food.

Best of all, we can afford to enjoy these beers every day. A good bottle of Barolo will set you back at least $60. A 750-ml bottle of Saison Dupont, a beer that makes Veuve Clicquot taste like Champale, is rather more reasonably priced at $5.99. We're talking luxury here, every day for the rest of your life. Sound good? Let's get started.

Aroma is one of the most important attributes of a beer, and brewmasters work hard to fashion an aroma that is inviting and tantalizing. Aroma is a beer's calling card, and it tells you what to expect on the palate. The aromatics of fine beer are virtually infinite, a fact that relates directly to beer's amazing versatility with food. Aromas range widely; they include floral (pilsners), ripe fruity (English pale ales), citrusy (American pale ales and Belgian wheat beers), hoppy (India pale ales), banana-like (German weissbier), clovey (German weissbier), smoky (German rauchbier), malty (doppelbocks and barley wines), sherry-like (barley wines and Flemish brown ales), herbal (Belgian tripels and French bières de garde), raisiny (Belgian dubbels), chocolaty (brown ales and porters), coffeeish (stouts), caramely (amber ales and bockbiers), earthy (lambics), and dozens of others. Scientists have identified thousands of natural aroma compounds in beer, and your nose is capable of distinguishing many more.

Flavor begins with aroma. Your tongue perceives only four sensations—sweet, sour, salty, and bitter—so your sense of smell is the key to flavor. Because some beers are more aromatic than others, it's worthwhile to get your nose into the glass. Swirl the beer around the glass, but be careful not to swirl it onto your shirt. Breathe in deeply—what do you smell? Some of the aromatics described in this book will sound wonderful, but others may sound strange, even unappetizing. You'll have to check them out for yourself, but it should be pointed out that you'd have a hard time finding nice-sounding descriptions for the flavors of many great foods and beverages. Stilton cheese is often described as "barnyardy," Sauvignon Blanc wines are said to have an aroma of "cat's pee," and great Riesling wines are said to be "petroly," meaning that they have gasoline notes. A great single-malt Scotch whiskey may be "seaweedy," with a "nose full of iodine." An open mind is essential for anyone who wants to explore great food and drink.

Where do the aromatics come from? Malt is the foundation of beer and makes a large contribution to aroma. Malt aromatics can be bready, honeylike, toasty, biscuity, toffeeish, nutty, caramely, chocolaty, coffeeish, or espresso-like. Add to this the very complex hop aromatics, which range from floral to fruity, grassy, lemony, grapefruity, catty (sorry, it's true), minty, piney, earthy, and a vast array of resiny aromas. If the beer is to be a lager, the yeast will make only a minor aromatic contribution, perhaps just a refreshing whiff of bathhouse sulfur. If an ale yeast is used, many more layers of aromatic complexity may be added. Yeast aromatics are virtually limitless, but they usually tend toward fruit. While the yeast consumes the sugars given up by the malt, it rapturously whistles while it's working, giving off aromas of peaches, pears, plums, bananas, spices, raisins, oranges, pepper, lemongrass, apples, butterscotch, damp earth, or whatever else it can think up. These may be combined in almost infinite variations.

Put all this together, and you can easily see that beer is an amazingly complex beverage, so it is not surprising that beer has so much to offer food. Don't worry—although the beer is offering a lot, this doesn't mean that you always have to be paying attention. There is much pleasure to be gained from simply going along for the ride. But if you want to put together food matches that go beyond pleasantness and approach epiphanies, then you'll want to pay close attention to what your nose is telling you. Harmonizing aromatics between the beer and the food is one of the guiding principles of matching. There's far more to beer than its aroma, but your nose will often lead you in the right direction. For example, if your dish is finished with a balsamic reduction sauce, you might want to consider a Belgian dubbel, which will have some acidity to match it, and appropriately raisiny aromatics. How will you know what to expect of the beer? Fortunately, beer rarely hides behind a veil of snobbish secrecy. Most of what you need to know will be right there on the label, usually in plain English. To unlock the pleasures of matching beer and food, you need to know only the elements of style.

Beer Styles

Beer labels are simple to read, and this takes away the guesswork of matching beer and food. Unlike wine, beer is generally categorized by style, a designation that gives you some precise information about the brew in the bottle. Wine labels often tell you very little about what's in the bottle—they can even seem to mock you. And for the privilege of finding out more, you're expected to fork over considerable sums of cash. "Oh, you don't know this little hill in this particular corner of the Loire Valley? Well, go away, then"—that seems to be the general attitude of many wine labels. Often, this attitude hides the fact that what's in the bottle isn't very good. If you don't believe me, talk to any wine expert about the difficulty of finding a decent bottle of Burgundy. Beer doesn't have these hang-ups and complexes—it's confident, it knows where it's coming from, and it's happy to tell you about itself.

The first thing a beer usually tells you is the most important thing for you to know—what style it is. Whether the style is German pilsner or imperial stout, that style describes what the beer tastes like, what the aromatics are like, how strong it is, what sort of body it has, how it was brewed, and even what its history is. That's a lot of information. Belgian tripel is an example of a classic style of beer. It was originally brewed by monks, and in some monasteries it still is. It's a beautiful sight—deep burnished gold, with a firm white head. Its aroma is a complex interplay of earthy herbs and spices with the flowery notes of the hops. Sipping it, you'll find pinpoint carbonation and a firm bitterness up front, which gives way to a round, medium-bodied, smooth, dry, spirituous palate that highlights notes of

peaches and pears. The beer is expansive on your palate and fills the senses. As the beer goes down, its strength, formerly hidden by elegance, becomes apparent. At about 9 percent alcohol, it's almost twice as strong as most other styles of beer. The finish is clean and clipped, with a hoppy bite. The aftertaste is warm and herbal, leaving a pleasant glow on your tongue. All tripels have their own personalities, emphases, and differences, but to a certain extent, they'll always fit this basic overall description.

Now that we know what tripel tastes like, we're ready to match it with food. We know that its herbal aromatics will complement dishes with herbs, particularly Provençal dishes with their profusion of thyme and rosemary, such as roast chicken with herbal stuffing. Also, a tripel's firm bitterness cuts through fat and strong flavors. It's going to be beautiful with sausages—there's some bitterness to cut the fat, and the herbal components of the beer and the sausage will harmonize.

"Cheat Sheet": Beer Styles and Flavors

ABBEY—Strong, fruity, spicy, aromatic, complex.
ALTBIER—Bronze-colored, snappy bitterness, full malt flavor.
AMBER—Color signals caramelized flavors in amber ales and lagers.
BARLEY WINE—Very strong, dark, bittersweet, malty, complex—a sipping beer.
BIÈRE DE GARDE—Full-bodied, herbal, flavors of anise and earth.
BITTER—Fruity and racy, subtle, low carbonation, robust hopping.
BOCK—Dark (usually), strong, malty, toffeeish, full-bodied, restrained bitterness.
BROWN ALE—Dark, caramelized, fruity, light chocolate and coffee.
DOPPELBOCK—Very strong, dark, toffeeish, with some sweetness.
DORTMUNDER EXPORT—Golden, dry, bready, moderate bitterness.
DUBBEL—Dark, fruity, complex, raisiny, spicy.
DUNKEL/DUNKLES—Dark, malty, juicy, bready, moderate bitterness.
ESB—"Extra special bitter," amber, fruity, slightly strong, hoppy.
FRAMBOISE/FRAMBOZEN—Beer made with raspberries; can be sweet or dry.
GUEUZE—Pale, dry, funky, wildly complex, quite tart.
HEFEWEIZEN—Wheat beer with yeast, light-bodied, spritzy, clovey, banana-like.
HELLES—Golden, light-bodied, malty, bready, restrained bitterness.
IMPERIAL STOUT—Very strong, dark, roasty, coffeeish, chocolaty, robust.
IPA—"India pale ale," amber, strong, dry, robust hop bitterness and aroma.
KÖLSCH—Very pale gold, bready, lightly fruity, restrained bitterness.

Again, thinking herbal—pesto! This tripel will be very nice with any pasta with pesto sauce, and it has the gusto to fend off garlicky assaults.

Once you know the style of a beer, you're off and running, and you'll have a pretty good idea of what it's going to do with food. If the label doesn't mention a style, don't worry. Some beers don't fit neatly into style descriptions, or the brewer may have chosen to mention the style on the neck label. You'll often find a flavor description of the beer there.

If the label says "IPA," or "India pale ale," this tells you to expect a pale amber beer with a relatively dry palate, sharp bitterness, and plenty of hop flavor. It's great with Mexican dishes. The name "doppelbock" tells you that the beer will be strong and dark, and it will have a slightly sweet, toffeeish malt flavor balanced against moderate bitterness. There's nothing better with pork. "Hefeweizen" will usually be a light-bodied hazy orange-colored beer with high carbonation, a big

KRIEK—Beer made with cherries; can be sweet or dry.
LAMBIC—Fermented by wild yeasts; tart base for gueuze and fruit beers; funky.
MÄRZENBIER—Amber, bready, round, malty, caramelized, juicy, medium-bodied.
MILD—Dark, lightly hopped, caramelized, raisiny, light-bodied.
OKTOBERFEST—Should be the same as "märzenbier," but sometimes paler.
OLD ALE—Somewhat strong, dark, caramelized, fruity, balanced bitterness.
OUD BRUIN—"Old brown," dark, sweet-and-sour, fruity, juicy, raisiny, complex.
PALE ALE—Amber, snappy, dry, fruity, hoppy, with some caramel flavors.
PILSNER—If genuine—golden, dry, sharply bitter, flowery, bready, snappy.
PORTER—Very dark, chocolaty, coffeeish, caramelized, hoppy.
RAUCHBIER—"Smoked beer"; smoky flavors and aromatics, juicy, caramelized.
SAISON—Dry, sharp, spicy, complex, refreshing, hoppy, slightly strong.
SCHWARZBIER—"Black beer," dark, bitter chocolate, dry, caramelized, bready.
SCOTCH ALE—Dark, sometimes strong, malty, full-bodied, restrained bitterness.
STOUT—Black, coffeeish, chocolaty; can be dry or sweet, strong or modest.
TRAPPIST—Made by monks; strong, fruity, spicy, complex.
TRIPEL—Pale, strong, dry, fruity, complex, spicy, rummy, spirituous.
VIENNA-STYLE—Bronze, sweetish, malty, bready, caramelized, light bitterness.
WEISSE/WEISSBIER—Wheat beer, usually with yeast. See "hefeweizen."
WITBIER—Belgian wheat beer, hazy yellow, light-bodied, citric, spritzy, slightly tangy.

CELEBRATOR
DOPPELBOCK
Ayinger

pillowy head, and aromatics of bananas and cloves. It's breakfast beer in Germany, but I usually wait until brunch. "Gueuze" will be pale, dry, funky, complex, and tart. It's perfect with tangy ceviches.

Each beer is different, but knowing a beer's style gives you all the information you need to get started. Brewers are a proud lot—they speak their minds and are not given to hiding. We leave that to the wine folks.

When we are matching beer and food, the most important thing we're looking for is *balance*. We want the beer and food to engage in a lively dance, not a football tackle. In order to achieve the balance we seek, we need to think about the sensory impact of both the beer and its prospective food partner. "Impact" refers to the weight and intensity of the food on the palate. Let's say we're having a barbecue. We've got some big, thick burgers, some saucy ribs, and some skewers of shrimp, tomatoes, and peppers. The shrimp develops a nice sweetness on the grill, as do the veggies. The flavors are delicate, though, so we want to complement them, not overwhelm them. Opening up the cooler, I reach for a Belgian wheat beer to serve with the shrimp. Belgian wheat beers are very light, bright, and spritzy on the palate and have low bitterness and a nice citrus aroma. On the palate, the beer and shrimp play off one another, and the result is delicious. The Belgian wheat beer is great with the shrimp, but what about the burger?

I'm using ground sirloin (only the best for my guests), and the burgers are big and juicy. On top of each one, I add onions, ketchup, mustard, tomato, and cheese. Now, that wheat beer is a lightweight. A burger would obliterate it. So my beer of choice is an American amber lager. It's medium-bodied and refreshing, with a snappy bitterness to cut through all those tasty toppings and some caramel sweetness to match the sweetness of the meat. These two are great together. The bitterness is sharp enough to clear the palate after each bite of the burger, accentuating the burger's appeal. Raw onions, mustard—no worries, the beer is loving every bit of it.

Now, the ribs are finally ready! Just the way we like them, with layers of sweet, spicy, tomato-based sauce cooked on and those crunchy burned bits around the edges. These ribs are intense—probably too intense for the amber lager, which might taste a little thin. There's a lot of sweetness in the sauce, which could make the beer taste drier than we'd like. We need to pull out the big guns—it's time for American brown ale. This is stronger than the amber lager, full-bodied and rich, with refreshingly sharp bitterness up front, and roasted malt flavors of caramel, coffee, and chocolate in the middle. Those roasted caramelized flavors match perfectly with the sweetness of the caramelized meat and sauce, especially those dark crunchy bits. (How come you ended up with all the crunchy bits?)

The brown ale is great with the ribs, but it wouldn't be so great with the shrimp. The flavors of the brown ale are so big that you'd barely taste the shrimp, and we don't want that. That's why impact is all-important—we're looking for a balance between our food and our beer. If one element seems likely to blow the other one away, it probably will. Try to pair light-bodied, lightly hopped, bright-tasting beers with delicately flavored food. As the impact of the food becomes bigger, you can go for bigger beers with snappier bitterness. Once again, you can refer back to the style of the beer to look at what kind of impact you can expect on the palate. For example, Belgian wheat beer will always have a relatively light impact, while American brown ale will always be considerably heavier.

If you're going to serve different beers with each course of a meal, here's another time you should pay some attention to the flavor impact of your prospective beers. Try to serve lighter-flavored beers before those with bigger flavors, and drier beers before sweeter ones. The reason is simple—something heavy will make whatever is served after it taste lighter. If you serve a big roasty coffeeish stout with the appetizer and then serve a light German wheat beer with the main course, you may find that the wheat beer ends up tasting watery, no matter how flavorful it actually is. This isn't any big deal—we tend to put meals together in order of flavor impact too, so it's easy to make everything fall into place.

Most Americans are familiar with beer as a pale yellow, fizzy drink with little flavor. But in the world of traditional beer not only does beer possess plenty of flavor, different levels and types of carbonation are characteristic of different styles of beer. Carbonation is a natural byproduct of fermentation. Carbon dioxide is created when yeast consumes sugar in its noble task of making beer. In finished beer, carbonation gives beer a refreshing lift, concentrates bitterness and acidity, and cleanses the palate. It also lifts the beer's aromas right out of the glass and presents them to your nose. With many dishes, carbonation gives beer a clear edge over wine. The carbonation in beer lifts and scrubs strong flavors from your palate, leaving you ready to enjoy the next bite as if it were the first. That's right—scrubbing bubbles! It is little wonder that in the wine world, only champagne can claim to be as versatile as pilsner or weiss-

bier. Carbonation allows beer to work with mouth-coating foods such as eggs, cheese, and chocolate, where wine frequently stubs its toe. Heavy dishes such as stews or one of my favorites, French cassoulet, are made to seem infinitely lighter by the palate-cleansing power of beer's carbonation. With food, beer is *refreshing*, in the very best sense of the word—it is a restorative for your palate. The power of carbonation should never be underestimated.

Few wines can handle truly spicy food, but the right beer can match perfectly.

At the low end of the carbonation scale are traditional English cask-conditioned pub ales, which, despite their reputation among Americans, should actually be served not warm and flat but lightly chilled and carbonated. These beers undergo a secondary fermentation in the cask, capturing a light natural carbonation. On the palate, it's just a prickle, but it allows all the subtleties of this style of beer to step forward without gassy interference. With straightforward foods like roast beef, it's hard to beat. At the other end of the carbonation spectrum are bottle-conditioned Belgian and German ales, especially wheat beers. They undergo a secondary carbonation in the bottle (very much like champagne), attaining a very high, creamy, pinpoint carbonation. Not only does this raise a beautiful head on the beers; it lends a light magnificent briskness. In some beers, such as Belgian saisons, the carbonation can be volcanic and sharpens the fine, dry bitterness of the beer. The acidity and aromatics of these beers are accentuated and form the basis of their food affinities.

Bright and Dark

We've already considered the intensity of the beer we're thinking of serving. Now it's time to look at how the food has been prepared. This is where the real fun begins—in the fine-tuning. Red snapper calls for a beer with a relatively light body. However, a Thai preparation with coconut milk, lime juice, and chilies will want a brightly flavored beer, while a Ligurian preparation with garlic, herbs, and olives will want something with dark flavors to play into these pungent, earthy flavors. What do we mean by "bright" and "dark"?

Brightness refers to a dry briskness on the palate, sometimes with a refreshing zip of acidity. It also refers to citrus or apple-peel aromatics, sometimes from the yeast strain used, but also from some hop varieties. The Cascade hop, for example, is prized for its aroma, which is redolent of grapefruit and pine needles. American pale ale, for example, has a zippy, focused bitterness to cut through the fat in the coconut milk and big Cascade aromatics to meld with the lime juice and stand up to the chilies. It's going to be very nice with the Thai-style snapper. There's going to be harmony between these flavors.

Darkness refers to roasted flavors such as chocolate, toffee, caramel, and coffee, as well as the flavors and aromas of dark fruits such as plums, raisins, and olives. Sweet spices such as cinnamon and nutmeg belong here too; this is one reason they are often added to stews. Mushrooms are a dark flavor and can work wonderfully with the right beer. If you're lucky enough to get your hands on some truffles, that's a dark flavor too, and you will want a very earthy beer. The Ligurian snapper preparation doesn't want to be overwhelmed by the beer, but it wants darker flavors to match its earthiness. Perhaps here we'll look to a Belgian dubbel. It's a dark beer but retains a light palate with low bitterness, a touch of sweetness, and a complex interplay of earthy, peppery, nutmeggy, raisin-like flavors that will work with the earthy flavors of the Ligurian-style snapper. Again, we're looking for harmony, and traditional beer has so many possible flavors that we can always find harmony if we seek it out.

Let's not confuse bright and dark *flavors* with light and dark *colors*, though. While most dark beers have darker flavors and most pale beers have brighter flavors, this is by no means always the case. For example, the French bière de garde style of farmhouse ale is often golden in color but is also very earthy, with aromatics of herbs, damp soil, and aniseed. Once again, a little familiarity with styles of beer will tell you what you want to know. Once you know, for example, that American pale ales have bright, citrusy aromatics and sharp, snappy bitterness, you'll see why they're a better match for your tacos than the French bière de garde. Citrus flavors work wonderfully with Mexican spicing, which often includes lime juice. Then again, if you're having a stuffed roasted chicken, the earthy, herbal French beer will provide a better match by linking its flavors to the herbs in the stuffing.

A wide range of beers can handle herbs nicely, but a few styles shine. American amber lagers have some herbal notes in their hop aromatics that marry nicely with herbs, especially thyme. Better still, go with Belgian saisons, tripels, golden ales, or French bières de garde, all of which have distinctly herbal aromatics that pair beautifully with powerful herb treatments such as pesto. Despite its Italian origins, pesto is the ruin of many wines, and few wines will work with it as well as the right beer will. Not only do these beers have the herbal component to match the herbs themselves, but the carbonation helps lift the olive oil from the palate and cool the burn of the garlic.

While I respect the can-do attitude of today's young hotshot sommeliers, I've got some bad news for them, and they might as well just accept it: wine and hot, spicy food just don't work very well together. Oh, sure, you can try, and the intellectual exercise is fun. You can get excited about how that New Zealand sauvignon blanc is going to match the dish with its bright flavors of limes and mangoes. The fun ends, though, when you actually put them in your mouth and your tongue reports to your brain what you already knew—"We have a problem." Hot spices distort and exaggerate wine flavors—tannins become tough and grainy, alcohol turns fiery, oak turns to furniture polish. Not to mention wine's almost total lack of affinity for cilantro, cumin, ginger, mustard, cinnamon, cardamom, and other spices common in a lot of the food we love. I'm not saying that a decent match with wine is impossible, but it is certainly difficult. Matching these dishes with beer is easy—beer leaps in where wine fears to tread. Beer has sweetness to counteract the heat, far less alcohol, and bubbles to soothe the palate and lift hot oils away. Hop and fermentation aromatics can do wonders with the spices I just mentioned, and the right choice will really sing. Weissbiers, witbiers, pilsners, American pale ales, and Belgian saisons all know the tune.

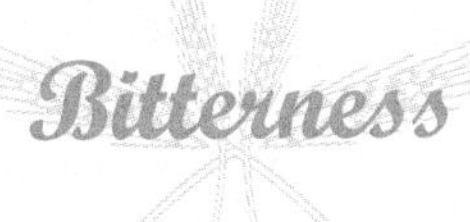

Ah, the dirty word. To the American mind, it suggests something to avoid—harshness or acridity. The Italians, however, who have a highly developed sense of flavor, love bitterness and realize that it can be refreshing and can stimulate the appetite. Look behind any well-stocked Italian bar and you'll see at least one row of *amari*, or bitters. Campari, Chinotto, and their brethren start off many Italian meals as aperitifs, and a sharp espresso signals the end of the repast. Perhaps we should have a closer look at bitterness. The Italians are pretty smart when it comes to flavor.

Well-applied hop bitterness makes a beer racy and refreshing. Like tannin or acidity in wine, this bitterness provides the counterpoint to the sweetness of malt and is the backbone of the beer's flavor structure. Just as we wouldn't usually want overly tannic or very acidic wine, we may not want very hoppy beer, at least not all the time. Too much bitterness can overwhelm delicately flavored food. Without bitterness, though, beer would be dead on the palate and, at best, would just wash down our food like soda pop. Mass-market beers have barely any perceptible bitterness; this is one of the shortcomings that renders them so insipid.

Well-hopped beers have the ability to cut through heavy sauces, fats, and oils, leaving the palate cleansed and refreshed rather than stunned. A medium-rare steak doesn't want a sweet, unctuous beer; it wants something sharp enough to slice through those deep flavors so you can enjoy the next bite. The same principle applies for sausages, smoked fish, smoked meats, or oily fish. Before the 1400s, English ales were unhopped and in fact were often sweet. Once hops came on the scene, the unhopped version of ale quickly died out, and it's not hard to imagine why.

Hops are not the only ingredient that can lend bitterness to a beer. Roasted malts can also add their own bitterness—just as espresso has a roasted bite, so does an Irish stout, and only partly from the hops. In beer, bitterness is focused and accentuated by lower serving temperatures, higher carbonation, and a low residual sugar content. Conversely, malt sweetness, warmer serving temperatures, and lower carbonation will temper bitterness.

Just as you can actually measure the spiciness of chilies in "Scoville units" by finding out how much capsaicin they contain, you can measure the bitterness of beer. The hops contain several bittering compounds, and they can be measured in International Bittering Units (IBUs). Some beer labels, especially if the beer is from the hop-happy Pacific Northwest, may actually give you this information, claiming, for example, a snappy 50 IBUs for their India pale ale.

Is this something you need to know? Not really. Not unless you're a brewer or a beer fan wearing a propellered beanie. Just as I don't need to know that habanero peppers have 20,000 Scoville units of heat to know that they're *really, really* hot, I'm not very interested in hearing beer explained to me in numbers either. Some chilies start off really hot, then mellow out over the course of a meal, while others slowly catch up with you until your mouth is on fire with the last bite. Scoville units don't tell you anything about that. Hops, too, have their own personalities. Some have a snappy, whip-crack bitterness that dissipates after a few seconds, while others have a bitterness that lies across your tongue like a carpet. In real life, numbers can't describe flavor. If you're interested in flavor, hops can be endlessly fascinating. All you really need to know about the numbers is that generally speaking, anything above 40 IBUs is likely to be fairly bitter.

In their attempt to appeal to the lowest common denominator, American megabrewers have removed almost all the bitterness from their products. What you're left with is an empty burst of carbonation with no flavor to back it up. Some mass-market beers actually advertise that their beer is "never bitter," trying to scare people away from real beer. That's too bad. Can you imagine a steakhouse boasting that its steaks are "never juicy"?

Malt, Sweetness, and Caramelization

Barley and wheat are the building blocks of most traditional beer. Both are full of warm, nutty flavors that conjure up notions of home, comfort, and purity. The warm, breadlike flavors of grain are more prevalent in some styles of beer than others, making them better companions for certain foods. Malty beers tend to be full-bodied and round on the palate.

A corollary to malt is sweetness. Perceived sweetness is a result of four main factors. First is residual sugar, malt sugars that the yeast didn't consume. Some of these sugars simply add body to the beer, but others actually taste sweet. These sugars can match up nicely with sweetness in a dish. Second is bitterness—the more bitter a beer is, the drier it will taste. Bitterness and sweetness balance each other—if you have more of one, you will taste less of the other. A beer with very little residual sugar may still taste slightly sweet if the bitterness is low. In this case, the beer will usually taste sweet in the center but dry in the finish. Even dry, bitter beers may have considerable malt aroma and flavor—northern German pilsners are a good example. In this case, we have a bready flavor and aroma but very little sweetness. This sort of beer is very refreshing and makes a fine aperitif. Third is carbonation. Carbonation expresses itself on the tongue as carbonic acid, increasing acidity and concentrating bitterness. The more highly carbonated a beer is, the drier and snappier it will seem. Conversely, if a beer loses its carbonation, it will seem sweeter. Fourth, temperature will affect your perception of sweetness. The colder a beer is, the drier (and more bitter) it will seem. This effect makes serving temperature as important for beer as it is for wine.

Grilled and roasted foods develop caramelized sugar flavors that we all crave. Our love for these flavors is probably hardwired into our brains and bred into our bones, because it's not hard to imagine that early humans who learned to cook their food thoroughly were likely to lead longer, healthier lives. The caramelized flavors in our favorite dishes are looking for a companion. In the sweetness of malt they'll find a willing partner, especially when the malts have been caramelized also. Wine has no partnering qualities for the caramelized flavors that we love—it can only provide a contrast. Caramel and crystal malts provide beer with flavors that link directly into the darkly browned surface of a steak, a roasted chicken, crispy duck, and even roasted vegetables. Conversely, accentuating the caramelized flavors in your food will provide a better match with your beer.

Many beers have a moderate level of sweetness on the palate, and this helps them match foods that have their own sweet elements. Sugar is an important ingredient in many Thai dishes, including the ubiquitous noodle dish, pad thai. German weissbier is a good choice here for many reasons, one of which is the beer's slight sweetness, which picks up on the sugar in the dish. Classic French duck preparations and many pork dishes rely on fruit to sweeten them. Dry red wines rarely meet with genuine success—the sweetness leaves them tasting thin and tough. German doppelbock can bring its own sweetness to the party, and the warmth of the malt flavors will melt into duck or pork beautifully.

Americans, brought up to fear the depredations of Thunderbird and Manischewitz, often run in the opposite direction when sweetness shows up in wine. This is a mistake when it comes to wine, and equally so when it comes to beer. Residual sweetness can be cloying when the beer has no food companion, but when desserts, stews, or cheeses hit the table, this quality can become a major asset. Most beers have enough residual sugar to match the sweetness in many dishes. When a dish has more than a dash of sugar in it, you should make sure your beer does too.

Roast

Beers made with roasted malts develop flavors of chocolate and coffee. Chocolate and coffee offer an amazing variety of flavors, and so do the malts these beers are made with. A beer can have a flavor of American milk chocolate or of French dark chocolate. A stout can taste like a biting espresso, or it can have the character of a sweetened latté. These roasted flavors in beer have a flavor "hook" that matches up perfectly with the char on grilled foods. The same flavors also provide a brilliant counterpoint to the saltiness of good ham or prosciutto. With desserts, strong roasty stouts can demonstrate true brilliance, perfectly matching chocolate and provid-

ing a wonderful contrast to ice cream and fruit desserts. Wine, being incapable of true roasted flavors, can't even come close.

After Dinner—Matching Desserts and Cheeses

Desserts

Quit chuckling and listen up, because I've got a secret for you—beer is brilliant with dessert. In fact, it's unbeatable. I once hosted a beer luncheon attended by New York's top sommeliers. The luncheon was held at the famous Gramercy Tavern, and to finish the meal, we served pastry chef Claudia Fleming's magnificent "trio of chocolate desserts." A chocolate and caramel tart shared the plate with a rich molten-centered chocolate cake and a tiny chocolate malted milk shake. As dessert was served, I issued a challenge—that none of the guests could think of a single wine that could match these desserts as well as either of the beers I was serving. The sommeliers were stunned by the bold challenge, but not as stunned as they were by the combination of the desserts with the beers. A few of them later said they'd had a beer epiphany.

My challenge was a bit unfair—wine never stood a chance. I served my own Brooklyn Black Chocolate Stout, an Imperial stout with a huge, complex dark chocolate and coffee flavor, and Lindemans Framboise, a sweet Belgian lambic fermented with outrageously fragrant raspberries. Dessert wines can be wonderful, but they can match only the sweetness of chocolate—the right beer can actually match the flavors, making for a far more profound taste experience. And the combination of raspberry and chocolate flavors is equally difficult to beat. When it comes right down to it, sweet wines should be served either by themselves or with cheese—they are almost always a poor match for desserts. The sommeliers conceded my challenge, and they hadn't even tasted my vanilla ice cream and chocolate stout float. Even with non-chocolate desserts, stouts can stand in for coffee, cutting across the sweetness rather than matching it, and adding an entirely different dimension of flavor. Well-made fruit beers can approach these desserts from an entirely different direction, opening up all sorts of wonderful possibilities. For example, we can serve Belgian kriek, fermented with Schaarbeek sour cherries, with a rich vanilla ice cream. Even better, we can serve it with cheesecake, with or without cherries on top. Who's laughing now?

Cheese

I suppose now you think I'm really deep behind enemy lines, in the middle of wine country. Not at all—cheese, especially great artisanal cheese, is solid turf for traditional beer. The dirty little secret of the wine world is that most wine, especially red wine, is a very poor match for cheese. Don't believe me? Ask an honest sommelier. One prominent wine writer, Brian St. Pierre, says in his book *The Perfect Match* that he's "had to conclude that the idea of matching red wine with cheese, basically, doesn't really work most of the time." He goes on to say that the relationship between wine and cheese is "more like a cordially wary relationship than a real marriage." Another wine writer, Joanna Simon, in the section on cheese in her book *Wine with Food*, laments at the outset, "Matching cheese with wine is fraught with confrontations. . . . The idea that wine and cheese are perfect companions is, I'm afraid, one of the great myths." Yet another says that "even apparently mild cheeses, such as Brie, can clash horribly, especially if you let them get too ripe and runny." Do you notice a pattern emerging here?

Many of us like to have good cheese after a meal, and we end up finishing our bottle of wine with the cheese; the liaison between the two is often accidental and awkward. Sweet dessert wines can be fine with cheese, but we often end up drinking dry reds and whites, which don't really work at all. Think about it—where do you usually see wine and cheese offered together? That's right—parties, weddings, and openings of art shows. The reason why many people end up serving wine with cheese, especially at parties, is that cheese coats the palate, blunting the flavor of the wine. This makes tougher wines taste pretty much OK, which is fine. For less-than-wonderful wines, cheese is the great equalizer, a fact that wine shops are fully aware of. Beer can do a lot better—it can find such harmony with cheese that you won't know where the beer ends and the cheese begins. Traditional beer and cheese are absolutely perfect together.

It's not very surprising, when you think about it. Beer and cheese are both traditionally farmhouse products, often made by the same person. (Have you ever seen a cow in a vineyard? Neither have I.) They both derive, to some extent, from grasses, though one could argue that the cow has a bigger effect on the grasses than the brewhouse does. They are both fermented and aged, and the type of microflora doing the fermenting greatly influences the outcome. They both balance sweetness and acidity with fruitiness and fermentation flavors. Many cheesemakers have become brewers and vice versa, and it's not hard to see why.

We're talking about serious cheeses with complex, often funky flavors and aromas. The secret to matching is that we can find harmony as well as contrast. For example, traditional aged cheddars such as Grafton Village (Vermont) and Montgomery (England) have a refined sharp acidity balanced by fruitiness and nuttiness. We'll look for a beer that has a sharp bitterness to work with the cheese's sharpness, some nice fruit character, and biscuity malt to match the nuttiness. India pale ale fits the bill perfectly—all the elements are in harmony, and the combination sets off fireworks on the palate. It's no surprise that this sort of combination is the basis for the traditional British "ploughman's lunch" of good cheese, cold meat, and bread. Belgian saison and aged Gouda are another great combination that works in a similar fashion.

Most American "Swiss cheese" is pretty bland stuff, but real Gruyère can have amazing depth. One of my favorites is a cave-aged version from Emmi, an excellent Swiss producer. It has a bold nuttiness with a latent acidity and funky concentrated grassy Alpine milk flavors. Roth Käse of Wisconsin also makes a great version. Doppelbock—strong, silky, toffeeish, and slightly sweet—matches it so well that you start to suspect that the cheese has doppelbock in it. The dominant malt flavor in the beer latches onto the nutty flavors in the cheese and doesn't let go.

I once hosted a tasting at Peter Kump's New York Cooking School (now the Institute of Culinary Education) called "The Cheese Wars—Beer versus Wine with Cheese." I wielded the beer, while in the other corner, my friend Paul Grieco, the brilliant former sommelier of Gramercy Tavern, brandished his wines. We served seven great cheeses, each paired with both a beer and a wine. When we got to the funkiest—no, let's be honest here, the stinkiest—cheese on the plate, everyone seemed to think that Paul would prevail. The cheese was Livarot, referred to in its native France as *les pieds de Dieu*, "the feet of God." (Trust the French to deliver the type of blunt culinary honesty that you really don't need.) Surely wine would be the best match for this most French of cheeses? I drew my secret weapon—Castelain, a French bière de garde, displaying a complex aromatic interplay of damp earth, herbs, and aniseed, wrapped around a soft golden beer with a warm, malty center. Eyebrows were raised. The match was perfect. The wine was vanquished. Paul is a wine genius, and he managed a few nice matches over the course of the evening, but I delivered the coup de grâce with the last cheese, the wonderfully pungent Colston-Basset Stilton. Paul deployed a very tasty dessert wine, but I had a secret weapon—J. W. Lees Harvest Ale 1988, a beautifully aged barley wine from Manchester, England. The beer was sweet and massively nutty, with flavors of dark fruit and earth—it embraced the cheese like an old friend. The beer had won. For the record, Paul didn't bring any red wines at all—his entries were all off-dry whites.

I love goat cheeses, especially aged ones. California's Cypress Grove Humboldt Fog is among my favorites. It has two cakes separated by a layer of ash, and it goes runny under the rind as it ages—that's when it's really good. Like most goat cheeses, this one wants some sweetness on the palate to balance the tang. A spicy Belgian beer with some residual sweetness would do the trick; but since the cheese is American, I'm moved to reach for Hennepin, a Belgian-style saison brewed in Cooperstown, New York. Hennepin is soft, round, and slightly sweet, with a yeasty earthiness and gentle spicing. Both bitter and sweet orange peel are used, and the beer has a distinctly orangey aroma. When this beer meets the Humboldt Fog, the flavors dovetail remarkably.

My favorite combination of beer and cheese is probably hundreds of years old. Barley wine and Stilton are a match so excellent that the British aristocracy kept it from the rest of us for generations. Of course, Stilton was originally meant to be eaten with beer, and that fact becomes immediately apparent when they meet on your palate. I'm a big fan of port wines; and port and Stilton are, I must say, a very nice combination. That match, however, is based on a simple contrast between the sweet fruitiness of the port and the salty pungency of the cheese; there's no actual harmony between them. When Stilton meets a barley wine, especially a nicely aged English barley wine, the harmony of flavors is nothing short of astonishing. Colston-Basset is my favorite; it's a buttery, earthy version that brings an entire barnyard of flavors to the table. A great barley wine just wraps around those flavors, caresses them with its sweetness, then subsumes them into its profoundly deep malt flavors, a riot of fruit, sherry, baking bread, and earth. Absolutely stunning—the perfect end to a great meal.

Traditional fruit beers open up a whole different set of possibilities, especially with sweet cheeses like mascarpone, stracchino, teleme, burrata, or fresh goat cheese. Here, the sweet versions work quite well. The New Glarus Brewing Company of Wisconsin produces two excellent fruit beers, Raspberry Tart and Wisconsin Belgian Red, the latter fermented with Wisconsin cherries. A combination of either of these with Peluso Teleme, a runny, sweet cow's milk cheese from California, shows the delicious potential of fruit beers with sweet cheeses. Once you get started, you'll find it difficult to stop. And why should you?

PART TWO: Brewing Traditions

4

Lambic

Paintings by Pieter Bruegel from the mid-1500s reveal a theme—beer, being joyously and copiously poured from pottery jugs.

The same beer is still being made today. The Payottenland district west of central Brussels is home to lambic beer, the world's oldest beer style. "Lambic" is probably derived from Lembeek, a small town in Payottenland that was once a small city-state and a stronghold of lambic brewers. Whereas most modern brewers take great care to exclude wild yeasts and bacterial strains from their brews, lambic brewers take the opposite route. They literally fling the windows open and invite nature in. This is the way beer was fermented hundreds, even thousands, of years ago, when even the most accomplished brewers didn't know what yeast was. Back then, all beers underwent "spontaneous fermentation" by wild yeast and bacteria. If I tried this in Brooklyn, I'd probably end up with an unfortunate result, but the airborne microflora in Payottenland produce some of the most complex and fascinating beers in the world. Some of the same wild yeasts make up the famous *flor* that graces fino sherry, and they help develop a similar character in lambic beer. The ancient process gives lambic beers fruity, funky flavors and sharp, acidic palates. Behind the sourness is a riot of earthy, toasty flavors and aromas, comparable to those of the finest blue cheeses.

Lambic beers have always been brewed with a portion of unmalted wheat, which by recent Belgian royal decrees must make up at least 30 percent of the mashing grist. The same decrees dictate the minimum concentration of the wort, the minimum acidity of the resulting beer, and that lambic beers must be spontaneously fermented. The majority of the grain in the mash is malted barley, which contains sufficient enzymes to coax the unmalted wheat into converting and releasing its sugars. Where most brewers want the freshest possible hops, lambic brewers prefer them aged. Aged hops have lost most of their bittering power, but their preservative abilities are left intact; this will promote a balance between yeast and bacteria during the fermentation. The lambic brewer has little need of hop bitterness—acidity will provide the backbone of his beer.

Up until this point, the process has been merely eccentric. But when the kettle boil is finished, things get stranger still, and the brewing process takes a sharp detour into the past. The wort is run out of the kettle into a "cool ship," a large shallow rectangular pan occupying most of a large room in the brewery's attic. Most breweries once had cool ships: the large surface area cooled the liquid overnight, and as soon as the temperature was safe the brewer's yeast was rushed into service—the brewmaster hoped that no uninvited guests had gotten there first. In a lambic brewery, the guests are explicitly welcomed. Broken tiles, missing roof slats, and hanging cobwebs are left undisturbed so that nature will take its course. Louvers in the roof direct the wind down onto the surface of the wort, cooling it while bringing in the airborne microflora of the countryside. By morning, the liquid is alive with activity, and it is transferred to wooden casks.

All beer was once fermented in wood, but lambic is the only type for which this remains the standard method. The wooden casks have usually been retired from sherry and port production and inherited by lambic brewers. Some casks are working into their second centuries as well as their second careers. They are

Bottles and oak casks of wild-fermented lambic beer rest quietly at Brouwerij Boon, in Lembeek, Belgium.

enormous—each one holds 11,220 liters of beer and is almost three meters tall at the end. Many are oval-shaped, allowing more casks to be placed in a limited space. Wood cannot be sterilized, but killing off microorganisms is the farthest thing from the lambic brewer's mind. Dozens of different organisms in the fermenting wort will meet a host of others as the fermenting beer flows into the casks. Here the beer will rest, perhaps for as little as four or five months, perhaps for years. The casks, many of them taller than a man, lie on their sides in long silent rows, caked in molds and dust. A complex chain of reactions and fermentations will be shared among the casks' microscopic denizens. Communities this complex lead different lives and make different decisions. One cask may become quite sour while the one next to it ages to a mellow, toasty quality. Yet another may veer toward rich fruitiness. The Brettanomyces family of yeasts is resident in each cask, creating its trademark musty, leathery, "horse-blanket" aroma. None is predictable. The conventional brewer would consider this a nightmare; the lambic brewer sees a treasure trove.

Some casks will be sold as straight, unblended lambic, but this has become rare. Straight lambic is very dry, amazingly complex, and almost without carbonation. When young, the beers tend to be honey-colored and boldly acidic—in this they are reminiscent of some traditional farmhouse ciders. Mature lambic tends to be mellower, trading its youthful acidity for greater depth. Fruit seems to leap out of the glass, but there's none to be found; the wild yeasts have done this themselves. Traditionally, straight lambic would be sold by the cask either to cafés or to blending houses. Blending houses, or *negociants*, were very similar to those still operating in France to produce champagne. After blending lambics from various sources to achieve a house character, the negociant would sell the resulting beer under his own name. Lambic blending houses were once very common, but there are only a few left today. Another common practice was for lambic brewers to sell wort to another house, which would then ferment the wort in its own cellars and blend its own beers for sale. Today, only Hanssens of Dworp continues this tradition of fermenting and blending.

If young lambic is tart and lively, and mature lambic is smooth, deep, and mellow, what might happen if the two were married? The answer is gueuze, which at its best combines the most alluring qualities of old and young lambic in a remarkably complex and refreshing beer. There are a number of stories about where the name comes from, though none of them is entirely convincing. Say "GER-ser" while clearing your throat, and at least you'll have the pronunciation down pat.

Gueuze is a blend of mature lambic with young lambic that is still fermenting. After the blending, the residual sugars contributed by the young beer will continue to ferment out, giving the gueuze a lively champagne-like carbonation. Like the blending of wine or Scotch whisky, the blending of gueuze is an art form. Every cask of lambic is different and evolving. The blender will seek to bring out the best qualities of each cask, to discover its unique talents. If a cask is developing particularly well, he may decide to keep it for years and perhaps sell it as straight lambic. Then again, he may wish to use it to ennoble a particularly fine gueuze. Other casks are best suited to an addition of fruit, resulting in kriek or framboise. The decisions are complex and difficult.

In each blend, the proportion of young beer to old will be critical. The young lambic may have been in the cask for only five or six months—it has little depth and plenty of acidity. The older lambic is mellow, aromatic, deep, and, naturally, more expensive. After all the casks are tasted and the decisions made, the proportion of young beer may be as much as 70 percent or as little as 15 percent. A lower proportion of young beer will tend to produce a very classy gueuze, freshened by carbonation and acidity, but retaining great aroma, complexity, and length. After the blending, a traditional gueuze will be bottled and then cellared at the brewery for at least six months and sometimes for much longer. The bottles are placed on their sides in wooden racks, just as bottles of aging wine are. Long, damp galleries of bottle racks share cellar space with aging casks.

Traditionally, all gueuze would have been bottle-conditioned and flintily dry, but many brewers have caved in to the public sweet tooth and added sugar to their beers. These versions are aged in stainless steel tanks before being sweetened, filtered, bottled, and pasteurized. They are usually mere shadows of their forebears. For a time it appeared that traditional gueuze would be swept away by the less challenging commercial versions, but there has been a revival of traditional gueuze in recent years. In some cases, a commercial producer, stung by criticism, has emerged with an excellent artisanal version of his beer. When the two versions sit side by side on a shelf, a reference on the label to "refermentation in the bottle" will lead you to the real thing. Otherwise, look for a dusting of yeast in the bottle. When pouring such a beer, you should decant it carefully, leaving the sediment in the bottle. The sediment is harmless but doesn't add anything pleasant to the beer, which should be perfectly clear when poured. Like good champagne, gueuze should be served moderately chilled rather than ice-cold—this allows the beer to release its full array of flavors and aromas.

Traditional lambic brewers and blenders are fiercely dedicated artisans climbing a waterfall of commercialism, money, and history. Their products are very much worth seeking out. I won't kid you—lambic beers are not for everyone. I find them delicious if undeniably funky, like many of my favorite cheeses. But they are an absolute riot of elegant, complex, brilliant flavors, and no one with a real interest in food and drink could fail to be fascinated by them. If you enjoy traditional farmhouse ciders or very dry vintage champagnes, you may very well enjoy gueuze. Like many great wines and sherries, these beers find their greatest glory in their combinations with food.

Most Americans who have had lambic beer first encounter it in the form of kriek or framboise. *Kriek* is Flemish for "cherry," and *framboise* is French for "raspberry" (*frambozen* in Flemish). Cherry and raspberry beer? Is this a joke? Certainly not. A gimmick? If so, it's been a gimmick for centuries. The border between wine country and beer country runs right through Belgium and also through its food culture. In the days before brewers discovered hops, they flavored their beers with all sorts of things, and the Belgians have retained more of that history than anyone else. They are not entirely alone. Even the Germans, who are conservative with regard to beer, have long added fruit syrups to their sharply sour Berliner weisse and blended lemonade and pilsner to create the popular Radlermass.

Cherries and raspberries grow wild, and before the days of freezing and canning, anything left unconsumed at the end of the season was destined to be lost. Heedless of any clear dividing line between wine and beer, brewers would gather the last of the fruit, which had often begun to dry on the tree or bush. They added the fruit to barrels of lambic beer, and the resident yeast went to work on the sugars, consuming the flesh of the fruit in a rush of new fermentation. A fistful of twigs would be placed into the bunghole of the barrel to prevent the fruit from being ejected before the yeast was finished. The result was a stronger, transformed beverage that sat squarely on the border between wine and beer.

At the most traditional lambic breweries, this technique has changed very little. The base beer is usually a blend of old and young lambic beers, but it is not destined to become a gueuze. Instead, fruit is added, and the fermentation starts anew. The most robust examples of kriek may require the addition of a pound of cherries for every few liters of beer. The local cherry of Brussels, the sour Schaarbeek variety, is preferred for the production of kriek, especially when the fruit has dried on the tree, concentrating the sugars. As the yeast consumes the flesh of the cherries, the pits are bared and start to add their nuttiness and bitterness to the beer. If the beer remains on the fruit for six or eight weeks, it will

retain a lot of fresh fruit flavor and color. If it remains longer, the beer will become drier, fruit flavors will mature into something deeper, and cherry stones will add some astringency. Just as the base lambic will often have been blended, different casks of kriek may be blended as well, as the brewer seeks the desired complexity and a fine balance of aroma, flavor, and acidity. Some more young lambic may be added before bottling to give the beer sufficient residual sugar for refermentation. The beer will then be cellared before it is released.

By the time a kriek or framboise is released, it may contain some beer as young as three months and some as old as two years. It will have been fermented at least three times—one beer fermentation, one fruit fermentation, and then a final fermentation in the bottle. Each fermentation has added to the beer's strength, which eventually ranges between 5 percent and 7 percent. Dozens of yeasts will invariably have been involved, each adding its influence. A blend of lambic beers may encounter a blend of fruit, and then the resulting beer may be blended again before bottling. It is little wonder that these beers can be amazingly complex.

Traditional kriek and framboise are sharp and dry, with exceptional length and depth on the palate. Less traditional versions are filtered, sweetened, or both, their complexity blunted along with their sharpness; fruit juices or purees may be used instead of whole fruit. Lambic aficionados are given to frothing at the mouth when the latter versions are mentioned, but I feel that both types have their place. Don't forget that some people always sweetened their beers, when they could afford it—sugar was once a luxury. While the traditional versions can be excellent aperitifs and very nice with savory dishes, no dessert wine can hope to rival sweetened kriek and framboise with desserts.

Lambics with Food

Lambics are quite low in bitterness, but they make up for it with plenty of acidity, which will drive their pairings with food. You won't find straight, unblended lambic outside Belgium's specialist cafés, so let's start with gueuze. While gueuze is undeniably acidic, this acidity is rarely uncompromising—many champagnes have a similar sharpness. And only the very finest champagnes can approach the complexity of a great gueuze. Gueuze makes a great aperitif, but this does not limit its appeal at the dinner table.

The acidity of gueuze lends it most obviously to seafood. *Moules frites* (mussels with fries) is a Belgian staple, and the mussels are often steamed in gueuze. The same beer provides an excellent accompaniment, as the sweetness of the sea meets the sourness of the beer. Along similar lines, this is the perfect beer

OPPOSITE: Most modern brewers would be appalled by cobwebs, but lambic brewers take care not to disturb the mini-ecosystems that produce their unique beers.

to have with escargots (a word that sounds much nicer than "snails"), especially if they're swimming in butter and garlic. Gueuze is also very nice with oysters, waking up the oyster's flavor like a burst of fresh lemon juice. Good crab cakes—I like them spicy—will enjoy an encounter with gueuze, which is bold enough to withstand chilies and works well with bright ingredients like lime juice.

Gueuze has cutting power that is perfect for oily fish—salmon, bluefish, sardines, and mackerel will make good matches. Smoked salmon is also a great partner. Better still is ceviche, the Spanish dish of seafood "cooked" by the acidity of lemon or lime juice. The Spanish spread ceviche throughout the Caribbean, to Mexico, and to Belgium, which they once ruled. At La Palapa, an excellent traditional Mexican restaurant in New York City, I enjoyed Boon Gueuze with a brilliant ceviche full of shrimp, avocado, and chilies. The match was absolutely perfect—at that moment, it was hard to imagine having the ceviche with anything else.

The Belgians don't confine gueuze to seafood. They also like it with tangy goat cheese, farmhouse terrines, sausages, and salads. Oddly, gueuze makes a fine match with Stilton—the beer and cheese, if they're at their best, have barnyard aromatics that link up perfectly. The acidity of the beer slices right through the fattiness of the cheese. With a bit of bread or some crackers, the two make a very satisfying afternoon snack.

Aside from gueuze, the only other type of lambic you're likely to find in this country is fruit lambic. Fruit lambics come in two basic types. Outside Belgium, you'll see far more of the modern variant, which blends lambic beer with fruit puree or juice to create a sweet kriek or framboise. With a bit more searching, you might also find the traditional versions of these beers, made with whole fruit that ferments out fully, leaving nothing behind but pits. These are sold unfiltered, and they are usually quite dry. They tend to be tart and austere, but extremely complex.

The traditional versions, lacking sweetness, are not always dessert beers, despite their encounters with fruit. They can be terrific with savory dishes. Duck and goose can be matched brilliantly by a traditional kriek—the acidity cuts the fat of the duck, while the subtle fruit flavors provide a beautiful counterpoint. Venison, which is often served with a sour cherry sauce, is also a good partner for traditional kriek. At t'Spinnekopke, a restaurant in Brussels famous for its *cuisine à la bière*, I once had a chicken prepared in a framboise-based cream sauce. It was delicious, though I have to admit that the bright lavender color of the dish was rather alarming. These beers are also delicious served with sharp, fresh goat cheeses.

When dry kriek or framboise meets Mexico's traditional chocolate-based mole sauces, prepare for a brilliant interplay of flavors. Real mole negro is austere, complex, and spicy, not sweet. Unsweetened chocolate is combined with ground chilies, nuts, seeds, and spices to create one of the world's great sauces, which is traditionally served on festive days. Pair it with dry fruit lambic, and you have fireworks. Both the acidity and the fruit are perfectly suited to the mole, and the complexity of the combination can be breathtaking. Both lambic beer and mole negro are many centuries old, but I doubt that they met until recently. Only in America.

Sweetened fruit lambics may be the bane of die-hard beer traditionalists, but they're a great friend to the pastry chef and the sommelier. As hard as some people try to convince us, the fact remains that wine is rarely good with dessert. No, not even dessert wines, which are best enjoyed on their own or with cheese. It is very sad to watch someone trying desperately to claim that zinfandel can match chocolate (it can't), when a sweet kriek or framboise will make a perfect match. Let's face it—you don't have to work very hard here. With any chocolate dessert, the sweetness of these beers will match that of the dessert. Then the combination of chocolate and fruit flavors, backed by lifting carbonation, will send your taste buds right into orbit. End of story. Foolproof. What else do you need to know? It's *perfect*. Port, Sauternes, Banyuls—no wine can come close to doing this. Among beers, only strong stout can rival such a performance. As far as I'm concerned, every restaurant that serves chocolate desserts owes it to the customers to serve these beers. Served in champagne glasses, these beers are deep red with a fluffy pink head, the very picture of elegance. Between courses, they make great palate-cleansing substitutes for sorbet.

Strangely, sweet fruit lambics rarely work well with fruit desserts. You'd think they would work perfectly, but the acidity and fruit in the beer and in the dessert are actually so similar that they cancel each other out, and the distinct flavors of each are lost. It's a strange case, in which the flavors are almost too complementary. Some other desserts work nicely, though. Cheesecake, for example, is an absolute revelation. In this case, you can have the cheesecake with fruit or without—it will work wonderfully either way. Panna cotta is also a brilliant match—the sweet-and-sour fruit flavors, backed by the complexities of the underlying beer, are enveloped by the pure sweet flavor of the cream. Sheer beauty.

In a similar vein, you can match these beers with a full range of fresh, sweet cheeses—mascarpone, teleme, and stracchino are all fine partners. Whether traditional or sweetened, fruit lambics are great food beers, a worthy addition to every cellar. Be creative, and you can have a lot of fun with them.

Notable Producers of Lambic

BROUWERIJ BOON A visit to Frank Boon's brewery in Lembeek is a trip in a time machine. You are catapulted back into the 1800s, when beer was truly handmade. The brewhouse is cobbled together from antique equipment—you can almost imagine that you hear steam engines at work. Behind the brewhouse is the "cellar," where row on row of giant oak *foudres*, or casks, sit on their sides, biding their time as the lambic ripens. The cobwebs waft gently between them as you walk by. The heads of the casks are marked with indecipherable alchemical-looking symbols, the meanings known only to Frank and his brewers. The casks themselves are ancient. Many of them were made in Germany almost a hundred years ago and were given to Belgium as reparations after World War I. The names of long-defunct German breweries are still stamped deeply in the wood.

Beer runs in Frank Boon's blood. His grandmother and her brothers owned a lager brewery when Frank was young, but the brewery fell on hard times and finally closed in 1970. Frank promised his parents he'd never become a brewer—it was a dead-end job, they told him. Still, the family brewed beer and made cider at home, and the process fascinated him. In 1972, the family moved to the Payottenland area, and the only person Frank knew there was a Mr. De Vits, the local lambic brewer. Frank and his friends liked to hang out at the brewery, drinking lambic and telling stories. Boon was nineteen, and De Vits was sixty-eight and expecting to retire soon. De Vits had no heir and planned to close the brewery when he retired. When Boon asked De Vits why he didn't sell the brewery, De Vits shrugged, saying, "Who would take up such a difficult business?"

Frank felt something stir—he decided that he was going to break his promise and become a brewer. He set aside his degree in social sciences and started a beer distribution business, selling fine Belgian beer to the cafés of Brussels. He was successful, and by 1977 he was able to buy the De Vits brewery. He wanted to make traditional lambic of excellent quality, knowing that no giant brewery would ever take up the labor- and capital-intensive production of this ancient style of beer. Lambic remains a small specialty, but Frank Boon is a success, both as a brewer and as a businessman. He wants to expand, and a partnership with the larger Palm brewery has given him the means to do so.

Geuze Boon (his own spelling) is a deep orange beer that opens with a lively pop of its cork. The beer has a lively champagne-like carbonation. The nose is pure lambic—French cider apples, wet wool, rose petals, ripe Brie, orange rinds, and a Riesling-like catty note. The palate is dry, with bitterness and acidity in perfect balance up front, falling back to reveal interlocked flavors of apples, hay, iron, and oak. A gorgeous example of traditional gueuze. This beer is great with mussels, shrimp, escargots, smoked salmon, ceviche, goat cheeses, oysters, and pâté de campagne.

Framboise Boon hides its hints of red behind a veil of brown. Earth, raspberries, and butterscotch aromatics fill the nose. The palate is lightly sweet up front, with mild acidity following through to a fruity finish. This beer is pleasant, but not big enough to take on deep chocolate—try it with a more delicate chocolate mousse instead. It would also be quite nice with a goat cheese salad.

Boon saves some of his best beer for the creation of his special **Boon Mariage Parfait** ("perfect marriage") **Framboise**, which carries a "vintage" date on the label. The raspberries aren't in hiding here—this beer looks like a Burgundy wearing a cap of foam. The aroma is outrageous—raspberries, butter, dandelions, roses, wet wool, vanilla, wood, and a faint funky note of ripe Brie. The combined acidity of the raspberries and the underlying lambic takes the forefront here, but some sweetness quickly jumps in to balance it out. Concentrated raspberry flavors in the center give way to a quick tart finish. Truly magnificent. Duck, goose, venison, venison sausages, foie gras, and country pâtés should try this on for size. Goat cheese ravioli would also set it off beautifully. It's just sweet enough for desserts—try it with dark chocolate cakes and tarts, vanilla or chocolate ice cream, and cheesecake. It's also a fine partner for goat cheeses and dessert cheeses such as mascarpone, stracchino, or teleme.

Kriek Boon is a glowing red beer with a startling blush-pink head. The aroma is pure cherries, with earth and a hint of butter. The palate strikes a fine balance of sweet and tart, with insistent cherry flavors driving right through to the finish. I feel that this is a more accomplished beer than his standard framboise. This beer is great with any chocolate dessert, panna cotta, chocolate-based pastas and sauces, magret of duck, and venison in a sour cherry sauce.

BRASSERIE CANTILLON Right in the center of Brussels, hard by the central railway station, is Brasserie Cantillon. Outside, modern Brussels dashes headlong into the future, but inside, time has stopped. Cantillon's gueuze bottles announce proudly that they contain "Belgium's most authentic lambic," a typical statement from the fiercely proud proprietor, Jean-Pierre Van Roy. Cantillon is known for the uncompromisingly dry quality of its lambics—Van Roy refuses to sweeten them at all. This dogmatic approach results in beers that live up to the swagger, and Cantillon is beloved among lambic purists.

Cantillon Gueuze Lambic is a deep orange beer with an insistent mousse. The aroma is full of toasty oak, apples, pears, and barnyardy horse blankets. This may not sound very nice, but it is actually reminiscent of a great vintage champagne.

It has a finely acidic palate, bone-dry with an ironlike hop bitterness. In the center swirls a maelstrom of citrus flavors combined with horse blankets, hay, damp earth, Stilton cheese, and wildflowers. It's so complex that you could spend days trying to tease it all apart. Great with shrimp, crab cakes, fish, oysters, and cheese, especially Stilton.

If the gueuze bottle is boastful, the label for **Cantillon Rose de Gambrinus** is sexy, with a watercolor depicting a Rubenesque blond woman sitting in a man's lap, a chalice of beer in her hand. His hand is busy too, wrapped lustily around her midriff. The cork on my bottle notes that the beer was bottled in 1996, making it six years old. Only the faintest pinkish blush gives away the presence of the raspberries and cherries that joined the lambic so many years earlier. The fruit shows more assertively in the nose, blending with deeply earthy aromas of wet sod, damp fallen leaves, ripe cheese, cherries, and vanilla bean. On the palate, the underlying lambic takes the driver's seat, rendering a bone-dry center wrapped in fruit aromatics. The finish is sharp and dry. The fruit lingers. This is an austere version of admirable complexity. Try it with venison or boar sausages, country pâté, or a goat cheese salad.

The color of cherries shows clearly in **Cantillon Kriek Lambic**, which glows a beautiful pinkish red, leading to yellow-brown at the edges. Aromatics of horses,

sour cherries, and Camembert waft from the glass. On the palate, the fruit's acidity combines with that of the beer and thrusts through the center with a massively fruity jab. The brain says "sweet," but the tongue says "sour." A brilliant and uncompromising rendition of kriek. Try it with magret of duck.

HANSSENS ARTISANAAL Hanssens of Dworp is one of the last freestanding blenders left in Belgium. Hanssens doesn't actually brew beer—it buys cooled, inoculated lambic wort from breweries to be fermented, aged, and blended in its own cellars. This is an art form unto itself, very much as affinage is for cheese or blending for Scotch whisky. Many champagne makers follow similar practices, buying grapes, must, or finished wine from other producers. Much of the character of lambic is determined in the cellar and the blending room, so the resulting beers are very much Hanssens's own creations. Like Cantillon, Hanssens is particularly loved by lambic purists.

Hanssens Oude Gueuze has a hazy gold color and an aroma of wet wool, preserved lemons, vanilla, and earth. The palate is sharply tangy and dry, opening up to a marvelously complex display of citrus and damp earth in the center. The finish is miles long and juicily acidic, with a final flourish of fruit. This would be brilliant with a good ceviche packed with shrimp and avocado.

Hanssens Artisanaal Oudbeitje introduces strawberries to lambic—this raises eyebrows, since strawberries are not traditionally used, and Hanssens is a very traditional producer. The beer is lightly carbonated and pours with a full gold color, although when the light catches it right, a pinkish hue emerges. The strawberries announce themselves in the nose, where they mingle with aromas of earth, sharp cheddar cheese, vanilla, yogurt, and a Riesling-like petrol note. The flavors turn out to be surprising—gentle sweetness quickly followed by fine acidity, and a wonderful fruitiness right through the center. It's not nearly as sweet as some fruited lambics, but just sweet enough to help it pair up with the right dessert. Panna cotta will be a fine match, as will cheesecake, fresh goat cheese, teleme, mascarpone, or Stilton.

Many traditional krieks are made from beer that is already a year or two old when the fruit is added. Hanssens leaves the beer on the cherries until they are reduced to bare pits, resulting in **Hanssens Oude Kriek**. This beer is then aged three years more in bottles before it is released. The color is almost heartbreakingly stunning; reds, roses, pinks, and oranges, all at once, like a beautiful sunset. The aroma opens up with a barnyard gambit, but this quickly dissipates, allowing complex aromatics of cherries, wood, earth, vanilla, and mold to come through. The palate opens sharply, with concentrated sour cherries right up front, showing skins, stems, stones—the whole fruit. The acidity, backed by just a hint of fruity sweetness, is gorgeously vibrant and juicy. The finish is long, tart, fruity, and finally drying. An absolute masterpiece. Serve this with magret of duck, roast goose, seared foie gras, foie gras terrine, gamy pâtés, aged goat cheeses, and sweet dessert cheeses. This beer is almost too good for dessert, but if you drink it with dessert, don't skimp. Go for the best very deep chocolate, very rich cheesecake, or a great panna cotta.

BROUWERIJ LINDEMANS The sleepy country hamlet of Vlezenbeek is only a fifteen-minute drive from Brussels, but it seems like a different world. This is rich Brabant farmland, and the Lindemans family once tilled it, but they've now turned their attention entirely to beer. The handsome farmhouse now houses the brewery's offices, and a ramshackle assemblage of new and old buildings stretches out into the fields behind it. From a small modern building next door, copper kettles gleam incongruously out onto the grassy Payottenland countryside. Inside, the activity is furious—the Lindemans are very busy and intend to expand. Their sweet, accessible fruit lambics have introduced a new generation to lambic beer, and they are scrambling to keep up with the demand. In a time when the bones of defunct lambic breweries dot the local countryside, this is a good problem to have. The brewery is a family affair, with the father, René, overseeing the work of his sons Geert and Dirk. When they built the new brewhouse, they kept the old, and both are still used. The sun shines in through holes in the roof of the old brewhouse, but no one is worried—here, nature is invited in. Rafters from this building were installed over the cool ship of the new brewery, in the hope of conferring some of the old brewery's precious microbes on the new one.

Lindemans Gueuze Lambic is a deep orange beer, edging into amber. The nose is of green apple peel and vanilla, with an earthy underpinning. On the palate, the beer starts tart but quickly sweetens. The beer is filtered and shows little depth. This sweetness is too much for me—I prefer traditional gueuze. This beer might be nice as a palate cleanser between courses. Lindemans's only traditional lambic shows the brewery's true mettle in the form of **Lindemans Cuvée René.** This beer is a hazy deep gold, with orange highlights. The nose is a complex riot of bright and dark aromas—green apples, Seville oranges, lemon zest, damp leaves, wet wool, and fino sherry. On the palate, the beer is as tart and bright as fresh lemonade, bone-dry and flintily fruity with an acidic pale sherry finish. Other beers may pay the bills, but René Lindemans likes this beer best, and he named it after himself. Try it with shrimp, crab cakes, or ceviche.

The beer that has made Lindemans successful and famous is **Lindemans Framboise**. This beer looks great in a champagne glass—it's a bright pinkish red, with a bright pink head. The raspberries, added to the beer in the form of pure juice, announce themselves even before you bring the beer to your nose. The aroma is almost pure raspberry, with just a hint of funkiness lurking somewhere behind it. The palate opens with a bite of acidity but instantly broadens into a full display of raspberry flavor and sweetness. The depth of the raspberry flavor is terrific. The acidity simply holds it all in check, driving it into a sweet, fruity finish. Traditionalists get their knickers all in a twist over this beer, but I think it's brilliant. I've never seen anyone fail to like Lindemans Framboise. There's a place for traditional framboise, but there's a place for this too; besides, some people always sweetened lambics at the table, and sugar sits out conspicuously on the tables of even the most traditionalist cafés. It's not for the coffee. This beer is spectacular with chocolate desserts of any sort. It's pretty much unbeatable with cheesecake as well. It also makes a nice sorbet-like palate cleanser—serve it in champagne glasses between courses.

Lindemans also produces the bright orange **Lindemans Pêche**, which does for peaches what the framboise does for raspberries. Not the height of complexity, but very tasty with peach desserts, vanilla ice cream, and chocolate anything. Pêche is a pretty pleasant way to start brunch as well.

5

WHEAT BEER

Beer is often called "liquid bread," and this description is particularly apt for beers made with wheat.

Throughout history, many grains have been used to make beer: emmer, spelt, oats, rye, millet, and sorghum are still used in various parts of the world even today. Brewers settled on barley as the best grain because it is relatively low in gums and proteins that can clog mashing vessels, making the wort difficult to drain off. Other grains, including wheat, tend to be full of these compounds. Barley also has a hard husk, which is useful to the brewer; it fluffs up the mass of grain in the mashing vessel, forming a filter bed and making the wort easier to drain. Wheat, on the other hand, has no husk, and is therefore tough to work with; it's very difficult to make a beer entirely from wheat.

The same qualities that make barley great for brewing make it poor for bread-making. Those gums and glutens that barley lacks are needed to make bread elastic; bread baked from barley tends to be dry, hard, and crumbly. Bakers would also need to get rid of the barley husk, unless they planned to make bran muffins.

So the brewer preferred to use barley and the baker preferred wheat, but it was not always possible to be choosy. Both brewer and baker have used blends of grains, and over time brewers discovered that wheat malt, when blended with barley malt, has some very pleasant qualities. Beers brewed with a good proportion of wheat tend to be brisk and light on the palate, with racy, thirst-quenching acidity. The proteins in the wheat form an intractable haze, giving the beer a particular glow that gave rise to the term "white beer." Wheat beers are usually at their best when young, and most have traditionally been left with their protein and yeast hazes intact. Most wheat beers are pale, though of course they are not actually white; like "white wine," "white beer" is a relative term.

MIT GARANTIERTER FLASCHENGÄRUNG
WEIZENSTARKBIER
Weizenstarkbier

In Bavaria, brewers developed a style of wheat beer that they paired with a particular strain of top-fermenting ale yeast. The wheat lends these beers a quenching quality, while the special yeast imparts flavors and aromatics of cloves, bananas, smoke, and bubble gum. These beers are called weissbier ("white beer") or weizenbier ("wheat beer"). They are enormously refreshing and spectacular with food. Around Berlin there is a variant called Berliner weisse, which derives its sharp acidity from a lactic fermentation. Berliners sweeten it with fruit and herb syrups, making a sort of beer cocktail.

In Belgium, there is a unique style of white beer called witbier in Flemish or bière blanche in French, brewed with a proportion of unmalted wheat and then spiced with the riches of Belgium's old spice trade. Curaçao orange peel and coriander are particularly favored. These beers are very pale indeed, and they are sometimes allowed to undergo a limited lactic fermentation, sharpening their fine acidity. If anything, these wheat beers, with their bright citric flavors, are even more refreshing than the German wheat beers.

Americans, of course, brew everything—the German style, the Belgian style, and a new American style, which tends to replace yeast aromatics and spicing with a more aggressive hop character. Wheat—light, fresh, slightly tart, brisk, and usually with a trademark haze—is what ties these styles of beer together.

In the spring of 1984 I had my first taste of Bavarian wheat beer in a gloriously sunny beer garden in Munich. The beer garden was so perfectly pleasant I seemed to be in a dream, or at least a very good movie. I was surrounded by ancient half-timbered buildings and happy-looking people who were drinking hazy golden beer out of what appeared to be flower vases. What was that stuff? I had to try it. After a brief flurry of pantomime and my bad German, the beer was brought to my table. The glass was a foot tall, and the beer had a three-inch fluffy white head. It looked great, but when I tasted it, the flavor stopped me in my tracks. There had to be something wrong here—the beer tasted like cloves and bananas. I wasn't at all sure I liked this beer, but Germany was clearly going to be more interesting than I'd imagined. As my time in Munich unfolded, I saw wheat beer everywhere—even at breakfast!

OPPOSITE: Glasses for Bavarian wheat beer are tall and flared at the top to hold the voluminous fluffy head. Schneider's strong Aventinus deserves an especially striking glass.

Making beer from wheat is an ancient tradition going back to the Babylonians. Wheat makes excellent bread, whereas barley does not, so each grain eventually gravitated toward its own talent. By the Middle Ages, most beer in Europe was being made from barley, though the use of wheat was not uncommon. The Bavarian house of Degenberg, a noble family, is thought to have brewed the first modern weissbier in the 1400s. *Weisse* means "white," though the beer was probably merely paler than the other beers of the day, which were all dark brown. Wheat beer gained in popularity, raising plenty of money for the Degenberger clan, but also arousing the jealousy of local dukes. After some years of feuding, the brewing rights for weissbier eventually fell to the dukes, and the royal Wittelsbach family started brewing at the site of the Hofbrauhaus in Munich. The Wittelsbachs declared that they alone had the right to brew wheat beers, and they had the muscle to back up their claim.

By the early nineteenth century, tastes had changed, and the wind fell out of weissbier's sails. Monastic brewing and scientific advancements had improved competing beers, and sales of wheat beer waned. In 1855, the brewer Georg Schneider leased the Weisses Bräuhaus in Munich and in 1872 he negotiated the end of the royal weissbier patent. Schneider set up a new brewery several streets away and concentrated on perfecting weissbier. The Schneider weissbier brewery in Munich was a casualty of World War II, but the Schneider family continues to brew some of the finest weissbiers in the world in nearby Kelheim. By the 1950s, very little weissbier was being produced; it was considered a drink for the elderly, much as Scotch whisky was until fairly recently. Starting in the 1970s, however, young people rediscovered weissbier, and this antique style has made a steady climb to claim about 30 percent of the beer market in Bavaria—no mean feat. All the major breweries in Bavaria now produce weissbier.

What makes weissbier so special? Let's start with the grains. Most weissbiers are made from a grist containing more than 50 percent wheat malt, with the balance made up of malted barley. The wheat imparts a certain fine acidity and a light delicacy on the palate. It is also full of protein, which helps the beer achieve its trademark pillowy head. The mash is complex and seeks to maximize the production of fruity flavors and aromas during the fermentation. The hops are used lightly, lending a restrained brisk bitterness to counterpoint the sweetness and fruitiness of the malt.

The yeast, however, is the star of the show. Most Bavarian-style wheat beer is unfiltered, and after the wonderful work this yeast has done, no doubt it deserves to remain. The German word *Hefe* means yeast, and *Weizen* means wheat, so you will often see these beers referred to as hefeweizen. The weissbier yeasts have an old lineage and are top-fermenting ale yeasts; among German beers, weissbier is a throwback. All weissbier yeasts will produce, in different intensities and combinations, flavors and aromas of cloves, bananas, bubble gum, smoke, green apples, and occasionally vanilla. Most weissbiers are of standard strength, about 5 percent.

The quality of the hops is very important. Head Brewer Miles Jenner inspects his hops at the Harveys brewery in Lewes, England.

TOP: Mechanized rakes move through the malt to keep it separated. Thomas Kraus-Weyermann checks on the barley's progress at the Weyermann Maltings, Bamberg, Germany. **BOTTOM:** This is "green malt," sprouted and ready for kilning.

TOP: Freshly kilned malt floods out of the roasting drums at the Weyermann Maltings. The room fills with a wonderful aroma. **BOTTOM:** Malt is processed and kilned to achieve various colors and flavors. These are some of the malts produced by Briess Maltings of Wisconsin. *(Courtesy Briess Malting Company.)*

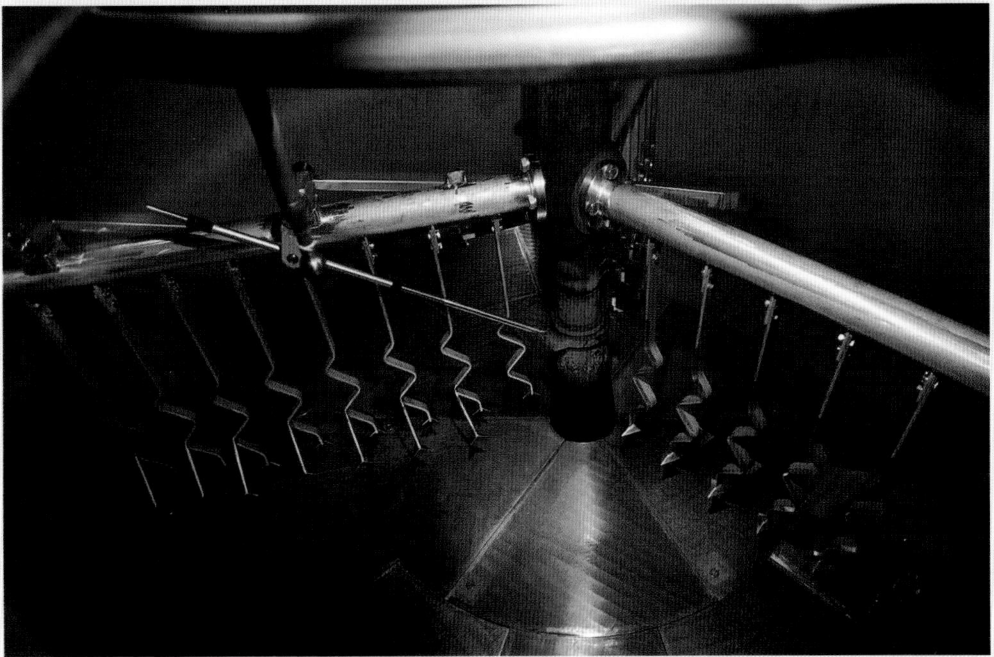

TOP: The malt gets to work—"mashing in" at the Brooklyn Brewery. **BOTTOM:** Inside a traditional lauter tun, the screens filter the husks away from the sweet wort. The rake assembly loosens the grain bed.

Lambic revivalist Frank Boon is dwarfed by his giant oak casks at Brouwerij Boon. OPPOSITE: The sharp acidity of lambic gueuze works wonders with a tangy Mexican ceviche.

TOP: Hot wort splashes through a strainer into a shallow pan at Lindemans. The wort will cool overnight, and then wild yeasts and bacteria will begin the lambic fermentation. **BOTTOM:** Patriarch René Lindemans and his sons brew popular lambic beers in their copper brewhouse in Vlezenbeek, Belgium. **OPPOSITE:** There's a hole in the roof, but never mind—it lets the wild yeasts in. Lindemans' old mashing vat has retired, but fresh wort cools nearby.

LINDEMANS
GUEUZE CUVÉE RENÉ

A sweet framboise is the perfect match for Waldy Malouf's signature chocolate soufflé at Beacon in New York City. **OPPOSITE:** Moules frites is the national dish of Belgium, and gueuze is the traditional accompaniment. **OVERLEAF:** Hanssens of Dworp produces the breathtakingly complex Oude Kriek.

HANSSENS

After the main fermentation is finished, the beer will be blended with additional malt sugars and bottled. The yeast consumes the additional sugars while carbonating the beer to an almost explosive champagne-like exuberance. The yeast remains behind in the bottle, adding body and earthy, nutty flavors to the beer. As if that weren't enough, the yeast is actually very good for you. It is chock-full of vitamins, particularly the B-complex vitamins. For this reason, German doctors have long recommended drinking weissbier and have even prescribed it to help clear up skin problems. Americans have been reduced to getting their brewer's yeast in nasty expensive little pills from health food stores—a long, sad journey from the joys of a glass of weissbier.

A proper glass of weissbier will catch your attention, just as it caught mine all those years ago in Munich. The classic weissbier glass is nearly a foot tall and is flared at the top. Once you try to pour weissbier, you'll understand why. It's so highly carbonated that it may try to climb out of the glass. A properly poured weissbier has nearly three inches of foam on top. There's a trick to pouring weissbier. The experienced drinker will slide the beer gently down the side of the glass until it's nearly full, then swirl the rest of the beer around the bottom of the bottle. This lifts up the yeast, which is then confidently poured into the center of the glass. The head will fluff up to the lip of the glass. Some showy bartenders in Germany will upend the bottle into the glass, letting the beer fall straight down into the center of the glass. Try this, and you're likely to get beer all over your table. Even if you're successful, you'll come off like Tom Cruise in *Cocktail*. That may seem appealing in America, but your German hosts will be noticeably unamused.

Most weissbiers range from full gold to hazy deep orange in color. As you drink the beer, the high carbonation tickles the palate. The bitterness is very light and snappy, followed by the slight sweetness of the malt, which is made almost candyish by the fruity aromas. The beer finishes cleanly with a hint of acidity. It's super-refreshing. Darker versions, called, somewhat confusingly, dunkelweisse ("dark white") or dunkelweizen ("dark wheat"), are russet-brown and tend to have more sweetness and fruitiness. Further down the same path are the weissbocks, dark and swarthy beers hiding an 8 percent wallop under brisk but heady swirls of fruit aromatics and bready grain flavors.

Weissbier with Food

When I host a beer dinner, it is often difficult to decide which course to pair with weissbier. Weissbier is so versatile that it could often accompany any or all of the dishes. If the flavors of weissbier appeal to you, then it's a great style of beer to have in your refrigerator pretty much all the time. Whatever you're having for brunch, lunch, or dinner, the odds are going to be pretty good that weissbier will match it. This beer is dancingly light on the palate yet packed with flavor and aroma, highly effervescent and brisk yet low in bitterness. On a hot summer day, it can be amazingly refreshing.

With Mexican dishes, weissbier shows the power of its scrubbing bubbles. It lifts the fat of cheese and avocados, cuts through the starchiness of beans and rice, parries strong spices with its malt sweetness, and then melds into the flavors of the dish. Cumin, cilantro, lime juice, pumpkin seeds, chilies, achiote, and other classic Mexican flavor components marry happily with weissbier. Mole poblano, with its dense interplay of nuts, smoked chilies, spices, and chocolate, picks up on the smoky flavors in weissbier. Dunkelweisse can be an even better choice here because the chocolaty flavors of the dark malts latch onto the chocolate in the sauce. Dishes that would turn red wines to turpentine and send white wines fleeing will find weissbier a perfect companion. Thai food, which tends to be light and spicy, is a good example. Thai cooking is all about freshness and the balance between sweet, sour, salt, and fire. Weissbier matches the sweetness with its malt and the sour with its tartness while lifting the salt and quenching the fire. It's an irresistible combination.

Indian food finds similar affinities, plus a few of its own. Many of the spices in Indian cooking are mirrored in the spiciness of weissbier. The banana and clove flavors that are weissbier's calling cards are often in the dish itself, and smoky flavors will pick up on the char from the tandoor. The acidity of the beer matches nicely with yogurt-based sauces as well. Dhal, an earthy lentil preparation often served as a side dish, is a beautiful partner. It's chicken tikka masala again? When made well, this is a very hard dish to resist. Weissbier has enough acidity to deal with the tomatoes, and the extra carbonation breaks up the sauce, which is delicious but heavy. With powerfully spicy dishes such as vindaloos, you should step up to the more hefty weissbocks, which can handle the heat while complementing the lamb. Weissbock is also best with lamb rogan josh.

I can't tell you how many times I have seen nearly full bottles of wine, especially reds, abandoned on the tables in fine Indian restaurants. The food had ruined the wine, and the wine had ruined the food. The diner had somehow imagined that a Barolo could hold its own against a vindaloo or had sent a California chardonnay to its death against a powerful chutney. What a shame! Weissbier would have saved those meals; in fact, it would have made them spectacular.

Bright, sunny Mediterranean dishes are good candidates for weissbier as well. Every Mediterranean country has a version of baccala or brandade de morue,

Georg Schneider I and his original recipe for weissbier. Georg Schneider VI runs the brewery today.

the classic dish of whipped salt cod. It doesn't sound very promising, but in the right hands this dish can be a revelation. The salt cod is often combined with potatoes, leeks, olive oil, and garlic into a mousse that's as light as it is rich with flavor. Weissbier is perfect here—it teases the flavors apart, highlights them with its acidity, and tramples nothing. These beers can also perk up the delicate flavors of octopus, whether grilled, boiled, or lightly ceviched.

Chinese food often has smoky mushroom flavors to which weissbier plays perfectly. Many Chinese teas are smoked, and I imagine that they also do the same for the food. Let's face it—not many of us are doing traditional Chinese cooking at home. If you are, good for you—and the beer will match your food wonderfully. With average Chinese restaurant take-out food, though, you really need weissbier. The volcanic carbonation will break up those cornstarch-based sauces and let you really taste the food, while the malt sweetness marries into the dish. With crispy duck, it's totally outrageous. I'm sorry, but as far as I'm concerned, wine really can't go here. Come on, now—Chinese food with wine? Yuck! Not only does weissbier match Chinese dishes well, but it also scrubs away some of the strong flavors of the food, leaving the palate refreshed afterward. You know what I'm talking about. Moo shu pork and General Tso's chicken taste great while you're eating them, but later . . . 'nuff said. Weissbier's what you need. If the restaurant allows you to bring in your own, do it. Pay corkage if you have to.

Weissbier is the brunch of champions, or at least the champion of brunch. Never mind the mimosa—weissbier covers the same territory with considerably more panache. It's light and refreshing, especially on a spring or summer morning. It's practically a cousin to yogurt and fruit and matches them perfectly. Having something more substantial? The typical Bavarian midmorning breakfast (*Brotzeit*, "bread time") is weissbier and weisswurst, the latter being a pale and rather bland veal sausage in a light broth, served with sweet mustard. I'm reaching for the eggs, myself. A cheese omelette presents two mouth-coating ingredients—eggs and cheese—but carbonation and a touch of acidity cut right through, and the fruity flavors seal the deal. Other egg dishes, especially eggs Benedict, are equally grateful for weissbier, which deals handily with runny yolks and Hollandaise sauce. Sausages, boudin noir, bacon, home fries—no problem. Afterward, the beer is so refreshing that you almost forget how much you ate.

If you're feeling repentant, you're in luck here. Weissbier is great with salads. It's light enough not to overpower the delicate flavors of good greens and lends its slight sweetness and fruity flavors to the mix. The bitterness is quite restrained, so it won't clash with endive or other bitter greens. The beer has enough acidity to stand up to dressings, even vinaigrettes. Weissbier can adroitly handle strong radishes, ripe tomatoes, anchovies, and even raw onions. If your repentance flags and you add some goat cheese, all the better. Remember, weissbier is chock-full of vitamins—this is health food!

Not surprisingly, weissbier is great with German food as well. Pork is the king of German cooking, and weissbier is an excellent match for roast pork, leg of pork, pork sausages, ham hocks, roast suckling pig, and dozens of other preparations popular in Germany. It's also very good with ham. The sweetness in the beer is a fine counterpoint to the saltiness of the meat, and the clove aromatics are just what you're looking for. And don't even get me started about prosciutto.

While poached or steamed seafood might look for something even more delicate than weissbier, fried fish and shellfish work very well. Frying develops caramelized flavors that meld with the malt, while the carbonation and acidity lift and cut through fat. The beer is light enough to allow the flavors of the food to show through. Sautéed softshell crabs, crab cakes, and seared scallops are particularly nice with weissbier. Lobster is also a great match—the beer has the perfect level of residual sweetness to match the meat and let its flavors shine through. Stronger, oilier fish such as salmon work even when poached, and better still when grilled or smoked. And although a pint of British bitter may be the more traditional accompaniment to fish and chips, weissbier is even better (though don't tell the British unless you want to be tossed out of the pub). Actually, the fish doesn't even need to be cooked—weissbier is excellent with sushi. It is not surprising that in Japan, where craft brewing has only recently taken a foothold, weissbier is among the most popular "new" styles. There are now Japanese breweries devoted exclusively to making weissbier. This is surely a bright side of globalization.

Venison and lamb dishes can be more delicately flavored than one might expect. The stronger weissbocks can be an excellent choice for them, particularly when they are garnished or sauced with stewed or sautéed fruit. Weissbock brings its own fruit to the party and is big enough to stand up to the flavor of the meat. The beer's chocolate and caramel flavors will find echoes in the meat itself. Similarly, the dark flavors in weissbock give it the ability to work well with mushrooms. I once had a dish of pan-seared turbot in a light porcini mushroom sauce, and I was surprised to find that Aventinus weissbock was a nice match. The dark malts worked with the mushrooms, and the caramel malts picked up on the seared surface of the fish. Despite its strength, weissbock remains light on the palate, so fish will not be overwhelmed.

If you want to avoid being tossed out of a Bavarian beer hall, don't toss lemon slices into your weissbier. Kristalweizen, the bowdlerized filtered version of weissbier, was once sullied with lemon slices in an attempt to make the beer more interesting or refreshing. Those who did this tended to be older people, and it was probably a throwback to the days when erratic beers were commonly mixed with fruit syrups to make them palatable. At some point, Americans, having seen elderly Bavarians flipping lemon slices into kristalweizen, started tossing lemon into perfectly good weissbiers. If you do this in Germany, not only will you ruin your beer, but you might as well stencil the word "tourist" across your forehead. Don't sit next to me.

Notable Weissbier Producers

PAULANER-SALVATOR-BRÄU Most American aficionados of weissbier were introduced to it by **Paulaner Hefe-Weizen**. The brewery was founded by Pauline monks, but Paulaner's monkish days are long over. Paulaner is now a large Munich brewer, recently swallowed up by the Dutch giant Heineken. Paulaner Hefe-Weizen is a deep orange beer with an impressively rocky white head. Clove and banana aromatics are well balanced, and a hint of bubble gum or Juicy Fruit joins the party as well. The palate is light and spritzy, with a fleeting touch of sweetness and refreshing acidity. The bitterness is restrained, but a bit hard. This is a good weissbier, and it makes a great jumping-off point for exploring the style. Paulaner is a big brewery, and there is a by-the-books corporate literalness to its weissbier, which is perfectly correct, though perhaps a bit lacking in flair. It makes up for this by being widely available. Its light, well-structured fruitiness makes it a perfect choice for brunch.

ERDINGER WEISSBRAU Erdinger, in the town of Erding just northeast of Munich, is Germany's largest producer of weissbier, which is the only type of beer it brews. As the weissbier style rebounded over the past thirty years, Erdinger reaped the rewards. Its style of weissbier appeals to a mass market—the beer is well made but rather neutral compared with many others. **Erdinger Weissbier** is pale orange and raises a pillowy white head. The aroma is very muted—faint malt and hops show through, along with the tiniest whiff of apple peel and oranges. On the palate, the flavor is dead clean, displaying fine acidity but very little fruit. The finish is suitably crisp. This is a good choice for very delicate fish, with which you might not want something more exuberant. **Erdinger Dunkel Weisse**, a dark version, is very similar, with a faint hint of chocolate and a bit more residual sweetness. Erdinger saves its exuberance for its **Pikantus Dunkler Weizenbock**, a classic strong weissbier weighing in at 7.3 percent. This beer has an aroma of malt and raisins. The palate is slightly sweet and warming, with pleasant raisin and date flavors. This would be very nice with duck, seared foie gras, pork, or venison.

WEIHENSTEPHANER Northeast of Munich, not far from Erding, is the pretty university town of Freising, which is home to Germany's most famous brewing school and its several breweries. Weihenstephaner, founded in 1040, claims to be the oldest brewery in the world. It is part of the Technical University of Munich, which is owned by the state of Bavaria. One would expect a brewery owned by a prestigious brewing school and displaying the crest of the Bavarian state to produce a very good weissbier. It does. **Weihenstephaner HefeWeissbier** is hazy bright orange and has nice clove, banana, and hop aromatics woven together with an intriguing note of nutmeg. It has a fairly dry palate with very clean bitterness and expansive fruit flavors. There's very little malt character, but that's fine—it's very refreshing, and the aromatics are terrific. An excellent all-around weissbier, particularly good with salads, Thai food, and brunch dishes.

AYINGER BRAUEREI INSELKAMMER The family-run Ayinger brewery, nestled a few miles south of Munich in the pretty village of Aying, is better known for its malty lagers but also makes two very nice wheat beers. **Ayinger Brau-Weisse** is a hazy medium-gold beer with orange highlights. The aroma is pleasantly bright, full of bananas and oranges. The bitterness is extremely light, and the palate shows nice malt sweetness and good fruit. The finish is clean and dry. I had this beer for *Brotzeit*, the midmorning "second breakfast," on a visit to one of the brewery's two beautiful restaurants. It was terrific with the weisswurst—I hadn't been a big fan of weisswurst, but that morning converted me. It's a great choice for brunch—go for a goat cheese omelette if you can't get weisswurst. It's also great with salads. Ayinger's other weissbier is quite different. **Ayinger Ur-Weisse** ("Ur" means "original") is an amber beer with an insistent foam and a remarkably deep toffeeish malt aroma. Bananas lurk in the background. The palate is slightly sweet but balanced, with caramel notes and a juicy malt center. Ayinger beers are known for the depth of their malt character, but you rarely encounter truly malty weissbiers. This is a great beer to pair with spicy Asian dishes, sausages, or good ham.

G. SCHNEIDER & SOHN The weissbier style had all but died out when the first Georg Schneider risked everything to start brewing weissbier again in Munich in 1872. He almost single-handedly resurrected the style, which enjoyed renewed popularity well into the twentieth century. The brewery in Munich was destroyed in World War II, and the Schneiders retreated to their brewery in Kelheim, in the Hallertauer hop country north of Munich. Weissbier had been produced on these premises since 1607, and the current brewery remains there, in a set of beautiful old buildings partially surrounded by a moatlike little stream. Today, Georg Schneider VI and his proud, talented brewmaster, Hans Peter Drexler, brew what is arguably the finest weissbier in the world.

Schneider Weisse is reddish-amber in color, much darker than most wheat beers. It has an exuberant carbonation and raises a very fluffy sustained head. The beer has an enticingly complex nose of bananas, bubble gum, and cloves, with a firm smoky backdrop and a whiff of caramel. The bitterness is moderate and balances out a juicy palate of lightly caramelized malt, zippy light acidity, raisins, bananas, and kola nuts. Despite its complexity, this beer still manages to be refreshing, and it has a long, quenching finish. It is a beer of truly majestic depth—a world classic. It will pair well with bolder fish preparations and is a big winner with Mexican, Indian, Chinese, and Thai food. This beer is extremely versatile, and I consider it a must-have, so there's always at least a case in my cellar.

As if one world classic weren't enough, the brewery also produces another classic: its weizen doppelbock, called **Aventinus**. At 8 percent, this beer carries its strength with remarkable grace. The beer is deep russet-brown and has a portlike aroma of raisins, dates, prunes, bananas, and cloves. The palate shows some sweetness, but it's remarkably dry for a beer of this weight. This allows it to remain light on the palate and almost dangerously refreshing. Close attention will reveal a slight warming quality in the finish. This beer is excellent with duck, venison, good pork or wild boar, and carbonnade flamande.

THE BROOKLYN BREWERY In the late winter of 1996, I had myself a shiny new brewhouse in Williamsburg, Brooklyn. I can no longer remember why, but there was never any doubt as to what the first beer was going to be. I had brewed weissbier at the Manhattan Brewing Company for many years, and it had proved to be a popular specialty. That version had been brashly hoppy—here I wanted to brew a softer, more classic weissbier. We dedicated our new brewery with the first brew of **Brooklyner Weisse** in March of 1996. The beer was instantly popular, and the new brewhouse revved up to a great start. I brought an assistant with me from Manhattan Brewing Company—the yeast. An Englishman, Mark Witty, Manhattan

Brewing Company's original brewmaster, had brought the yeast from Germany many years earlier. Now it traveled to Brooklyn and started fermenting Brooklyner Weisse, which has a hazy orange color, a voluminous white head, and an aroma of bananas, cloves, and bubble gum with a hint of smoke in the background. The bitterness, from German Perle hops, combines with the high carbonation for an insistent snappiness, followed by a wave of sweetish malt. Banana flavors are concentrated in the brisk juicy center, from which the beer springs into a drying, fruity finish with a wheaty acidic twist. We're planning to bottle Brooklyner Weisse someday soon, but for now it's available on draft at finer bars and restaurants in the Northeast. Try it with brunch dishes, salads, crab cakes, fish dishes, and Chinese, Thai, Vietnamese, and Indian cuisine.

These days, hops are usually the only spice in beer, but that was not always the case. In the 1500s, spices from far-flung lands started to become available to Europeans through trade or colonial outposts. The spices quickly found their way into Europeans' cooking, and into their brewing as well. Brewing could be very inconsistent back then, and spices not only introduced new flavors but also disguised bad ones. Brewed from barley malt and raw wheat, and spiced with coriander and Curaçao bitter orange peel, Belgian-style wheat beer is one of the few survivors from those days. Very pale and hazy with yeast, it is called witbier ("white beer") in Flemish and bière blanche in French. Although this style of wheat beer is quite popular today, only a few decades ago it came perilously close to vanishing.

The Brabant region east of Brussels had brewed wheat beer for hundreds of years, peaking in the 1800s. The city of Leuven and the provincial village of Hoegaarden competed for dominance in the witbier trade. By the 1950s, witbier was nearly extinct—a victim of wars, fashionable lagers, and brewery consolidations. In 1966, a milkman, Pierre Celis, established the De Kluis brewery on the site of a defunct brewery next to his house in Hoegaarden. He brewed the old style of wheat beer that the town had once been known for, and people came flocking back to their native beer. The brewery became very successful, but a devastating fire in 1985 put it in financial straits, forcing its sale to the giant international brewing conglomerate Interbrew. Pierre Celis moved to Texas, founded the Celis Brewery in Austin, and began brewing the characterful Celis White. The Celis Brewery did not survive its eventual takeover by Miller Brewing, but the brewing renaissance that Pierre Celis started is alive and well. Dozens of breweries in

Belgium and the Netherlands now produce witbier, and the style has come full circle, embraced by young people throughout the Low Countries and beyond.

Witbier's charms are easy to grasp. The beer is attractive, a pale hazy glowing gold capped by a rocky white head formed by wheat proteins and high carbonation. The aroma is bright, citric, and lightly spicy, sometimes showing apple notes and a refreshing whiff of mineral sulfur. It smells and tastes like a summer breeze on a lazy, happy day.

On the palate, restrained bitterness gives way to a very light-bodied center combining the sweetness of the orange with a fine, drying acidity and the smooth, grainy flavors of the wheat. The beer finishes with a slightly tart edge, clean and clipped. The beer is almost ludicrously refreshing and fairly light in alcohol, rarely topping 5 percent. Ah, the lemon again. It's back, this time carrying some credentials. While the Belgians rarely add a slice of lemon to a glass of witbier, the Dutch often do; sometimes restaurants and bars even provide a nifty candy-colored plastic muddler. Unlike weissbier, witbier is actually brewed with citrus, so the combination seems less jarring. A good witbier should stand on its own, but a slice of lemon can be a pleasant addition.

Witbier is traditionally refermented in the bottle and never filtered. It is usually brewed from an evenly split blend of very pale barley malt and raw wheat. The raw wheat adds its proteins to the haze and also an almost pasta-like wheat flavor to the beer (the mash for witbier smells just like a boiling pot of spaghetti). The coriander and orange peel are added in the kettle and are often joined by a "secret spice" or two of the brewmaster's choosing. Grains of paradise, chamomile, and white pepper are probably the most common, but no one's entirely sure of brewers' recipes—when the Belgians say "secret," they mean it. Warm fermentation by ale yeasts give witbiers a pleasing overall fruitiness, but none of the clove or banana notes of German weissebiers. In witbier, we look to its refreshing, racy acidity and to its citrus and spice notes to drive its remarkable affinity for food.

Witbier with Food

As nice as some other beers are with salads, witbier has to be the overall winner. Basically, witbier will match any salad brilliantly, as long as the dressing isn't overly sweet. (Does anyone really want those sugary "French" dressings anymore? I've certainly never seen them in France.) Even with a sweet dressing, you can get away with it—just don't drown the salad with the dressing. Witbier is great with vinaigrettes and can handle anything you want to toss onto the salad—cheese, ham, eggs, anchovies; go right ahead.

When on vacation in Provence a few years ago, I rented a massive stone farm-

It's hard to beat Belgian wheat beer with salads.

house with a shaded yard and a big pool. We made salads every day with the great local produce. If you've ever seen a French provincial market in the summer, you know how amazing everything is. The only time we visited the supermarket was to pick up beer. Our favorite was Brugse Tarwebier, known in the United States as Blanche de Bruges. Vineyards surrounded us, and though some of them turned out decent rosé wines, we found the wheat beer infinitely more refreshing and elegant in the hot Provençal sunshine. The air was perfumed with lavender, and the beer was perfumed with orange peel and coriander. Somehow, it all seemed to fit together perfectly.

At brunch, witbier tastes better than the best orange juice you've ever had. The orange aromatics awaken the senses and then provide a beautiful counterpoint to egg dishes, especially my summer favorite, goat cheese omelettes. Bacon and sausages will swoon before its quenching acidity. The great French sandwich croque monsieur—grilled swiss cheese and ham (with frites and mayonnaise, please)—finds a perfect partner here. In Amsterdam, sitting at the edge of a canal in the dappled summer sunshine, I was once served an open-faced grilled salmon and Gouda sandwich on ciabatta bread with a squeeze of lemon. The witbier glowed in the sunshine, then melded its orange peel into the lemon, cut through the Gouda, and wrapped itself around the salmon. The wheat flavors married the ciabatta. A gentle breeze rustled the trees. It's one of those combinations I still have dreams about—it was all so beautiful. That day, I briefly considered moving to Amsterdam. Those houseboats, I later discovered, are very expensive.

Witbier is a real star with fish. It is light enough to complement even the most delicate fish such as turbot or sole, while its citric notes and tartness enhance the natural flavors of a dish. Lobster, shrimp, and crab find it equally friendly, even in fairly spicy preparations. Sushi, sashimi, and smoked salmon find perfect expression in combination with witbier, which lifts oils and brightens flavors without disturbing the essential qualities of the fish. Bursts of pickled ginger and wasabi will be withstood. This is another style of wheat beer that is being enthusiastically adopted by Japanese craft brewers. Fish dishes prepared with citrus will provide stellar matches. I once hosted a beer dinner where the chef prepared striped bass in a mandarin orange sauce brightened with thin strips of mandarin zest. It was a great dish, and the beer pairing was perfect. Orange peel met orange peel, and the combination was truly brilliant.

Mexican and Thai dishes, which often have citric notes in their flavor profiles, find an echo in the orange peel in witbier, while cumin and cilantro partner with the beer's coriander. Pork in sour orange and achiote sauce is a good example of a classic Mexican dish that really sings with witbier. Indian food, with its complex interplay of spicing brightened by tamarind and lemon, can match very nicely. In any of these cuisines, you'll want to avoid anything with truly scorching chilies—witbier is versatile, but it isn't bold enough to weather really serious heat. Generally speaking, any chicken or pork dishes with brightly flavored preparations will work nicely, especially if they have lemon, lime, or orange flavors.

Notable Witbier Producers

HOEGAARDEN When I recently ran into Pierre Celis at a brewing conference, I hoped that perhaps he'd decided to reenter the world of brewing. No such luck, though I was glad to see that the twinkle in his eye was undiminished by his seventy-plus years. It must be the yeast, I thought. Now owned by the giant Belgian-based brewing conglomerate Interbrew, Brouwerij De Kluis is an unbridled success story, selling its wheat beer from the fashionable cafés of Europe to the beaches of Martinique.

Hoegaarden Original White actually has a hazy translucent pale yellow color with an almost greenish tinge. The nose is beautiful—oranges, lemons, and a whiff of coriander. A mousse-like carbonation opens the beer up on the palate; it is very light-bodied and spritzy, as light bitterness melds with a fine acidity to support a dry but orangey center. The finish is brisk and clean, leaving impressions of oranges, sweet spices, and pasta. Hoegaarden manages to be superlight on the palate while delivering plenty of bright, citrusy flavor. It no longer seems quite as full-flavored and smooth as it did when Pierre Celis brewed it, but it remains a classic nonetheless. Combined hops, acidity, and high carbonation provide enough cutting power to match oily fish such as salmon and sardines. The fish doesn't need to be oily, though; delicate fish like turbot will show its best when chaperoned by something this elegant. This beer makes a great aperitif and is also perfect with summer salads.

DE RIDDER Wheat beers are almost as popular in the Netherlands as they are in Belgium. De Ridder of Maastricht, a division of Heineken, produces a very nice Dutch version called **Wieckse Witte**. It has an earthy aroma of orange peels, coriander, yeast, and boiling spaghetti. A quick smack of bitterness opens onto a light-bodied tableau of earthy yeast, tangy oranges, and light sweet spices. The dry but fruity center leads through to a clean, sharp finish. Wheaty pasta flavors linger. On a sunny summer day in Amsterdam when you are parked in a chair along a canal, Wieckse Witte tastes particularly amazing. I recapture that feeling in my Brooklyn roof garden by grilling up some salmon steaks and serving them with a salad and a glass of Wieckse. I'll be damned if it doesn't work like a charm, though I do miss the boats gliding by. It's also terrific with the Indonesian cuisine that is so ubiquitous in Amsterdam. Thai and Vietnamese dishes can also make good partners, as long as they're not superspicy.

DE GOUDEN BOOM In the beautiful medieval town of Bruges, Paul Vanneste's Gouden Boom (Golden Tree) brewery produces one of my favorite versions of the witbier style. In Europe, you're more likely to see it under the name Brugs Tarwebier (*tarwe* is Flemish for "wheat"), but in the United States it is sold as Blanche de Bruges. It has a very pale yellow color with a slightly greenish glow. The nose shows a whiff of sulfur along with luscious orange peel and honey, countered by pungent coriander notes. It opens up light and sweet, the malt balanced out by very light bitterness and fine acidity. It remains fruity through the center and goes out in a short, clean finish. This beer is remarkably refreshing and a perfect choice for delicate fish and salads. It's also a terrific accompaniment to my favorite summer brunch dish, a goat cheese omelette with sautéed Granny Smith apples.

BRASSERIE LEFÈBVRE The Lefèbvres have been brewers since at least the 1870s, and six generations later the family is still going strong. The brewery is in Quenast, southwest of Brussels, a quarry town where stone was once cut to make into prized Belgian cobblestones. Their **Blanche de Bruxelles** has a full hazy yellow color and big orangey aroma with notes of green apple peel. The bitterness is light and brisk, and it's quickly followed by sweet malt, which rolls through the fruity center. The long, sweet finish shows some balancing acidity. For some reason, this beer has sometimes been marketed in the United States as **Manneken Pis**, after the famous fountain in Brussels of a little boy tinkling into the water. The Belgians seem to find this cute—I don't. The beer is very nice, though, and an excellent accompaniment to goat cheese salads, especially with orange segments and pine nuts. It's also very good with firm white fish and shellfish.

THE BROOKLYN BREWERY I have to admit that when I was asked to brew a Belgian-style witbier, I was less than thrilled with the idea. I loved witbier, as long as I didn't have to brew it. If I was going to make this beer, it was going to be brewed traditionally, and this meant working with unmalted wheat. Unmalted wheat is rock hard and full of mash-clogging proteins; my head swam with visions of frustrating twelve-hour days trying to squeeze wort out of recalcitrant mashes. Spices could be tricky, and how was I supposed to get the orange peel out of the kettle? When it came time to brew the beer, though, I was seduced by the medieval nature of it all. I found that there were mashing techniques that would make the raw wheat workable, and I loved the way the brewhouse filled with a wheaty aroma like boiling pasta when we mashed it. For the orange peel I found large mesh bags, which we dunk up and down in the kettle like giant tea bags. Now, when we brew witbier, I have visions of Bruges or Amsterdam in springtime.

Our witbier, called **Blanche de Brooklyn**, has a pale hazy yellow color and a perfectly white head. The aromatics are bright and citric, with honey notes alongside the Curaçao oranges and the light coriander. We use very little hop, and the bitterness is very light; but high carbonation makes for a brisk, dry, refreshing palate showing light fruity malt through the center, where it mingles with the oranges. It sprints into a clean, bright finish with a sparkle of acidity. Fresh bready wheat flavors meld with marmalade in the aftertaste. This is one of our draft-only beers, and it's quite popular in restaurants. I'm particularly fond of it with baked, grilled, or smoked salmon. It's also excellent with eggs Benedict, and, oddly enough, with real barbecued pulled pork, where the beer's orangey flavors work wonderfully with the sweet, nutty pork flavors. This has become one of my favorite beers of ours, and in 2000 it won the international World Beer Cup competition as the best witbier in the world. I'm not sure whether I agree, but you could probably convince me over brunch.

ALLAGASH Founded in Portland, Maine, in 1995 by the brewer Rob Tod, Allagash Brewing Company specializes in Belgian-style ales, all of them bottle-conditioned. **Allagash White** has a glowing hazy gold color and a big aroma of fresh oranges with just a dash of spice. Snappy sharp bitterness gives away the beer's American origins, then settles into a very dry, brisk, wheaty palate. It finishes with a flourish of bitterness, leaving the palate scrubbed clean. A distinctly American interpretation that makes a nice choice when more cutting power is called for. It's very good with fried fish, sardines, Arctic char, and salmon. The hops will also give this beer the muscle to stand up to spicy Thai and Mexican dishes.

When Napoleon's troops entered Berlin during the Franco-Prussian war, they were very pleased to find an approximation of their native champagne. But the drink they dubbed the "champagne of the north" was not a wine at all; it was a local beer called Berliner weisse. Berliner weisse is a very pale top-fermenting wheat beer with a subtle fruity aroma; a thin, dry effervescent palate; and a whipcrack of acidity virtually unchallenged by hop bitterness. Just as short cold days coax refreshing acidity out of the grapes of Rheims and Epernay, lactic fermentations do the same for this beer. While lactic bacterial fermentations are no longer common in beer, they are widely used by vintners of white wines to turn the harsh crabapple-like malic acid into the softer (flabbier, some would say) lactic acid. Whatever its appropriateness for white wine production, it has a dramatic effect on this beer. After months or even years of aging, the beer emerges with a floral lemony fruitiness and fine, knifelike acidity.

The comparison to champagne deepens when one considers that nearly all champagne starts out too acidic for the average palate—a dose of sugar before bottling calms all but the rare "brut sauvage" varieties. So too with Berliner weisse—the bracing acidity is a bit much for most people, who decide to soften it with herbal or fruit syrups. This is probably a throwback to the days when many beers were flavored with fruit or an herbal mixture called gruit. Raspberry and woodruff essence are the most common syrups, the latter being a bright green concoction derived from a local herb called *Waldmeister* in German. Raspberry is one thing, but woodruff? Think Grandma's hard candy tray, with lemon, lawn clippings, and a startling blend of Robitussin and Jagermeister. It's more pleasant than it sounds, but no less strange. Thus sweetened, Berliner weisse turns out to be quite refreshing. Since it has a modest strength of only about 3 percent by volume, you won't mind drinking it out of the enormous stemmed bowl that it is often served in.

There were once more than 700 weissbier breweries in Berlin, some of them quite large. Between 1870 and 1900, production of Berliner weisse virtually doubled, even as more modern styles from Bavaria were entering the market. Berlin's reputation for brewing was jealously guarded, and "Berliner Weisse" remains an "appellation controlée"—no beer produced outside Berlin is allowed to carry the name. Two world wars left Berlin in ruins and combined with changing tastes to leave its famous wheat beer on the ropes. There are now only a few producers of true Berliner weisse left, though versions pop up from time to time in other towns under different names.

Berliner Weisse with Food

This is a tough one, because almost no one drinks Berliner weisse on its own—it's always mixed with a flavored syrup to balance out its lactic acidity. The beer's food affinities will depend almost entirely on which syrup you decide to add, and how much of it. Light additions of raspberry or lemon syrup will make a fine refresh-

A beer cocktail—Berliner weisse is always served with herb- or fruit-flavored syrups to blunt its acidity.

ing drink to serve with salads. Just a touch of lemon, and you'll have a very nice accompaniment for citrus-based fish dishes and for eggs at brunch. With a dash of lemon syrup, it can also be terrific with Thai food—you can custom-sweeten the beer to match the sweetness of the dish. Finally, there's something to match mee krob, those addictive sweetened fried noodles.

If a dish is made with raspberries or cherries, a dash of raspberry syrup may be called for. Many Berliners seem to favor adding the green essence of woodruff to accompany their curries, though I'm not sure I can go there. The woodruff thing eludes me—you'll have to decide for yourself.

Go a little heavier on the fruit syrups, and you'll have a semisweet dessert beer, suitable for serving with anything chocolate. A bit less, and you have a sorbet-like palate cleanser. The word with Berliner weisse is to get (or make) your own syrups and have a good time with it.

Notable Berliner Weisse Producer

BERLINER KINDL BRAUEREI Kindl was founded in 1872 as an independent brewery but is now part of a large national group. It brews a wide range of styles but is best known as one of the last two major producers of the old Berliner weisse style. **Berliner Kindl Weisse** comes in fat, stubby bottles of a sort that were once common in the United States; somehow, it seems to be part of the time warp in which this beer exists. It has a pale hazy yellow color with an almost greenish glow. The aroma is hauntingly alien, a strange mélange of preserved lemons, ripe melons, flowers, and a faint whiff of candle wax. The spritzy, light-bodied palate is breathtakingly acidic with a sharp citrus tone, like lemonade without the sugar. No hop bitterness is noticeable—the beer finishes quickly, with scouring acidity leaving the palate refreshed. By itself, this beer is interesting, but frankly it's something that not even Berliners are prepared to brave. A dash of the traditional woodruff syrup renders it Day-Glo green, with the acidity blunted by sugar as the woodruff lends flavors of cough drops and Grandma's hard candies. Raspberry syrup will push the beer in a more familiar direction, making a tasty, tangy, refreshing cocktail. It's a bit hard to give food matches here—the possibilities depend on what you decide to add to the beer, and how much. A dash of orange juice, and it's ready to handle eggs Benedict at brunch. A big shot of raspberry syrup, and it makes a nice foil for panna cotta. Some beer purists are offended at the idea of such beer cocktails, but they need to get a historical grip. Beer, like wine, has always been used to make mixed drinks. When was the last time you tasted straight vermouth?

6

THE BRITISH ALE TRADITION

AFTER GRADUATING FROM COLLEGE IN 1983, I MOVED TO LONDON FOR A YEAR. IT TURNED OUT TO BE A YEAR THAT WOULD CHANGE MY LIFE.

It was in London that I truly fell in love with beer. Oh, yes, I drank beer in college—lots of it. There was only one problem—even though I drank it, I didn't actually like the stuff. What was there to like? American mass-market beers, the bland concoctions of bean-counters and chemists, were the only beers I had any access to. My roommates and I basically bought the least foul beer we could afford at any given time. When we were truly poor, it was Haffenreffer, accurately known as the "green death." Otherwise, it was Knickerbocker, a ghastly beer named after a big brand once brewed in New York City by Jacob Ruppert. Ruppert also owned one of the city's basketball teams and named it after his beer. If we were a bit flush, we bought Budweiser, which at least had the advantage of tasting almost like water rather than chemicals. We'd buy a bottle of Guinness stout and blend it in, to add a bit of taste. I enjoyed college, but in terms of beer those were dark years. For me, England changed everything.

As I met people in London and my group of friends expanded, I started to spend lots of time in the pub. One of the first things I noticed was that beer was usually the first topic of conversation when we got together. "Nice pint tonight." "Pint's spot-on." "Cracking pint." Or, more ominously, "dead pint," which meant we'd be leaving shortly. The beer wasn't the same in every pub, even when it was the same beer from the same brewery. Beyond that, the beer wasn't the same every day, even in the same pub. Somehow, this made the beer interesting and mysterious. It wasn't just beer—it was more like the weather. If the pints were "spot-on," the weather was beautiful, and we'd bask in the sunshine. If they were bad, we fled as if before an oncoming storm. These guys didn't consider themselves beer aficionados—this was a normal topic of conversation for just about everyone. American mass-market beer was the same all the time—what was up with this English stuff? The answer my friends gave me was startling. The beer was different every day because it was *alive.*

Britain is the last great bastion of the days when the brewing process was finished at the pub or tavern where the beer was consumed. This type of beer is called "cask-conditioned" beer, and it is the basis for all traditional British brewing. While styles and vessels may have changed, the basic methods for producing cask beer are the same as they were centuries ago. Traditional British beers are all ales, and they undergo a rapid, warm fermentation, often in open vessels. When the fermentation is finished, the yeast floats to the top of the liquid and lies there in a thick viscous mat, whereupon it is skimmed off. The yeast will be used to ferment the next batch, and the beer is transferred to barrels or casks. Despite the skimming, there is still plenty of yeast in the beer, and it has more work to do. If there is still some residual sugar left in the beer, the yeast will work with that—if not, a bit more sugar will be added. Finings will be added—either gelatin or isinglass—to encourage the settling of the yeast. Then the cask will be sealed with a wooden or plastic bung. The yeast continues to work, nibbling away at the sugars and "conditioning" the beer with the resulting carbon dioxide. Rough flavors evolve away and turn mellow. Now the beer is on the move.

When it arrives at the pub, it is propped up on a cradle called a stillage. After a day or two, the cellarman takes a wooden peg and taps a hole through a thin spot in the center of the bung. Excess gas is expelled, and foam surges up through the hole. A porous peg is tapped into the hole, allowing gas to escape, and the beer churns away until the cellarman decides that the level of carbonation is just right. Then he taps in a nonporous peg, trapping the remaining gas. Out comes the mallet, and a tap is driven through the other small stopper in the head of the cask. The cask is left to rest on its side, as the yeast settles to the bottom and the beer "drops bright."

Up at the bar, pubgoers are unaware of the masterful work going on right under their feet. The finished beer is drawn up to the taps by means of a "beer engine" or hand pump, directly into the pint glass. As the beer is propelled into the glass, it mixes with air and loses some of its already light carbonation. In some country pubs, the beer is still decanted by gravity, directly from the casks into the glass. As the beer settles, it should be bright, appearing as clear as if it were filtered. But this beer is "alive," and the subtleties that filtration tends to remove are intact. If the cask remains tapped for a few days, it will evolve over time as the yeast continues to exert influence and the beer comes into contact with the air drawn into the cask. Cask ale is best when consumed quickly—more than a few days of contact with air will start to degrade the carbonation and flavor. Many Americans have described these beers as "warm and flat," but when they are served properly, they are at cellar temperature—lightly chilled—and retain a faint

OPPOSITE: Fuller's is one of London's two great family-owned breweries, and its London Pride is one of England's finest ales.

GRIFFIN BREWERY
FULLER'S
CHISWICK
LONDON
PRIDE
Outstanding
BEST BITTER
Alc.4.1% Vol.

A visiting brewmaster in the brewer's tasting room at the Greene King brewery. Cask-conditioned "real ale" can be wonderfully nuanced.

but important prickle of natural carbonation. Overchilling will kill this beer, rendering it thin, empty, and harsh. When the beer is at the right temperature, the palate is caressed by waves of malt, fruit, and hop flavors, all dancing alluringly in a wonderful interplay. This beer demands that some attention be paid, lest you miss everything the brewer worked so hard to attain. In a fast world, it remains a slow drink, a remnant of a more civilized age.

Cask beer was the national drink of the United Kingdom up to World War II, but soon thereafter, change was in the air. Starting in the late 1960s, the fast world started to catch up with cask-conditioned ale. Brewing and serving it properly required dedication, and large corporate brewers started to feel that such dedication was too expensive. Cask-conditioned beer is fragile and is generally meant to be drunk within a few weeks of brewing. Managing stocks of such a perishable product is not easy. Cellarmanship is an artisanal craft and takes time to learn. The bean-counters piped up. Wouldn't it be so much easier and cheaper if they just filtered and carbonated the beer and served it cold, as the Americans did? Who would notice? Who would care?

Well, it turned out that many thousands of people cared, and they were getting angry. They had good reason. By the early 1970s, the large British brewers, who also owned the pubs, had withdrawn traditional cask beer from the market, replacing it with bland filtered shadows of their former products. These beers didn't change from day to day and required no training to serve properly. They were consistent, stable, boring, and very profitable. Many British pubgoers mourned the beers they had loved, but what could they do? On November 20, 1972, the answer came in the form of the first branch meeting of the Campaign for Real

Ale (CAMRA). The campaign codified the traditional brewing and serving methods of cask beer and dubbed it "real ale." Then the campaigners took to the streets, staging mock funerals outside breweries that had killed their favorite beers and boycotting breweries and pubs that had stopped producing and serving them.

By 1979, CAMRA had more than 28,000 paid members and had become a sophisticated organization exerting considerable economic, political, and social pressure on the offending breweries. By the early 1980s CAMRA had produced a stunning reversal of fortune for traditional British beer, which became widely available once again. Today, the Campaign for Real Ale can boast more than 50,000 paid members and is arguably the most successful consumer organization in the world. Cask-conditioned ale remains under corporate attack for the same reasons it was almost killed off in the 1960s. Huge sums of advertising money have pushed characterless mass-market lagers into even the smallest village pubs. Yet "real ale" endures because it has a unique depth of both flavor and history. More than 300 small breweries have opened in Great Britain since 1971, every one of them brewing traditional cask-conditioned ales. Traditional beer is bred in the bones of Britons, and it is hardly surprising that many of them would rather fight than give it up. You'd sooner wrest champagne away from the French.

There was a time when the word "bitter" was considered appealing rather than frightening. The Italians still feel this way—their bars are stocked with Campari and all manner of "bitters," drinks made from herbs and botanicals that are meant to whet the appetite. Espresso is certainly bitter as well, and it is looked on lovingly. English-speaking people seem to have a tougher time—no one wants to hear the "bitter truth" or to be handed a "bitter defeat." But if you spend any amount of time in an English pub, you are almost certain to be handed a pint of bitter, and you should be glad of it, for it can be a fine thing indeed. While bitterness provides the backbone of this style of beer, it has many other qualities to offer.

Despite the inroads made by heavily marketed bland lagers, bitter is still the national drink of England. Every brewery in England produces at least one bitter, and often several. True bitter is always cask-conditioned; when filtered and bottled, it becomes "pale ale" and takes on a different character. Bitters are highly individualistic—they range from golden to mahogany in color, from a low 3.5 percent to a sturdy 5.5 percent in strength, and from lightly hoppy to truly bracing. Lightly toasted pale malt forms the base of these beers, sometimes with an addition of caramelized malts for color and additional flavor. Some brewers also use invert sugar, which has a mild, toffeeish flavor. Invert sugar is actually more expensive than malt and is used for the distinctive flavor it gives to the beer.

The traditional British hop varieties Fuggle and Golding, prized for their gentle bitterness and their piney, fruity, and earthy aromatics, still predominate here. Most bitters are fairly dry, though there is a tradition of residual sweetness that still holds sway in the west Midlands, Yorkshire, and Scotland. Each brewery has its own special strain of yeast that will strongly influence the beer it ferments. One brewery's yeast may create a citric orange marmalade character (Fuller's of London), while another's will suffuse the beer with a light aroma of bananas (Bateman's of Lincolnshire). In southern England, bitter will usually be served with only a wisp of a head on it, just a thin cap of lacy foam, the liquid pulled right up to the brim. In the north, people prefer a substantial head, which is produced at the tap by using a sort of spray head on the hand pump. Naturally, northerners and southerners are equally disdainful of each other's serving practices. It's best not to get in the middle of this one.

All good bitters have a distinctive grain flavor surrounded by fruit and supported by relatively robust hop bitterness. Some brewers will add a handful of whole hops to each cask, allowing extra hop aroma to suffuse the beer. This is called dry-hopping. The particular talent of British brewers is their ability to coax huge amounts of flavor out of beers that are relatively modest in strength. Subtlety is the key here. These are not wild, flashy beers, and they are not meant to age. They are produced quickly and should reach your glass with the earthy, yeasty smell of the fermentation room still intact. Americans often fail to understand bitter—they find it weak, even watery. We need to pay a bit of attention and stop sipping. Bitter is not a sipping beer; it's a drinking beer, a beer to stick with for the whole evening.

For me, it's hard to detach bitter from the British pub. A good pub is a truly sociable place, the sort of homey refuge that is rarely seen in America. Winter will often see a real fire in the fireplace, surrounded by couches and overstuffed chairs. Beers of modest strength give you the ability to stay as long as you like. Or at least until 11 P.M., when most British pubs will pitch you unceremoniously into the street. They need to work on that bit.

Unlike German lagers, British bitters are hard to codify. As a style, bitter is very broad, but it has come to be loosely subcategorized by strength. A brewery will usually produce a light bitter of about 3.5 percent, sometimes referred to as "ordinary." (You have to love the classic British restraint. "Ordinary bitter"—sounds great, no?) A somewhat more substantial "best bitter" will usually display a bit more hop and weigh in at about 4 percent. From here, a "special bitter," often somewhat darker and slightly sweeter, will approach 5 percent, followed perhaps

by an "extra-special bitter," snappy and full-bodied, at about 5.5 percent. Anything stronger than this is generally considered to be something other than bitter, perhaps an old ale or a strong ale. The definitions are fluid and self-referential, and I've never quite figured out which is to be more prized, a brewery's "best bitter" or its "special bitter." Perhaps the answer is at the cash register—the stronger beer is almost always more expensive, a result of the strange practice of taxing beer according to its strength.

A quiet moment at the pub. The pub, or public house, is a British institution, a sort of state of mind. The British speak of "going to the pub"; Americans never say that they're "going to the bar."

A word here about bitter in America. Many brew pubs brew versions of bitter and serve them properly on the hand pump. These beers can be terrific, but American exuberance tends to creep in, and they're often stronger than the English ales that inspired them. Many English bitters come to the United States only in bottled form, presented as pale ales with a fuller carbonation and slightly higher strength that changes their character. This fact presents a conundrum, which I have neatly (if not quite honestly) solved by merging the tasting notes for British bitters, pale ales, and India pale ales. I've decided to keep the notes on food matching separate, because the fuller carbonation of bottled bitters and pale ales tends to affect their food affinities.

Some English bitters come to us in the now ubiquitous "widget" can or bottle first developed by Guinness. The widget package takes a lightly carbonated filtered beer and injects nitrogen into it, forming a dense creamy head on your pint. The idea is to imitate the light carbonation and mouth feel that you get from a pint served by a hand pump. This is an impressive piece of technology, and beers thus served can be tasty. But the sad fact is that to get real English bitter, you have to go to a good pub—in England. The widget package can deliver the aroma and flavor framework of bitter, but not its soul. The soul of the beer resides with the yeast in the cask, and it is shorn away by the depredations of modern packaging, except in the few happy cases where the beer is bottle-conditioned. So enjoy the beer here, but realize that you're still missing something. And keep your eyes peeled for a cheap flight to London.

British Bitters with Food

When I lived in London, one of my roommates had an international cookbook written by a British author. I distinctly remember that in her introduction the author lamented, "You will notice that there is no chapter here on British cuisine, as alas I consider it to be a lost art." Fortunately for the British and their millions of yearly visitors, this is no longer the case. While London's food scene probably won't rival that of New York, Rome, or Paris anytime soon, excellent restaurants have opened throughout Britain. Food markets brim with fresh produce, and pubs, ever mindful of the increased competition, have stepped up their efforts. Cheap air travel and open borders among the European states have caused millions of Britons to rethink their culinary lives. Suddenly, good food is sexy. Native British bitters are frisky and up to the challenge.

While cask-conditioned bitter doesn't have the full carbonation of most beers, it has many other attributes to work with when it encounters food. Lighter, breezier bitters can be excellent with fish, matching sea sweetness with light malt. Even delicate fish will find an excellent match—these beers will accentuate fresh fish flavors rather than overwhelm them. The best British malts are made from "maritime" barley varieties that are grown close to the sea. Perhaps this accounts for the whiff of sea air that characterizes several of my favorite bitters, most notably Adnams of East Anglia. Not surprisingly, these aromatics meld effortlessly with seafood. Seared tuna, especially with a bit of cracked black pepper, is terrific. The sweetness of crab, lobster, and shrimp is similarly well supported by the sweetness of malt.

When the fish is stronger and oilier, more robust bitters can step in. Beers labeled "best" or "special" bitter will tend to work very nicely with salmon, which likes beers with a well-developed hop character. Smoked and kippered fish are also fine companions to best bitters. Of course, one of Britain's most famous dishes, fish and chips, is magnificent with bitter. Everything works here—the bitterness in the beer cuts through the fat while the malt flavors find a friend in the batter coating and light up the flavor of the fish itself. I really love properly made British "chips"—they can give Belgian frites a run for their money, which is saying a lot. They're usually served with malt vinegar and salt, a Spartan-sounding treatment to say the least, but actually very tasty and great with a pint of bitter. Malt vinegar was beer once, and it seems to remember.

More full-bodied bitters are excellent with pork, roasted or fried poultry, and red meat. Bitters with apple notes, such as Yorkshire's famous Samuel Smith's Old Brewery Bitter, are particularly nice with roast pork or pork chops. Some bitters show slight sweetness on the palate; these are very good with ham, providing a pleasant counterpoint to the salt. The hard mineral tang of Burton bitters such as Bass or Marston's is very nice with a juicy medium-rare steak and can handle the poivre sauce, melted Stilton, or béarnaise sauce you're thinking of putting on it. The caramelized malts that give many bitters an amber hue also give caramel flavors, which pick up on the caramelized flavors in roasted meats. Strong bitters are also a good accompaniment to game, particularly venison, duck, and wild pheasant. (Wild is best, but if you're going to roast a farm-raised pheasant, slather it with olive oil and then wrap it in prosciutto before you roast it. It'll be moister and brilliant with the beer.) Roast beef, pork, and chicken are all wonderful with stronger bitters as well. Frying will intensify the caramel flavors even more and add some fat as well—these beers are very nice with fried chicken, cutting through the fat while matching the flavors in the crunchy skin.

One of my favorite pubs in London is run by the venerable Fuller's brewery. It's called The Churchill, and while it's a terrific pub in its own right, it is particularly notable for having a very good Thai restaurant in the back. Before I went to The Churchill, I wouldn't really have thought of British bitters with bright, spicy Thai food. But sure enough, the resinous earthy hop character of the Fuller's beers finds a willing partner in lime, galangal, and lemongrass. Jasmine rice echoes the fruit and biscuit grain flavors in the center of the beers. Malt sweetness matches the sweetness in many of the Thai dishes. When the spices really get going, bitter shows one of its hidden strengths—quaffability. The low carbonation means that you can douse the fire without feeling full afterward.

Fish and chips may be Britain's most famous dish, but another is even closer to my heart—bangers and mash. This simple dish of sausages and mashed potatoes can be revelatory, especially when served with a pint of good bitter. Britain is home to some of the world's finest and worst sausages. The great ones are usually made from pork and bursting with juices, herbs, and glorious pork flavor. The bad ones are made with some cereal called rusk—don't bother eating these pasty imposters, which taste like wartime rations. I don't know what rusk is, and neither does anyone else. Seek out a good butcher or a pub that has already found one. A full-bodied premium bitter with good sausages and mashed potatoes is one of those combinations that can make you forget all about fancy restaurants. The flavors are in perfect harmony, and you want the meal to last forever.

Almost as good is shepherd's pie, which is usually made with lamb but can also be made with beef. No, not the stuff dished out to you in school cafeterias—real shepherd's pie, with buttery mashed potatoes floating on a sea of lamb, fresh vegetables, and herbs. The beer matches almost every element of this dish, which is the British answer to the French cassoulet.

In 1752, George Hodgson opened the Bow Brewery in London's East End. Hodgson sold pale ale successfully for years, but his business really took off when he started shipping a special pale ale to India in 1790. We'll have a look at India pale ale later, but the modern form of pale ale is a descendent of Hodgson's East India Pale Ale, which became famous and successful not only in India but also back home in England.

Burton-upon-Trent, an industrial city in England's Midlands, was once known for strong, sweet dark beers, but when the Napoleonic wars blocked its Baltic trade in 1806, it turned to India for new markets. Hodgson was well entrenched in the Calcutta market, but he was about to be usurped. Pale ale was all the rage among India's British colonists, so the Burton brewers began to brew pale ales. In fact, they became so good at it that Burton quickly became known for the quality of its pale ales. Great wines are often said to possess terroir, the flavor of the local earth. Beer often has a certain kind of terroir as well, and Burton is a good example. The town of Burton sits on a substrate of limestone, and the well water used by the breweries is pulled up through it. As a result, the water is suffused with calcium sulfate (gypsum), and it is extraordinarily hard. This turned out to be perfect water for brewing sparkling pale ales—the yeast loves the calcium and ferments out the sugars completely, producing a very dry beer. Beers brewed with Burton waters were paler than others of the time and tended to be clearer as well. The water also produces a clean, dry, sharp hop bitterness with a quality that I like to refer to as "clipped." The bitterness finishes with a sudden snap that is remarkably refreshing and helps hold together the flavor structure of the beer. Brewers in other cities, attempting to capture the Burton flavor, started "Burtonizing" their water by adding gypsum.

Today, the modern British pale ale is an amber beer of moderate strength, usually about 5 percent. British pale ales are almost always bottled (kegged Bass Ale, which is brewed only for export, is a notable exception), and they are often filtered, fully carbonated, slightly stronger versions of a brewery's premium bitter. They are brewed largely from pale ale and crystal malts, the latter giving the beer nice caramelized flavors and sometimes a touch of sweetness. Bitterness is usually moderate as well—British brewers prize balance and subtlety—but the beer is also zippy. Many brewers still "Burtonize" their water to achieve a snappy hop character. Most of their beers have a classic earthy English hop aroma and varying degrees of fruitiness, depending on the brewer's house yeast strain.

To some extent, it is British pale ale that helped launch the revival of craft brewing in the United States. Most American professional brewers, myself included, were once amateur brewers. I would wager that Samuel Smith's wonderful Old Brewery Pale Ale was among the first great beers that most of us ever tasted—and some of us later tried to imitate at home. Great American craft breweries such as Sierra Nevada picked up the ball and ran with it, creating a whole new style of pale ale along the way.

India Pale Ale

By the 1790s, the British were established in India and needed beer, which was considered a staple in every household. India, however, presented serious problems for brewers. Brewing in India was impossible—it was too hot (this was before the advent of refrigeration), water supplies were poor, and the basic ingredients were unavailable. Attempts to ship beer out of Britain to Calcutta failed. The sea voyage from Britain to India could easily take four or five months, much of that time spent in hot climates. The sweet, dark ales of London, shipped in large wooden barrels called hogsheads, arrived in India flat, sour, and unsalable. The British navy had tried to tackle this problem for decades, but with little success. Beer was also a staple for sailors, and they tended to get very upset when they were forced to go without it. Beer rations for ships stationed in the English Channel were generous—each man received a gallon of strong beer a day! The navy tried onboard brewing with concentrates, and though it was successful in cooler climates, it failed in warmer ones. The navy eventually settled for grog, a mixture of rum, citrus juice, and sugar that was considerably less healthful than beer (as many of us can probably attest to from our college days).

The British in India were not about to be reduced to drinking grog. Enter George Hodgson of London, who had a bright new idea. He produced a pale ale of greater strength and bitterness than those he sold in London. The hops helped protect the beer from spoilage, as did the increased alcohol content. He aged his beer in London for months, until the yeast had consumed almost all the sugars in the beer. This meant that there was little left for spoilage organisms to eat. On top of this, he added hops to each hogshead of finished beer—this gave an added degree of protection from spoilage. This beer turned out to be a very inhospitable environment for anything that was looking to sour it. It had an alcohol content of 7 percent or more, and Hodgson hoped it would be sturdy enough for the challenge.

Hodgson's India Ale arrived in Calcutta in fine shape—clear, strong, and bitter, with a big, resinous hop aroma. Back in Britain, however, people who had never been to India were unfamiliar with India pale ale. This changed suddenly in 1827, when a ship bound for India was wrecked in the Irish Sea. Some of the ship's 300 hogsheads of India pale ale were recovered and sold at auction in Liverpool. Soon, people throughout England were clamoring for the wonderful new "India beer." Brewers were happy to oblige, and India pale ale, or IPA, became famous throughout Europe and even in the United States. Versions of IPA were brewed in Norway and even Germany, and by the late 1800s several breweries on the East Coast of the United States were brewing it as well. Ballantine's IPA, brewed originally in Albany, New York, and later in Newark, New Jersey, retained some of the character of the original IPAs as late as the 1970s. Other breweries, both here and in Britain, faltered far sooner. By the 1980s, IPA was just another name for a low-strength bitter in Britain and was nearly forgotten in the United States.

It took American craft brewing to resurrect truer renditions of India pale ale. A few brewers, most notably Samuel Smith and Fuller's, have recently tried to reclaim the mantle for the British, and their beers are quite nice, though not as bold as they should be. Young's of London produces a true IPA in its Special London Ale, though it doesn't actually use the term IPA.

A true India pale ale should be light amber in color; have a big, earthy, fruity hop aroma; and wield a whipcrack hop bitterness, held together by sturdy malt at a strength of at least 6 percent. The hard water should give a clipped, refreshing mineral finish. It doesn't sound like a beer for the fainthearted, but a well-crafted IPA goes down with remarkable ease. Perhaps the appetizingly bright blast of hops emboldens the fainthearted to mend their ways. I can't tell you how many times I've hosted beer tastings and dinners where avowed drinkers of Coors Light have excitedly told me how much they

Courtesy Merchant du Vin.

loved the IPA and asked where they could get more of it. I'm always thrilled, but vaguely jealous—it took me years to make this leap, and they do it in three minutes flat. Go figure. Good for them!

British Pale Ales and India Pale Ales with Food

Fuller carbonation and higher strength take these beers in a slightly different culinary direction from their cousins, the bitters. Softer versions, such as those of Samuel Smith's of Yorkshire, retain bitter's easy relations with roasted meats, particularly beef, lamb, and pork. Steaks will do nicely, but prime rib is even better—there's something in the pink juiciness of the meat that a good pale ale just latches onto. Roasted chicken and turkey are also good companions, the sweet

caramelized skin picking up on the caramel malt in the beer. Grilled meats—especially steaks, pork chops, and lamb chops—are very good with pale ales. Again, caramelization is the key, and the beer has the bitterness and carbonation to lift the fat. Later, when any of the above meats presents itself as cold leftovers, British pale ale remains a great choice. Let the beer warm up for ten or fifteen minutes outside the refrigerator; this will allow all the subtle fruity flavors to come forward. Cold meats also have subtle charms, and these beers will work perfectly with them.

Carbonation allows more direct encounters with spicy foods, and drier, sharper pale ales are in their element here. Not surprisingly, India pale ale is quite good with Indian cuisine, and it brandishes the cutting power to slice through creamy dishes like chicken tikka masala. These beers are sturdy enough to handle powerful spices, and their hop flavors will meld with the coriander, cardamom, and curry common in Indian food. You certainly want some carbonation working for you when you encounter dishes prepared with ghee, the ubiquitous Indian clarified butter. Ghee is one reason why many Indian dishes taste so good that you can't stop eating them, even though you know you should. Unfortunately, many Indian restaurants carry only Indian pilsner beers, which are boring at best—they lack the full flavor and hoppy snap of the German and Czech originals. See if a restaurant will let you bring in your own beer, or at least encourage the restaurant to expand its beer horizons.

Cajun food is better known for riotous flavor than subtlety, and robust pale ales are suited to the fray. For jambalaya—the Creole rice, meat, and seafood dish—you can go for a hoppy pale ale, saving IPAs for spicier versions. Blackened pork and chicken are excellent with IPAs; the bitterness of the beer will not only handle the spices but cut neatly through the side dish of black-eyed peas.

British pale ales are hard to beat at lunchtime—they seem to be ready to handle almost any sandwich (except, somehow, tuna salad). They are excellent with roast beef, turkey, chicken salad, ham, Italian cold cuts, burgers, and just about any toppings that you can think of. If you're going upmarket for lunch, these beers are also great with pâtés and quiches. Good full-flavored sausages, which work so nicely with bitters, will do just as well with pale ales, which will easily handle even fiery mustards on the side. Going downmarket for lunch? You can try to pretend that you don't want that meatloaf, but of course you do—with a side of macaroni and cheese, no less. British pale ales will understand, and they're the essence of discretion; they won't tell anyone they saw you.

Pasta with cream-based sauces will partner well with British pale ales, especially those with restrained bitterness. Alfredo, carbonara, Gorgonzola, and primavera sauces all will match nicely, but don't forget to get good Italian durum wheat pasta if you can find it. Cream gives all these sauces a slight sweetness, and the caramel sweetness in the beer picks up on that. At the same time, it lifts the cream and the cheese, making the dishes taste far lighter. If you're going to fill up on the garlic bread, the beer will deal nicely with that too.

For seafood, British pale ales are best with darker-flavored preparations. Roasted monkfish is a good example, as is any fish prepared with olives. Seared scallops can make a remarkable match with sweeter, less bitter versions, as can sea urchin. Frying also brings seafood into pale ale territory, so you will certainly enjoy your pale ale with classic British fish and chips. Fried calamari can work equally well, as will fried clams.

Some wintry foods like old-fashioned chicken potpie (don't laugh—if you make your own, this dish can be awesome) and shepherd's pie (same here) are terrific with these beers. When the dishes are heavier, look for versions with more residual sweetness. Spicy and sprightly dishes will prefer the hoppiness of India pale ales.

Notable Producers of British Bitter, Pale Ale, and India Pale Ale

GREENE KING When I lived in England, I got a real kick out of the place names, and one of my favorites was always Bury St. Edmunds. The name sounds like an instruction, but it actually reflects a piece of local history. East Anglia was once a kingdom, and in the ninth century King Edmund was slain here and an abbey was built over his bones. The abbey certainly brewed beer. East Anglia is barley-growing country (much of the malt I use for Brooklyn Brewery's beers originates here), and Bury St. Edmunds became an influential center of religion, political power, and brewing. Fragments of the abbey remain, but the powerhouse Greene King brewery is now the center of influence here. Benjamin Greene, an ancestor of the writer Graham Greene, bought the brewery in 1800. Much of the brewery is built over the old abbey—a rabbit warren of centuries-old tunnels surrounds the brewery's tasting room and cellars. From the roof of the brewery, it seems that Greene King envelops the entire town.

The brewery's monastic roots are celebrated in the name of **Greene King Abbot Ale,** which is sold in the United States in a can with a floating widget. The widget does its job, producing a cap of creamy foam on top of the honey-colored beer. The aroma is full of biscuity malt, hay, dried oranges, and earthy hops. The initial impression is of sweetness, but this is quickly countered by broad bitterness. The beer is full-bodied and creamy, showing nice malt flavors in the center and a bone-dry hoppy finish. This is snappy and versatile; it'll be fine with plain roast beef, but can also handle spicy Thai and Mexican dishes.

Established in 1711, Morland brewed fine ales in Oxford for nearly 300 years, but rising real estate values forced the brewery off its property a few years ago. Greene King swallowed up the Morland brands and equipment. Beer enthusiasts howled justifiably, but some directed their invective at Greene King, which is a bit unfair. At considerable trouble and expense, Greene King retained the Morland yeast strain, giving the Morland beers a different character from those produced under the name Greene King. The brewers at Greene King have a great respect for the distinctive character imparted by yeasts—they've been using theirs in an uninterrupted line for 190 years and have never recultured it. The best-known of the Morland beers is **Morland's Old Speckled Hen**, which comes in a clear bottle and is named after a particularly beautiful wood-clad antique car. This beer has a full amber color and a lively aroma of fresh hops and bright fruit—oranges, peaches, and apricots. Bitterness is very light up front, allowing malt sweetness to show through on a silky, round palate. From the center, it drops to a quick off-dry finish. It is delicious and elegant. I'm looking for garlic Toulouse sausages (the British make them almost as well as the French), pork, or veal. This is also a great beer to have with sandwiches for lunch, though I'd avoid the tuna salad.

TETLEY Tetley is a large national brewer that has been variously allied with or owned by several international brewing groups over the years, most recently Carlsberg. The main brewery is still in Leeds, and cask-conditioned Tetley Bitter is a major brand in its native Yorkshire. Here, a filtered version of Tetley Bitter makes an appearance in a widget can, where it's simply called **Tetley's English Ale**. This is a full amber beer with a lacy head and a very subtle aroma of hay, fruit, and hops. It's very light-bodied and dry, with a mouth-coating bitterness, a bit of biscuit, a touch of fruit. The finish is very dry, with lingering hops. The hops give this beer backbone and make it sturdy enough for steak, burgers, or even barbecue.

SAMUEL SMITH For many American beer lovers, Samuel Smith's Old Brewery is a sort of touchstone. Many of us were introduced to classic English beer styles by Samuel Smith's versions, which are handsomely presented in (but left unprotected by) clear low-shouldered bottles. These beers have become famous the world over, true ambassadors of British brewing prowess. Samuel Smith's is very much a family affair, and the colorful Smiths are famous for their insularity and eccentricity. Tadcaster is a small Yorkshire town located between Leeds and York, and the Smiths bought the brewery, which was founded in 1758, in 1847. The Smiths opened a second brewery in Tadcaster, but sibling rivalry soon split brothers Samuel and John. Samuel took the original brewery and John got the other one. John Smith's brewery is still in Tadcaster, but it has been owned by a procession of big international brewers, the latest of which is the family-owned Coors of Colorado.

While many Americans consider the soft, round, butterscotchy flavor profile of Samuel Smith's beers as typically English, it would be more accurate to describe them as typical of Yorkshire. Samuel Smith's is one of the few breweries to retain the old "Yorkshire square" system of fermentation. This system involves double-decker fermenters, a sort of duplex system with a hole in the floor between the two levels. As the yeast rises, it emerges through the hole into the upper floor, but as it settles, the beer withdraws into the lower chamber, leaving unwanted weak yeast and residues stranded in the top chamber. This system may have been developed to produce cleaner beers and stronger yeast, but it also seems to help develop the flavor profile. Another oddity is the actual material that the fermenters are made of: not stainless steel, copper, or even oak, but Welsh slate. Stainless steel versions of this system survive at a few English breweries, none of them very far from Tadcaster.

The brewery's flagship beer is **Samuel Smith's Old Brewery Pale Ale**, a copper-colored beer with a big fluffy head. There's that Yorkshire nose—hay, apples, butterscotch, and hops. The beer hits the palate with a mineral tang, then softens and rounds out to a dry biscuity malt center. The finish is clean and flinty. This beer is big enough for steak, juicy enough for roast beef, and subtle enough for lamb. I also enjoy it with terrine en croûte, as do the British, though terrine en croûte sounds a lot better than "pork pie." A slightly more concentrated version of this beer is produced for the holiday season, under the name **Samuel Smith's Winter Welcome**. It has similar flavors and aromatics, but both are punched up and the palate is even more juicy. It is a very fine beer also.

Samuel Smith's was among the first English breweries to answer the call for a return to the original India pale ale style. Its **Samuel Smith's India Ale** is a pale amber beer with an intense aroma of earthy English hops, Granny Smith apples, and a hint of garden mint. The palate is light-bodied, with a high thin wail of bitterness floating above a biscuity, buttery, bone-dry center. The finish is long and dry, and grain flavors cavort in the aftertaste. This is a very tasty beer, though Smith's, unlike the American brewers, couldn't bring themselves to amp up the strength to the levels of old. They are British, after all, and balance is everything to Smith's. Try this beer with oily fish, spicy merguez sausages, grilled shrimp, and spicy Indian dishes.

YOUNG'S If you live in London and love beer, you are probably either a Fuller's person or a Young's person. If you're a sophisticate, you'll appreciate the charms of each—London's two independent brewers have distinctly different styles. In my youth—living, as I did, in Fuller's country—I was unimpressed by the more austere flavor profile of Young's beers. Now that I'm quite grown, the Young's house character impresses me greatly. Beer has been brewed continuously on Young's site in Wandsworth, south London, since 1581. The Young and Bainbridge families bought the brewery in 1831, and the Young family has been involved with the brewery ever since, though it became a public company in 1898. When filtered beers threatened to wipe out traditional cask-conditioned ales in the 1970s, John Young was one of the few brewers to stand firm.

The brewery casually mixes old equipment with new—a modern kettle sends wort to hammered-copper open fermenters built in the 1800s. Rather than shred out all their historic equipment, Young's developed a few rooms into mini-museums for tour groups. Before the redevelopment of the old kettle room, I was once left there in semidarkness by a brewer who excused himself to take a phone call. The dusty riveted copper kettles seemed like gargantuan bullet-shaped black totems; I felt a strange ripple of fear as if they might suddenly make demands of me. There was a lot of history in that room, and it was palpable. I'm glad it's still there; there's something about family involvement that can preserve the heart and soul of a brewery. The Youngs keep a magnificent stable of shire horses on the grounds; until recently these horses made local deliveries, drawing a dray through the crowded streets of Wandsworth. Their duties are occasional now, but they are still frequently shown.

With typical British understatement, Young's refers to its everyday bitter as "ordinary," though it is wonderfully refreshing and dry, with a bright blend of fruit and hops. Young's Ordinary doesn't leave London; the traveling is left to **Young's Special Bitter**, which is bottled and sold in the United States as **Young's RamRod**. The name refers to the brewery itself, which is officially known as the Ram Brewery, and also to the company mascot—a burly ram with massive curved horns. RamRod has a full amber color and a fresh aroma of hay, hops, and wild-flowers with a bubble-gummy fruit lilt in the background. Gentle carbonation and appetizing, finely tuned bitterness lead the way to a very dry, biscuity palate, giving way to a flinty finish. A few minutes after you drink this beer, the aftertaste emerges; it's a wonderful grain flavor, reminiscent of fresh-baked bread. This is a

OPPOSITE: An etched-glass door welcomes visitors to the tasting room at Young's.

SAMPLE
ROOM

fine bottled rendition of British bitter and exemplifies Young's dry, subtle, balanced brewing style. This beer is magnificent when fresh, but its delicacy doesn't age well—the back label is helpfully freshness-dated and is worth paying attention to. RamRod is a particularly great lunch beer—it'll pair up happily with a wide range of sandwiches. At dinner, go for really good sausages, lightly spicy Indian or Mexican dishes, or a simply prepared steak.

Young's Special London Ale is one of the few true nineteenth-century India pale ales that have survived undiluted to greet the twenty-first century. In England it's called "Young's Export," and it was clearly built to travel. In the past several years, Special London Ale has returned to its roots and is once again bottle-conditioned. The full amber beer shows a dusting of yeast in the bottle and an exuberant earthy-fruity aroma of English hops. The bitterness is broad and expansive, but seamlessly matched by a thick backbone of malt in a dry but sturdy rounded center. The beer finishes quickly with an almost salty dry mineral tang. The hops linger cleanly, and the palate buzzes. A brilliant beer—muscular and powerful at 6.4 percent, but confident enough to be subtle and full of finesse. A great beer to pair up with a pan-seared hanger steak in shallot sauce, broiled or grilled shell steak or porterhouse, prime rib, rack of lamb (this beer will shrug off the mint sauce), spicy pork chops, and barbecue. After dinner, reach for Stilton, or the biggest, baddest, oldest farmhouse cheddar you can get your hands on.

FULLER'S In my London days, I lived in South Ealing, a quiet bedroom community at the edge of London, on the way out to Heathrow Airport. This is Fuller's country; the brewery is located in nearby Chiswick. Beer has been brewed on Fuller's site in Chiswick for nearly 350 years, though the current firm of Fuller, Smith, and Turner dates from 1845. The Fuller and Turner families are still involved; Sir Anthony Fuller has recently handed the reins to a member of the Turner family. The brewery is a handsome assemblage of brick buildings, one of them embraced by one of England's oldest wisteria plants, with a trunk the diameter of a telephone pole.

Fuller's "ordinary" bitter, called **Chiswick Bitter,** is a pale amber beer with a flowery, fruity aroma and a quick smack of hops. It's light and refreshing, but it doesn't travel—you'll have to go to London to try it. The brewery's most popular beer is **Fuller's London Pride,** which is served as a bitter in London but comes to the United States in a bottle, labeled as a pale ale. This beer has a light amber color and fairly low carbonation. The nose reflects the Fuller's house character, a blend of earthy hops and homemade orange marmalade. On the palate, the beer is juicy and full-bodied but dry throughout, showing a touch of caramel in the center before heading into a long, dry finish. I really enjoy this beer with duck, even

British breweries sometimes have secondary names based on a family heraldic symbol or simply the old name of the brewery. The symbol for Fuller's is the mythical griffin.

Chinese take-out crispy duck. It's also nice with roast beef, sausages, and pork chops. At The Churchill, one of Fuller's London pubs, the beer pairs up very nicely with the house Thai food, the orange character in the beer linking up harmoniously with the lime juice in the dishes.

If London Pride is popular, **Fuller's ESB** (Extra Special Bitter) is both popular and famous. Its fame is built partially on its successes at the Great British Beer Festival, where it has taken a profusion of prizes over the years. It is widely copied, especially in the United States, where ESB has become a common name for a craft brewery's strong, malty, hoppy bitter or pale ale.

The original is a pale copper beer with light carbonation and a big nose of earthy, fruity English hops combined with a cartload of oranges. On the palate, dynamic fruit, malt, light caramel, and hops all show through to a dry hoppy finish. A toasty, biscuity grain flavor lingers. A distinctive beer—no wonder it's so widely copied. It's big enough to handle venison and game birds, particularly wild pheasant. It's also great with steak and lamb. At 6 percent, it's a pretty big beer for lunch, but if you have a relaxing afternoon in front of you, try it with a roast beef sandwich or a good burger.

Several years ago, Fuller's decided to celebrate the 150th anniversary of the firm by releasing **Fuller's 1845**, the first bottle-conditioned beer it had offered in decades. The beer was popular enough to be kept on. This beer has a deep maple syrup color, and there's plenty of fruit in the nose. It sits with quiet confidence.

The nose leads you to expect that there's a crouching tiger in the glass—will it bite? When the beer pounces, it's lighter than expected but muscular, coating the mouth with earthy, peppery bitterness. Then it drives a train of juicy malt sweetness and tangerines right through the center, heading for a dry, mineral finish. This is a great beer for prime rib and roast beef au jus, and also a fine partner for venison. It's also brilliant with England's farmhouse cheddars—seek out Montgomery cheddar or Lincolnshire Poacher.

ADNAMS As we drove into Southwold, a pretty seaside village in the barley-growing region of East Anglia, we noticed a small tanker truck with a fading image painted on the back. It depicted a deliriously happy pig with a pint in its hoof, obviously having a very fine time. The truck, we later learned, was used to transport beer from the Adnams brewery to the bottling facility. Excess yeast, still containing some beer, was routinely fed to local pigs, apparently making them tipsy (and, no doubt, delicious to eat). The brewery wanted to repaint the fading "happy pig" onto its trucks but was afraid that animal rights activists might take notice and protest against the pigs' "happy meals." The other farm animals should be so lucky.

Adnams Sole Bay Brewery was founded in 1890, and the town of Southwold seems hardly to have changed since then. The brewery still makes local deliveries by horse-drawn drays. **Adnams' Extra** has a pale honey color and a marvelous fresh aroma of resiny hops, green apple skins, green grapes, new-mown hay, soil in early springtime, and seaside breezes. A halo of crisp bitterness surrounds a biscuity malt core carrying a juicy burst of fruit, leading out to a flinty dry finish. When it's in peak condition, it's one of the most magnificent beverages I've ever tasted. It's terrific with fish, stuffed calamari, sausages, cold duck, cold roast beef, and ham. **Adnams' Broadside** has a full amber color and shows a similar hay and sea air character, backed up by more malt in the nose. The palate is off-dry up front, with balancing hops sliding down the sides of the tongue. In the center, it combines nice fruit with light caramel, leading into a dry, crisp finish. It's brilliant with sausages, lamb, and roast beef.

I'm not sure exactly how the nearby sea manages to insinuate itself into Adnams beers. These beers are famous for not traveling well, though the head brewer, Michael Powell-Evans, feels that this is due to less salubrious cellarmanship outside the local area. When the beer is tasted near the brewery, the seaside tang is powerfully evocative. I once ordered some fish and chips and a pint of Adnams' Extra in a pub in Southwold, and by the time the food arrived, I was so enraptured by the beer that I asked the waiter to take the food away. The beer was absolutely perfect that day, and I didn't want anything to interfere with it. Nothing did. I had that pint more than a decade ago, but a great pint of Adnams' Extra is a time machine for me, depositing me instantly back in that pub, the food leaving the table, the pub dog in frantic anticipation of his stroke of luck. It's pure magic.

HARVEYS The town of Lewes is a fairy-tale confection of Victorian splendor near the southern Sussex coast, not far from Brighton. A castle overlooks the town, and cool breezes make their way over the low hills that separate Lewes from the sea. The river Ouse moves lazily through the edge of town, and a brewery was built here in 1790. John Harvey bought the brewery shortly thereafter and brought it to local prominence. He moved across the river to the brewery's present site in 1838, and the current brewery was built in 1881. The Harveys brewery, known affectionately to locals as "Lewes cathedral," is one of the most beautiful in England. Designed by the famous brewery architect William Bradford in the Victorian industrial gothic style, it is a classic tower design. Before the days of electric pumps, liquids were moved through the brewery by gravity. The mash tun would be on the top floor, the kettle below it, the fermentation rooms below the kettle, and the casks in the cellar. By 1985, Harveys had outgrown the building and so expanded it, taking great care to match the gorgeous iron and brickwork of the original.

The head brewer, Miles Jenner, is a quiet but intense man, descended from a family that has been brewing since the mid-eighteenth century. His father came to Lewes in 1938 and worked for Harveys for the next sixty years as head brewer, managing director, and finally chairman. Miles Jenner joined the firm in 1980 and has been head brewer since 1986. He and his family live in a house on the brewery grounds. Members of the Harvey family, John Harvey's sixth and seventh generations of descendents, are still very much involved in the day-to-day business of the brewery.

Harveys Sussex Bitter has a pale amber color and an aroma of hay, damp wood, yeast, earthy hops, and a touch of barnyardy sulfur. If that doesn't sound nice, believe me, it smells wonderful, just like the brewery's room full of open fermenters. The beer opens up with crisp hops and a dash of acidity supporting a light, juicy, racy malt center. The finish is short and dry. It's perfect with fried fish, calamari, octopus, and veal.

ROOSTER'S Many British breweries make strictly traditional British beers, which means, among other things, that they use only traditional English varieties of hops. In England, American hops are commonly looked down on as weedy and loud

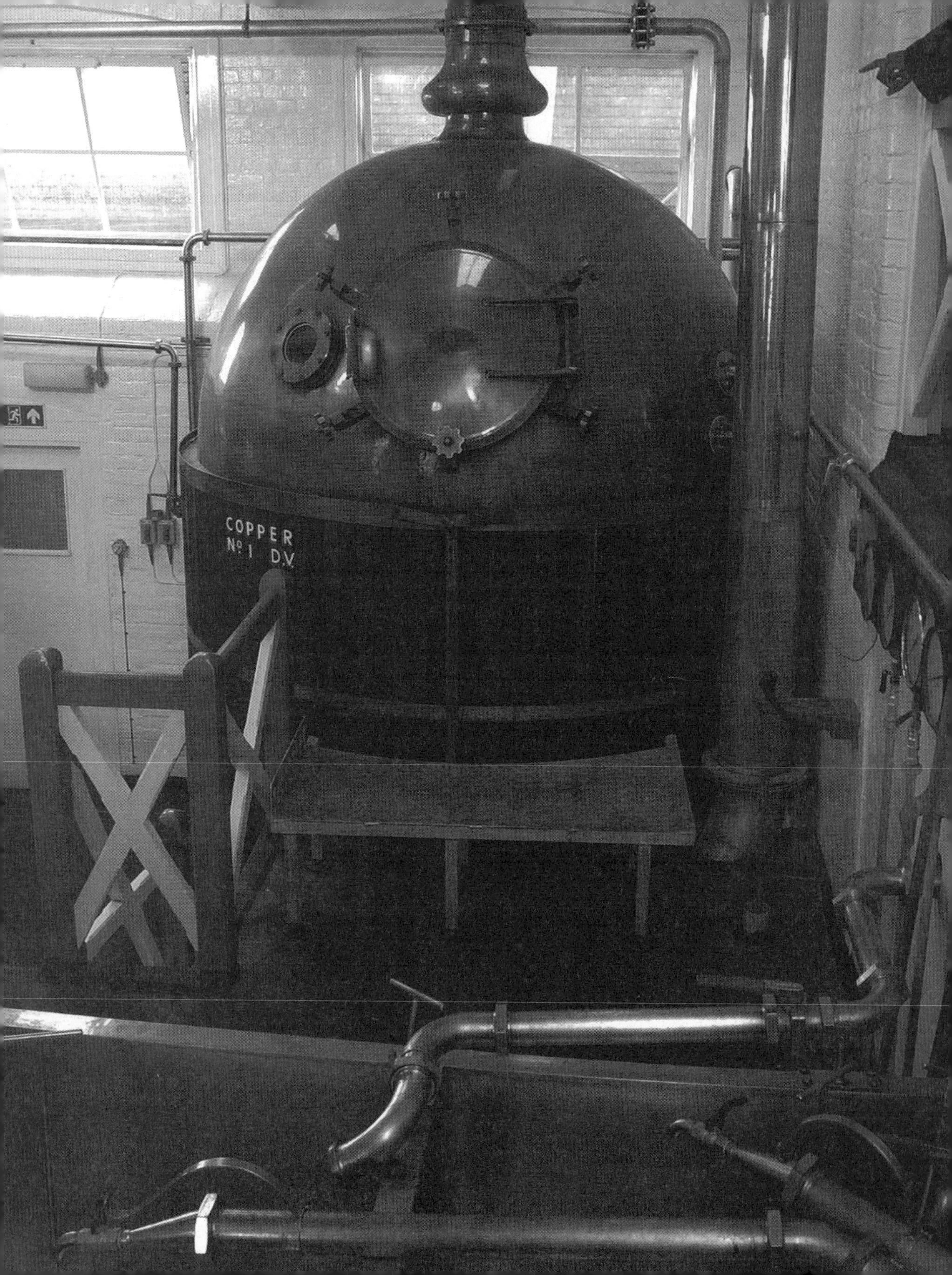
COPPER
Nº1 D.V.

in flavor. Yorkshire seems to produce the odd iconoclast, however, and few are more ornery than Sean Franklin of Rooster's Brewery. Sean is a tall, lanky, soft-spoken but opinionated Yorkshireman who has been well served by his stubbornness. He established Rooster's Brewery in 1993 in the affluent North Yorkshire town of Harrogate, and he's had to expand his brewery twice to keep up with demand for his excellent beers, which frequently veer off the path well trodden by other British brewers. He's brewed cask versions of wheat beer, used copious amounts of American hops, shocked people with intense bitterness and hop flavor, and thrived. His beers, which are all fruity and well balanced, are an eloquent argument against timidity in traditional brewing. **Rooster's Yankee** has a full gold color, with peaches and mangoes leading the charge in the nose, surrounded by a flotilla of citric American hop aromatics—pine needles, limes, and spices (it's reminiscent of an Alsatian Gewürztraminer). After that display of hops, it's surprisingly round and soft up front, with a big burst of peachy fruit in the center and sneaky moderate bitterness. The finish is long and fruity, trending dry. It's brilliant with Thai and Vietnamese food, latching onto sweetness and citric notes in the food. Fish dishes such as lemon sole would also be nice. You'll have to go with what's on offer in the pub—for now, Rooster's beers are available only from the cask.

TIMOTHY TAYLOR Keighley, West Yorkshire, is in dale country, and hard clear water runs fast down out of the Pennines. The Taylor family established a brewery in 1858 and moved it here to the Knowle Spring in 1863. The brewery is still family-owned, and the brewing of its award-winning beers is presided over by the head brewer, Peter Eels. In the mid-1970s, Fritz Maytag, the owner of San Francisco's Anchor Brewery, visited the Timothy Taylor brewery, and he now claims it as one inspiration for his own excellent Liberty Ale. The inspiring beer was **Timothy Taylor's Landlord**, a bitter with a color of pale honey and a wonderful aroma of hay, earthy hops, and orange peels. Nice acidity and broad bitterness strike the palate first, leading to a soft, round Seville orange center. A long, dry finish features bitter marmalade, with hops and bready grain lingering. Landlord is wonderful with fish and chips, Thai and Vietnamese dishes, salmon, roast beef, and duck.

OPPOSITE: Harveys kettle has a traditionally British bullet shape. This kettle is new but is an exact replica of the one it replaced. Kettle shape can influence beer flavors, and Harveys didn't want any changes.

BASS BREWERS Bass is by far the best-known brand of British beer in the world. Founded by William Bass in 1777, the brewery became famous for the pale ales and India pale ales made at its massive complex in Burton-upon-Trent in the English Midlands. Bass's red triangle was England's first registered trademark. Over the centuries, Bass has bought and subsumed many other breweries, but in recent years the company has itself been divided into bits and sold off. The original company now runs hotels, pubs, and other "leisure properties," and the Bass brand has been purchased by the Belgian giant Interbrew. While the recent history of Bass is convoluted, difficult to follow, and often rather depressing, the beers live on. Bass's best beer is found only in British pubs.

Cask-conditioned **Draught Bass** is an amber beer with a gorgeous aroma of fresh hay, saddle leather, apples, and earth. Fruitiness asserts itself first on the palate, seeming momentarily sweet but turning suddenly dry, with hay and biscuits in the center. The finish is short and mineraly, with an almost salty tang. If you're in a pub, it's an excellent beer to stick with for the evening. If the pub is serving good food, all the better—go for ham, sausages, shepherd's pie, or saltimbocca. If you're in London, seek out The White Horse, on Parson's Green (District Line, Wimbledon Branch). You'll be rewarded with Draught Bass aged and conditioned to perfection and excellent food to accompany it.

Bass is also famous in the United States, but the beer sent over here is completely unknown in Britain. The export beer is simply known as **Bass Ale**, and it's widely available in bottles and on draft. Bass Ale has a full amber color and a distinctive fruit and leather nose developed by the house yeast strain. Crisp bitterness up front gives way to a light-bodied, brisk, bone-dry beer showing a quick burst of fruit and biscuits in the center before signing off with a hard mineral snap. Impressions of hops and wet stone waft through the aftertaste. Many British pale ales have far more flavor than Bass Ale, but given the size of the company, the beer retains a surprising amount of character. With food, take advantage of Bass Ale's dry snappiness and don't get too fancy. Try it with oily fish, crab cakes, grilled shrimp, plain steaks, roast beef, and burgers.

WH BRAKSPEAR & SONS I'm vaguely disturbed that I seem to have many happy memories of drinking beer outdoors, and I don't mean in beer gardens. I first encountered Brakspear's ales when I lived in London in the early 1980s. At the time, the now-famous Neal's Yard dairy was literally a yard—it had a tiny market in a London alley on weekends. Among all the delectable cheeses, honeys, and jams, my friend Tim Murphy and I spied jugs of **Brakspear Bitter**. The jugs were plastic, but they were shaped and colored like old-fashioned stoneware. The lids had ingenious little pressure-relief valves, in case the live ale inside should decide to continue its fermentation. We grabbed ourselves a jug—it must have held at least six pints—and repaired to a good people-watching location. I still remember the taste of it, sharply hoppy and resiny, with a backdrop that tasted like a whole field of ripe barley on a sunny day. The jug didn't last long.

Brakspear Bitter has a light amber color and a wonderful aroma of hay, oranges, apricots, and earthy hops. Carbonation is very delicate on a dry, light-bodied frame featuring beautifully subtle malt flavors. Robust bitterness, a Brakspear trademark, rises up behind the malt and dominates through the long, flinty finish. At only 3.4 percent, this is an excellent example of what the British call ordinary bitter. This filtered version is available here in bottles, and if you find it in fresh condition, Brakspear Bitter is probably your best opportunity to experience an ordinary bitter on this side of the Atlantic. The uninitiated may find it thin, even watery, but drink deep and pay a little attention and you'll be well rewarded. Try it with cold lamb, roast beef, fried battered fish, sausages, or a nice ploughman's lunch of Stilton and cheddar cheese, ham, cold beef, brown bread, and pickle.

MARSTON, THOMPSON, & EVERSHED Marston's was founded in 1834, during Burton-upon-Trent's boom years. It is the last brewery in the world to use a curious form of fermentation called the "Burton union system." The name derives from the use of oak fermenting casks joined—or united—by pipework. In the union system, yeast rises to the top of the large fermenting casks and forces itself up out of the casks through pipes fitted to the cask bungs. This yeast settles in a trough above the casks, while the beer itself is directed back into the casks. By the end of the fermentation, the casks have expelled almost all their yeast, leaving the beer quite clear. Many brewers in Burton, including Bass, once used this old fermentation system, but it proved too expensive to maintain. Marston's, believing that the fermentation system is critical for the flavor development, invested more than £1 million in new "union rooms" in the early 1990s. Marston's was an independent brewery at the time but has since been swallowed up by another brewery. It remains to be seen whether the union rooms will still be a working part of the brewery or will become interesting but sad museum pieces.

These days, only one beer is put through the unions, the brewery's flagship **Marston's Pedigree**, one of the top-selling cask ales in Britain. The beer has a bright burnished deep gold color, and it proudly displays Burton's hard water in the form of a sulfurous aroma of which the locals are very fond. The sulfur blends in with fruity peppery hops and apple notes to form a unique nose. The beer is light and dry on the palate, showing broad, well-balanced bitterness and orangey malt in the center. The finish is clipped and mineraly. Many great drinks show a sulfur character—some Rieslings are prized for it. If the big sulfur aroma doesn't bother you, this is a great beer to stick with for an evening. It's racy, complex, and marvelously refreshing. Enjoy it with roast beef, roast pork, and fried fish.

Until the late 1600s, just about all beers were brown. Malt was dried with heat from wood fires, which were notoriously difficult to control, and malts were almost always dark and smoky. This all changed in the late 1700s with the advent of controllable coke fires in malting kilns and the resulting introduction of pale malts. As pale ales became the rage in early nineteenth-century England, brown ales started to step out of the crowd of porters and stouts.

Pale ales were expensive from the start—coke for drying the special pale malt was costly. As the eighteenth century drew to a close, pale ales strutted their stuff as the bright young things of Britain's beer world, and the emerging middle classes loved them. Brown ales held sway among the working classes, who came to see the expensive pale ales as effete beers best suited to office clerks. The brown ale style is quite broad, and it eventually developed into at least four distinct variants.

In northern England, where people imagined themselves made of stronger stuff than affluent southerners, a hefty version of the style developed, fueling the men who spent their days in the mines and shipyards and their evenings at the pub. Northern brown ales tend to be deep amber to light brown in color, with a malty aroma, a crisp moderate hop edge, a nutty caramel palate, and a dryish finish, weighing in at between 4.2 percent and 5 percent. These days, the most famous example of this variant is Newcastle Brown Ale, which was first brewed by Colonel Jim Porter in 1927. "Newkie Brown" is now as inextricably linked to Newcastle as coal once was. Newcastle Brown Ale is not particularly brown, which is typical of the northern variant, and a bit thin compared with its competitors, which include the warm, appropriately nutty Samuel Smith's Nut Brown Ale (locally called Old Brewery Brown Ale) and the richly flavored Double Maxim from Vaux. All are brewed from pale and crystal malts, but Newcastle Brown Ale is made by a throwback technique: it is a blend of a lighter amber ale and a stronger brown ale, the former sold as Newcastle Amber and the latter brewed for the blending. Newcastle Brown Ale enjoys the kind of cult following that Rolling Rock had in the United States in the 1980s.

In the south and Midlands, a version called "mild" was once prevalent, and it outsold pale ale and bitter throughout Britain until the 1950s. Milds are generally dark brown in color with very soft hop bitterness and slightly sweet, rounded caramel and chocolate flavors, pleasantly fruity aromatics, and clean finishes. Milds are generally quite light in alcohol, at about 3.2 percent. At one time, they were considerably stronger—in the late 1800s, milds were often about 7 percent. Like most British styles of beer, they lost considerable strength during World War I, when the government discouraged the use of barley in beer. Modern versions of mild are the ultimate "session pints," fermented quickly and designed for quaffing. Hard work makes for thirsty people, and mild was perfect sustenance for coal miners and dockworkers. The postindustrial English economy has been unkind to mild—office workers are not nearly so thirsty as coal miners, and they want to avoid the working-class image of mild. England's west Midlands is probably the last real stronghold of mild, though the style occasionally shows signs of a long-promised comeback.

The south of England is also home to a variant of brown ale, similar to mild but often sweeter, and sometimes stronger, though rarely above 4.2 percent. These brown ales will typically include a bit of chocolate malt in the mash for flavor and color, and today they're hard to find, even though many breweries produce them. They are usually bottled, and they are found stashed behind the bar at the better pubs owned by breweries. Though I am a veteran drinker of Fuller's fine ales, I discovered only a few years ago that Fuller's still produces a brown ale. An elderly man ordered it at a pub as I looked on, somewhat crestfallen that I'd never even heard of Fuller's Brown Ale, despite my half-dozen trips to the brewery. Fortunately, no one stepped up to strip me of my credentials as a "Fuller's man."

British Brown and Mild Ales with Food

While British brown ale tends not to have bitter's affinity for seafood (diver scallops are a notable exception), it makes up for this by being particularly good with cured meats, red meat, barbecue, game, and cheese. Bitter is very good with steak, but brown ale reaches for perfection. The chocolate and caramel notes from roasted and caramelized malts link up with the char developed in the broiler or on the grill. Want some Stilton or Gorgonzola on that steak? Brown ale is a team player, equally at home with the steak and the cheese. Barbecue will show a slight preference for British brown ale's more muscular American cousins, but it certainly won't kick the British version out of the smoker. The pairings can be great—you'll just want to go a little lighter on the sauce if you want the match to be perfect.

Brown ales will match virtually any beef dish, whether it's grilled, stewed, or roasted. Braised short ribs or beef cheeks are always a very nice match. If you're looking at a Brazilian churrascaria or an Argentine parillada—both classic South American beef fests—this is the beer for you. Tell them to bring you the whole cow—you're ready. If the cow's already been dealt with and turned into chili, brown ale still makes a fine companion, whether you go for the version with beans or not. (If the spices get serious, though, go for the more robust American brown ale instead.)

Softer, rounder brown ales are excellent with sautéed sweetbreads and seared scallops, the caramel of the beer matching the sweetness from the browning of the dishes. Milds and sweeter brown ales are also very nice with seared foie gras—instead of running roughshod over the delicate flavors as most wines do, the beer seeks a gentle and pleasant harmony, and almost invariably finds it. These beers are voluptuous enough to harmonize with the gamy flavors of venison, boar, wild pheasant, squab, and quail. Brown ale can work well with intense reduced sauces, but it is also perfectly comfortable with simple pan gravy.

The classic ploughman's lunch features a pint of brown ale, which is great with cold roast beef, lamb, pork, ham, and a wide variety of cow's and sheep's milk cheeses. Almost any pork dish is delicious with brown ale, especially roast pork loin, preferably butterflied and stuffed. Even spicy pork dishes such as Mexican puerco en pipián will be very nice with brown ale. The classic pâté de campagne works well, as do various liver-based pâtés, including good old-fashioned chopped chicken liver. Other liver dishes, like calf's liver with bacon and onions, appreciate the beer's warm roasted flavors and cutting power. Most brown ales are easily firm enough to handle roast duck and goose, as long as the meat is not immersed in a sweet sauce. Don't worry about a dash of duck sauce with the Chinese crispy duck—you'll be fine there. The roasted flavors in brown ale just love that crunchy, crunchy skin.

Brown ale forms a fine base for a beef stew and then happily joins it at the table. Other stews, including cassoulet, are also fine matches for brown ales. My version of cassoulet takes about three days to prepare but is worth it. The white beans are joined by duck confit, ham hocks, garlic Toulouse sausage, salt pork, and sometimes the odd bit of lamb. A nice brown ale just sails through it all, playing with each ingredient as it goes, then moving on to the next. Brown ales form a particularly fine relationship with mushrooms, especially shiitakes or morels—the lightly roasted character of the beer picks up on the earthiness. Almost any dish featuring mushrooms will pair with British brown ales, from mushroom risotto to lamb with a morel sauce. One of the nicest pairings I ever had was brown ale with a lusciously buttery wild mushroom strudel at one of chef Scott Bryant's restaurants in New York. The strudel was beautiful—it spoke eloquently of the earth, and the beer echoed everything it said.

Notable Producers of Brown and Mild Ale

HIGHGATE & WALSALL Highgate's tower-style brewery has stood since 1895, and in that time it's seen a lot. It was taken over by another brewery in 1938, and Bass later owned it for decades, allowing it to sink slowly into obscurity. Bass spent years considering "rationalizing" the brewery out of existence until a management buyout saved the brewery in 1995. The brewery, proud of its renewed independence, has built its own pubs and a loyal following. The town of Walsall is in the coal-mining Black Country of the West Midlands, one of the last strongholds of mild. There aren't nearly so many coal miners as there once were, but Highgate has stuck by the style that was once the favorite of workingmen throughout England. **Highgate Mild**, the brewery's flagship beer, has a deep russet-brown color and a complex aroma of chocolate, coffee, wet stone, wood, and damp leaves. The beer is dry and smooth, showing lean, juicy malts supported by beautiful roast acidity melded with a thin girder of hops. The finish is short, with a fruity, pruney aftertaste. It's a remarkable beer, blending malts, grains, brewing sugars, and two old house yeast strains to achieve considerable complexity in a beer of only 3.2 percent. It's excellent with plain grilled steaks, venison, roast beef, pork loin, lamb chops, sausages, ham, sandwiches, and almost any dish featuring mushrooms.

SCOTTISH AND NEWCASTLE BREWERIES The recent history of this brewing group is a tangled affair, beginning with the merger of McEwan's and Younger's of Scotland with a brewing group called Newcastle Breweries Ltd. in 1960. Since then it has been through a succession of mergers and ownerships. It is now a national powerhouse in the United Kingdom, owning several breweries and thousands of pubs. I dare not predict who will own the company or even what it may be called by the time you read this. Perhaps the only thing that has remained steady over the past several years is **Newcastle Brown Ale**, which is still the best-selling bottled ale in the UK. Newcastle Brown Ale has a fine mahogany color and a light aroma of fruit, malt, hay, and burnt sugar. The carbonation is quite low, and a restrained broad bitterness balances out fruity malts in a medium-bodied, winy center showing some caramel and just a suggestion of chocolate. The finish is short and dry with a final banana-like flourish. This is a very good partner for "bangers and mash," the old British standby of sausages and mashed potatoes. It's similarly pleasant with shepherd's pie or a hearty ploughman's lunch. The beer's caramel flavors also give it a nice hook to latch onto the flavors of mild tandoori lamb and chicken dishes.

SAMUEL SMITH'S There is something particularly hearty-sounding about "nut-brown ale." In many old British books, people wax rhapsodic about nut-brown ale. I've read more than one poem dedicated to its virtues; if the verse is to be believed, a man might live by nut-brown ale alone. Many breweries once produced beers by that name, and the Yorkshire brewer Samuel Smith's decided to revive it for export bottlings of its Old Brewery Brown Ale. **Samuel Smith's Nut Brown Ale** has a deep copper-brown color and a fine thick head. The nose is a seamless blend of caramelized malts, apple pie, haylike hops, and butterscotch. The bitterness is restrained but brisk, opening up a medium-bodied dry palate showcasing nice caramel flavors in a fruity center. The finish is dry and mineraly. This is a classic northern English brown ale, flavorful and well balanced. The drying mineral character derives from the hard water used; the town of Tadcaster sits above a water table suffused with limestone. The mineral quality combines with an attractive caramel character to give this beer terrific versatility. Try it with fried chicken, roasted poultry, steaks, roast beef, grilled sausages, or good homemade meatloaf.

GEORGE GALE & COMPANY Gale's is the largest family-owned independent brewery in Hampshire, with an estate of more than 150 pubs. The brewery's beers are distinctive in the best sense of the word, and I feel that family ownership has helped promote the brewery's individuality. Individuality is the source of the brewery's strength; without it, Gale's would certainly not have thrived for more than 150 years. **Gale's Festival Mild** is a good showcase for the house character, derived in large part from an old yeast strain. This beer is very dark brown, verging on black—only the slightest red highlights punch through. The aroma shows caramel and licorice against a haylike backdrop. The yeast shows itself on the palate, producing a light, winy acidity that carries flavors of raisins and chocolate through the center. The finish is long and winy, and it's only on the aftertaste that you really notice the hops. An ironlike bitterness lingers. This is an old-fashioned stronger version of mild, weighing in at 4.6 percent. It's a fascinating beer that seems destined to accompany stewed beef, short ribs, game birds, or vension.

WOODFORDE'S NORFOLK ALES Founded in 1980, Woodforde's is among the most successful of the modern British microbreweries. It started off in Drayton, near Norwich, and then moved in 1989 to larger premises in the village of Woodbastwick. It brews a wide range of beers from its own well water, local East Anglian malt, and Kentish hops. Among its most popular beers is **Woodforde's**

Norfolk Nog, a bottle-conditioned ale with a deep garnet-brown color. The aroma is redolent of raisins, prunes, and chocolate, with an earthy overlay of hops. The aroma would lead you to believe that the beer will be heavy, but quite the opposite is true. The palate is very light-bodied, with low carbonation and a broad restrained bitterness, holding chocolate and dark fruit flavors in a lightweight frame. The finish is brisk and dry, showing a touch of caramel and roast acidity. Grain flavors linger attractively. This is an easy-drinking beer possessing what the British admiringly call "moreishness" and "sessionability," meaning that you'd like to drink plenty of it and it's light enough so that you can do so without undue peril. At 4.6 percent, you can consider it an old-fashioned, stronger version of mild. Enjoy Norfolk Nog with ham, roast beef, cold meats, and sandwiches.

Asking the bartender to blend beers in the glass for you is an old tradition. To this day, many people still walk into American bars and ask for a "black and tan," a pint with pale beer below and Irish stout floating mysteriously on top. When I was living in London, my friend Jon and I were devotees of a blend we called the "Peacemaker." One day, I asked a barman to fill half my pint with Fuller's sturdy ESB bitter and then top it up with a small bottle of Fuller's very strong Golden Pride barley wine. He put the pint down on the bar, regarded me from under bushy eyebrows, and solemnly informed me, "You'll not be having many of those." We did have many of those, but we were young then.

In the early 1700s, many people had their own particular blend of beer that they enjoyed. A bartender might end up blending beers from as many as six different barrels to get the flavor a customer wanted. Not surprisingly, this was a rather labor-intensive practice, but the barkeep gave the customers what they wanted lest they go elsewhere. In 1722, the brewer Ralph Harwood in London came up with a single beer that mimicked the flavor of one of the most popular blends, a three-beer mixture known as "three threads." He called this beer Mr. Harwood's Entire, apparently referring to the fact that it had the best qualities of all the others. Harwood's Entire was moderately strong, fairly dark, and reportedly tasty, and it could be served quickly, which satisfied both the barmen and their customers. London's porters, hardworking men who slaked their thirst with copious amounts of beer, particularly favored Entire, which became known as "porter beer." The name Entire fell into disuse, but you can still see it engraved in the stone exteriors of some old London pubs.

As "porter beer" became the most popular style in London's pubs, dozens of breweries jockeyed to dominate the market. Porter was so popular that it became possible to make a fortune brewing just this one style. But brewers needed economies of scale to do this, so those in London started building large breweries with gigantic wooden storage vats to hold fermenting and aging porter. When Whitbread built its porter brewery in Chiswell Street in 1745, it installed vats that would hold more than 160,000 U.S. gallons each. The new vats were often "dedicated," with lavish promotional dinners held inside them just before they were filled with beer. In 1790, the Meux brewery constructed a vat large enough to hold 200 dinner guests. Five years later, Meux erected a vat with a capacity of 860,000 U.S. gallons, the largest in the world.

All this was bound to end in tears. These vessels, impressive as they were, were made of wood, and wood has its limits. Those limits were discovered in October 1814, when one of Meux's porter vats burst, breaking down the brewery's walls, sending a raging flash flood of porter through London's streets, and demolishing nearby buildings. Eight people died "by drowning, injury, poisoning by the porter fumes or drunkenness."

When Arthur Guinness opened his brewery in Dublin in 1759, he made other styles of ale, but he soon turned his hand to porter, which had become as popular in Ireland as in England. Until the 1790s most porter in Ireland was imported from England, but the Irish brewers then recaptured their local market. By 1803, Guinness had given up on other beer styles and brewed only porter, and by the 1830s Guinness porter was being widely exported. Guinness porter is the ancestor of the present Guinness stout beers, and the continued popularity of Guinness around the world is based on those early exports. Versions of porter still remain in some European countries—Poland, Sweden, Denmark, Finland, and Russia all have breweries that make porter.

Americans also enjoyed porter, originally importing most of it from England. George Washington enjoyed both English and local-brewed porter until 1769, when he gave up the English stuff—he'd decided that nothing from England suited his palate any longer. Thomas Jefferson brewed and sold porter; we still have his letters complaining of how difficult it was to find good corks for bottling his beer. By the time the American colonists declared independence, American porter brewing was in full swing. Robert Hare of Philadelphia opened a porter brewery in 1776, just in time to be driven out by the British occupation. By 1778, however, he was back at it, and he later supplied Hare's porter to George Washington's presidential mansion. Even when German immigrants brought lager styles that swept through the Northeast in the mid-1800s, many of

Porter brewing has returned to London—this beer is a recent addition to Fuller's line of fine ales.

them brewed porter for their non-German customers, though they used the new bottom-fermenting lager yeasts to make it. This variant of porter still survives, produced by the D.G. Yuengling Brewery of Pottsville, Pennsylvania, America's oldest brewery.

By the 1960s, changing tastes, the world wars (malt roasting used up much-needed energy reserves), and Prohibition nearly killed off porter in the United States; and by the 1940s, it had already died out in England, replaced by mild brown ale and stout. Even Guinness stopped producing porter in the 1970s, though you'll still hear older Irish people refer to Guinness stout as "porter." The craft-brewing movement, first in England and then in the United States, has rediscovered the porter style in the past twenty years. English porter remains relatively rare, but American craft brewers are fond of the style and have added their own flavorful flourishes.

Modern English porters are still dark, full-bodied ales showing more roasted character than brown ales, but less than stouts. Most porters aren't quite black—reddish-brown highlights are usually visible in the glass. Porter doesn't have stout's aggressive espresso-like roast bite but shows its roast in a smoother, more chocolaty flavor. As with most English beers, hop bitterness is nicely balanced against malt flavor and sweetness, with the brewery's yeast strain adding fruit aromatics. At about 5 percent, porters are not nearly so fearsome as they appear, and they are particularly seductive on chilly evenings.

British Porters with Food

British porters are rich, elegant beers that carry their roast with grace and ease. Bitterness tends to be more restrained here than in the exuberant American versions. They are often surprisingly silky and are capable of matching many more dishes than one might imagine. A few years ago, I hosted a beer dinner for the Association of Westchester Country Club Chefs at the Bronxville Field Club in New York. One of the dishes was seared diver sea scallops. Much to the surprise of the forty chefs in attendance, I served Samuel Smith's Taddy Porter with the scallops. They hadn't imagined that I'd be serving such a dark beer—wouldn't this overwhelm the dish? Not at all. Good diver scallops have a delicate natural sweetness, and searing caramelizes the sugars. The roast and caramel in the porter echoed those in the scallops, and the sugars in the beer matched the sweetness of the scallops. The porter was quintessentially British—it played out on the palate with smoothness, subtlety, and finesse. A few of the chefs later told me that it was one the most perfect matches of food and beverage they had ever experienced.

Many of porter's affinities are more obvious than that. Porter has plenty of roast to pick up on char flavors from the grill. Grilled steaks and burgers are natural partners, with chicken and pork following close behind. Even grilled vegetables on a skewer will team up with this beer, the smoky sweetness of the veggies latching onto the roast in the beer. Grilled or barbecued ribs will be a nice match for porter as well, with sweeter porters doing the best job of matching the sauce. Meatloaf is perfect with porter, as is shepherd's pie. Venison and boar are also on porter's dance card, whether they are seared, grilled, roasted, or stewed—the gamy red-meat flavors work nicely with the beer's dark malts.

Good sweet Italian sausages are delicious with porter, but venison sausages are even better. (D'Artagnan, the excellent purveyor of foie gras and game, makes a terrific venison and cherry sausage—I buy it online at www.dartagnan.com.) Pot roast and slow-braised short ribs are also good companions. At lunchtime, porter can be really wonderful with a Reuben sandwich or almost anything on pumpernickel bread, which features harmoniously chocolaty flavors.

Chocolate doesn't often show up in savory dishes, but when it does it's likely to be delicious, and porter should be there to greet it. Several traditional Spanish and Italian dishes are enriched with dark chocolate, and porter will work especially well with them. The match is magical. Mole poblano, the classic complex Mexican sauce featuring spices, chilies, nuts, and chocolate, turns chicken into a great partner for porter. Some game has its own chocolaty qualities—squab and wood pigeon come to mind, especially when wild. Porter can be a fine accompaniment to these powerfully flavored meats, as well as to buffalo and moose.

With desserts, especially those made with chocolate, porter can really shine. Many porters are brewed with "chocolate malt," so called because it is roasted until it attains the flavor of dark chocolate. No wine can match chocolate desserts nearly as well as the right beer. As Joanna Simon, a prominent British wine writer, laments, "Death by chocolate is a common form of wine extermination." Not to worry—beer rides gallantly to the rescue. If the chocolate in the dessert is very intense, you might want to go for an imperial stout, but if it's subtle to medium in intensity, porter will be the best choice. For example, British porters are very good with chocolate soufflé and mousse. Light chocolate cakes will also enjoy a pleasant encounter with porter.

Black and implacable, topped with a cloud of pale foam, the appearance of a pint of stout never fails to impress. It is no great surprise that Guinness produces television commercials showing nothing but a pint of Guinness Stout—as we watch, the famous head forms and settles.

No other style of beer is as married to one brewery as stout is to Guinness. In 1759, thirty-four-year-old Arthur Guinness signed a 9,000-year lease on a defunct brewery at St. James Gate, Dublin. He'd had three years of brewing experience in Kildare and had moved to Dublin to make his fortune. His first years were difficult—Ireland was under English rule, and imported English beers were taxed far less heavily than local Irish beers. Guinness held out until the tax laws were changed, giving him a fair shot at both the Irish market and the overseas trade. He hired an expert porter brewer from London and soon was exporting his porter to England. By the early 1800s Guinness West Indies Porter was finding its way to the Caribbean, and the end of the nineteenth century saw Guinness in Europe, Africa, Australia, Asia, and North America. Today, Guinness brews nineteen versions of stout in more than forty countries and sells it in 135 countries. In 1947, Guinness even opened a brewery on Long Island, New York. It closed seven years later—apparently American stout drinkers wanted their beer to come from Dublin rather than Long Island.

Stout is a direct descendent of porter. Porter brewers, Guinness included, began brewing a stronger, roastier version called stout porter, indicating a heavier brew. Eventually, the word "porter" was dropped, and the beer became known simply as stout. In 1817, Daniel Wheeler's patented roasting machine was introduced. This device allowed precision roasting of malts and raw barley, giving rise to black beers with a high-roast flavor. Guinness started using highly roasted raw barley in its beer, giving the beer a distinctly dry espresso-like bite and setting it apart from others. While Guinness was highly successful, it had robust competition in Ireland from Beamish and Crawford, which was established in Cork as the Cork Porter Brewery in 1792. Beamish was surpassed by Guinness in 1833, and it continues to brew a very fine stout today. Murphy's Brewery, established in 1856, is Beamish's crosstown rival. It brewed porter when it first opened but soon found that the local taste had turned to stout and began brewing that instead. Today, Murphy's still brews stout and is favored over Guinness by many people in Cork.

Classic Irish stout, despite its stark appearance, is a very friendly style of beer. It's very dry, brisk, and light. That's right, light. Don't be fooled by the color—that's a result of the heavy use of roasted grains in the mash. It is no indication of strength. All the major labels of draft Irish stout contain less than 5 percent alcohol by volume, even lighter than mass-market American "pilsner." This is a beer designed for evenings at the pub, where it can be enjoyed in copious quantity. The amazingly sturdy, creamy head on a pint of Guinness is the result of an ingenious tap system that forces dissolved nitrogen from the beer under very high pressure. Guinness and its rivals combine a robust hop bite with a bone-dry, slightly acidic light-bodied palate showing roasted flavors of espresso and dark chocolate. The hop bite is combined with a roast bite—once again, the comparison to espresso is apt. If the beer is quite fresh, an earthy hop aroma will greet the nose. There's a good reason why this beer is exported around the world. It's light but flavorful, it's marvelously refreshing, and it tastes great cold or at room temperature. The heavy hopping would at one time have preserved the beer on its journeys. Guinness has been remarkably successful over the years, so it has, thankfully, seen little reason to change its beer. If you're in Dublin, check out the local brew pubs, The Porterhouse in Temple Bar and Mssrs. McGuire on the Liffey, both brewing wonderfully full-flavored versions of classic Irish stout.

In England, stout brewers have historically favored a far sweeter style. In both England and Ireland, stout was widely considered a healthful tonic—"Guinness Is Good for You" was a famous advertising slogan. The Irish even referred to stout as "mother's milk" and prescribed it to nursing mothers, who were supposed to benefit from its high iron content (and, no doubt, babies benefited from tastier milk). Seeking to boost its healthful qualities, British brewers took this allusion more literally and added milk sugar to many stouts, which became known as milk stouts or cream stouts. Labels boasted of the nutritious qualities of these beers and often featured robust-looking milk churns. Yeast cannot ferment milk sugar, so it remained in the beer, giving a rounded, sweeter palate. Since some of the sugars remained unfermented, the alcohol content was generally low, and the beer was sometimes served to people recuperating from an illness or injury. Workmen enjoyed stout as an energizing pick-me-up after long days in mines and shipyards. The ranks of England's mines and shipyards are depleted these days, and sweet English stouts have become hard to find.

Another variant of stout, now widely made by American brew pubs and craft breweries, is oatmeal stout. Oats are rarely used in brewing, and for good reason—they turn sticky and gummy in the mashing vessel, the same as they do in your cereal bowl. This makes oats a very tough grain to work with, but brewers probably started using them hundreds of years ago when other grains ran short. Added in relatively small proportions, oats can make a fine contribution to a slightly sweet stout, giving the beer a round, silky, almost oily quality.

Imperial Stout

Catherine the Great fell in love with the flavor of stout while on a trip to England and asked for some to be sent to her at the Russian court. When the beer spoiled on its way to the Baltic ports, Catherine was not amused. She wanted stout, and Catherine was the sort of person who generally got what she wanted. If she didn't get her beer, heads could roll. The Barclay brewery of London came to the rescue, making a particularly strong, bitter stout sturdy enough to make the long sea voyage. At 10.5 percent, this was a beer that could take care of itself. It showed up at the palace in fine condition. This beer was an instant sensation at the Russian court and became known as imperial Russian stout.

Similar beers were made by other breweries and shipped to Nordic ports and throughout the Baltic states. Baltic breweries eventually started to make their own versions, which they usually preferred to refer to as porters. These were sometimes bottom-fermenting lagers, coaxed into an ale-like intensity of flavor by warmer fermentations and concentration of malt. Imperial stout is still made by a few breweries in England and many more in the United States, including my own. It is beer of singular intensity, often combining flavors of dark chocolate, coffee, licorice, burnt fruit, hops, and tar into a complex powerhouse.

Imperial stout was also the basis for beers brewed in the eighteenth and nineteenth centuries for shipment to the Caribbean, where it provided nourishment and refreshment to workers, overseers, and merchants. Guinness's West Indies Porter was the forerunner of today's Guinness Foreign Extra Stout, a strong bitter beer with a distinctive acidic edge. One might think that a strong black beer would be the last thing you'd want in the heat of the Caribbean, but the beer remains remarkably popular there; it is thought of as a restorative and even an aphrodisiac. This beer isn't available in the United States, and many Caribbean immigrants pine for it—it's occasionally even smuggled in. On a vacation in St. Kitts, I found the Foreign Extra Stout remarkably refreshing, even in the blinding Caribbean sun. After I'd had two or three bottles, though, the locals started to eye me warily, seeming to wonder if I was up to no good. What was I planning after three bottles of a love potion?

English and Irish Stouts with Food

Stouts are surprisingly versatile with food. Irish stout in particular has the ability to pair beautifully with dishes you'd never expect. The pairing is usually more a matter of stark contrast than seamless harmony, but it can be brilliant nonetheless. A good example is the classic combination of Irish stout and oysters. The waters around England and Ireland once teemed with oysters, and, like lobsters, they were inexpensive and widely consumed by the working classes. Oysters and porter made a tasty and cheap meal for many thousands of people every day. Today, overfishing and pollution have made oysters a relative luxury, but the combination of stout and oysters is as nice as ever. Chophouses and seafood palaces from London to New York still serve stout to accompany oysters on the half shell. The dry, assertive bitterness and roast of the beer intersects with the brininess, texture, and sea flavors of the oyster in a way that nothing else can. One can almost imagine the beer as the knife that cracks the oyster open—there seems to be a primal connection between them. The flavor of the oyster is magically magnified and fills the senses. Guinness hosts a massive oyster festival in Galway, Ireland, every year, where thousands celebrate this centuries-old combination of beer and food.

Irish stout is also wonderful with mussels, lobster, crab, clams, scallops, and calamari. All of these have a certain sea sweetness that Irish stout accentuates wonderfully. It's hard to say why this affinity doesn't transfer to most fish, but the beer does seem to overwhelm almost everything but tuna and salmon, which are big enough to stand up for themselves. Bluefish, sardines, anchovies, and mackerel are a few other exceptions—the beer is great at slicing through their essential

"fishiness" and teasing out the pleasant sea flavors. Smoked fish works well, too. Irish stout is great with smoked salmon, lox, trout, and kippers.

Like lobster, oysters were once considered food for the poor. These days oysters earn respect, and stout is still the traditional accompaniment.

Irish stout is as happy on land as at sea, and it finds a perfect partner in ham. Once again, the dry intensity of the beer draws out the salt and magnifies the essential flavors of the ham. The more intense the ham, the better the match—prosciutto di Parma, pancetta, and Serrano ham are all explosively delicious with Irish stout. Corned beef, a one-time Irish staple, is great with stout, as is pastrami. There are few things better with a classic Reuben sandwich than a pint of stout. Steaks, preferably covered with cracked pepper, coarse salt, and olive oil before hitting the broiler or grill, are excellent. The beer matches the char while cutting the fat and melding with the juices. Naturally, the same goes for burgers. While it seems best that oysters and stout meet only on your palate, beef and stout can happily share a pot. It seems that someone in every Irish household has an old recipe for Guinness stew, a dish that I imagine is almost as old as the brewery. The basic recipe is as simple as it sounds—Guinness, beef, and just about any vegetable or tuber you happen to have on hand. Served with its namesake, it's exactly what you want on a cold, blustery winter evening.

For sheer versatility, English stouts, tasty as they are, are rarely as breezily successful as Irish stouts. Irish stout uses flavor contrasts to make its uncompromising bone-dry assertiveness into an asset with food. English stouts tend to be sweeter, more chocolaty, and a bit more subtle. This means you may want to look for harmony more than contrast. That said, English stouts are still excellent with food, just in a different way from their Irish cousins. Oatmeal stouts and other off-dry variations can be excellent with beef, venison, and lamb, especially when these meats are served with savory sauces, which tend to have some sweetness. Soft oatmeal stouts can be particularly good with sweetbreads and seared scallops, for the same reasons—the slight sweetness and nuttiness to match the dish and the almost oily, silky quality of both the meat and the beer. Taste as they disappear into each other.

English stout's chocolate flavors will find happy partners in chocolate-based mole sauces as well as those strange but delicious Italian pastas made with chocolate. Felidia, Lidia Bastianich's excellent Italian restaurant in New York, makes a wonderful bitter-chocolate ravioli. It's stuffed with roasted pumpkin squash and sautéed with butter, marjoram, and pumpkin seeds. It's magnificent with imperial stout, which provides a clear harmony with the chocolate in the pasta, the sweetness to match the squash, toasty malt flavors to match the pumpkin seeds, and cutting power to set aside the butter.

Chocolate flavors are also a big note in small game birds like squab and wood pigeon, especially if they're wild. Oatmeal stout will play along nicely.

Of course, when we think of chocolate, we usually have dessert in mind. Sommeliers and diners alike flail about, trying their best to believe that there's a wine that matches chocolate. There isn't. Chocolate is sweet, and it coats the mouth. Neither of those qualities is something wine is equipped to handle. Put away the California zinfandel—that's not a partnership, it's a wrestling match, and you're certainly not going to win it. Put away the sweet dessert wine, too—aside from being sweet, what does it have to offer chocolate? The harmony between stouts and chocolate desserts is so big and so wide and so obvious that every restaurant that serves desserts should have at least one stout on its list. If you get only one thing from this book, make this point the keeper—*stouts are an absolutely perfect match for chocolate desserts.*

There are two ways to go here, and each has its merits. The first way is to have a semisweet or sweet stout. Here you're matching sweet with sweet, and chocolate with chocolate. This works best when the dessert is not terribly sweet, and the chocolate is more milk than dark chocolate. A chocolate soufflé is a good example of a perfect match for a sweet stout. You want to make sure that the stout has at least some bite to it, though—otherwise, the match is actually so close that the flavors cancel each other out. When the chocolate in the dessert is more intense, it's time to bring out the big guns—imperial stout. This is the second way to make the match, using a beer that provides harmony and contrast at the same time. Imperial stouts tend to have considerable residual sweetness, but it's balanced by roast acidity and hop bitterness. In combination, say, with one of those little French dark chocolate cakes with the molten center, the bitterness and roast cut right across the sweetness like espresso. Then the chocolate and coffee flavors of the beer embrace the same flavors in the cake and your eyes roll toward the ceiling. You can get as intense as you want with the chocolate—imperial stout will be right on the money. Chocolate truffles? Perfect. Trust me—once you taste this, you will never, ever drink wine with chocolate again.

With other desserts, imperial stouts provide chocolate and coffee flavors and produce very tasty contrasts. The old rule that the wine must be as sweet as the dessert does not apply to beer. Beer has the bitterness and carbonation to lift sugar and cut through fat, which gives the palate both a flood of flavor and a welcome break with each sip. An intense raspberry or strawberry tart welcomes the chocolate flavors—I don't need to tell you what fine partners fruit and chocolate are. Imperial stouts work equally well with creamy desserts such as classic caramel flan, crème brûlée, and panna cotta.

Notable Producers of English and Irish Porter and Stout

ARTHUR GUINNESS & SONS Though it is very good at projecting a handmade image, Guinness has long been a globe-straddling behemoth. At various times, the brewery at St. James' Gate in Dublin has been the largest in the world. Guinness is now a jewel in the crown of the gigantic multinational Diageo, which has always sounded to me like the name of some prehistoric landmass. You have to admire Guinness, though. It has carved out a nice niche for itself, selling huge amounts of sharp black beer in a world awash in golden fizz. Guinness claims that its beers are sold in 135 countries, and in the past several years it has made great strides in the American market. In Italy, where people value the appetizing bitterness of their espresso and their traditional aperitifs and digestifs, Guinness has recently enjoyed a sudden and well-deserved popularity.

Guinness Stout Draught, despite its stark appearance, is one of the lightest beers on the market, barely clearing 4 percent. Guinness invented the "widget" can, which squirts a stream of nitrogen gas into the beer as the can is opened. This forms the famous creamy trademark Guinness head on the beer when it's poured into a glass. It's an ingenious trick, much imitated, though usually not very well. The beer has an earthy haylike English hop aroma, with just a hint of malt aroma peeking

Guinness Foreign Extra Stout is a Victorian beer that's still popular in the Caribbean, where locals feel that it puts a certain spring in one's step.

through. Bitterness is broad, assertive, and mouth-coating on a very light malt frame. The hops merge with an espresso acidity and race toward a flinty dry finish.

The widget can contains essentially the same beer that is served on draft both here and in Ireland. Properly served draft Guinness has a nicer hop flavor and more coffeeish depth in the center than the canned version does. Freshness counts for such a light beer, and Dublin Guinness is legendary for that reason. I once judged a beer competition with the woman who was then in charge of quality control for Guinness. She told me that Guinness once had a very slight flavor problem in one of its batches and sent out a team to investigate. Though the offending beer had left the brewery less than forty-eight hours previously, all they could find in Dublin was empty barrels—the beer was already gone.

Draft Guinness is brilliant with oysters, crabmeat, and the famous Dublin Bay prawns. It's also excellent with ham, prosciutto, pastrami, corned beef, steaks, burgers, barbecue, and Mexican dishes.

Guinness Extra Stout, at least in the United States, is an entirely different beer. At 6 percent, it's much stronger than the draft or canned versions, and it's available only in a bottle. (Confusingly, though, there is now a bottled version of the widgetized "draft" as well.) The label says "Imported" in big letters, but it protests too much. It's imported, all right—from Canada, Toronto to be precise. This beer has an aroma of hops and sulfur. The bitterness and acidity are right up front on the palate, bracing and powerful. The scouring bitterness drives a sharp coffee flavor through to a long bitter finish. This beer is a real throwback—it's astonishingly assertive. It once would have been bottle-conditioned, and that would have lent it far greater depth than it has now. I doubt that most oysters would survive an encounter with this beer. I'd save it for powerfully fruity aged hams and robust sausages.

BEAMISH & CRAWFORD Beer has been brewed on Beamish's site in Cork, Ireland, since 1650. Richard Beamish and Arthur Crawford purchased the brewery in 1792 and relaunched it as the Cork Porter Brewery. The brewery grew explosively, and by 1805 the output grew from 12,000 barrels to 100,000 barrels per year, making it the largest brewery in Ireland and the third largest in the British Isles. It could have been a contender, but **Beamish Irish Stout** now just nips at Guinness's heels. Still, it's well loved in its native Cork, and it has recently been reintroduced into the United States, both on draft and in a widget can. The brewery has passed through the hands of a number of international brewing groups and is now part of Scottish and Newcastle's portfolio.

Beamish Irish Stout has a light aroma of hops and chocolate. The palate is light-bodied, creamy, and bone-dry, with a thin whack of bitterness. There's a dusty flavor of coffee and cocoa in the center followed by a flinty, hoppy finish. If the beer is particularly fresh, it distinguishes itself with a very pleasant aroma of hops. Otherwise it relies on a fine-tuned bitterness to be quite refreshing. It's great with oysters, burgers, or ham and Swiss on rye.

MURPHY BREWERY In the Christian tradition, it is a miracle if holy water is turned into wine. In 1856 James, Jerome, Francis, and William Murphy built a brewery intended to turn consecrated water into beer. The blessed well was in Cork, and the Murphys built their brewery alongside it and drew their brewing water from it. The brewery is still known as the Lady's Well Brewery, even though it now uses the town water supply. In 1983, Murphy was bought by Heineken, which has helped give the beer a wider international presence. The canned and bottled beer that we get in the United States is brewed not in Cork but in England, where Whitbread brews it under license.

The Murphy Brewery once produced porter but now has only one product, **Murphy's Irish Stout**. This beer is black with a thick cap of foam and has a pleasant aroma of earthy, floral hops and chocolate. The palate features light bitterness seamlessly integrated with the bite of the roast, leading into a dry, winy center. From there, it's gone in a flash, leaving behind only dry, clean bitterness and a coffeeish ghost. Murphy's is less assertive than Beamish and far less assertive than Guinness. A few years ago, Guinness had an amusingly muscular advertising slogan, "Guinness, the beer you've been training for." Soon afterward, Murphy's sly retort appeared on the sides of buses: "Murphy's Irish Stout—No Experience Required." That witty exchange pretty much sums it up; what Murphy's lacks in acidity and snap, it makes up for with mellow smoothness. It's very pleasant with delicate oysters, ham and Swiss cheese sandwiches, and a wide variety of Mexican dishes, especially those featuring black beans or mole negro sauce. Its mellow hopping also makes it the best stout to use for making a traditional Irish stew of beef in stout.

SAMUEL SMITH This famous family-run ale brewery in Tadcaster, Yorkshire, brews three roasty beers with distinctly different characters. **Samuel Smith's Taddy Porter** is solidly black and floats an aroma of caramel, ripe plums, chocolate, butterscotch, and licorice. Moderate bitterness greets the tongue along with a juicy burst of berry-like fruit. The palate is light, round, and soft, developing muted chocolate and coffee notes. The finish is long and dry. A great match for seared diver scallops, earthy monkfish preparations (especially with morels), steaks, and beef stews. For desserts, go for fruit tarts or chocolate soufflés.

Samuel Smith's Oatmeal Stout has a light fresh hop aroma with a chocolate backdrop. The palate is full-bodied and semisweet, with sturdy hopping and racy acidity balancing caramelized malts. The roast lies broadly across the tongue like a lash of Italian coffee. The sweetness persists into a quick finish. A terrific beer to serve with chocolate desserts, fruit tarts, cheesecake, and ice cream.

While these first two stouts each weigh in at about 5 percent, **Samuel Smith's Imperial Stout** tips the scales at 7 percent. The darker head signals a heavy concentration of roasted malts in the mash. The nose is a heady perfume of dark French chocolate, vintage port, passion fruit, and licorice. The beer coats the palate with a deep cushion of velvet, lush, juicy, and silky. The bitterness rises behind it with ironlike rigidity, a rod to hang all that velvet on. Chocolate, espresso, and ripe fruit fill the senses before exiting gracefully in a long, drying finish. This is a must-have for serious chocolate desserts—flourless chocolate mud cakes and chocolate caramel tarts. It's almost as good with cheesecake, especially cheesecake with fruit on top. The list goes on: butter shortbread cookies,

Georg Schneider I started brewing weissbier in Munich in 1872. Today, Georg Schneider VI carries on the family tradition in Kelheim.

TOP: Brewmaster Hans-Peter Drexler brews the beautifully structured weissbiers at the Schneider brewery. **BOTTOM:** A group of friends meets for morning brotzeit at Ayinger's inviting gasthaus. **OPPOSITE:** Breakfast of champions—weissbier with weisswurst is the traditional midmorning meal in Bavaria.

Weissbier is wonderfully versatile with food. The smoky aromatics in Schneider Weisse link up nicely with the bacon in this delicious spaetzle. **OPPOSITE:** Weissbier can also handle spicy dishes with aplomb. Chef Floyd Cardoz, a genius with Indian spices, with his Goan-Spiced Crab Cake at Tabla, New York City.

Tabla

SCHNEIDER WEISSE

The brisk flavor and bright aromatics of Belgian wheat beer make this variety perfect with many fish dishes. **OPPOSITE:** Chef Rick Moonen with friends at Oceana. A master with seafood, Moonen now pairs weissbier with dishes at RM and Branzini in Manhattan.

Classic pub architecture in Manchester, England. The Marble now houses a small brewery in its cellar, producing traditional cask ales. OPPOSITE: Master cellarman Mark Dorber ages cask ales to perfection at the White Horse, Parson's Green, London. Dorber has taught the art of cask conditioning to legions of

TOP: Biscuity English malts wait their turn at the Harveys brewery. **BOTTOM:** A quiet moment with a pint of bitter at the Marble brew pub in Manchester. **OPPOSITE:** Bitter chocolate blends with spices and chilies in this duck with Oaxacan mole negro at La Palapa. A beer with roasted, chocolaty flavors makes an excellent partner.

Samuel Smith

Head Brewer John Keeling brews award-winning traditional ales at Fuller's of London. **OPPOSITE:** This beautiful 1930s copper kettle still reports to work at Greene King in Bury St. Edmunds, England.

COPPER
DO NOT

Old riveted mashing vats at the Harveys brewery in Lewes. OPPOSITE: A barman pours a pint at the White Horse, London. Cask-conditioned ales are usually drawn from the cellar by a simple hydraulic hand pump.

Young's Ram Brewery sits right in the center of bustling Wandsworth. Should you visit the brewery, you may well meet the company mascot, a burly ram.

strawberry shortcake, carrot cake—in short, anything that would taste great with strong French or Italian coffee.

FULLER'S The London brewer Fuller's is best known for its excellent bitters, but a neglected brown ale has always lurked behind the bar at its pubs. Now the brewery has made a more wholehearted commitment to **Fuller's London Porter**, its first heavily roasted beer in many years. This beer appears very dark brown rather than black—pretty ruby highlights shine through the glass. It has a full, rich milk chocolate aroma, but we're talking about Lindt, not Nestlé's. Hop aromas drift in the background. Bitter hops glide up the sides of your tongue, and then everything fills in: the juicy acidic roast, the fruity caramel center, the warm coffee and chocolate platform. The finish is clipped and dry. A delicious beer brewed with the equivalent of perfect pitch—the structure is flawlessly harmonious, and everything works, like a great symphony or piece of Palladian architecture. Serve this with authentic Mexican mole negro, light chocolate desserts, fruit desserts, or vanilla ice cream.

YOUNG'S Fuller's' friendly crosstown rival in London—Young's—entered the fray with **Young's Oatmeal Stout**, which is available in both a bottle and the now ubiquitous widget can. This beer has an appetizing aroma of chocolate, coffee, hops, and dried fruit. A first impression of sweetness dries out quickly, revealing a very soft, round, almost oily palate showing light chocolate and licorice flavors. The finish is chalky and dry. A very light, easygoing stout that will be as happy with a ham sandwich as with sweetbreads. It will provide a light touch to match chocolate soufflés and is very good with cheesecake. Aside from that, it's a beer you can easily stick with for an entire evening all by itself.

HARVEY & SON Starting in 1781, Thrale's Anchor Brewery of London was preeminent among the dozen breweries that made strong porter for export to the Baltic countries. In 1796, one author wrote that Thrale's Entire ("entire" was the original name for porter) was known far and wide:

> *The reputation and enjoyment of Porter is by no means confined to England. As proof of the truth of this assertion, this house exports annually very large quantities; so far extended are its commercial connections that Thrale's Entire is well known, as a delicious beverage, from the frozen regions of Russia to the burning sands of Bengal and Sumatra. The Empress of All Russia is indeed so partial to Porter that she has*

ordered repeatedly very large quantities for her own drinking and that of her court.

Upon its owner's death, Thrale's brewery became Barclay Perkins, which grew to become London's largest brewer of dark ales. Barclay Perkins shipped its beers to Europe and beyond through a network of agents. One of these agents was a Belgian named Albert Le Coq, who had a handsome trade in imperial stout, which he shipped from England to Russia and the Baltic ports. Le Coq donated large quantities of stout to Russian soldiers who had been wounded at the Crimean front. In gratitude, the czar awarded him the imperial patent. In the early 1900s, import duties for the Baltic region increased dramatically, and the czarist government suggested that Le Coq brew his stout within the Russian Empire to avoid the hefty import taxes. His company purchased a brewery in the town of Tartu, in a province then known as Livonia, the present Estonia. In 1912, the brewery in Tartu produced its first bottles of Imperial Extra Double Stout.

Le Coq's venture did not remain in the company's hands for long. In 1917, the brewery, which had strong czarist connections and even featured a crown on its labels, was nationalized by the new Bolshevik government and shut down. It later reopened, and it produced Baltic-style strong porters well into the 1960s. In 1974,

Courtesy B. United International.

The crowning glory of both England and Russia, A. Le Coq's Imperial Extra Double Stout has recently been resurrected.

Norwegian divers came on the Prussian ship *Oliva*, which had sunk to the bottom of the Baltic Sea in 1869. The divers surfaced with several bottles from a large consignment of beer. The labels bore the signature of A. Le Coq. Research began into Le Coq's legacy, and decades later the beer he had shipped from London to Russia was reborn.

This famous beer was revived several years ago when Matthias Neidhart, owner of the American specialty beer importer B. United International, initiated a collaboration between the Tartu brewery and Harveys of Lewes, England. Records still existed of the old imperial stout recipes, and Matthias took them to Harveys' head brewer, Miles Jenner. They decided to accept the challenge of re-creating the beer under Tartu's auspices. The result is a masterpiece. **A. Le Coq Imperial Extra Double Stout** is packaged in the original low-shouldered, tall-necked bottle and carries the original logo on its label. The 1999 bottling is as black as night and scarcely raises a head as it slides into the glass. The powerful aroma is astonishing—figs, prunes, burnt fruitcake, hot tar, black cherries, dark chocolate, espresso, saddle leather, burning wood, and pine needles. The palate does not disappoint—it goes all the way, and then some. It opens up still, sweet, soft, oily, and silky. Juicy dark fruit and powerful espresso gather into a storm and flood the palate with flavor. Hop bitterness rises like a wave behind it all, blending in with the roast and drying out the center. Roasty, raisiny acidity floats over the maelstrom. The finish is long and espresso-like, and sweet malts reemerge in a final juicy display of dark fruit. The aftertaste is of the finest dark chocolate, fruity and winy.

There isn't one false note here, and you truly feel that you're tasting a piece of history. The beer is aged for at least a year before bottling, and during that time it develops some lactic acidity, just like the old vatted stouts. At the end of its maturation, it achieves a strength of 9 percent: strong, but modest for its incredible depth of flavor. A. Le Coq Imperial Extra Double Stout is a towering achievement, on the same level as a great old Barolo or vintage port. It makes a mind-boggling match with venison in sour cherry sauce and is a fine accompaniment to game sausages, particularly wild boar. Otherwise, pair it with fine deep chocolate desserts, chocolate truffles, intense fruit tarts, or Stilton cheese. As for cigars, only the finest, strongest Cubans will do, unless you have an Arturo Fuente Opus X. In that case, I'll be right over.

GEARY'S **Geary's London Porter** is brewed in Portland, Maine, by David Geary, who says that it derives from an eighteenth-century English recipe. Geary uses the old English Ringwood yeast strain, an assertive producer of spicy-fruity aromas. His London Porter is a black beer with fruit, hops, and spice nearly obscuring chocolate notes in the nose. On the palate, the beer is bone-dry and mouth-coating, with an insistent pinpoint carbonation. Bracing bitterness is featured in a beautiful structure built of high caramel, chocolate, coffee, and fruit. The finish is dry, with a refreshing snap of acidity and licorice as it signs off. This is very skillfully brewed and is quite English in character, thanks to that distinctive yeast. Serve it with oysters, roasted lobster, crab cakes, good ham, assertive chocolate desserts, and vanilla ice cream.

BROWAR OKOCIM Founded in 1845 in Brzesko, Poland, by an immigrant from Bavaria, Okocim grew to supply the entire Austro-Hungarian Empire by the turn of the century. The Okocim logo, a coat of arms featuring a billy goat drinking from a frothing glass of beer, is quite reminiscent of the designs of many bockbier labels from Germany. Poland has had a tumultuous history since 1845; the country actually disappeared for decades. This history runs through the local beers. Strong imperial porters and stouts were at first imported from England and later brewed locally. German and Austrian brewers were often hired to run Polish breweries, and eventually they turned to using lager yeasts. The result was a distinctive style of bottom-fermented strong porter that was eventually brewed from Scandinavia to the Baltics into eastern Europe, all distantly related to the beers that emerged from London in the 1700s.

Okocim Porter is a fine example of the style, and the label shows the cross-cultural currents; the word "Porter" appears above the old German billy goat bockbier symbol, and the word "Stout" appears below it. The beer is opaque, with a big tan head. It has a huge aroma of caramel, toffee, chocolate, licorice, and raisins, with a tiny hint of black truffle. The palate is smooth and sweet, with robust hopping stepping in to balance the candyish malts. Juicy chocolate and raisin flavors develop in the middle, before the beer sweeps out to a long, drying, hoppy finish. Cold fermentation restrains the fruit, yet at 8 percent it is not a doppelbock—it has far more roast flavor than any German beer. It's a great match for duck, pork, venison, robust sausages, and even chocolate desserts, so long as they're not terribly sweet.

The Scots are fortunate that barley is such a hardy plant. From September through May, temperatures in Scotland rarely struggle out of the 50s, making for a short growing season. Barley and oats can tough it out, and Scotland grows plenty of both. If the term "Scotch" brings whisky to mind, remember that whisky is simply distilled beer and that the Scots didn't take to it until the early 1800s. By that time, they had been brewing beer for thousands of years. Scottish monasteries established commercial breweries in medieval times, and many female brewers, known as "browster wives," sold beer out of their homes. Public breweries began to appear by the late 1400s, followed by commercial guilds that sought to protect the local market against intrusions from England. By the 1800s Scotland was a major exporter of beer to Europe, North America, the Caribbean, and India. The cities of Alloa, Edinburgh, and Glasgow were packed with breweries.

From the earliest days, Scottish beer was different. The hop cannot grow in cold, blustery Scotland, and early brewers used blends of spices, herbs, and roots to balance out the sweetness of the malt. Flavorings included bog myrtle, bitter gorse, ginger, dandelion root, orange peel, juniper, wild licorice, spruce, wormwood (the active ingredient in absinthe), quassia bark, and heather. Even when the Scots started to import hops, they did so grudgingly and at considerable expense. Not only were hops expensive, they were English; this did not exactly endear the hop to the Scots, who constantly sought to blunt arrogant England's expansionism. Scottish beer drinkers cared little for the taste of hops, and brewers used them, sparingly, only for their preservative qualities. Malt flavors were emphasized, as they are to this day.

Scottish beer even fermented differently from English beer. Colder ambient temperatures led to slow, cool fermentations by ale yeast strains that could stand the northern chill. Long cool fermentations tend to produce malty beers with muted fruitiness, even when ale yeasts are used. Scottish beer took weeks rather than days to ferment, and then settled in for a long cold storage before being served. In this regard it resembled Bavarian lagers more than it did English ales. Cool temperatures also tended to force the yeast to settle out early, leaving the beer with plenty of residual sweetness.

Modern Scottish brewing still echoes these early influences. Although closures and consolidations have greatly reduced the number of breweries in Scotland, the remaining Scottish beers retain a regional character. Roasted barley is heavily used, and the beers tend to be dark, though they rarely show strong roasted flavors. They are rich, smooth, deeply malty beers with biscuity flavors at the center. Scotland's indigenous Golden Promise variety of barley lends a faint vanilla-like character to the malt flavors in many Scottish beers. The fruity flavors and aromatics typical of English ales are muted up north, and a toffeeish sweetness dominates stronger styles. Light butterscotch notes are common. Hop bitterness tends to be moderate at most, and hop flavors or aromatics are rare.

Scottish ales have their own nomenclature as well, brought back from the past by revivalist brewers. Beers were once priced according to strength, and the name reflected the price, in shillings, of a barrel of the beer in question. A 60-shilling ale (written as 60/-) would be a fairly light beer, while a 90-shilling ale would be heftier. Other names are more direct. "Light" will indicate a slim body and low alcohol, "heavy" indicates a bitter of average strength, "export" starts to show some muscle, and "wee heavy" swaggers with a strength above 7 percent. Somewhat confusingly, Scottish beers of average strength are referred to as "Scottish" ales, and the term "Scotch" ale tends to be reserved for strong versions. At least one brewery has revived the old tradition of brewing with heather, and the results are wonderful. Some American craft brewers, wanting to give their beers some essential Scottishness, have started brewing their "Scottish ales" with peat-smoked whisky malt. The Scots themselves seem to be secure in their Scottishness; they leave whisky malt to distillers.

Cask-conditioned versions of traditional styles of beer are served in many Scottish pubs. The Scots have their own way of doing this, too—they don't use the English hand pump, preferring to push the beer to the tap with air compressors. If you encounter draft versions of Scottish ales in the United States, they'll usually be served normally, though they will usually have relatively low carbonation and an almost creamy texture on the palate. When served fresh and not overchilled, they are quite delicious.

Scottish Ales with Food

Haggis aside, the fact of the matter is that the Scots have been eating well for years. In the mid-1980s, when London was a vast wasteland for anyone seeking decent non-Indian food at reasonable prices, Edinburgh bustled with perfectly good French and Italian restaurants. Just as Scotland's brewing style is vaguely European, so is its sense of food. Perhaps this is a happy consequence of the Auld Alliance, Scotland's long-ago partnership with France against England. Certainly Scotland has generally regarded the continent with far less suspicion than have the English, and this has been to their culinary benefit.

Lighter Scottish ales can be gentle enough to accompany salads, particularly if the salad includes meat or nuts. The classic endive salad with Roquefort cheese and walnuts is one example. Any salad topped with beef carpaccio will also find a good partner here. The light hopping and soft, nutty sweetness of other Scottish beers make them terrific with roasted meats, especially roast beef and lamb. Scottish beef is much prized for its sweetness, and the malt in these beers just melts into the beef flavors and textures. The beer's affinity for lamb is at least as profound, especially when the lamb is prepared simply, allowing its naturally herbal, gamy flavors to show through. Lamb chops, liberally covered with olive oil,

The thistle, a symbol of Scotland, is recalled in this Scottish ale glass. These days, some Scottish brewers are once again brewing with local plants, particularly heather.

rosemary, cracked black pepper, and a dash of sea salt, then roasted in a hot oven, are the essence of simplicity. Scottish ales sing in the company of dishes like this, the beer's light fruitiness and sweet malt finding deep resonance in the food. Stronger Scottish ales can rekindle the Auld Alliance in their partnership with one of my favorite dishes, cassoulet.

Game birds also pair up nicely with Scottish ales. Pheasant, partridge, and quail are especially good matches, and Scottish wild game is available in the United States from D'Artagnan. If you get your hands on some, you're in for a great treat. You can taste the land in the meat of these birds—a diet of heather, nuts, and berries suffuses them with flavors you won't find in farmed birds. The Scottish barley grows on the same land, and you can taste it. When everything meets up on the table, the results can be magical. The next day, take the leftover meat from the pheasant, make a pheasant salad sandwich, and pour yourself a Scottish ale to go with it. Simple, yes, but so tasty you'll be virtually giddy. Your only question will be whether the pheasant in the sandwich might be even better than it was the night before. That's why you'll have to try it again and see.

With less esoteric food, Scottish ales are easygoing and versatile. Their lack of hops denies them the cutting power to deal with some spicier dishes, but their juicy malt character more than makes up for any deficiencies. Almost any sausages will happily pair up with them, and they are great with ham. Meatloaf virtually demands a beer like this, and the match is soft and comfortable. Pork and chicken are easygoing themselves, so it's hard to go wrong—roasting them will develop some sweetness that will accentuate the partnership. The silky-smooth, restrained malt sweetness of Scottish ales makes them fine partners for gratins and cream sauces such as Alfredo and carbonara. Cream and butter also have a smooth, restrained sweetness that finds an echo in the beer, which melds seamlessly with the sauce. The softness of the beer also makes it a good match for roasted, grilled, or steamed vegetables, which won't have to shout to be heard.

Stronger, sweeter Scottish ales can be very nice with venison, and they will work with classic concentrated reduction sauces. Seared foie gras is also a nice pairing—the harmony of the flavors can be so close it's almost eerie. Fruity, mild cheeses go very nicely with these beers, especially after dinner. Finally, we shouldn't forget dessert, where the sweet maltiness of classic strong Scotch ales is excellent with crème brûlée, and, of course, Scottish butter shortbread cookies.

Notable Producers of Scottish Ales

TRAQUAIR HOUSE Traquair House, parts of which were built in 1107, is the oldest inhabited house in Scotland and the seat of the Stuart family. Mary Stuart, better known as Mary, Queen of Scots, spent time here, as have twenty-six other kings and queens of Scotland and England. After Prince Charles Edward Stuart rode out through the house's imposing iron Bear Gates in 1745, the fifth earl of Traquair closed them, vowing that they would not be opened again until a Stuart regained the throne of Scotland. Bonnie Prince Charlie was defeated outside London, and the Bear Gates have remained closed ever since. Peter Maxwell Stuart, the twentieth laird of Traquair, inherited the house in 1965 and discovered that it had an abandoned brewery in the cellar. The brewery had been installed in the 1500s and had been refitted with a new kettle in the mid-1700s. The laird put the brewery right back to work, brewing an eighteenth-century recipe for strong ale. The beers are still fermented in unlined oak vessels, just as they would have been 200 years ago. Peter Maxwell Stuart died in 1990; his daughter, Lady Catherine Maxwell Stuart, is now in charge of the brewery.

Traquair House Ale has a vibrant brown color, very light carbonation, and an aroma full of malt and fruit, with an oddly appetizing whiff of bacon. The bitterness is moderate and well integrated into a dry, malty palate, showing flavors of biscuits, chocolate, and rum. The finish is short and dry. At 7.2 percent, this beer is very

The Windsors still hold the British throne, and the Stuarts brew while biding their time at Traquair House.

graceful for its weight. It's a fine partner to full-flavored beef, venison, wild pheasant, partridge, and wood pigeon. It would also be very good with sweetbreads.

Traquair Jacobite Ale is much darker, deep brown with red highlights. The label shows Scottish thistles, but this beer is spiced instead with coriander, which is nicely integrated into a malty nose with a fruity backdrop. Malty, sweet, juicy, round, chewy, roasty, and powerful, the palate bursts into full flower right up front, then dives into a long drying finish. The coriander lingers in the afterglow. A gorgeous beer that will provide a perfect match for venison. It wants full-flavored gamy meats—duck, goose, wild boar, or wood pigeon will do nicely. After dinner, pair it with Stilton or a nutty full-flavored aged Gruyère.

MCEWANS The international brewing giant Scottish & Newcastle had its beginnings in the William Younger and William McEwan breweries, which both enjoyed great success in the late 1800s. They swallowed up many of their competitors before merging in 1931 to form Scottish Brewers. They've continued to annex many breweries since then and may yet be swallowed up themselves. Brewing continues at McEwans old Fountain Brewery in Edinburgh, though it is now a very modern operation.

McEwans Scotch Ale is a dark brown beer with a typically Scottish aroma of butterscotch, muted fruit, and a faint hint of peatiness. The palate is very sweet and shows a bit of caramel, with just enough bitterness to keep it from being cloying. I'd prefer more malt development in the center. That said, this beer would be very nice with a classic caramelized onion, bacon, and goat cheese tart. It's also a fine dessert beer—serve it with flan, dulce de leche, crème brûlée, panna cotta, or vanilla ice cream. The original McEwan brewery had a very successful overseas and colonial trade, shipping its strong ales as far as Calcutta. McEwan's Scotch Ale is a sort of holdover from those days—the beer is brewed only for export and is known elsewhere as Younger's Double Century. It's brewed under license in Belgium, which has shown a fondness for Scottish beers dating back to the 1800s.

BELHAVEN BREWERY In the 1300s there was a monastery at Dunbar, a coastal town in the Scottish border country south of Edinburgh. The monks once brewed, but by 1719 brewing had passed to a commercial concern on the same site. In the 1980s Belhaven was briefly owned by an international banking conglomerate, but a management buyout secured the brewery's independence in 1993. Belhaven is now the oldest independent brewery in Scotland. Its beers remain distinctively Scottish in character.

Belhaven Scottish Ale has the color of maple syrup and an evocative nose of rich malts, sulfur, leather, vanilla, and earthy haylike hops. There is a certain aroma that arises from the very walls of an old British brewery, a smell of centuries. I've often envied that; my brewery smells terrific, but it has yet to earn that depth of aroma. Belhaven manages to put this aroma into its beer. Light-bodied malts vault unencumbered across the palate—the beer is not nearly as heavy as the nose might suggest. The hops are light, broad, and brisk, allowing malt to show through in a dry setting. The finish is short and clean. When fresh, this beer has a famously distinct malt character that provides an excellent match for the classic ploughman's lunch of roast beef, ham, Stilton or cheddar cheese, Branson pickle, and brown bread. Its leathery, earthy aroma also lends this beer to dishes prepared with mushrooms.

Belhaven Wee Heavy has a very similar nose, but it's far richer and more concentrated, adding layers of honey and treacle. The color is mahogany, and the head is thick and rocky. Delicious sweet malts take center stage on a juicy, round palate that relegates hops to a supporting role. Chocolate and burnt sugar develop in the middle, and the finish is short and drying. This is a classic Scottish ale, showing wonderful malt character and traditionally restrained hops and fruit. It's terrific with short ribs, duck, venison, leg of lamb, and stuffed pork loin, and it even has enough sweetness to work beautifully with a good panna cotta.

ORKNEY BREWERY The Orkney Islands, off the north tip of the Scottish mainland, are a world unto themselves. My friend Larry once visited North Ronaldsay, a tiny speck of an island at the northern end of the group. He returned with tales of fields of an ancient grain variety the locals called "bere" and of sheep that were fenced out onto the island's beaches, to circle the island eating seaweed instead of grass. When one of the residents told Larry that he visited the mainland about once a year, it took a while for Larry to realize that the man was referring to mainland Orkney, not mainland Scotland. Even mainland Orkney is remote, and the village of Quoyloo is more remote still, about an hour removed from the island's capital, Kirkwall. A former publican, Roger White—an Englishman—had the temerity to establish a brewery here in 1988, using a one-room nineteenth-century schoolhouse to house his equipment. By 1995, he had done well enough to build a new set of buildings and modernize the brewery. The beers, some of which have won national awards, retain a distinctly Scottish character.

Orkney Dark Island is a very dark reddish-brown beer with a remarkably rich nose of malt, molasses, chocolate, leather, and hay. After the huge nose, the beer itself is surprisingly light. The carbonation is subdued, and the bitterness is almost undetectable; but the beer remains dry, with caramel and chocolate playing through the center. The finish is short and dry, with a quick burst of raisiny acidity. Despite its dry flavor, this beer is typically Scottish; I've never had an English beer that used so little hop. Orkney is sheep country, and this beer would make a fine accompaniment to spring lamb or rare roast beef.

Orkney Skullsplitter is supposedly named after a historical figure, though at 8.5 percent it might lead one to take the name as a threat. This is a very good example of the strong Scotch ale style. It has a dark amber color and a hugely deep malt nose with leathery notes. The palate is soft and silky, with no hop bite at all; the hops merely prevent the malt from cloying. Even so, the beer is round and only semisweet, moving its full malt flavor in a linear fashion straight out to a long finish, where hops reappear to provide a drying close. Despite its strength, chilly Scottish fermentations have left this beer with very little fruit character. The palate really has only one note, but fortunately it's a great note. Try Skullsplitter with full-flavored pork dishes, game birds, and pungent buttery cheeses.

HEATHER ALES Heather—*fraoch* in Scots Gaelic—grows abundantly in Scotland and was once a favorite beer flavoring. In 1992 Bruce Williams, an owner of home-brew supply shops, decided to revive the ancient heather ale style. He set up shop in a closed brewery in Argyll and began producing a beer flavored by heather flower tips added during the boil of the wort and in a strainer on the way to the fermenter. He soon moved his production to the family-owned Maclay brewery in Alloa. Williams set up a new brewery at Strathaven in 1997 but still contracts some production to Maclay's.

Froach Heather Ale has a hazy orange color and a fluffy white head. The nose is sweet and richly floral, with notes of mint, hay, ginger, honey, jasmine, bubble gum, orange flowers, and bergamot. On the palate, the beer is quite light, with a ghostly tongue-coating bitterness that quickly fades. A dry, floral center gives way to a long finish. This is obviously not a typical Scottish ale—at least not anymore. It's a completely fascinating beer, and the heather is a powerful presence. Fraoch has become quite popular in Scotland, which is blessed with plenty of wild game. Fraoch is excellent with wild quail, partridge, or pheasant. In Provence and Liguria, rabbit is sometimes prepared with lavender, and this beer would make a perfect accompaniment.

Barley Wines

. . . It must be observed that there is an essential difference between drinks brewed tolerably well, and such as are at the same time intended to be of the vinous kind, calculated for health and pleasure, and to bring malt drinks once more into vogue, by exalting the taste, flavor, and power of dilution equal to wine, without any of the ordinary bad effects usually resulting from malts or wines. Laying aside vulgar opinion, that foreign wines are used by the rich, rather from vanity than taste, it must be observed that experience will always be superior to custom. Our business then is to prepare our malt drinks, as nearly as possible to answer the like purpose as foreign wines. . . .

"The Method of Manufacturing Pure Malt Wines," from *Every Man His Own Brewer*, London, 1768.

Malt wine? Well, not quite. From the Norman conquest onward, England's brewers have regarded France's vintners with a somewhat envious eye. Shakespeare said that "a quart of ale is a meal fit for a king," but England's kings were now French-speaking foreigners—and wine drinkers. Wine was the drink of the Norman aristocracy, while ale remained the drink of the Saxon masses. England is too chilly and cloudy to grow wine grapes, so the Norman aristocrats imported their wine from Europe. In the early 1700s the emergence in England of a wealthy merchant class, the development of pale malts, and a more scientific approach to the brewing process gave rise to ales that rivaled the finest wines in their finesse, complexity, and strength. These beers were not for the masses but for the aristocracy, who had grown tired of having their wine supplies cut off by pesky wars with France. These strong beers were variously referred to as October beers, Dorchester beers, malt liquors, or malt wines; and by the early 1800s the term "barley wine" had been coined. The brewers' envy faded, eventually replaced by pride and satisfaction. People began to write prose and poetry about these beers and increasingly vowed to "leave water and wine to France." Now, mind you, most of this prose and poetry was quite bad, but once you've tried a great barley wine, you may be given to song yourself.

A barley wine is a very strong top-fermented ale, with an alcohol content ranging from around 8.5 percent up to 14 percent. At this strength, the beer shows genuine power on the palate and a warming quality usually associated with wine, sherry, or port. Barley wines are traditionally brewed from pale malts, sometimes with an addition of sugar in the kettle. A large, thick mash will yield a wort of uncommon strength, and the wort will often be sent to the kettle undiluted by any rinsing of the grain. The concentration of sugars, combined with a long boil in the kettle, often darkens the beer to a deep amber color. The ale yeast that normally spends its days fermenting ordinary bitters will often become deliriously active when pitched into a very strong wort. As the fermentation proceeds, the alcohol content rises, and eventually the yeast is stunned by its own handiwork. The brewer must coax and cajole the woozy yeast into finishing its job, lest the beer be left too sweet. The fermentation can take weeks, but eventually the brewer will allow the yeast to settle into a long sleep.

It's hard work, but the skillful brewer is rewarded with a beer showing great depth of flavor, unparalleled richness, and a fruity, heady aroma. The beer will be aged for months, if not years, before it is released. A great barley wine has all the depth, complexity, smoothness, body, and power of the finest tawny port. The aromatics are a rich swirl of deeply toffeeish concentrated malt, warm spices, dark fruits, and sherry. Carbonation is usually quite low, and the palate is semisweet, round, and juicy. As the beer ages, it will become less bitter, as all its flavors marry and evolve into something sleek, elegant, and almost austere. These are beers for contemplative sipping. To many brewers, barley wine represents the pinnacle of their art.

From the beginning, barley wines were much coveted; those who brewed and served them were highly admired. By and large, these beers were first brewed by butlers to wealthy families, who were unfettered by commercial pressures and could undertake the expensive aging crucial to the flavor and aroma of a fine barley wine. A butler's ability to brew such beer was no small matter. In *A Practical Treatise on the Nature of Brewing* (1806), butlers are told, "As most Noblemen and Gentlemen take great pride to outvie each other in having superior articles about their tables than their neighbors, you cannot be too curious in malt liquors under your management." In other words, if you want to keep ahead of the Joneses, you'd better serve excellent barley wine at your estate. It's nice to know that serving lack-luster beer has apparently been a social faux pas for more than 200 years.

A modern variation of barley wine, making its appearance over the past half-century, is exemplified by Whitbread's Gold Label and Fuller's Golden Pride, honey-colored beers with strengths of more than 10 percent, but no yeast in the bottle. They are generally matured for less than ten weeks at the brewery, and they have a smooth, fruity palate balanced by moderate hopping and warmed by alcohol. They are pleasant but not profound, and when advertising them, brewers have sometimes shown an unfortunate tendency to boast about their strength rather than wax poetic. The new generation of American barley wines, which we'll explore in another section, would be virtually unrecognizable to English brewers. The American version is a peacock display of malty power and bright hop flavor. Subtlety and balance, the hallmarks of British brewing, are often tossed out the window when Americans brew barley wine. That's fine—these beers offer different pleasures for different moods.

You would think that the same government which allows the term "champagne" to appear on wines from upstate New York would have no trouble with the historic term "barley wine." But no. American regulations prevent barley wines from being called by their proper name; instead, you'll see the ungainly term "barleywine-style ale" on the label. Apparently, the government bureau determining these things thinks that consumers might otherwise become confused. This ruling comes, of course, from the same people who allow the appellation "Hearty Burgundy" for crude California jug wines. Go figure.

Old Ale

By the 1840s, brewing had become a big business, owing to the popularity of porter and then pale ale. Aging was no longer taken for granted; many beers were now produced from kettle to tankard in under a month. It was only then that the term "old ale" started to appear, describing precisely the same sort of beer as had been described as "malt wine" a century earlier.

For some time, "old ale" and "barley wine" were synonyms, but they have diverged over the past century. Whether as a result of innocently fanciful whims or the machinations of marketers, "old ale" is today a virtual catchall term. The only common elements among old ales are a somewhat dark color, a tendency toward fruitiness, and some residual malt sweetness. After that, all bets appear to be off; many beers marketed as old ales are simply hefty milds or slightly stronger brown ales at 4 to 5 percent. Another corner is occupied by the classics such as Theakston's Old Peculier—these are dark, fruity, full-bodied porterish ales ranging from 5 to 7 percent. None of them is particularly well aged, but perhaps they derive their titles from a wistful idea of old-fashioned heartiness. Some beers sold as old ales do hold to the original meaning, notably the wonderful Gale's Prize Old Ale.

British Barley Wines and Old Ales with Food

Until a few years ago, I'd looked on barley wine principally as a digestif, a beer best suited to my favorite old French club chair, which is parked strategically in front of my fireplace. No food need apply, I thought—this was a beer for sipping on its own. As wonderful as good barley wine is by itself, it turns out that barley wines have some brilliant food affinities. Barley wine is powerful and unctuous rather than refreshing, so we look for dishes that will play to its considerable strengths.

Sweeter varieties are an excellent choice for foie gras, whether seared or served in a terrine. The malt sweetness of the beer provides a fine counterpoint to the subtle gaminess of the foie gras, while the hops provide cutting power and light carbonation lifts fat and resets the palate for the next bite. If you'd like to eat the rest of the duck too, look for lighter barley wines such as Fuller's Vintage Ale or classic old ales like Gale's Old Ale or Harveys Elizabethan Ale. These also have some fine acidity to help cut through the fattiness of duck skin.

Classic barley wines, especially with a bit of age, work very nicely with lamb, venison, and wild boar. The concentrated malt flavors and fruity aromatics can easily handle any likely sauces, and these meats are sturdy enough that we needn't fear overwhelming them. The gamy flavors of the meat meld seamlessly into the silky pillow of malt. Beef flavors are more delicate than we often assume, but mushrooms, always a great friend of malt, will bring beef into the fold as well.

Great cheese is the crowning glory of barley wine, and vice versa. Powerfully flavored cheeses are the bane of any honest wine sommelier, but the brewer finds a true friend here. The list of cheeses that are wonderful with barley wine could fill an entire book, but there are some matches you should absolutely not miss. Classic cheddars such as Montgomery from England and Grafton Village from Vermont are great with almost any type of barley wine. These cheeses have enough acidity and fruitiness to stand up to young barley wines, which may display more exuberant power than subtlety. In a similar vein, but showing more milk flavors and nutty depth, aged Gruyères are excellent as well. My favorite is Emmi, a cave-aged Gruyère from Switzerland—try it with Young's Old Nick or Theakston's Old Peculier. Sweeter versions are excellent with aged goat cheeses such as Chavignol, Coach Farm, or Cypress Grove Humboldt Fog.

When great Stilton meets a well-aged British barley wine, we reach the pinnacle of flavor combinations. Everything here dovetails—the barnyard Stilton character finds the earthiness of the malt, and the two disappear into each other, becoming one perfect married flavor. The fruit and sherry flavors sail over the top, brightening everything. Even port can't do this. Go for the best: Colston-Basset Stilton with J. W. Lees Harvest Ale, the older the better. Bliss out.

If you still have any room, barley wines are excellent with caramelized desserts such as crème brûlée and crêpes with dulce de leche. Stronger, sweeter barley wines are also very nice with tarte Tatin, especially with good vanilla ice cream.

Notable Producers of Barley Wine and Old Ale

GREENE KING The 200-year-old Greene King Brewery is a regional powerhouse in East Anglia, owning more than 1,000 pubs and dominating the town of Bury St. Edmunds. Given the brewery's size and ambition, it is laudable that the beautiful old brewhouse equipment, and some very interesting specialty beers, have been retained. The most interesting of these beers, Strong Suffolk, is sold in the United States as **Olde Suffolk**. This beer is a blend of two very different ales, neither of which is ever sold straight. The first is a very strong old ale known at the brewery by the mysterious-sounding name 5X. It is aged for one to five years in sixty-barrel uncoated wooden vats. The vats reside in a barely accessible attic space in the brewery, and their lids are coated with a bed of local soil known as Suffolk marl. The surface of the liquid in the vats eventually comes into contact with air, and the marl is said to filter out unwanted microscopic visitors. 5X is brewed to a strength of 14 percent or more and has a powerfully winy, oaky flavor reminiscent of oloroso sherry. The second beer, a malty amber ale of standard strength, is known simply as BPA. The two are blended to create the 6 percent Olde Suffolk, which the brewery considers to average at least two years old at bottling. The practice of blending a very old "vatted" beer with a younger beer meant to freshen and enliven it is centuries old, but these days it's rarely seen outside Belgium, where such blends produce lambic gueuze.

OPPOSITE: Perched up in the rafters of an attic at Greene King, this oak vat is used to age the mysteriously named "5X" for two years or more. Local soil called Suffolk marl rests protectively on top.

Olde Suffolk has a beautiful dark mahogany color and a malty aroma with a dash of sherry and more than a suggestion of an oaky Rioja. A unique combination

VATS

of hop bitterness, winy acidity, and oak tannins greets the tongue before the soft, dry malts emerge in the middle. The center is juicy, making a suggestion of bitter marmalade before sliding out to a long, dry, ironlike finish. This beer is excellent with rare roast beef and cold lamb and would also be very good with a steak grilled over wood charcoal.

THEAKSTON'S In the Middle Ages, the small Yorkshire town of Masham (pronounced "Mass-um") was a center of the local wool trade, a status that made it wealthy and powerful. The wool trade has moved on, but the town retains an anachronism from those medieval days, an ecclesiastical court called a peculier, meaning "special" or "extraordinary." The court still occasionally sits to dispose local church matters. The Theakston family bought an inn and a brewery in 1827 and has named its most famous beer after the peculier of Masham. The Theakstons expanded in the 1870s, building their own maltings and brewery. In the 1980s, flush with success, they overextended themselves and were acquired by the international giant Scottish & Newcastle. Their beers, now brewed in both Masham and Newcastle, have retained considerable character.

Theakston's Old Peculier has a dark reddish-brown color and a thick tan cap of foam. The aroma is chocolaty and appetizingly malty—it reminds me of a chocolate cake in the oven. Earthy hops show through the malt. As the beer strikes the tongue, there's an initial impression of saltiness, followed by malt sweetness offset by moderate hopping. The center is racy and dry, showing caramel and a touch of chocolate on a zippy palate that dashes out to a quick, mineraly, dry finish. I remember Old Peculier well—it was one of the first dark beers that I drank regularly, and it was the inspiration for the name of New York City's first serious beer bar, the Peculier Pub. This beer was not always in such a hurry; it's lost some depth in the center over the years. But it's still very pleasant. It will make a perfect match for a good classic shepherd's pie. Try it also with meatloaf, sausages, steaks, and roast beef.

SARAH HUGHES BREWERY Brew pubs were once very common in England, and even small hotels often had their own breweries. The Beacon Hotel in Sedgley, near Dudley, was built in 1850, and the hotel's small brewery was built in a yard behind it. In 1921, Sarah Hughes bought the hotel and brewery, and she ran it until her death in 1951. In 1957, the Hughes family stopped brewing at the Beacon Hotel, and the hotel's century-old brewing tradition seemed to have ended. Thirty years later, in 1987, Sarah's grandson, John Hughes, found her recipe for a strong mild ale in a cigar box and decided to revive the brewery.

Sarah Hughes Dark Ruby Mild has a very deep red color and a voluminous tan head. The aroma is fascinating, a complex mélange of chocolate, hops, sherry, port, plums, and raisins. The palate is rich, round, and sweet, with the malt balanced by light bitterness and a drying lactic acidity. Caramel and raisins burst from the juicy center. The finish is long and drying, with a distinctively acidic twang. This beer is a real throwback, recalling the days when "stale" was a term of endearment for beer that had developed some appetizing acidity with age. Notable acidity is now rare in English beers, but it remains appetizing. Ruby Mild is called "mild," but these days its acidity and its 6 percent strength put it comfortably in the category of old ale. Ruby Mild is brilliant with sautéed foie gras, magret of duck, roast goose, braised short ribs or beef cheeks, and venison.

YOUNG'S Young's, a brewer in London, shows a deft hand along the entire range of British styles, from "ordinary" bitters to strong ales and stouts. **Young's Old Nick** is a particular favorite of mine. The Old Nick in question isn't the jolly Christmas elf—it's the other guy, the one you'll end up with if you've been bad. Old Nick has a deep garnet-brown color and a wonderfully malty-fruity aroma, like a fruitcake in the oven. The palate is round, juicy, and sweet, with hops stepping in firmly to pull the flavors into an excellent balance. The center is packed with nutty, caramelized malt flavors, and the finish is long and drying, winding up with a mineraly snap. This beer is a minor masterpiece—firm, beautifully structured, and supremely confident. It seems to know that it's a perfect version of itself. The brewery calls Young's Old Nick a barley wine, and I'm not going to argue, though at 8 percent it can be classified as an old ale. It's a great accompaniment to roast suckling pig, porchetta, wild boar, or venison sausages. At dessert, it's very nice with crème brûlée and other custards. When the cheese cart arrives, try it with buttery blues like Stilton or Berkshire Blue.

FULLER'S As the twentieth century drew to a close, Fuller's head brewer, Reg Drury, contemplated retirement. He'd worked for the venerable London brewer for decades, and he wanted to wind up his active career with a flourish. Fuller's produces a modern-style golden barley wine called Golden Pride, which is available only in small bottles. This beer is smooth and strong but has little else to recommend it. Drury wanted to brew a true barley wine that would improve nicely with a bit of age. What he conjured up was **Fuller's Vintage Ale**, which is handsomely packaged in individually boxed, numbered bottles. It is brewed from the most recent crop of award-winning barley and hops and then bottle-conditioned before leaving the brewery. Fuller's Vintage Ale has a gorgeous deep amber color and a deep, evocative aroma of haylike hops, earth, and marmalade. As I tried to figure out what memory the aroma had evoked, I realized that this beer smells just like the Fuller's brewery, with its centuries of aroma permeating the walls. The beer is sweet at first; it takes a few seconds for the sharp bitterness to rise up behind the malt. The center is round and juicy, full of caramel and oranges, reminiscent of a great tawny port. The finish is miles long, drying, hoppy, and warming. It's wonderful. The label on the 1998 "vintage" says that the beer is best before the end of 2001, but that date is long past and the beer clearly has at least three great years left in it. Younger bottles will show more sweetness and less integrated flavors, with the hops further forward on the palate. Reg has retired, and the present head brewer, John Keeling, will surely add his own flourishes to this excellent ale. Serve this with powerfully nutty cheeses like cave-aged Gruyère or aged Gouda, or you can go for buttery blue cheeses like Stilton or Berkshire.

J. W. LEES & COMPANY In 1828, John Lees retired from the textile business he ran in the Manchester suburb of Oldham. He was only fifty years old, and he soon became bored. So he bought a row of old cottages and converted them into a brewery. John's grandson, John Willie Lees, was a railway stationmaster when he inherited the brewery. He was a flamboyant and industrious man, and his business thrived. He built the current brewhouse in 1876 and eventually became mayor of Oldham. His brewery is still in the family, run by Richard Lees-Jones and his sharp, business-minded son William, who represents the sixth generation in the brewing trade. John Lees's cottages, enveloped by later buildings, are still visible on the site of J. W. Lees's rambling Victorian brewery. The brewery, which is very traditional, still delivers beer in wooden casks to local pubs. Large, deep, beaten-copper open fermenters sit right outside the office of the head brewer, Giles Dennis.

In 2002, I visited Giles to brew my Brooklyn Best Bitter, a very hoppy premium bitter made with only American hops. As the open fermenter filled with the Brooklyn-inspired wort, the fermentation hall filled with the alien aroma of grapefruity, piney Cascade hops. Giles seemed intrigued, if worried, by the aroma. I later heard that the brewery made the beer on three more occasions. The locals, more used to Lees's soft, full-flavored malty bitters, apparently enjoyed their introduction to brash American flavor. A couple of months later, Giles Dennis came to Brooklyn to brew a version of a recipe from the J. W. Lees archives, a strong porter called "Star," last brewed in 1884. Several weeks later, New Yorkers got a taste of old Manchester—I like to think that John Willie Lees would have recognized the beer.

J. W. Lees brews a wide range of excellent ales, but none so striking as its

barley wine, **J. W. Lees Harvest Ale**. At 11.5 percent, it is brewed to age for many years, and it does so beautifully. J. W. Lees Harvest Ale 1988 has a rich amber-red color and a heady, spirituous aroma of pound cake, orange and lemon rinds, baking bread, dried fruit, maple syrup, and concentrated malt. Nothing else tastes quite like this—medium-bodied, sweet, incomparably juicy, with fruity acidity combining with hop bitterness to balance. The center explodes in a riot of fruit and malt flavor. The hoppy, fruity, off-dry finish is endless. Ghosts of tropical fruit roam through the aftertaste. My favorite port houses are Ferreira and Niepoort—their twenty-year-old tawny ports approach, but never quite reach, this level of elegance, complexity, and power. Harvest Ale is a tour de force, a world classic. The beer is filtered, but like many filtered wines it manages to age wonderfully, with younger bottles showing syrupy sweetness and a more awkward balance. As it gets older, the elements marry, sweetness recedes, acidity and fruit step forward,

Whether young or well aged, J. W. Lees Harvest Ale is brilliant with Stilton cheese. 1988 was a very good year.

bitterness softens. Drink young bottles with crème brûlée, panna cotta, custards, dessert soufflés, and blue cheeses, especially Stilton. When young, this beer is also brilliant with cigars. Drink older bottles by themselves; they're too special to share the stage. Decant the beer carefully because old bottles will throw a harmless but unattractive sediment. If you get some in your glass, close your eyes and drink it anyway.

THOMAS HARDY BREWING In 1837 Sarah Eldridge founded the Green Dragon Brewery. That colorful name was later changed to Eldridge Pope, when the Pope family became involved in 1870. Sarah Eldridge was a contemporary of the writer Thomas Hardy, and when the Thomas Hardy Society asked the Eldridge Pope Brewery to make a special beer to commemorate the fortieth anniversary of his death, the brewery looked to one of his stories for inspiration. In his tale "The Trumpet Major," Hardy describes the local Dorchester Ale: "It was of the most beautiful color that the eye of an artist in beer could desire; full in body, yet brisk as a volcano; piquant, yet without a twang; luminous as an autumn sunset; free from streakiness of taste; but, finally rather heady." **Thomas Hardy's Ale** was first released in 1968 and quickly became a cult classic. In 1996, the Eldridge Pope Brewery sold off its brewing operations, which became known as Thomas Hardy's Brewery. Then, in 1999, it was announced that production of Thomas Hardy's Ale was too small and too expensive to continue. Beer connoisseurs the world over went into mourning. It is still fervently hoped that some brewery will one day bring this beer back to life.

There are still bottles out there, which is why I'm writing about it. Every "vintage" of this beer has its own personality. Let's have a taste of the 1992 bottling. Thomas Hardy's Ale 1992 has a deep red color and little carbonation—it looks like an old Burgundy. The aroma is so beautiful that it makes me want to cry. It contains universes. How to describe it? Oranges, raisins, plums, wildflowers, basil, old leather, freshly chopped wood, fallen leaves, black truffles. In my experience, only great vintages of Barolo can come close. The beer enters softly, sweet and round, but it's a ruse. Massive, gripping bitterness rises up behind the sweet, fruity malt and makes a bid for dominance. The malt, a sweet, juicy, swirling storm of flavors, shoves the bitterness back, plays through the center, and then jets out to a long, languorous finish, where the hops reassert themselves in a bittersweet aftertaste. The label claims that Thomas Hardy's will improve for at least twenty-five years, and that's not hard to believe. It's bottle-conditioned, and after a few years the fermentation of residual sugars will bring the strength up to about 12 percent. This is the classic English barley wine, brewed, fermented, and aged exactly as described in brewing books of the mid-1800s. If you find a bottle, there's no telling how it's been treated, so you're taking a chance. Bad storage conditions will damage fine beers as surely as it will fine wine. Old bottles of Thomas Hardy's have commanded princely sums—at a charity event, I once auctioned off a bottle that fetched more than $200. You may yet find old bottles for only a few dollars. Snap them up—the risk that the beer has been mistreated is small compared with the pleasure of finding a bottle in great shape. There are no young bottles of Thomas Hardy's right now, so anything you find will be several years old and ready to drink. If you have patience, it will improve with age. I do believe that some great brewery will restore Thomas Hardy's Ale to the world. In the meantime, drink the bottles you have with Stilton cheese, reverence, and hope.

GEORGE GALE & COMPANY In the hamlet of Horndean, just inland from Portsmouth, England, the Gales have been brewing for more than 250 years. George Gale built a brewery here in 1847 and reconstructed it after it burned in 1869. The grand Victorian edifice is the most striking building in an otherwise charming but modest village. Behind the brick walls is a blend of modern brewing equipment and ancient museum pieces. Some open fermenters, dating back many decades, are lined with uncoated pine, and there's a copper kettle, fabricated in 1926. The older, smaller equipment is kept in use for the production of **Gale's Prize Old Ale**, a throwback that George Gale himself surely would recognize. Gale's Prize Old Ale 1998 is almost still, and it pours dark brown with a thin collar of foam. The aroma is dark and complex—Madeira, sherry, malt, rum, kola nut, plum pudding, leather, wool, and wildflowers. The palate is round, soft, and dry at first, full of fruity, juicy acidity. Austere, hard hops step in to balance out the malt, keeping it dry and racy through the center. The finish is short and sherry-like, with a slightly acidic, woody aftertaste. This is a genuine classic, brewed just as it would have been 200 years ago. It is quite strong at 9 percent, and it will age nicely for several years. Connoisseurs prize this beer for its juicy acidity and stunning complexity. It's beautiful with short ribs, beef cheeks, hanger steak, venison, Manchego cheese, and good ripe farmhouse cheddar.

7

THE BELGIAN ALE TRADITION

Everyone else seemed to have a bicycle, so I rented one and went cruising through the dappled sunlight in the gorgeous medieval town of Bruges.

It was the spring of 1984, and I had just left London, which had been my home for a year. I'd fallen in love with English ales in London and thought that I now knew everything about beer. I pulled up to a café, locked up the bike, and walked in. There must have been a dozen taps, and I didn't recognize the beers pouring from any of them. There were dozens more beers in bottles on the back bar. The barkeep then poured a drink with a startlingly pinkish hue and handed it to the fellow next to me. "What is that?" I asked, assuming that it was some sort of soft drink. "It is kriek," he answered, "a beer made with cherries." I stood there like an idiot, dumbfounded and staring. He smiled, poured me a small glass, and handed it to me. "Welcome to Belgium," he said.

Nestled between France, the Netherlands, Germany, and the North Sea, tiny Belgium is home to 12 million people, three languages, and some of the finest, most complex beer in the world. Belgium was once ruled from Burgundy but while Belgians retain an appreciation of fine wine, they save their passion for beer. Visit a Belgian café and this passion is evident, even palpable. Beers in dozens of styles, each with its own special glass, will be lovingly displayed even in the most modest establishments. Look past the ever-present industrial pilsners, and you'll see the ones we're looking for. Some will be swaddled lovingly in tissue paper. Some will stand tall in champagne bottles with the full regalia of a cork and wire hood. Many boast a secondary fermentation in the bottle and sit on a fine sediment of slumbering yeast. Some have been married with fruit and stand on the border between wine and beer. Some have been fermented spontaneously, using techniques thousands of years old. Others are redolent of herbs and spices. Some have been reverently brewed by monks. For the beer lover, Belgium is truly heaven on earth.

The kindness of my first Belgian barkeep notwithstanding, the Belgians are an ornery people. The Burgundians, Dutch, Germans, Austrians, and Spanish all

Among the buildings on the magnificent Grande Place in Brussels is the Brewer's Guild building, dating from 1696. Beer has always enjoyed an exalted position in Belgium.

rolled armies through this country for centuries, but that has only made the Belgians tougher, prouder, and more prickly. This personality follows through into their beers, which are some of the most individualistic in the world. Many of the beers defy neat categorization and stand alone, perfectly happy with self-definition. The number of varieties is staggering. The population of Belgium is scarcely larger than that of the New York metropolitan area, yet the country has more than 100 breweries producing at least 400 beers.

The Belgians have retained more of their ancient brewing culture than any other country, and their brewers seem to be the most immune to the supposed charms of modernity. Since the advent of the European Community, Belgian beers have gained popularity throughout Europe, and they can now be found everywhere from Copenhagen to Hong Kong. Recent years have seen Belgian beer becoming popular among aficionados in the United States, and in some cities Belgian restaurants have sprouted, invariably featuring beer at center stage. Belgian cuisine marries refined French technique with Dutch sturdiness, and the complexity of many Belgian ales makes them amazingly rewarding with food.

BELGIAN PALE ALE

As pilsner swept through Europe in the late 1800s and early 1900s, it sometimes seemed to be following a scorched earth policy, wiping out native beer styles as it spread. Belgians responded with their own top-fermenting beers. These were not as pale as pilsner, but they were bright and refreshing and offered their own rewards. It is a bit of a leap to refer to these beers as pale ales, or indeed to try to name them at all. The Belgians certainly don't make any such effort. Sometimes they are referred to as *spéciales belges*, sometimes simply *Spécial*, sometimes *belges*, and sometimes, in English, simply "ale." Though the term "pale ale" is not actually used, the beers bear more than a passing resemblance to the English beers of that name. Somehow, though, they manage to be distinctly Belgian. I suspect that all the major producers of Belgian pale ale are using yeast strains that are not-so-distantly related, and this results in many of the characteristics they have in common.

Belgian pale ales are pale bronze to copper-colored and are usually filtered. They tend to be brewed entirely from barley malt, avoiding the sugar that has found its way into many English ales. They are fairly standard in their strength—about 5 percent. Hopping tends to be moderate, both in bitterness and in aroma, supporting a medium-bodied biscuity malt center and leading to a clean, dry finish. The gentle smoothness of Belgian pale ales makes them almost ludicrously drinkable. What makes them distinctly Belgian is a certain round softness of malt character married with the spicy contributions of their yeast strains. A delicate fruitiness is often met by light notes of licorice, aniseed, fennel, orange peel, or cinnamon. The yeast ferments at very warm temperatures but then treads lightly, and these subtle flavors don't dominate or overwhelm. Rather, they play along, telling a complex story over the course of an evening or a meal. They are delicious by themselves, but when these flavors meet their counterparts in food, the recognition is instant and powerful.

Belgian Pale Ales with Food

I'd always thought of choucroute as an Alsatian dish. Modeste Van den Bogaert, the patriarch of the De Koninck brewery in Antwerp, begged to differ. "It is not only from Alsace—it is also from Antwerp," he said firmly. "You should order it—it's very good here." We were sitting at De Pelgrim, a warm, earthy café across the street from the brewery. It seemed a bad idea to resist Van den Bogaert or the choucroute, so I did as I was told and ordered it.

If you're looking for a nice match with beer, sausages are rarely a stretch, but this match was extraordinary. The sausages had a beautifully porky flavor, and the sauerkraut was only mildly acidic, allowing it to dovetail perfectly with the fine hoppy edge of the beer, which is simply called De Koninck. Better yet, a few flecks of aniseed or fennel in the sauerkraut tied into similar flavors in the beer, making the match amazing.

At the time, I'd have sworn that nothing could match a Belgian pale ale as nicely as choucroute, but that wouldn't be giving the beer its due. These beers show excellent versatility with a wide range of dishes. The soft spicy-herbal flavors are an excellent foil for lamb, whether it's a slow-cooked leg of lamb or a rack of lamb chops. A bit of rosemary enhances the match. Braised short ribs or beef cheeks are also wonderful matches—the beer wraps around the meat and virtually melts it on your tongue, lifting away the fat and sending in subtle flavors of cinnamon and nutmeg to seduce the meat. The earthiness of these beers also gives them an affinity for beef dishes featuring mushrooms.

Need I say pork? Almost any pork dish—except, perhaps, a citric or vinegary Mexican or barbecue preparation—is going to work splendidly with Belgian pale ale. Roast suckling pig, pork chops (even Cajun-style, which are spicy but not citric), roast loin of pork, pork tenderloin, breaded pork cutlet, pork shoulder, puerco en pipián—take your pick. The combination of aromatic biscuit flavors and herbal-spicy aromatics makes matches with pork virtually foolproof, as long as you avoid too much acidity. Otherwise, go for it.

A good Belgian pale ale can turn a simple roasted chicken from an ordinary meal into a culinary event. Herbs are the key. Some sage, thyme, or rosemary on the skin, under the skin, or in the stuffing will link up with the herbal flavors in the beer and really light the meal up. The caramel and biscuit flavors in the beer will match the browned skin, and you'll be on a roll. Something in the biscuity center of these beers particularly loves potatoes, so how about some on the side? Now I'm thinking of brussels sprouts, blanched and then sautéed in butter with a bit of shallot. OK, you can still just have the simple roasted chicken, but this is starting to get really good.

And here's something to remember—Belgian pale ales are very good with turkey. Turkey has a mild nutty flavor, and so does the beer, which can also make use of its herbal qualities to match stuffings and trimmings. I feel that French bière de garde is the all-around champion at the Thanksgiving table, but Belgian pale ale is certainly a close second.

These beers can be very nice with some fish, especially white-fleshed varieties (snapper, cod, monkfish, flounder) prepared with herbs, olives, or mushrooms to match the beer's earthy character. Battered fried fish is another good match—the biscuity flavors in the beer will echo flavors in the coating, and the beer will have a clean, dry edge that will suit the fish nicely. Again, stick with white fish for the best matches—darker, oilier fish will call for more cutting power and brighter flavors.

Notable Producers of Belgian Pale Ale

BROUWERIJ DE KONINCK Just as Dublin is synonymous with Guinness, it would be impossible to think of Antwerp without De Koninck. De Koninck is the name of both the brewery and its flagship beer, which is the unchallenged everyday drink of the people of Antwerp. So ubiquitous is this beer that it is often referred to by its trademark goblet, called a *bolleke* (pronounced "boll-uh-kuh"). In Antwerp, simply ask for a *bolleke*, and you'll get a chalice of De Koninck. The name De Koninck, which conveniently (and accurately, at least in Antwerp) means "the king," derives from the original owner, Joseph Henricus De Koninck. He owned a beer garden here in the early 1800s, and in 1833 he added a brewhouse of his own. In 1919, the Van den Bogaert family joined the enterprise. De Koninck remains a family affair, with Modeste Van den Bogaert at the helm—an imposing man who manages to seem both rustic and baronial and is clearly very proud and fond of his beer. At the café De Pelgrim, across the street from the brewery, he can be found every day at lunchtime, drinking a De Koninck and reading the *Financial Times* in English. He spent part of World War II in England, and he retains a soft spot for the English and their ales. When I last had lunch with him, I was prepared for his inevitable question. "Are you having the yeast?" he asked. Every day, a bucket of De Koninck yeast is brought across the street to De Pelgrim, where the locals either drink it out of shot glasses or add it to their beer. There can be no doubt that it's an excellent tonic, but I'm not a local. Nonetheless, I took my shot of yeast, which has a bitter, earthy flavor. Modeste smiled his approval.

A new brewhouse, built in 1996, is impressively reminiscent of a set from a science fiction film, the kettle towering like a rocket in a vast hangar. Behind the walls, the old brewhouse is being cleaned up and lit for tours, rather than being discarded. Compared with the new brewhouse, the former one looks like a charming old set of outsized copper pots and pans.

De Koninck has a full amber color and raises a thick, sturdy head. The aroma is wonderfully appetizing, a heady mélange of biscuity malts, cedar wood, cinnamon, anise, melons, and hops. The hop bitterness is bracing but graceful and gives way to a fruity palate that is both dry and juicy, underpinned by caramel and biscuit flavors. The finish is quick and dry, and the spicy anise flavors linger. The beer is not spiced, but the house yeast makes a big contribution to the flavor and aromatics. This beer is very nice in bottles, and fresh on draft it is nothing short

of remarkable. If you start your evening in Antwerp drinking De Koninck, you're likely to find it so delicious that you'll forget to try anything else. That would be a shame, since Antwerp is a great city for beer, but you could do worse. De Koninck is great with the local choucroute, potato croquettes and frites, pork, roasted or fried chicken, fried fish, veal, saltimbocca, and all manner of sausages.

BROUWERIJ PALM Founded in 1597, Palm is now the largest independent family-owned brewery in Belgium. It was originally a farm called De Hoorn, located in Steenhuffel in the province of Brabant. There is evidence of a farmhouse brewery from the mid-1700s, though the farm almost certainly brewed much earlier. The Van Roy family has owned and run the brewery for at least 250 years. The family retained the old name De Hoorn until 1975 but then renamed the brewery after its principal product, **Spéciale Palm**. The brewery sits on a small estate, which includes a farm and a moated chateau that belonged to the duke of Brabant in the 1400s. The chateau is now the brewery's visitors' center.

Speciale Palm has a pretty amber color and an aroma of biscuits, anise, hops, and orange marmalade. Hop bitterness is crisp but light, allowing biscuity malts to step forward in the dry, round, creamy center. There is a burst of juicy, orangey fruit before the beer moves into a quick, dry finish. Hops and spices glow in the aftertaste. Speciale Palm is quite versatile, and I find it particularly good with pork sausages, roasted chicken, breaded veal cutlets, and breaded fried fish.

OMMEGANG Ommegang, which brews Belgian-style beers in a set of farmhouse-style buildings in Cooperstown, New York, produces an ale in the classic style of Brabant. As fond as I am of Ommegang's other beers, especially the saison Hennepin, I feel that **Rare Vos** may be its most beguiling brew. Rare Vos, which means "sly fox," is a tribute to a great café of that name in Brussels. The beer is bottle-conditioned, but it pours bright copper and shows a brilliant display of classic Belgian aromatics. Sweet oranges dance with aniseed, biscuits, caramel, and hops in the tantalizing nose. The palate shows restrained bitterness and racy acidity in a medium-bodied fruity frame with very little residual sugar. The finish is quick, hard, and mineraly, with a slight metallic tang. Rare Vos is great with mussels, grilled shrimp, oysters, fried clams, sausages, and choucroute.

NEW BELGIUM BREWING COMPANY As he rode his fat-tired mountain bike from one brewery to another across the mercifully flat Belgian countryside, the American electrical engineer Jeff Lebesch had an epiphany. Belgian beer, he decided, was the finest liquid on the face of the earth. He desperately wanted to

OPPOSITE:
De Koninck's patriarch, Modeste Van den Bogaert, enjoys a quiet "bolleke" of his ale at De Pelgrim. The beer is very fresh—the brewery is visible across the street.

make some of his own. When he got home, he started to brew Belgian-style beers in his kitchen. He was quite good at it, and no one was surprised when he started a tiny commercial enterprise out of the basement of his home in Fort Collins, Colorado. It was very much a family affair, with his wife, Kim Jordan, helping out on the bottling and their son making deliveries. The word got out that the beer was excellent, and the business soon outgrew the basement. In 1995, the family put Lebesch's engineering skills to work and built a large state-of-the-art brewhouse in Fort Collins. It seemed absurdly large at the time, but New Belgium Brewing Company experienced explosive growth over the next several years. It outgrew its equipment the way babies outgrow clothes, shedding molted tanks to put in ever larger ones. Kim Jordan became a marketing powerhouse, and New Belgium's beer became famous and popular in the western states. The brewery's blend of community involvement and environmentally friendly policies (it is the only wind-powered brewery in the country) endeared it to its neighbors. Other craft brewers have watched New Belgium's meteoric rise with bewilderment; it is now one of the top-selling craft brewers in the country.

While New Belgium brews many fascinating beers, its success has been largely built on just one, the easy-drinking **Fat Tire Amber Ale**. Fat Tire has a full amber color and a faintly spicy aroma with notes of yeast and biscuits. Very restrained bitterness provides balance on a relatively light-bodied, soft, biscuity frame, showing a touch of fruitiness but finishing clean and dry. There is a hint of spice in the aftertaste. This beer is a version of a Belgian pale ale, but it once showed its Belgian roots far more proudly. It has shed considerable complexity on its way to superstardom. That is a fate avoided by few artists, and only a curmudgeon could begrudge this beer its success, especially since it seems to underwrite some brilliant experimental beers that are full of traditional flavor. Like Samuel Adams Boston Lager, Fat Tire has introduced thousands of people to better beer, and that is important work. Fat Tire is very drinkable and has an easy versatility. Try it with earthy Mexican dishes, roasted pork loin, roast chicken, turkey, sausages, and burgers.

FLANDERS BROWN AND RED ALES

The city of Oudenaarde and its environs, in east Flanders, are home to a unique style of brown ale known as *oud bruin* ("old brown"). "Old" doubtless refers to the throwback quality of these beers, whose distinctive sourness links them to the even older lambic tradition. Belgian lambic brewers don't add yeast to their wort, but rather allow souring wild yeasts in the air to take charge of the fermentations, just as they would have done thousands of years ago. Brewers of oud bruin don't go quite so far into the past—these beers are fermented by a blend of house yeast and bacterial strains that produce extraordinary flavors. At one time, many English beers would have been fermented by similar yeasts and acquired a much-prized sour edge. That practice has largely departed from England, but it has come to rest in Oudenaarde. Oud bruins are brewed conventionally from a blend of pilsner, Vienna, and Munich malts, with some roasted malt or barley added for color. By the time the yeast is finished, however, the beer is anything but conventional. Beyond its dry caramelish maltiness it develops a distinctly acidic tartness and winy, sherry-ish, raisiny notes worthy of a fine amontillado. The beer is dark, but roasted flavors rarely show through in a coffeeish fashion; rather, they play out as a firm nuttiness or a hint of chocolate. There is hardly a hint of hops—they're used, but the bitterness isn't discernable and there is rarely any hop aroma. Some sweetness remains in the center, but most beers dry to a crisp finish brought on by water high in bicarbonates. The dance of sweet and sour lingers on the palate. Strength is usually between 5 and 6 percent but occasionally drifts higher. Liefmans of Oudenaarde is by far the best-known producer of Flanders brown ales.

Liefmans bottles are dressed to thrill, lovingly wrapped in tissue paper. Liefmans adds fruit to its sourish brown ale to create excellent versions of kriek and framboise.

Like many old styles of beer and like the sherry it so closely resembles, Flanders brown ale is traditionally blended. Before refrigeration, brewing was a seasonal affair. In early spring, before warm weather prevented further brewing, a strong version of the beer would have been brewed for use through the summer. The extra strength was meant to help preserve the beer from spoilage, but it only slowed the inevitable march of acidic yeast and bacterial strains. The "stock" beer would become tart and sherryish by autumn, when it would be blended with fresh, lively beer. Constant blending throughout the year brought some consistency of flavor, though there is little doubt that the beers once had different flavors, depending on the season. These days we look for consistency in our beers, but there's something distinctly charming about the old seasonality, which connoisseurs still enjoy in other natural products—cheese, for example. Though this solera-style blending technique is no longer driven by the seasons, it is still widely used to produce the traditional oud bruin flavors and is important in maintaining a modern level of consistency.

The addition of fruit is usually saved for lambic beers, but a few breweries add cherries to their oud bruins, creating *kriek*—"cherry" in Flemish. The yeast attacks the fruit, breaking down the pulp, fermenting the sugars, and drawing nutty flavors from the pits. The beers can emerge with a wonderful interplay of fruit aromatics, sweetness, sourness, and sherry notes. They are wonderful with desserts, are also excellent with savory dishes, and are great to cook with.

The brewers of west Flanders make no reference to "red ale," though the style certainly exists. Flanders red ale is also a throwback, but it is still brewed in respectable volume, especially by Rodenbach of Roeselare, the largest and most famous producer. The brewers, indifferent as ever to attempts at categorization, prefer to refer to their beers as the "Burgundies of Belgium." Burgundy once ruled this area, but the local beers bear little resemblance to pinot noir. The reddish color comes largely from the use of specially caramelized malts. The red ales of west Flanders are closely related to the brown ales of east Flanders, but there are some notable distinctions. The most important is the tradition of aging the red ales in huge vats of unlined oak. The wood, which cannot be sterilized, is home to dozens of wild yeast and bacterial strains that attack the residual sugars in the beer. Over the course of its aging, which can last as long as two years, the beer takes on its characteristic acidity, along with oak flavor and color. Sherry and passion fruit notes develop and deepen as oxygen slowly seeps in through the wood.

Like the oud bruins, these beers are usually blends of young and old beer. The young beer is fermented in stainless steel tanks by a house "yeast" that may contain more than a dozen different strains. This yeast blend will include some lactic acid–producing bacteria and Brettanomyces yeast, which produces an underlying earthiness. Even the young beer is not terribly young—fermentation usually lasts for more than a month. The younger fresher product is then blended with the wood-aged stock beer, the brewer seeking a balance of youth and experience. The resulting blends, which are between 4.5 percent and 5.5 percent, are light-bodied and zesty, with complex fruity and earthy aromatics, malt caramel and sweetness balanced with refreshing acidity. An ironlike finish cleanses the palate. One would think that the sweet-and-sour flavor of Flanders red ale would be an acquired taste, but many open-minded people fall in love with its perfect synthesis of complexity and refreshment as soon as they taste it. These beers may be throwbacks, but they are once again growing in popularity, lovingly brewed by people of rare vision. Burgundy should be so lucky.

Flanders Brown and Red Ales with Food

Vibrant acidity is the defining characteristic of the brown and red ales of Flanders. The red ales in particular have a very light touch that makes them a perfect foil for shellfish. Rodenbach, for example, is so nice with lobster that its label ought to depict one. The beer has the acidity to brighten the lobster's flavor, the carbonation to lift the clarified butter, and the underlying sweetness to meld with the natural sweetness of the meat. It's a natural choice, since the Belgians seem to have a particular love of shellfish. A Belgian friend once served me a heaping plateful of delicious tiny shrimp—for breakfast. His mother had dutifully peeled each one, blazing through them with quiet deftness as I looked on in awe. We spread them on fresh bread with a bit of butter and poured small glasses of Rodenbach to wash them down. It was an extremely tasty meal, though I think I would have preferred it for lunch. I certainly didn't have the heart to tell her that most Americans don't really eat shrimp for breakfast. (Where were the Belgian waffles I'd heard so much about?) Then again, if I'd had them for lunch, I wonder whether I'd still remember those shrimp so vividly all these years later.

Perhaps brunch is more like it. Flanders red ales are excellent with omelettes, and that is more than you can say for a kir royale. Goat cheese omelettes make a particularly nice match—the beer matches the acidity in the cheese but also provides a nice contrasting sweetness. Another nice match is eggs Benedict; the beer slices joyfully through the hollandaise sauce and heads straight for the bacon. I enjoy brunch at French restaurants in New York City, and it's always a difficult choice—do I go with an egg dish, or will it be the croque monsieur? Croque monsieur, a grilled Gruyère sandwich with a slab of good ham in the center, is also perfect with red ale, so at least my choice of beer is easy.

Flanders red ales are excellent with crab, whether it's a simple dish of picked crabmeat, softshell crabs, or crab cakes. Again, the acidity is just like a squeeze of lemon, and the level of sweetness is perfect. The same is true of oysters, and the beer won't flinch at spicy sauces, so go right ahead. Moules frites—mussels with fries—is such a popular dish in Belgium that entire restaurant chains have been built around it. Red ales are a brilliant accompaniment and can also be used in the broth for the mussels, making the match better still. Squid and octopus are good partners, regardless of the cooking method. Ceviche is an obvious choice—the beer has the acidity to match the citric marinade and can easily handle any spices you want to throw at it. Acidity is also an asset for matching salty dishes—Flanders red is very nice with brandade (or bacala, whipped salt cod). Smoked salmon is also a nice match, as is gravlax, which is cured with sugar and salt. The beer will happily welcome the traditional sprig of dill and dab of honey-mustard sauce.

Not surprisingly, Flanders red ales are excellent with a wide variety of fish and will match most preparations. If a dish contains citrus or vinegar, or is one that you would consider squeezing a lemon over, you're likely to have a very fine match. I'm partial to sautéed monkfish served with a lemon shallot sauce. If you pair the monkfish with red ale, you may find it hard to shake the impression that the beer was invented for this dish.

Flanders brown ales bear considerable similarity to their red cousins, but roasted malts bring darker flavors of raisins, chocolate, and toffee into the mix. Red ales certainly don't have to stick to brunch and seafood, but I feel that their greatest talent lies there. The brown ales retain a similar acidity but have the heft to match meat dishes confidently. Flanders brown ale is the classic base for carbonnade flamande, a stew of beef, onions, and beer that virtually qualifies as the Belgian national dish (the other contender is moules frites). The raisiny quality of the beer is often intensified by adding raisins or prunes to the dish. Naturally, the brown ale then provides the perfect partner for the dish.

Pork is another good partner for these piquant brown ales. Animal breeders seem to be working hard to get all the fat out of pork—I work hard to find pork that retains old-fashioned flavors. Belgian pork is still full of flavor, and these beers lift and cut through the fat, leaving the glorious pork flavor to commune with the raisiny, pruny flavors of the malt. Wild boar is never fatty, but it is still full of gamy flavor, and these beers can work very well with it, especially with wild boar sausages. Somehow, no one has managed to dumb down the fat and flavor of duck (a fact for which I am profoundly thankful), which is wonderful with

Flanders brown ale. The beer also makes a nice base for an accompanying sauce, especially one made with sour cherries. Speaking of cherries, let's not forget venison, which also enjoys both the beer and a good sour-cherry sauce.

Notable Producers of Flanders Red and Brown Ales

BROUWERIJ RODENBACH The inland port of Roeselare straddles a canal that runs across the flatlands of Belgian Flanders. Here the Rodenbach family, originally from Germany, has flourished for more than 200 years. Ferdinand Rodenbach arrived here as a military doctor during Austrian rule in the 1700s, and his family produced famous authors, politicians, and inventors. Alexander Rodenbach, who was instrumental in the movement for Belgian independence, bought a brewery in 1820, and the family established the Rodenbach brewery in Roeselare in 1836. The brewery's most striking building, a conical malting tower, dates from that period; it is now part of the brewery's museum. In 2002, the gorgeous old multilevel brass, copper, and tile wedding cake of a brewhouse built in the 1920s finally gave way to a modern stainless steel brewhouse on the other side of the brewery grounds. This brewhouse has a special airlock system for adding the hops to the kettle. When I asked the brewmaster, Rudi Ghequire, why this system was necessary, he smiled and gave me a typically conspiratorial Belgian response. "Don't worry—*we* know why we do it."

Nothing prepares the visitor for the sight of the maturation halls, featuring row upon row of huge oak vats ranging in size from 120 hectoliters (about 100 U.S. barrels) to 600 hectoliters. There are 300 of these vats, arranged in eleven halls, far more than those of any other producer of traditional tart Flemish beers. Here the beer silently ages for two years or more, taking on wonderfully complex flavors from the wood and the microorganisms living within it. Many of these vessels are more than 100 years old, and the oldest dates from 1868. The brewery employs a team of coopers. When a vat needs repairs, the coopers remove it from its stand and dismantle it in their shop; they then do traditional work with reeds and beeswax until the vessel is again ready for service. A multimillion-dollar investment from Rodenbach's new owner, the Palm brewery of Brabant, has transformed the building housing the maturation halls into a beautiful and informative visitors' center. The rows of vats are visible behind glass, and a handsome bar sells Rodenbach beer and serves local food.

The brewery's main product is called simply **Rodenbach**. It is a blend of two beers: 75 percent young beer, fermented and aged with a complex blend of yeasts in stainless steel tans for four or five weeks, and 25 percent aged beer, which emerges from the wooden vats after years of slumber. The beer has an alluring red-orange color and a stunningly complex nose of passion fruit, dried lemons, vinegar, vanilla, and wet wool blankets. The palate opens up light, sweet, and juicy, with only the slightest hint of bitterness, before lactic acidity grabs the tongue and pulls everything into balance. Some caramel and oak show in the center, and the finish is long and tart, with an ironlike twang at the end. It's strange, startling, and complex, but remarkably refreshing. Seafood leaps instantly to mind, especially lobster, shrimp, and crab dishes. This beer is a natural with ceviche, and the acidity is also a nice counterpoint to full-flavored fish. With a salad, Rodenbach virtually acts as its own vinaigrette, and it is particularly nice with goat cheese salads.

The beer aged in wood is not all destined for blending—it is also bottled "straight" as **Rodenbach Grand Cru**. This beer is somewhat stronger, 6 percent as opposed to the blend's 4.6 percent. Everything here is riper and more assertive—the color is a deep red, edging into brown, and the nose shows plenty of vanilla-like oak (the interiors of the vats are shaved down to fresh wood after every use), preserved lemons, lemon zest, damp earth, passion fruit, apricots, sherry, and horse blankets. The palate is round and sweet, with caramelized malts quickly countered by a firm acidity. Sherry, fruit, and oak play through the juicy center to a long sweet-and-sour finish. This beer has enough heft to work with game, especially wild wood pigeon and partridge. It's also a fine accompaniment to beef cheeks and short ribs: the acidity helps slice through the unctuous fat. Similarly, it's also nice with gamy liver pâtés. Once again, pickled dishes, especially ceviches and herring, have a natural affinity for this beer.

The family history of the Rodenbachs is closely intertwined with the history of Belgium. The family saga is played out at the Rodenbach brewery's beautiful visitors' center.

LIEFMANS The most famous of the Flanders brown ales lead interesting lives. They are brewed by the Riva group, which produces the wort in Dentergem, west Flanders. The wort is then trucked across the flat countryside to the town of Oudenaarde, in east Flanders. There, the Liefmans brewery, which once did the entire production itself, ferments, ages, blends, and bottles the Liefmans beers. Liefmans, which has been producing beer since at least 1679, struggled to continue production in its aging brewery in Oudenaarde until Riva bought it in the late 1980s. Creditably, Riva made a considerable investment in Liefmans and expanded the popularity of the traditional beers. The odd practice of trucking the wort across Flanders is a matter of necessity—Riva wants to ensure that the Liefmans souring yeast blend doesn't come anywhere near its other beers, which use more conventional yeasts. The house yeast originated at the Rodenbach brewery of Roeselare, which is famous for its red ales.

Liefmans Goudenband is by far Liefmans's best-known beer. It is available in small bottles, but the large corked bottles, lovingly hand-wrapped in printed tissue paper, are particularly popular. The beer itself is gorgeous, a dusky garnet-brown color reminiscent of an old Barolo. The nose is startling and intense; it exudes waves of sherry, chocolate, wood, raisins, prunes, nutmeg, leather, and horse blankets. The palate is sharply acidic, with fruity sweetness stepping in to provide balance. There's a flavor of sour cherries, although none have been used—cherries are saved for the brewery's kriek. The center is tart and juicy, leading to a long, winy finish with a slight ironlike tang. Goudenband, like many other traditional Flanders beers, is a blend. Four-month-old beer is blended with year-old beer. The yeast is then removed and sugar and fresh yeast are added for bottle-conditioning. Sharp, funky, and 8 percent to boot, this is not a beer for the faint-hearted, but it is certainly complex and fascinating. It is a very good aperitif and makes an excellent palate cleanser between courses of a meal. It's also delicious with fresh tangy goat cheeses, grilled shrimp, crabmeat salad, and braised beef, and as a base for the stock in a traditional carbonnade flamande. Liefmans also produces excellent kriek and framboise, by adding whole cherries or raspberries to a brown ale base.

BAVIK The Bavik brewery is in Bavikhove, Belgium, where the De Brabandere family has been brewing since 1894. The brewery runs a successful chain of cafés, where its traditional beers remain popular. A few of its beers are sold under the Petrus label, a fact that seems to have sparked only mild amusement at the venerable château of the same name in Bordeaux.

Petrus Oud Bruin has a beautiful red-brown color and aromatics redolent of amontillado sherry, dried lemons, vanilla, fruit compote, and wool blankets. Light mouth-coating acidity is paired with fruity sweetness to create a tasty sweet-and-sour confection in a light-bodied frame. The finish is long, winy, and refreshing. This is a very complex beer for its modest strength of 5.5 percent. The complexity is achieved by blending pale and dark beers, the dark beer having been aged in oak casks for two years. This technique seems to promote a certain mellowness; the acidity is well integrated and approachable, but nothing here has been dumbed down. Petrus Oud Bruin is terrific with tangy cheeses, crispy duck, carbonnade flamande, sausages, and hanger steak with shallot sauce.

NEW BELGIUM BREWING COMPANY Behind the juggernaut that is New Belgium's Fat Tire Amber Ale, more traditional Belgian beers lurk in the background. The brewmaster, Peter Bouckaert, was imported from Belgium, where he worked at Rodenbach. He evidently missed his local Flemish beers, because he soon set about re-creating one at New Belgium. He named his experiment **La Folie** ("The Folly") and set to work. After prolonged tinkering, he finally bottled it in 2000. The 2000 bottling of La Folie has a stunning color, deep red with brown and orange highlights. The nose is big and funky, with sherry and ripe cider apples taking the lead on a barnyardy backdrop of leather, earth, damp wool, vanilla, oak, and black truffles. Malt sweetness and bright, sharp acidity are in perfect balance on the palate, neither threatening to overwhelm the other. The center is juicy, somehow sweet and tart, woody and drying all at the same time. It is very reminiscent of rhubarb pie. The finish is long and rhubarby, finally becoming clean and dry. La Folie is fermented with a blend of special yeasts and bacterial strains, then aged from one to three years in barrels previously used to age Burgundy wine. It's a wonderful accomplishment, every bit the equal of the Flemish beers that inspired it. It's a very limited product for now—you can buy it only from the brewery in Fort Collins, Colorado. It may soon be more widely available. La Folie is a brilliant accompaniment to sautéed foie gras. Also, try it with game terrines, braised short ribs, and aged goat cheeses.

The flat farmlands of Wallonia, the French-speaking region of southern Belgium, are home to one of the world's most refreshing and enigmatic beer styles. Ask someone in Antwerp what a "saison" is and he may respond with a shrug, but a century ago this regional specialty was known far and wide. Saisons are traditionally farmhouse ales, rustic beers produced by small artisanal brewers in the Wallonian province of Hainaut.

These were originally provisional beers for the farmhouse table—light, brisk, refreshing, and sustaining. Nutritionally, they were as important as milk or bread.

Saison means "season," and the season in question was the end of winter and the beginning of spring. As mild March weather breathed life back into the countryside, the brewing season drew to a close. In the days before refrigeration, brewing was impossible in warm weather—fermentations would get out of hand, and the beer would spoil. Besides, the farmer would be busy with his crops and would have no time to brew. The beer brewed in March had to last through the heat of the summer, through the early autumn harvest, and into the next brewing season, which generally started in October. It needed to be robust enough to keep for months, yet light enough to quench the thirst of farmhands. Once the harvest was over, the farmers would start brewing again—the beer could be sold to provide a secondary income as the fields lay fallow. Some saison breweries are still attached to farms where you can pick up eggs and cheese along with your beer.

Only a few saisons are still produced today, but they are some of Belgium's most exciting beers. They are brewed largely from pale malts, sometimes with oats or a dash of sugar. A wide range of spices and botanicals may be used in the kettle, from white pepper to dried orange peel. At one time, these beers would have been fermented in wood and served directly from casks, but that practice has died out. These days, a warm, robust top-fermentation is usually followed by a secondary fermentation in a heavy champagne-like bottle, which is sealed with a cork and wire hood. The bottled beer is almost always laid down for at least two months before being released. These beers have their own distinct personalities, but most have a sunny orange color; explosive carbonation producing an impressive rocky head; bright, spicy, fruity aromatics; a refreshing hop attack; and a dry, slightly tart finish. The heavy hopping that would once have helped the beer survive the summer now provides a resinous aftertaste. The strength is usually about 6.5 percent.

I consider these beers truly glorious and endlessly interesting. As with wheels of great artisanal cheese, every bottle of saison is very slightly different—it lives its own life, tells its own tale. The siren song of saison has proved irresistible to some of America's most creative craft brewers, who are devoted to keeping the spirit of this style alive, both in Belgium and elsewhere. With food, the best saisons are beyond versatile—they are virtually invincible.

Saisons with Food

People ask me all the time, "What's your favorite beer?" I always answer, truthfully, that it depends on the weather, where I am, what I'm eating, what mood I'm in, and what I have to do tomorrow. What I don't tell them is this—if I were forced to choose one style to drink with every meal for the rest of my life, saison would have to be it. At any given time, there is at least one case of saison in my cellar. Saison is not just versatile—it's downright promiscuous. It seems to go with almost everything. The combination of dynamic bitterness, scouring carbonation, bright aromatics, spicy flavors, pepper notes, dark earthy underpinnings, and racy acidity gives these beers a hook to hang their hat on for a wide range of dishes. I love to slather my rib-eye steaks with olive oil, cracked pepper, and coarse sea salt before broiling them to juicy medium-rare perfection. Saison has the bitterness to cut through the fat and salt, the high carbonation to lift them off the palate, peppery flavors to meet the cracked pepper, fruity notes to mingle with the juices, and earthiness to pick up on the essential flavors of the meat. It's not just a match; it's a torrid embrace.

I give salmon steaks, a summer favorite, a treatment very similar to that for the rib-eye, minus the salt. Saison, which gives a bravura performance with the rib-eye, is equally brilliant with salmon steak. It lifts the oiliness of the salmon and slices into the fish with a crackling wave of bitterness and lemony acidity. As the pepper echoes the peppery note in the beer, the salmon flavor is lifted and defined. Everything falls into place. It doesn't get better than this.

Except, perhaps, with shrimp salad. I coat peeled shrimp with olive oil, cumin, and a dash of hot habanero chili sauce, then toss them in the wok. They're done in scarcely a minute, and I add them to a salad of mesclun greens, sliced red onion, avocado slices, sweet red peppers, and ripe tomatoes. A simple oil and balsamic vinegar dressing, some cracked black pepper, and I'm done. (Fifteen minutes flat, mind you—this is a terrific fast meal.) Now here comes the saison, which meets the acidity of the dressing with its own, waves hello to the pepper, parries the onion, cuts through the avocado, quenches the habanero sauce, and reaches the shrimp, where its own coriander notes play with the cumin. The sweet flavors of the shrimp linger undisturbed, while the habaneros glow on my tongue. Beautiful.

Saison is great with all but the most delicate fish; it's too big, for example, for a simply sautéed filet of sole, flounder, or turbot. But if we're talking about Thai red snapper with spicy tamarind sauce, bring it on. The same goes for fried fish—especially with a squeeze of lemon—clams, and calamari. Saison is tremendous with crab cakes—make them as tame or as spicy as you like. Even the delicate turbot can play along. I once had it pan-seared with a celery puree and porcini mushroom reduction sauce, and it was very nice with Saison Dupont. The match seemed improbable, but it worked because the pan searing picked up on the toastiness of the grain while the mushrooms matched the earthiness at the center of the beer. Some other affinities were playing there too—I still haven't finished figuring this one out. Saisons never stop beguiling and astonishing me.

Saison is a fine partner to sausages of every imaginable description. Italian, merguez, chorizo, seafood, Toulouse, bratwurst, venison, boudin noir—I can't think of a single variety of sausage I've ever had that wouldn't be enjoyable with these beers. Pork sausages seem to find a particularly nice match. Many saisons possess a strong note of green apple peel, an attribute that really sings with pork dishes. Pork chops, cooked just like that rib-eye steak, are a favorite of mine. Some sautéed Granny Smith apples on the side will make them even better.

Saison is a real star with Thai food. Thai cuisine pits bright flavors (lime, tamarind, cilantro, and chilies) against dark ones (nam pla fish sauce, soy sauce, and mushrooms) and sweetness against salt and acidity. Saison has bright citric notes to match the bright notes in the food and earthiness to meet the darker flavors. The result is a fireworks display, not of disparate elements but of remarkable harmony. All my favorite Thai dishes work with saison—crispy duck in red coconut curry sauce, chicken massamun curry, tom yung gai, beef satay, and the ubiquitous pad thai.

You will find the same with Vietnamese food, which has similar flavors at work. I once had dinner with a small group of friends at the Slanted Door, an excellent Vietnamese restaurant in San Francisco. When I discovered Saison Dupont on the menu, I ordered a large bottle. The others at the table had not tasted saison before, so they were in for a treat—I poured a little for each of them. To make a long story short, we cleaned the restaurant out of every bottle it had—more than a dozen. The beer went with every dish. It defied chilies, matched mint leaves, and performed dozens of minor miracles on our palates. Everyone went nuts over the beer. The food was brilliant and we had a ball. After we'd depleted the saison supply, the other patrons glowered sullenly at us as the laughter bounced between our empty bottles. They'd missed something absolutely essential, and they knew it. I almost felt guilty for a minute or two. Then the feeling went away. It always does.

Notable Producers of Saison

BRASSERIE DUPONT The province of Hainaut, near the French border, is largely flat farmland. Tourpes, which is so small that it hardly counts as a village, was not easy to find. As we pulled up to the brewery, members of a family were loading beer into the back of their station wagon. The beer wasn't in cardboard cases; the corked bottles were carefully laid on their sides in plastic milk crates. The family loaded every free bit of space in the car with beer before taking to the road, the car lumbering under the weight. Many decades ago, the same scene would surely have been played out with an unhappy horse doing the lumbering. Saisons are provisional beers, and local people have come here to stock up since 1850. The Duponts bought the brewery in 1920, and two generations later a family member, Marc Rosier, runs the business. Marc's two sisters and other relatives also work for the brewery; Marc's young nephew, Olivier Dedeycker, is in charge of brewing. The farm, called Moinette ("little monk"), offers cheeses and breads, some of them containing spent malt or minced hops. The farm sits on land where an abbey is believed to have stood.

When I told Olivier Dedeycker that I regarded my visit as a pilgrimage, he looked a bit puzzled. I revere the Dupont beers, and I had approached this place with some trepidation. I didn't want to be disappointed, to find that things were not as I'd imagined. I needn't have worried. The brewhouse vessels, made of riveted copper and iron, are strictly traditional, and the kettle is direct-fired. During World War II, the family buried the vessels in the adjoining fields to save them from being melted into armaments by the invading German army. The brewhouse is a classic farmhouse assemblage, worthy of a museum, but put to work every day. Here, gravity does work that more modern breweries leave to pumps. They have spent money only where it will improve the product—for instance, on the modern bottling line. This is the very picture of artisanal brewing.

The best-known beer in the Dupont range is **Saison Dupont Vieille Provision** ("old provision"), which comes in a heavy champagne-style bottle fitted with a cork and wire hood. The cork invariably lets go with a mighty pop, and Saison Dupont leaps forth like a force of nature, a bright golden orange with a magnificent pillowy white head. Granules of yeast and protein bob and swirl in the glass, propelled by convections of the powerful carbonation. The nose is astonishing—lemon zest, apple peels, black pepper, anise, coriander, damp earth, peaches, and earthy-fruity East Kent Golding hops. The beer expands into a mousse on the palate, at first slightly sweet and then breathtakingly dry, as snappy, bracing hops race in. The whole thing explodes into a riot of bright citric fruit, dark loam, herbs, malt sweetness, and refreshing acidity. The finish is dry, fruity, hoppy, and quick as the crack of a whip. It has an exquisite balance of stunning complexity and sheer thirst-quenching drinkability. It's impossibly delicious.

OPPOSITE: Saison Dupont, brewed on a small farm in Hainaut, is a jewel in Belgium's brewing crown. It's refreshing, has remarkable depth of flavor, and goes with almost everything.

I've probably had more than 500 bottles of Saison Dupont, and I'm still awestruck and humbled by every single one. No two bottles are exactly alike, a trait it shares with other beautiful living things, be they flowers or raw-milk cheeses. By itself, this beer is obscene; with food, it is a miracle. I hardly know where to start, but try it first with well-peppered salmon steaks, Thai food, spicy Mexican dishes, Vietnamese food, steak au poivre, fiery Cajun dishes, and well-

Product of Belgium
Vieille Provision
SAISON DUPONT
Unfiltered
Belgian Farmhouse Ale
Brewed by Brasserie Dupont,
Imported by Vanberg & Dewulf,

aged Gouda cheese. Aside from desserts and very acidic tomato sauces, it's hard to find anything that Saison Dupont doesn't match. It's so complex that it has a flavor hook for almost any dish. To me, it's a desert island beer, something that I have no intention of ever living without. I took six bottles with me to Mexico once, and I laughed as I blasted each cork into the warm surf. The beer was unbelievable with the quesadillas.

Forêt, known in Belgium as Moinette Bio, is made from organically grown hops and barley. It's very similar to the Vieille Provision, but doesn't have quite the same racy vibrancy and hop attack. I suspect that organic brewing ingredients still have a way to go. It's still an excellent beer, though—it simply suffers slightly by comparison. It's strong at 7.5 percent, but light-bodied and flinty, a fine accompaniment to seafood, especially monkfish, crab cakes, and mussels (with frites, of course).

The brewers at Dupont swear that their beers aren't spiced, but Belgian brewers tend to be evasive when asked too many questions. I'm suspicious. Besides, I can't think of any other way to explain the little brown flecks in the head and the deeply spicy aroma of Dupont's **Moinette**. Saison Dupont is strong but quaffable at 6.5 percent; Moinette's full gold color belies an 8.5 percent wallop. It has a powerful aroma of coriander, passion fruit, damp earth, dried orange peel, lemon curd, and peaches. The bitterness is brusque and sharp, providing a counterpoint to the Juicy Fruit malt sweetness residing at the center. Bitterness and acidity dry out the finish, and the fruit lingers. Another tour de force, perhaps not quite as refined as the Vieille Provision, but beautiful in its own right and big enough to take on any dish it pleases. Try it with salmon steaks, grilled sardines, spicy Thai snapper, coconut curries, gamy sausages, steaks, and barbecue.

Olivier Dedeycker is endlessly inventive, and the brewery experiments constantly. A few years ago, the Duponts found a label for a beer produced by the brewery before they owned it. This was a honey beer, and it inspired them to brew their own **Bière de Miel**, a beer with a large addition of aromatic honey to the kettle. The honeys change from time to time, but the versions of Bière de Miel that I've tasted all have the house character of black pepper and fruit, backed with a powerful perfumy aroma and flavor of beeswax and honey. The beers have been dry—honey is very fermentable—with an acidic twinge in the finish. This beer is particularly wonderful with wild game.

The strength of the Dupont beers tops out at 9.5 percent with their Christmas beer, **Avec les Bons Voeux de la Brasserie Dupont**. The name offers the brewery's best wishes, and the beer sets out to fulfill them, showing a full, deep orange color and an aroma of herbs, musty fruit compote, black pepper, hops, and sweet spices.

The power is more obvious now on a round, sweetish palate just bursting with fruitiness. The finish is long and resinous. This beer is terrific by itself or with spicy foods, especially jerk chicken, lamb vindaloo, and Thai snapper with chili sauce. It's also great with cheese—try it with Parmigiano Reggiano or an aged Gouda or farmhouse cheddar.

BRASSERIE À VAPEUR Many breweries in Belgium use very old equipment. Rather than toss out an old vessel or machine as obsolete, they lovingly repair it. The Belgians are artistic brewers, and artists require inspiration. Perhaps the soul of the beer resides partly in the walls, the rafters, the kettle, the engines. It's a spirit I've felt more than once.

In the town of Pipaix, a stone's throw from the Dupont brewery at Tourpes, a steam engine dating from 1885 huffs to life and the flywheel starts to spin, driving the mash mixing paddles and rakes of the Brasserie à Vapeur—the "steam brewery." There was a farmhouse brewery here in the early nineteenth century, and the Biset family ran the brewery until 1985. Jean-Marie Dits, who taught school during the day and brewed beer at home in the evenings, then took over the brewery, which by that time was nearly in ruins. He had dreamed of owning a brewery since a fateful school outing to the nearby Dupont brewery in 1967. This was his big chance. It took him two months of hard work to rehabilitate the antique plant, and he started to brew on weekends, supplying only the local area. He brews truly artisanal beers, full of spices and rooted in the ancient local brewing culture. His first wife, Anne-Marie, died tragically in an accident at the brewery some years ago, but Jean-Marie pressed on. One of his daughters will one day run the brewhouse.

The brewery is best-known for its **Saison de Pipaix**, much of which is aged for years in its cellars. Seventeen years after bottling, Saison de Pipaix 1985 has a hazy orange color and a wildly funky aroma with anise, black pepper, and orange peel out front and leather, horse blankets, lemons, and decaying leaves underneath. The palate is bone-dry and sharply tart, with a fruity sourness driving straight through the perfumed, honeyed center to an oddly clean finish. This is reminiscent of a great lambic gueuze and would make a perfect match for a good Mexican ceviche.

The brewery produces many variations on the saison theme. Another, **Vapeur en Folie**, has the brewery's old steam engine on its label. At eight years old, it had a gorgeous burnished antique gold color and an aroma of funky cider apples, damp earth, and wet cast iron. The palate is momentarily sweet and then suddenly acidic, with a lime and bitter-orange fruitiness in the center, and a long ironlike finish. The overall impression is reminiscent of a dry Normandy farmhouse cider or a hard-edged sauvignon blanc, perhaps a young Sancerre. Try it with lobster and shrimp salads made with soft-flavored greens, and with ceviches and goat cheeses.

BRASSERIE D'ACHOUFFE One could be forgiven for thinking that all the products of this brewery are Christmas beers—after all, one of Santa's elves appears to be on the labels. Closer inspection will reveal that he is carrying malt and hops, a sure sign that he is not an elf but a *chouffe*, a legendary gnome living and brewing in the forests of the Ardennes. The brewery was founded by two brothers-in-law—Pierre Gobron and Chris Bauweraerts—in 1982 in the little village of Achouffe, in the Belgian province of Luxembourg. They were homebrewers, and they originally cobbled together a brewery out of bits and pieces, installed it in a 200-year-old farmhouse, and ran it as a part-time hobby. Gobron, a production engineer at an ice cream plant, left his job to work full-time at the brewery in 1984. Bauweraerts, a computer engineer, joined him in 1988, and the partners have built a loyal international following and a succession of larger and larger brewhouses for their popular artisanal beers.

Their flagship beer is called simply **La Chouffe**. It is a pale orange beer with an exuberant aroma of oranges, pineapples, mangoes, apple peels, and hops. The brewery doesn't call this beer a saison, but it surely fits the description of the true farmhouse style, strong at 8 percent, and virtually chunky with yeast. Moderate bitterness is up front on the palate, followed by a fruity core that seems sweet at first, then dries into a long bitter-orange finish. Despite its strength, it remains medium-bodied, light on its feet, and almost dangerously drinkable. I've often enjoyed it in restaurants with Indian dishes, but it is very versatile and a great partner for barbecue, Thai food, duck, cassoulet, and rustic sausages. The brewery has its own popular restaurant overlooking the brewhouse, specializing in Belgian *cuisine a la bière*.

BREWERY OMMEGANG In Cooperstown, New York, a town best known as the home of the Baseball Hall of Fame, Wendy Littlefield and Don Feinberg—a wife-and-husband team—produce some of the finest Belgian-style beer in the United States. Their flagship beer is called simply Ommegang, but I feel that their finest creation is **Ommegang Hennepin**, a strong (7.5 percent) bottle-conditioned saison. It has a full gold color and a sweet nose of oranges, coriander, and star anise. Broad, sharp hopping balances a sweet-and-sour center combining juicy, fruity malts with a refreshing light acidity. Herbs and spices tango at the center before sashaying out to a short, dry finish. Fruit and sweet spices glow in the aftertaste.

This is a truly excellent rendition of the saison style. The sweetness in the center makes it a great choice with barbecue, jerk chicken, Cajun dishes, pork loin, and duck. It's also an excellent accompaniment to one of my favorite American cheeses, Cypress Grove Humboldt Fog, an aged goat cheese from California.

BIRRA BALADIN Like France, Italy brings wine to mind, but young Italians now seek flavorful beer in a way that their parents never did. Perhaps it's the newness of the flavors, perhaps the novel flashiness of beer's image, probably a bit of both. When I've hosted beer tastings in Italy, I've always found the audiences to be hungry for new taste experiences—the Italians are a lot of fun to drink beer with. Today there are more than ninety small craft breweries in Italy, some of them producing excellent beers. My favorite is the brew pub Birra Baladin, run by Teo Musso, a talented brewer in the tiny Piemontese hilltop town of Piozzo, a quick drive from the famous wine villages of Barolo and La Morra. He spent some time at Brasserie à Vapeur in Belgium, and its influence shows clearly. Musso's well-balanced beers are largely brewed in Belgian styles, and he certainly has a Belgian sense of creativity, using herbs, spices, and unusual grains with abandon. Piozzo is usually a sleepy place, but on weekend nights people travel from miles around to crowd into Baladin, which takes on the air of a superhip party.

Beer is brewed at the pub but fermented several blocks away. Musso obtained permission to run a pipeline under Piozzo's streets; it carries wort from the pub to a small building full of fermentation vessels. Many of the vessels wear giant earphones fashioned out of speakers and foam rubber—Musso says that the yeast enjoys listening to music. He is unabashedly eccentric, but he brews elegant beers with a personal sense of style. He also has a head for business. He has started to export his hand-bottled beers, and although he's starting small, I have little doubt of his future success. Musso designs his own bottles and labels, both of which are handsome and striking.

At least two of Baladin's bottle-conditioned beers can be broadly viewed as saisons. **Nora**, which is named after Musso's wife, has a hazy pale orange color and a thin but persistent head. The nose is quite fruity, showing citrus, sweet spices, and a whiff of iron. It is on the palate that this beer reveals its secret—there are virtually no hops. In their place Musso has used an array of bitter herbs and spices, a practice reaching back to the days when people brewed with fruit. Reaching back even further, he's also used unmalted kamut, a grain that was widely used for brewing in ancient Egypt. The palate is very dry, with a thin quininelike bitterness and fine acidity. Some orangey sweetness bursts out through the center and then the beer dries into a long winy finish. It's fascinating and elegant, and would make a fine match for duck à l'orange or pork served with a fruit sauce. Nora has the classic strength for saison at 6.8 percent. At 8 percent, **Super Baladin** is somewhat stronger and has a hazy pale amber color and an aroma of oranges, apples, and hops. Fine light bitterness combines with fruity acidity at the front of the palate, and the beer blooms briskly across the tongue. It's very dry, but the fruit flavors give a fleeting impression of sweetness. Light wheaty flavors occupy the center and the beer slides into a long, dry, slightly tangy finish. The aftertaste has a warming glow. Super Baladin is beautifully balanced and it's perfect for baked or grilled salmon or arctic char.

TRAPPIST AND ABBEY BEERS

Those of us living in the secular world rarely think about monks. When we do, the image that comes to mind is a robed figure deep in contemplative prayer, perhaps with a ray of sunshine falling reassuringly on his shoulder. There may be a manuscript and a quill in the picture, and perhaps a chunk of bread to keep him going. Oh, yes, and then there's the chanting. There is little room in this image for a goblet of beer, still less for an entire brewery. What are monks doing brewing beer? Aren't they supposed to be praying and avoiding pleasure and the temptations it inevitably brings? Will not drinking beer lead to eternal damnation? "Don't be silly," say the monks. When I talk to them about brewing, I can't help feeling that modern religion has lost something in the translation, something essential that the monks have retained behind their stone walls.

All over Europe, pubs and beer halls have always been built next to churches, and midday on Sunday will often find the flock streaming from one into the other after services, sometimes with the pastor in the lead. The Old Testament is awash in wine, and when most monasteries were still in southern Europe, most of them had vineyards to provide wine for their own sustenance. We have the French monk Dom Perignon to thank for champagne. When monasticism spread to the beer-drinking countries, the monks naturally took up brewing. In the Middle Ages, water supplies were poor, and everyone knew that drinking water might sicken or even kill you. Beer, having been boiled and then fermented, was perfectly safe and a staple food for many Europeans.

One of the basic tenets of monasticism is self-sufficiency. Saint Benedict of Monte Cassino developed the rules of monastic life in the sixth century. Not only would the monks spend many hours praying, but they had to work as well. The monastery needed to be maintained. The monastery should be constructed, he said, to provide all the necessities of life for the monks. Their needs thus provided, they would never have to venture outside to face the temptations of secular life. There were, however, other temptations. Local lords, looking to secure their places in the afterlife, constantly curried favor with the abbots, and this inevitably led to some straying from the path set by St. Benedict.

In the 1100s, St. Bernard broke with the Benedictines and founded the strict Cistercian order, the rules of which call on monks to perform manual labor. Despite St. Bernard's intentions, this provision was largely ignored until the seventeenth century, when the Abbaye de la Trappe was founded in Normandy. Its monks were known as Trappists, and they soon spread to other areas of northern France. The Trappists sincerely believed in both self-sufficiency and manual labor for monks. Local lords ceded land to them, and the monks worked in the fields, growing wheat and barley. All the Trappist monasteries brewed beer, both for themselves and for sale.

The monks made great beer. They were serenely patient, well educated, thorough, and motivated by faith. Their costs were low, so they were able to use better ingredients than commercial brewers. In the 1700s the Trappists were driven out of France by the revolution and resettled in Belgium and the Netherlands. They resumed brewing in the 1830s, and the reputation and availability of their beers have increased ever since.

There are five Trappist breweries left in the world, all in Belgium: Chimay, Westmalle, Orval, Rochefort, and Sint Sixtus-Westvleteren. Until recently, there

Demandez sounds rather pushy, but in French it is less demanding. No doubt people politely asked the monks for their "Speciale 1956."

was a Trappist brewery in the Netherlands, Schaapskooi, but it has now licensed its brewing to a secular brewery. A non-Trappist Cistercian monastery, Val-Dieu, has recently installed a brewery, and its beers are starting to become available. These are all enclosed communities, and the brewing takes place within the walls of the abbeys. The term "Trappist," when applied to beer, is similar to an *appellation controleé* in wine—only these five breweries may use it, and only they may affix the seal "Authentic Trappist Product" to their bottles. Technically speaking, Trappist ales are not a single style of beer but a family of styles. Those styles have had a profound influence on brewing in Belgium and beyond. Since life has scarcely changed inside the walls of the monasteries for centuries, the beers reflect styles of brewing that no doubt otherwise would have been lost. Among them, the Trappist breweries make about twenty different beers. Trappist beers are all top-fermented and bottle-conditioned. They tend toward sweetness, but some are dry. Most are dark, but four are pale. All are strong, fruity, spicy, earthy, and aromatic. All are complex and wonderful with food.

While some of the Trappist beers defy neat categorization, dubbel and tripel have become styles unto themselves. However, the Belgians can't seem to decide how to spell these terms. *Dubbel* is alternatively spelled *dobbel* or *dobbelen*, and some brewers throw in an extra "p" to create *trippel*. There are also varying theories as to what the names originally meant. Some people say that the names refer to the number of fermentations these beers have, but that answer is unsatisfying—many Belgian beers have multiple stages of fermentation. Other people, perhaps closer to the mark, believe that the names refer to the strength of the beers, though the math doesn't quite work out. More likely, casks were once marked "X," "XX," or "XXX," in ascending order of strength.

Whatever the truth is, the two styles at least are clear. Dubbels are deep russet-brown beers, a bit strong at about 6.5 to 7 percent. They are brewed from pale and dark malts, but they usually also include dark candy sugar, a special type of cane or beet sugar that has been caramelized. The caramel flavors follow through into the beers, which tend to show plummy dark fruit aromatics, with chocolate, spice, rum, and raisin notes. The palate is medium-bodied and somewhat sweet in the center but tends to finish dry. Bitterness is light to moderate, and the better examples are bottle-conditioned.

Tripels have a more innocuous appearance, but they pack a bigger punch at about 9 percent. They have a sunny golden-orange color; a rocky white head; lightly hoppy, fruity, and spicy aromatics; and a brisk, lightly malty palate showing some sweetness in the center and a dry finish. Bitterness is restrained but snappy. Tripels are brewed from pale malts and white candy sugar and are almost always bottle-conditioned. At this strength, the alcohol becomes part of the flavor profile, but pleasantly so—the beer remains refreshing and light on the palate.

The beers produced by the five Trappist breweries are much admired and imitated. When a brewery takes the name of a saint or a nonbrewing abbey for its products, the beer is referred to as an "abbey ale." If an abbey is involved, it needn't be Trappist; Benedictines and other monastic orders once brewed beer as well. Sometimes, the beer is brewed on behalf of an abbey that no longer has a brewery, and sometimes there is no genuine connection to any existing monastery—breweries have named beers after centuries-old ruins of monasteries. These beers almost always mimic the characteristic flavors of the Trappist originals. Westmalle Tripel, for example, has spawned dozens of imitators. Despite being secular, many abbey ales are excellent.

Never serve any of these beers below 50 degrees Fahrenheit; it would be like going to a symphony concert wearing earplugs. You'd miss the whole thing, and that would be a shame—these are some of the finest, most complex beers in the world. Serve them at cellar temperature, 50 to 55 degrees Fahrenheit, in a large wineglass (meant for red wine), a brandy snifter, or—best of all—the brewery's own chalice.

Chimay: Abbaye Notre-Dame de Scourmont

Little more than ten years ago, the name Chimay was seen or heard in the United States only rarely, and then only in reverent, hushed whispers. As an appreciation of traditional beer swept the country, this Trappist beer helped lead the charge. The name Chimay is now bandied about freely in bars and restaurants from Houston to Hong Kong. Chimay has become by far the most famous and widely distributed of the Trappist beers.

The monks named their beer after the nearby small town of Chimay, only a few miles from the French border. The abbey is nestled in a patch of Ardennes forest, which opens up to a tableau of dairy pastures where the monks' cows idle away their hours; their milk will become Chimay cheese.

The monastery was established in 1850 and began commercial brewing in 1862. Demand for Chimay beer grew steadily, forcing the monastery to replace its gorgeous traditional copper brewhouse with a less aesthetic functional assembly in the early 1990s. Softly acidic brewing water is pumped from the abbey's own artesian wells and blended with local Belgian malts, candy sugar, and German and American hops to create the three Chimay beers. The house yeast strain ferments at very warm temperatures, creating very dry beers with distinctive notes of dark fruit, pepper, and a hint of nutmeg. All three beers show some sweetness in the center of the palate, but this is due to fruity aromatics rather than residual sugar.

Critics have complained that the new brewhouse has cramped the style of the exuberant yeast, leading to beers with cleaner, less spicy flavors. It is true that at one time the beers were more boldly aromatic, but a bit of aging will bring out the yeast's best work, and the Chimay beers are still of the highest quality. Chimay identifies its beers by the color of the cap on the bottle, and all three are available in distinctively shaped standard-size bottles or larger heavy champagne-style 75-centiliter bottles finished with corks held in place by wire hoods. All the beers are bottle-conditioned and sit on a sediment of live yeast. If laid down properly, they will become fruitier and drier over time.

The original Chimay beer is called **Chimay Rouge** ("red") and is brewed in the dubbel style. It is russet-brown with a fluffy white head and shows light aromatics of malt, black pepper, prunes, black currants, and hops. The bitterness is pointed but restrained, leading to an expansive, lightly fruity medium-bodied palate and a dry finish. In its larger, cork-finished bottling, this beer is labeled "Premiere." Chimay Rouge carries its strength, about 7 percent, with considerable grace. The other Chimay beers are stronger still, though the monks do produce a simple golden beer at about 4.5 percent for their own day-to-day sustenance. This beer has no label and is never sold to the public. When I've tasted it at the abbey, I've been fascinated by how the house yeast still manages to show its influence in a beer of such modest strength.

Chimay also brews a golden beer for the outside world, but it is certainly not modest. **Chimay Blanche** ("white") is a radical departure from the other Chimay beers and may be viewed, broadly, as a tripel. It has a burnished honey color, raises a rocky white head, and displays a magnificently bright hop aroma. On the palate, the beer is quite dry and sharply hoppy, with flavors of caramelized sugar in the center, combined with a fine acidity. The finish is clean and dry, leaving a lingering impression of hops and peaches. In 1986, the town of Chimay celebrated its 500th anniversary, prompting the abbey to put Chimay Blanche into a larger bottle and call it Cinq Cents. At 8 percent, and carrying a robust blast of hop character, this is a brash, muscular beer brewed with admirable confidence. Rumor has it that this is the monks' own favorite, but they are characteristically silent when asked to choose. Chimay has started to produce this beer in kegs, making it the second Trappist beer to become available on draft. The draft version is even more aromatic, with hops leaping out of the goblet. It's bright, snappy, and intense—perhaps even an improvement over the original bottled version.

Chimay Bleu ("blue") is the abbey's strongest beer, and probably the most popular Trappist beer in the secular world. A dark reddish-brown, it strikes me as a concentrated version of Chimay Rouge, edging up to just over 9 percent. At this strength, the yeast combines with dark malts to produce a wealth of subtle port-like dark fruit aromatics, backed by notes of nutmeg and black pepper. The bitterness is firm but stands aside for the rich, plummy malt center and then reasserts itself in the dry finish. In the large bottling, this beer is known as Grande Reserve, an appropriate name for a beer that ages very gracefully. Many aficionados prefer Chimay Bleu when it has been cellared for five years or more, taking on sherry and port notes as the spiciness intensifies. This is the only Chimay beer that carries the year of production on its label.

Chimay owns a small inn near the monastery, called Auberge de Poteaupré. For lovers of Chimay beers, there can be no better place to taste them. In front of the inn is a patch of thick Ardennes forest—the monastery is hidden behind the trees. In the back is a solarium and a patio opening onto an idyllic pasture backed by a line of trees. Auberge de Poteaupré is run by Vincent Sacré, a boyishly exuberant fellow gifted with culinary talents that could challenge some of the best restaurants in Paris. After a spectacular dinner matched with Chimay beers, he brought out some aged bottles of Chimay Bleu. We'd been feeling tired after the meal, but suddenly everyone perked up. The 1997 bottling showed a subtle fruitiness—plums, raisins, nutmeg, some apple peel, and a burst of black pepper. In a bottle from 1993 these characteristics were intensified, even though the beer seemed lighter on the palate. It was silky and soft—the hops had dropped back and the beer had become sherryish, showing burnt oranges along with the apple peel and dried fruits. It was stunning, but Vincent Sacré had more up his sleeve, and a bit of cajoling pried loose a bottle of 1988. It was worth the wait. The yeast had dried the beer out and made it stronger—the strength was apparent but well integrated into a portlike palate. Caramel flavors came to the fore, carrying stewed fruits and nutmeg. It was truly magnificent.

Chimay produces a wonderfully medieval goblet for its beers, and there is a graphic on the bottle label that apparently forbids you to pour the beer into an ordinary tumbler. Given the provenance of the beer, it seems wise to comply, and the beer certainly tastes better in a goblet. The same label urges you to serve the beer between 59 and 65 degrees Fahrenheit, and far be it from me to disagree, though I will point out that Chimay Blanche will easily survive a gentle chilling to 48 degrees Fahrenheit or so. Chimay Rouge and Bleu should certainly not be over-chilled, as their subtle aromatics will be dulled.

Orval: Abbaye Notre-Dame d'Orval

The natural beauty of the Gaume valley, running between the Chier and Semoy rivers at the border with France, would inspire spiritualism in the stoniest heart.

More than 900 years ago, Benedictine monks traveled here from Calabria and established a monastery. The Benedictines didn't last; a half century later, Cistercian monks from Champagne reestablished the monastery as Abbaye Notre-Dame d'Orval. Orval means "valley of gold," a pretty but odd-sounding name for a religious community of ascetics who have given up all worldly possessions. The name derives from a local legend that a countess, Matilda of Tuscany, once lost a gold ring in a pool near the site of the abbey. She knelt at the edge of the pool and prayed for the ring to be returned to her, promising that she would build a monastery there if her wish was granted. A trout rose miraculously from the water, carrying her ring in its mouth. The princess kept her word and built Abbaye Notre-Dame d'Orval. The trout clutching the gold ring, an intriguingly pagan-looking heraldic symbol, still decorates Orval's handsome art deco label.

Perhaps, while she was at it, the countess should have also asked for divine protection for her monastery. Despite the fairy-tale nature of the legend, medieval Europe was a rough place, and over the centuries the Orval monastery was gutted by fires and savaged by wars. As the eighteenth century drew to a close, the French Revolution drove Louis XVI from the throne, and he fled toward sanctuary at Orval. He never made it. Neither did Notre-Dame d'Orval, which was sacked and destroyed. In 1926, the Trappist order built a new monastery amid the ruins of the old. The present abbey buildings, built in glowing golden local sandstone, are a powerful blend of Romanesque and art deco influences. The beautiful copper brewhouse, which occupies its own small building, was built in 1931 to help finance the reconstruction of the abbey. Orval's commercial director, François de Harenne, is a descendent of Countess Matilda. His family was once quite wealthy, but remembering the countess's promise, the family donated its fortune to help rebuild Orval in the 1930s. François, a monkish man who is clearly proud of his beer, doesn't seem to have any regrets.

Unlike the other Trappist breweries, Orval produces only one beer, named simply **Orval.** The distinctive bottle, shaped like a little bowling pin, is austerely decorated with an elegant neck label. The beer inside is distinctive as well. Orval is famous for what both the monks and beer enthusiasts refer to as the *goût d'Orval. Goût* literally means "taste," but a better translation here might be "essence" or perhaps even "spirit." The beer is a sunny golden orange and raises a pillowy white head. Like many Belgian breweries, Orval has its own glassware, and its grail-like goblet is my favorite of all.

OPPOSITE: An art deco influence is strongly evident in Orval's 1930s architecture.

A well-poured chalice of Orval is a magnificent sight. The aromatics are wonderfully complex, an herbal blend of hops, sage, hay, flowers, damp earth, and saddle leather. On the palate the beer is stunningly dry, with an appetizing knifelike bitterness opening onto a fruity herbal center. Hops bring up the rear, and the finish is clean and snappy. Orval has a flavor revered not only in Belgium but the world over. There is absolutely nothing like it.

Orval is brewed from a blend of European barleys, some of them specially malted to the brewer's specifications. Candy sugar, which looks just like the chunky "rock candy" I used to love as a kid, is added to the kettle. (I can't believe I used to eat pure sugar on a string, but I did.) The sugar ferments out completely, lending the beer a light-bodied dryness. Then follows a succession of fermentations. The first is carried out by a regular top-fermenting ale yeast and takes several days. Then a blend of ten yeast strains is added, one of them particularly special—Brettanomyces. The whiff of "saddle leather" that raised your eyebrow earlier is developed by this yeast strain, which becomes more dominant as the beer ages. Brettanomyces is also able to consume sugars that other yeasts can't, causing the beer to become drier still. Dry hops are also added at this stage, adding their floral aromatics to the mix. The beer rests on the hops for three weeks or so before being bottled with some fresh yeast and priming sugar. At this point, the bottles are placed in a special temperature-controlled aging room. During the next nine weeks, the beer finishes its refermentation in the bottle and the *goût d'Orval* emerges. The beer is then ready to leave the closed, silent monastery and step out into a wider world.

Orval is available only in its neat little bottle—no kegs are produced. Aside from their beer, the monks at Orval produce some very nice cheese and excellent bread. It seems they truly do have everything they need.

Like all bottle-conditioned beers, Orval changes over time. When fresh, it shows bright, lemony hop notes in the nose. As the beer ages, it becomes drier and the fresh hops diminish, replaced by earth, leather, horse blanket, and herbs. As the yeast consumes the remaining sugars, the beer also becomes stronger; it will leave the brewery at perhaps 6.2 percent, but that strength will eventually rise to about 7 percent. By this time, the beer will have very high carbonation, supporting a monumental cap of foam. Connoisseurs will each have their preferred stage of the beer's development, and the fact that it ages so interestingly is part of its charm. From bright hoppy youth to earthy, leathery age, it leads a fascinating life. We are lucky to share it.

Westmalle: Abdij Trappisten van Westmalle

Of all the Trappist breweries, Abdij Trappisten van Westmalle has arguably been the most influential. Strong beers marked "XXX" on the barrel or bottle have probably long been referred to as tripel, but it is Westmalle Tripel that has defined this style of beer. Golden, fruity, dry, and spirituous, Westmalle Tripel is a world classic.

The abbey, officially named Our Lady of the Sacred Heart, was founded in 1794 near the town of Westmalle, just northeast of Antwerp. Brewing began in 1836, but the beer was for consumption only by the cloistered monks. It first escaped from behind the monastery's high walls in the 1870s, when it was sold in the village to raise money for the projects and maintenance of the abbey. Around 1920, Westmalle began commercial production on the monastery grounds, and its famous Tripel emerged shortly after World War II.

Most of the abbey and its defensive-looking walls were built around the turn of the twentieth century. The brewhouse itself was built in the 1930s and has racy art deco flourishes. Inside, a copper brewhouse gleams, set into beautifully tiled floors in a striking pattern of ochres, greens, russets, and grays. It's one of the most beautiful brewhouses I've ever seen. Underneath the gleaming floors is a set of gas jets to fire the kettle. Direct-fired kettles are now rare—steam heats the kettles of most modern breweries. Direct firing leads to hot spots where sugars in the wort are caramelized. As a result, Westmalle's beers have a distinctive background note of burnt sugar. Many brewers have attempted to capture this flavor in steam-fired systems, but so far without success.

Brewing water, high in mineral salts, is drawn from the abbey's own well. This is blended with malts from Belgium, Germany, and France. Dark malts complete the brewing grist for the dubbel, and dark candy sugar is added in the kettle. **Westmalle Dubbel** is the definition of the dubbel style. The beer is russet-brown with a fluffy tan head and shows aromatics of raisin-bread toast, plums, dates, and bananas. On the palate, it is soft but insistently expansive, showing complex fruit, chocolate, and an overall impression of juicy tawny port. The finish is clean and dry, with a moderate lingering bitterness. Westmalle Dubbel has stunning complexity for a beer of its strength—only 6.5 percent.

A keg-conditioned version of Westmalle Dubbel is supposedly available at only three establishments in the entire country. (However, there are plans to expand the draft production.) One of these is a tiny bar called Vieux Bon Temps ("good old days"), down a narrow dark alley near the Grande Place in Brussels. On one trip my colleague Steve and I found ourselves here, and the matronly barkeep revealed in conspiratorial but proud tones that she had Westmalle Dubbel on draft. As she poured her treasure into Westmalle's sparkling cut-crystal chalices, her satisfied smile spoke volumes. So did the beer. We never did make it to dinner.

Westmalle Tripel, at 9.5 percent, achieves an elegant spirituous quality. A strong wort derived from pale malts joins white candy sugar and half a dozen hop varieties in the kettle. The beer is bright and golden, raising a creamy white head. The nose is an interplay of hops, wet iron, tangerines, and preserved lemons. There is an abrupt burst of hops up front on the palate, but this quickly gives way to a cleanly malty center with a hint of sweetness and a beautiful mélange of fruit and hops. The finish is hoppy and dry, with a clean mineral bite. The aftertaste is interestingly herbal, with a slightly sulfurous vegetable-like quality, a mixture of hops and bell peppers. It is intensely appetizing.

Rochefort: Abbaye Notre-Dame de Saint-Remy

I wasn't having much luck in my attempts to arrange a trip to Abbaye Notre-Dame de Saint-Remy, the monastery that brews the brilliant Rochefort Trappist ales. Frustration was setting in. Some Trappist monasteries are more closed than others, and this one seemed to be sealed tight. I decided to call the abbey myself and plead my case directly. At the other end of the line was Father Abbot Jacques Emmanuel, the "head monk." When I told him that I had enjoyed his beer in New York City, he suddenly warmed, saying, "I don't know how you managed to get it. You must be quite clever."

The Rochefort beers are difficult to find, but they are worth the effort. The abbey sits near the small town of Rochefort, in the picturesque countryside of the

A brewers' conference over a chalice at Abbaye Rochefort.

Ardennes. Saint-Remy was established as a convent in 1230 and was converted to a monastery in 1464. Brewing began in 1595 but was brought to a halt by the French Revolution, which forced the abbey to close in 1794. The Trappists reoccupied the abbey in 1887 and built a new brewery in 1899. Parts of the abbey have a distinctly medieval look, although the oldest buildings are later, dating from the 1600s.

Built in the 1960s, Rochefort's brewhouse is stunning and pristine, a Jules Vernesque symphony in copper, stone, beige tiles, and stained glass. It remains the most beautiful brewery I've ever seen. I felt the sin of envy creeping over me as I stepped into the room. Saint Arnold, the patron saint of brewers, stared silently down at me from a wall plaque—I quickly banished my envy. Frère Luc, a tall, sprightly man with an easy smile and a sense of grounded calm, showed us through the brewery as another monk sat patiently in front of the kettle, waiting to add the next charge of hops.

All the Rochefort beers are dark. They are known simply as Six, Eight, and Ten—names indicating the concentration of the corresponding worts, as they would once have been expressed in the now abandoned scale of Belgian brewing degrees. A blend of malts, some of them caramelized, represents imports from all over the world. Caramel flavor and color are further developed from dark candy sugar added to the kettle. German Hallertauer and Styrian Golding hops are added for both bitterness and aroma. All the Rochefort beers undergo a very warm rapid fermentation followed by a period of bottle-conditioning. The abbey does not age the beer before releasing it, preferring to allow commercial concerns to age the beer as they see fit. Rochefort's beers are released about a month after they are brewed. When young, they can be slightly hot, but this character calms within months, and the beers age wonderfully.

Rochefort Six is brewed in the dubbel style and is dancingly light on the palate despite a strength of 7.5 percent. Pale brown with a hint of red, it raises a fine cap of tawny foam. The aromatics are full of dark fruits with a hint of hop. The palate is soft, slightly sweet, and subtle, with a round mouth feel and herbal flavors bordering on mintiness. Plummy dark fruits develop into the finish.

Rochefort Eight is more concentrated, at 9.2 percent, with a full russet-brown color and figgy aromatics. The palate shows a firm, broad bitterness wrapped around a dark fruit center of prunes and figs. Caramel and warm malty flavors play throughout, until it pulls up dry in the finish.

Rochefort Ten is a powerhouse at 11.3 percent, and it uses that power to drive a palate of astonishing complexity. The beer is deep brown with red highlights under a rocky tan head. The malt is forward in the nose, joined by raisins, prunes, dates, figs, sherry, burnt sugar, and Grandma's hard candies. The bitterness is firm and mouth-coating, supporting a sweet center with a portlike intensity. The dark fruit flavors come in waves, the whole show wrapping up with a mouthwatering twinge of acidity. Hops linger in the warm glow of the aftertaste. It is a truly magnificent creation.

Frère Luc kindly offered lunch at the abbey, which we gratefully accepted. We were shown to an elegant room decorated with religious imagery. Frère Luc dashed off for noon prayers, but eventually someone showed up with a big tureen of soup. We ladled it out and found it tasty, if austere; it was a smooth blend of pumpkins, onions, carrots, and other vegetables. It was very nice with the Rochefort Six, which we drank from the abbey's handsome chalices. We were famished, but somehow it seemed very monkish to have a simple soup and a Trappist beer for lunch. As we prepared to leave, the fellow came back with more bowls, followed by a big pot of stew. The aroma made our heads swim. It was essentially a bacon stew, made of lardons, pork, and onions, with some tomatoes, cream, and plenty of pepper. I've never had anything like it—it was a true farmer's dish, something to keep you through a long, cold, rainy Belgian winter. We tried not to eat too much of it, but we were helpless—it was so delicious that we couldn't stop. Rochefort Eight was a perfect accompaniment. The meal finished with a fluffy chocolate *gâteau* with ice cream. Someone at the abbey is a very good cook indeed. As we finally rolled ourselves out to our car, our hosts waved merrily from the front door. They seemed happy, and it was easy to see why.

Westvleteren: Abdij Sint Sixtus

The competition for the title "rarest Trappist beer" is very close, but in this respect Westvleteren wins out even over Rochefort. Westvleteren's beers are available only from a drive-up hatch at the abbey gates or from the café In De Vrede, across the road. Even then, not all the beers are sold at any given time. At the hatch, the beers are rationed to drivers, and long lines can form when the strongest beer is available. Owners of specialist cafés line up to stock their establishments. Occasionally someone collects up enough cases to ship overseas, and several hundred bottles make it into the United States.

At one time, the abbey's beer was widely available, but this was not a true Trappist product—it was made under license by a brewery nearby. The abbey beer—St. Sixtus—took the proper name of the abbey itself, which is Abdij Sint Sixtus. The licensing arrangement ended several years ago, and Westvleteren now sells only what it needs to support the needs of the abbey. The needs of monks are modest—the brothers brew only once a week.

The abbey, which was founded in 1831, sits in the open fields of west Flanders, in the township of Westvleteren, near Ieper (Ypres). The brewery was built in the mid-1830s but never became a truly commercial establishment. A modern brewhouse was installed in 1990, replacing a rustic setup nearly a century old. Wort is derived from pale malts, which join white and dark sugar in the kettle. German hops spice the beers, which are fermented with the same yeast used by the monks' counterparts at Westmalle. The beers have extended maturation periods—up to three months—before being reyeasted, primed with sugar, and bottle-conditioned.

If you ever catch sight of a bottle of Westvleteren beer in the United States, it is almost certain to be the strongest of them, which has a yellow cap and is known as Twelve. The name corresponds to its strength in the old Belgian scale. It is also known as Abt ("abbot"). **Westvleteren Abt** has a rust-brown color and wears a tight-knit rocky head. The aroma is toffeeish, deeply malty, and yeasty, with notes of dates, cherries, and faint smoke. The bitterness is sharp, with a metallic edge that coats the palate as sweet malt bursts through the center, showing raspberries, strawberries, and rose petals. Hop bitterness reins in the sweetness, and the beer finishes sharply, with a spirituous glow brought on by its considerable strength. The beer goes into the bottle at about 10.5 percent but may eventually reach 11.5 percent. It is a powerful beer in all respects, combining refined complex malt and fruit aromatics with an aggressive hop attack.

Trappist and Abbey Ales with Food

Belgium's Trappist ales and their secular offspring are some of the most rewarding beers in the world to pair with food. Their complex flavor gives you many reference points to work with in seeking harmony with a wide range of dishes. Some matches will be quite simple, and these can be delightful. There also exists, however, the possibility of an epiphany, one of those moments when all the planets seem to align on your palate and you suddenly understand the true meaning of life. Somehow, it seems appropriate that these beers in particular should possess such powers. For the truly brilliant matches, you'll need to use your imagination and creativity, matching beer flavors to food flavors in myriad combinations. If it sounds daunting, relax. It isn't intimidating—it's fun! And when you hit the jackpot, believe me, you'll know it.

Let's start with the beers that actually fall into style categories. Dubbels are always dark in color and have dark flavors—caramel, toffee, rum, chocolate, raisins, plums. Bitterness is moderate, but there's more than enough cutting power for most dishes, and carbonation is high. All dubbels show at least some sweetness in the center, though many finish dry. The best are wonderfully complex. They are at their best with gamy red meats. Dubbels are particularly good with lamb, which combines gamy flavors with some sweetness and an affinity for herbs. The caramelized flavors will work with the surface of the meat, and the fruity flavors will dive in to meet the rest of the dish. Fruit sauces will lead you to sweeter dubbels, which will add their own fruit flavors.

Duck, which I categorize as a red meat, is another great combination with dubbel. Unlike chicken, duck has yet to be made bland by modern farming methods. Dubbel's burst of dark fruit flavors suits it wonderfully. Nicely crisped duck skin is one of the most perfect pleasures that the world of food has to offer. The caramel flavors in the dubbel will surround the duck with raisins, rum, and prunes, while the carbonation lifts the fat from your palate. A great dubbel is the best thing you will ever have with braised duck legs or duck confit. Foie gras, my favorite part of the duck (after the skin), is also a great partner with dubbels, for similar reasons. Here you'll want to pick sweeter dubbels to work with the richness of the foie gras and the sweetness of its usual accompaniments. The classic seared foie gras in grape sauce (a reduction of sautéed green grapes, wine or beer, duck fat, and demiglace) is terrific with dubbel, which not only matches the flavors of the dish but also resets the palate with its fluffy soft carbonation. This makes every bite as good as the first one, which is a very neat trick with something this rich. Dubbel is a much better partner for this dish than sweet wine, which not only bogs down the palate after the first bite but also puts far too much sweetness on the palate early in the meal—foie gras is usually served as a starter. Dubbels are also a fine partner for sweetbreads, which are usually served with a rich sauce. Sweetbreads themselves are very rich, so the palate-cleansing quality of the beer is certainly appreciated, and the dark fruit and malt center of the beer is just what this dish is looking for.

Dubbels are perfectly nice with a steak but even better with beef stew. My favorite beef stew is the classic carbonnade flamande, which is essentially the national dish of Belgium (though you could also make a good argument for *moules frites*—mussels with fries). In the carbonnade, all the liquid in the stew is beer, preferably a Belgian dubbel or Flanders brown ale. It is finished with a pinch of sugar, a hint of sweet spice, and apples or prunes. It's a simple but spectacular dish, and the flavors of the beer latch onto all the flavors in the stew. On a cold winter day, it's hard to think of anything better. And, of course, carbonnade is better yet after a day or two in the refrigerator. Another classic Belgian-French dish, rabbit stew with prunes, is also wonderful with dubbel, which has its own plum, raisin, and prune flavors to echo those in the dish.

A contemplative moment—Brother Luc in the brewhouse at Abbaye Rochefort.

TOP: The term Trappist may be used only for beers brewed within monastery walls. The appellation controleé is fiercely protected. **BOTTOM:** Abbaye Notre-Dame de Scourmont is still very much a monastery, despite the fame of its Chimay beers. **OPPOSITE:** At Auberge de Poteaupré, Chef Vincent Sacré's signature dish is duck breast in a Chimay Blue sauce.

CHIMAY
CHIMAY
Auberge de Poteaupré
CHIMAY

Verboden
te roken
DE KONINCK
DE KONINCK

TOP: The brewhouse at Orval. The beer travels the world, but the monks remain here. **BOTTOM:** François de Harenne's family donated their worldly possessions to rebuild the abbey at Orval. **OPPOSITE:** De Koninck patriarch Modeste van den Bogaert enjoys a laugh and a few beers at De Pelgrim.

TOP: Production director Philippe van Assche in the beautifully tiled brewhouse at Westmalle. **BOTTOM:** Au Vieux Bon Temps in Brussels proudly serves Westmalle Dubbel on draft, a rarity even in Belgium. **OPPOSITE:** In his element—Philippe van Assche in the tasting room at Westmalle. **OVERLEAF:** Rochefort's classic brewhouse is a Jules Vernesque fantasy in copper. Rochefort's beers are difficult to find but worth the hunt.

Trappist
Westmalle

TOP: Brewmaster Rudi Ghequire is flanked by giant oak vats at Rodenbach. **BOTTOM:** The old brewhouse at Rodenbach. It's no longer used but will be maintained as part of the visitors' center. **OPPOSITE:** Chef Mario Batali at his flagship restaurant, Babbo, in New York City. Mario is fond of saison, which is a perfect match for his house-made mussetto, a Friulian pork sausage.

OMMEGANG
BABBO

The malting tower at Rodenbach is now part of the brewery's museum. It is a classic piece of Victorian brewery architecture. **OPPOSITE:** Chef Michael Romano with his melt-on-your-tongue short ribs at Union Square Café in New York City. When he tasted the dish with a Belgian dubbel, he said, "Wow, that's perfect. The raisiny flavors in the beer tie everything together."

nion Square Café

RESTAUREZ-VOUS
AU
BRU
orval

Duvel is much imitated in Belgium, and its signature glass is a national icon. **OPPOSITE:** The bright, hoppy character of Orval makes a nice match for the pork chops at Café de Bruxelles in New York City. **OVERLEAF:** Some parts of the cloistered grounds at Abbaye Rochefort resemble a medieval village. The oldest buildings date from the 1600s.

Sausages, especially those made of venison, wild boar, or lamb (lamb, rosemary, and mint sausage is a favorite), are great choices with dubbels. Once again, dark fruity flavors in the beer meet dark gamy flavors in the meat, and herbal flavors in each complete the embrace. Other preparations of venison and wild boar can also be great matches, depending on the sauce (if any), the accompaniments, and the gaminess of the meat. More powerfully flavored renditions might be better matched with dubbel's bigger brothers, which we'll get to shortly.

With white meats, look for preparations compatible with dark fruit and caramel flavors. Roast suckling pig is a good example. Dark, cracking skin has flavors that link up with caramelized malts and dark candy sugar in the beer. Prune and raisin flavors dive into the meat. Perfect harmony is not difficult to achieve here. Even without the skin, you can get some great caramelized flavors from other roasted pork dishes, such as stuffed roasted pork loin.

I like to make fun of chicken, partly because I used to love it so much when I was younger. Chickens were still chickens in those days. I know I sound like a curmudgeon when I say that I can remember when chickens were full of flavor—but I can. These days, your average supermarket chicken doesn't taste like much. (What do you want for three bucks?) Mr. Purdue has a lot to answer for. But a good free-range or organic chicken, properly prepared, can make a stunning dish, and it's well worth the few extra dollars. With dubbels, once again we want caramelization in the skin of the chicken. Simple roast chicken with stuffing can be excellent, especially if you use a high oven setting toward the end of the roasting—this results in a dark, flavorful skin. Herbal flavors in the beer can pick up on the stuffing. Use some prunes in the stuffing, and you've got a really great match. Some chefs will pan-sear chicken that's been roasted or braised, pressing it flat to a very hot skillet. It's a great technique, which can transform an ordinary bird into a work of art. Dubbel is a great partner to the delicious flavors that result.

For bigger dishes, you can step up to beers that I'll call Trappist-style dark strong ales. It's a mouthful, I'll admit. But this is Belgium we're talking about, and Belgians don't like to be pigeonholed. The beers I'm referring to are the top of the range for strength and complexity, brewed in the style of Chimay Grande Reserve (or Bleu), Rochefort Eight and Ten, and Westvleteren Twelve (Abt). Think of these beers as concentrated dubbels. More malt flavor, more fruit, often more bitterness, sometimes more sweetness to balance, and the warming effect of higher alcohol content are hallmarks of this style. Some of these are the true Trappists mentioned above; others are secular abbey ales brewed in the same style.

These are the big guns you'll pull out to take on that rare gamy venison in a sour-cherry sauce or rustic pâté de campagne served with stone-ground mustard.

They can match the deep chocolaty game flavors of duck, goose, squab, and wood pigeon (especially if wild); cut through heavy reductions; and seduce the side dishes. Braised short ribs or beef cheeks, with their dense, fatty, flavorful meat, need this level of cutting power and intensity. Roasted malt flavors will echo the surface flavors of these dishes, which are often nearly black from early searing, long slow heat, or both. Then raisin, prune, and dark spice flavors can go to work with the essential flavors of the meat. There's also an earthiness in these beers that gives them a fine affinity with mushroom sauces. Oxtail, whether presented in a stew or a terrine, is a great match with these beers as well. I once had Rochefort Ten with a terrine of oxtail and foie gras, which was shot through with pistachio slivers. It was a mind-boggling combination.

Golden, herbal, fruity, rummy, and powerful, tripels are big enough to take on boldly flavored dishes but elegant enough to dance with refined flavors. Firm bitterness and herbal aromatics make tripels perfect for good sausages, particularly garlic Toulouse, bratwurst, duck, and Armagnac, and chicken truffle. Just about anything from artisanal sausage makers like D'Artagnan, Aidell's, or Trois Petits Cochons will work very nicely. Tripel will play along beautifully if you want to serve the sausages as an Alsatian choucroute, complete with pickled cabbage—the beer can handle the acidity. If you put the sausages into a cassoulet, all the better (I'm always in favor of duck). Cassoulet, wonderful as it is, can be as heavy as wet cement—all those sausages, ham hocks, duck legs, and beans are delicious but daunting. Tripel has the power to lift away the beans, while its herbal flavors link up with the thyme, garlic, and meat. Suddenly, the dish seems much lighter and even more flavorful.

The herbal character of tripels makes them a fine partner to wild game birds, especially pheasant, partridge, and quail. A bit of lemon or orange zest in a stuffing will make the match even more profound. Tripel is an excellent accompaniment to herb-crusted veal dishes such as classic Wiener schnitzel or sage-crusted saltimbocca. If you don't have or don't want veal, either of these dishes can be made with pork (which is even tastier). Gamy hams like prosciutto di Parma, Serrano, and Bayonne are wonderful with tripel. (For a great hors d'oeuvre, wrap these hams, sliced thin, around a piece of ripe Brie and serve with tripel. Watch guests swoon.) At La Palapa, a terrific traditional Mexican restaurant in New York, I had Chimay Blanche with quesadillas rajitas poblanas, stuffed with cheese, chili poblano peppers, and onions. The herbal character of the beer linked up with the strong green vegetable flavors in the poblano peppers, while the firm hops cut through the cheese. The match was spectacular.

Almost anything in a pesto sauce, from pasta to fish, will work quite well—tripels really dig basil. Thai chicken with holy basil is a very nice match. Because tripels tend to have citric notes, anything served with an orange- or lemon-based sauce will tend to work well, as long as the sauce is not too sweet. Even then, sweeter tripels may still do the trick. A fish dish with mandarin sauce is a good example, as is lemon chicken.

For seafood, you'll largely want to stick to stronger, oilier fish like salmon and Arctic char, fish in sauces (monkfish in lemon sauce is a favorite), or fish that's been grilled or fried. Most poached fish will be overwhelmed by tripel, but fried fish has fat to blunt the beer's hop attack and some caramelized flavors to work with the malt. Tripels often have a faint flavor of burnt sugar in the background, and it can find some nice echoes in grilled fish. Tuna, swordfish, and sardines are strong enough to stand up for themselves and will make very pleasant matches, especially if they're grilled. Grilled octopus seems to appreciate the hard mineral edge of these beers, and the sea-sweetness of the meat finds a nice harmony with the malt sweetness. Sweeter tripels are also fine matches for seared scallops. When seafood gangs up in the form of bouillabaisse, tripel makes a nice foil, especially if the broth is fairly herbal.

Along with the herbs and citrus, tripels often show a refreshing whiff of sulfur. Don't run away—there's some sulfur character in almost all beers (and wines, for that matter), and it can be an important part of the overall aromatic blend. In tripels, the sulfur tends to play out as a distant vegetable note—a hint, perhaps, of bell pepper. This gives tripel a surprising affinity with slightly sulfurous vegetables in the cabbage family, like cauliflower, broccoli, and brussels sprouts. Some people have noted that tripels are quite nice with asparagus. So eat your veggies.

I've left Orval for last, because it is an entirely idiosyncratic beer. There are many tripels and dubbels brewed in Belgium, and quite a few beers brewed in the dark strong Trappist style typified by Chimay Grande Reserve. The *goût d'Orval* is unequalled.

Where to start? Let's begin at the beginning—Orval is the perfect aperitif. Bone-dry, bitter, and aromatic with a zippy acidity, it has everything that the French and Italians would look for in a predinner drink. It's mouthwatering, and few beers set you up for a good meal the way this one does. Serve it moderately chilled in champagne glasses with hors d'oeuvres, and you'll have an instant conversation piece to start your party. Few champagnes show this level of complexity (and those that do, you'll want to keep for yourself). Orval has a complex nose of citric hops, lemon zest, sage leaves, saddle leather, wet wool, and damp earth.

Courtesy Merchant du Vin.

Orval's skittle-shaped bottle, diamond-shaped label, and elegant chalice are as distinctive as the beer itself.

Funky, salty flavors will provide a brilliant counterpoint to the beer. Orval will draw the salt out of well-aged prosciutto and then send its funky earthy flavors in to commune with the gaminess of the ham. The band-saw bitterness will slice through the oil of grilled sardines, while the lemon-zest aromatics ramp up the flavor of the fish and the damp earth meets the open sea on your palate. If you want to take it a step further, serve the grilled sardine filet on a homemade potato chip cooked in olive oil. This can be dangerous, mind you—your guests may want to move in.

I suppose it's obvious by now that Orval is great with fish. The beer has cutting and lifting power but remains fluffy and light, the perfect foil for a wide variety of fish preparations. Because Orval has bright aromatics (lemon zest) and dark aromatics (damp earth and leather) in a unique interplay, it goes with almost everything. It will work just as well with stuffed trout drizzled with fresh lemon juice as it will with roasted monkfish in a porcini mushroom sauce. The beer's lemon and earth components are great with Ligurian or Provençal fish preparations, like snapper with herbs, olives, and lemon. With strong, oily fish like salmon, char, and bluefish, it cuts through the fat, lifts the oil, and exposes the full flavor of the fish, working extra magic with its citrus components. Smoked salmon also makes a nice partner, and Orval can handle mackerel and herring, even when they are kippered. Another terrific match is bacala or brandade de morue, the Mediterranean dish of salt cod whipped with potatoes. Orval's acidity allows it to work very nicely with lime- or vinegar-cured fish, whether it's the Spanish escaveche or its descendent, the spicy Caribbean "ceviched fish."

Back on land, Orval is excellent with coarse gamy sausages, especially venison or wild boar. Sweet Italian sausage, which is often spiced with fennel seeds and sage, is also a great partner. Saltimbocca, which combines flattened veal or pork paillard with prosciutto and sage leaves, is perfect with Orval. As I noted earlier, Orval has an excellent affinity for mushrooms, so you can try it with any dish served with a mushroom sauce. I've particularly enjoyed it with a buttery, flaky wild mushroom strudel.

Notable Secular Producers of Abbey-Style Beers

DE GOUDEN BOOM I owe the town of Bruges a debt of gratitude. Bruges introduced me to the wonders of Belgian brewing. I first went to Bruges in 1984, and it remains one of the most beautiful towns I've ever seen, a medieval confection of canals, little bridges, and gabled architecture. Here the Vanneste family has run this brewery since the 1870s, though it has taken on larger partners along the way. De Gouden Boom ("the golden tree") is probably best known for its excellent witbier, known in the United States as Blanche de Bruges and in Europe as Brugse Tarwebier. De Gouden Boom also brews two very good tripels, one for itself and another for an abbey. Its own **Brugse Tripel** is darker than most tripels, with a full pumpkin orange color and a firm rocky head. The aroma is a complex blend of dark fruits (dates, figs), hops, and sweet spice. The palate is soft, rich, and creamy, dry but showing plenty of fruit. Hops pull everything into a pleasant balance, and the finish is warming, long, and dry. This beer will be very nice with herbal preparations of rabbit, partridge, or quail and would also be a good partner to monkfish and lobster.

For the monastery Steenbrugge, De Gouden Boom brews **Steenbrugge Tripel Blonde**, a full gold beer with a fluffy white head. The nose is gorgeous—herbal, hoppy, and spicy, with a whiff of hot-spring sulfur that quickly dissipates. The palate is well balanced, with light bitterness supporting restrained malt sweetness. The finish is dry with a mineral tang. An excellent rendition—try it with seafood dishes, game birds, herbal poultry dishes, pâtés, and sausages. The abbey dubbel, **Steenbrugge Dubbel Bruin**, displays a light mélange of raisins, hops, and rum in the aroma. This beer has a light touch; bitterness is restrained, and the palate opens up sweet, with a burst of raisiny fruit and chocolate in the center, then pulls back to close bone-dry with a slight acidic tang. A very elegant beer, and a fine partner to rack of lamb with rosemary and olives, venison, braised beef dishes, beef stews, Mediterranean rabbit preparations, and duck in mole negro.

VAN STEENBERGE Not to be confused with Steenbrugge, this brewery is located in Ertvelde, east Flanders, and produces a wide array of beer under many names. In the 1390s the royal estate at Corsendonc passed into the hands of the Augustinian order and became Corsendonc Priory, a reknowned center of ecclesiastical scholarship. The priory was sacked in the 1420s, restored in the 1600s, and closed in 1784. The lovely buildings remain, but the abbey is no more. The current Corsendonk beers are made at two different breweries by Jef Keersmaekers, whose family has long been active in Flemish brewing. Perhaps it's a good thing that he has no monks peering over his shoulder—the monks might look askance at the name of Keersmaekers' Corsendonk Pater Noster (Our Father), brewed for him by Van Steenberge. In the United States, this beer is known by a more boring name, **Corsendonk Abbey Brown Ale**; America's religious fervor seems to have made the brewery nervous. This abbey dubbel is a deep reddish-brown with an aroma redolent of port, raisins, figs, dates, prunes, dark rum, and chocolate with a smoky backdrop. The bitterness is light, and the beer is expansive on the palate, combining sweet flavors of dark fruit with a fine acidity in the center, sailing through to a long, dry finish. Chocolate lingers in the aftertaste. Wonderfully complex, and great with carbonnade flamande (for which it also makes an excellent base), short ribs, venison, game pâtés, wood pigeon, and wild pheasant.

DU BOCQ To create his tripel, Jef Keersmaeker left Flanders and went south to Purnode. Here the Du Bocq Brewery produces a profusion of beers, including the tripel Corsendonk Agnus Dei (Lamb of God). In the United States, this beer has the bowdlerized name **Corsendonk Abbey Pale Ale**, which is confusing but avoids trouble in the Bible Belt. This beer has a full gold color and an orangey aroma showing hops in the background. On the palate, it's round, silky, and smooth, caressing the tongue, with hops perfectly balanced against candyish sweet malt. The finish is very long and drying, leaving a lingering impression of fresh bread. A stylish, almost slick rendition with no rough edges. Try this with prosciutto, pasta carbonara, pasta in a Gorgonzola sauce, bass in a mandarin orange sauce, lemon chicken, or good pork sausages.

BROUWERIJ MOORTGAT Best known for the strong golden ale Duvel, the family-owned Moortgat brewery of Breendonk also produces a line of beers named for the

Benedictine abbey of Maredsous. **Maredsous 8 Dobbel** derives its number from the old scale of Belgian degrees, referring to the strength of the original wort. The beer has a beautiful garnet color and raises a rocky tan head. The aroma is terrific, a dance of biscuits, rum, and raisins. The beer opens up on the palate with foamy pinpoint carbonation and a light bitterness. It seems sweet at first but then dries as flavors of concentrated raisins, dark sugar, and dark rum combine with a winy acidity to bring the beer to a long finish. At 8 percent, this beer is a bit stronger than most dubbels. A fine beer to match short ribs, beef cheeks, leg of lamb, venison sausages, country pâtés, and wild boar. **Maredsous 10** is paler but stronger, at about 9.5 percent. This deep amber beer has the same basic flavor structure as 8 but leans away from raisins, preferring apricots. The finish is long and warming.

VAN HONSEBROUCK I first encountered this brewery's products in the form of a strong ale called Brigand. Since then, the brewer Luc Van Honsebrouck and his family have bought a castle called Ingelmunster in the Flemish town of the same name. The castle suggested the name for the brewery's dark Kasteelbier, and more recently for its **Kasteelbier Golden Triple**. This beer has a very pretty color—a sort of burnished antique gold, with an aroma of white rum, raisins, and oranges.

The flavor structure is reminiscent of a good dry German Riesling—very fruity and complex up front, with an impression of considerable sweetness, suddenly drying into a fruity finish. The impression of sweetness is false—the beer is actually dry, but fruity and quite strong at 11 percent. Enjoy this with monkfish, lobster, bouillabaisse, or chicken dishes made with herbs and fruit.

The Belgians are constantly struggling with the complexities of dealing with both French and Flemish labeling. Sometimes this has amusing results. *Donker* means "dark" in Flemish, and *foncée* means the same in French. Thus the name **Kasteelbier Donker Foncée**, a deep reddish brown beer with a prune-like aroma. The beer is very sweet, mustering barely enough bitterness to prevent the sugar from running amok. You get a mouthful of raisins and prunes, leading into a long, sweet finish. Try this with seared foie gras or foie gras terrine. Otherwise, I'd reserve it for cheeses, especially Stilton, or caramelized desserts such as crème brûlée or flan. This beer is filtered—if it were bottle-conditioned, the yeast would continue to consume the sugar, overcarbonating the beer while drying it out.

HET ANKER Founded in Mechelen more than 600 years ago, Het Anker ("the anchor") brewery is best known for its **Gouden Carolus**, a strong dark ale that is widely considered a classic. Gouden Carolus ("golden Charles") refers to a gold coin on which the head of Emperor Charles V, a native of Mechelen, was imprinted. The name also appears on the label in French, "Carolus d'Or." Gouden Carolus has a gorgeous deep mahogany color and a pronounced rum-raisin aroma. The beer sneaks softly onto the palate and then blooms into sweet, raisiny splendor, does a light pirouette on your tongue, then exits drily with a warming spirituous flourish. An astonishingly elegant beer that doesn't put a foot wrong. Get some very good lamb chops and roast them medium-rare.

Het Anker's tripel is known as Toison d'Or in Belgium, but in this country it is marketed, somewhat confusingly, as **Gouden Carolus Triple**. This fluffy beer is deep gold with a floral perfumy aroma featuring some interesting notes of mint and lavender. Some sugar has caramelized in the kettle, and you can taste it clearly. The palate is smooth, round, and rummy, with sweetness showing only momentarily. The beer dries out in a long, bready mineral finish. An outstanding example of the style. Pair it with rabbit, pork loin, pork chops, cassoulet, Thai basil chicken, grilled octopus, or sushi.

VICTORY BREWING COMPANY Downington, Pennsylvania, might seem like an unlikely place to seek out a tasty Belgian-style tripel, but Victory Brewing Company's brewmasters, Bill Covaleski and Ron Barchet, deliver the goods.

Victory Golden Monkey is a bottle-conditioned pale orange beer with an eager carbonation. The nose is rich and distinctly Belgian—oranges, spices, and hops in a nicely meshed interplay. The American influence shows up front—a thin whack of hops wakes up the palate. Then Belgium takes over and drives this beer through a dry, full-bodied fruity center and a graceful dry finish. Victory indeed—this is a great rendition from one of the best producers on the East Coast. Have this beer with grilled bass, cold duck, cold lamb, prosciutto, Serrano ham, monkfish, crab cakes, or pasta carbonara.

ALESMITH BREWING Northern California has been a center of American craft brewing for decades, but until recently southern California lagged far behind. That's starting to change, and San Diego is becoming a hot spot for great brewing. Alesmith is a small producer brewing some rather big beers, including its **Alesmith Horny Devil Ale**. The large bottle hides a grayish plastic wine cork under the crown cap. The color of the beer is very deep gold, and the carbonation is light. The nose is beautiful—rum, oranges, and sweet spices. Hops take a backseat as the beer opens up fruity and semisweet on the palate. The center is fat and round, and the finish is long and drying, with fruit and grain flavors lingering. The name "Horny Devil" seems to allude to Belgium's famous Duvel (Devil), but it is not in the same style. The label doesn't call the beer a tripel either, but it's clearly in that tradition, and a very good interpretation. At 10 percent, it's slightly stronger than most tripels, and it's a touch sweeter. The seamless blend of fruit, spices, and sweetness will make it terrific with seared foie gras, duck, spicy quesadillas, country pâtés, and seared scallops.

OMMEGANG It seems like a mad vision as you come around a curve in the road—a traditional Belgian farmhouse, blazing white in the sunshine falling on the fields outside of . . . Cooperstown, New York. Don Feinberg and Wendy Littlefield had spent years importing some of Belgium's finest beers, and their passion for Belgian beer and food eventually resulted in Brewery Ommegang. The brewery is named after a colorful annual processional in the Grande Place in Brussels, and was originally a joint venture between Feinberg and Littlefield as importers and Brouwerij De Smedt and Brouwerij Moortgat as importees. The brewery's flagship beer is called simply **Ommegang**. It has a gorgeous color of aged Burgundy—red, leading to brown at the edges. The aroma is a potpourri of fruit and spices: orange peel, star anise, raisins, dates, and coriander. Feinberg and Littlefield, like most Belgian brewers, are evasive on the subject of the recipe, but the beer is surely spiced. The palate is sweet, round, and juicy, outrageously fruity in the center, then turning drier and slightly astringent into the long finish.

At Fleur de Sel, an elegant little French restaurant in New York, I was once served saddle of venison in a black licorice sauce—it sounds strange, but it was delicious. This beer would be a perfect match. Since you're unlikely to encounter black licorice sauce anytime soon, I suggest other venison dishes, hanger steak in a shallot sauce, well-peppered rib-eye or shell steaks, carbonnade flamande, and pâté de campagne. The people at Ommegang are as passionate about food as they are about beer—you can have a look at their website, www.belgianexperts.com, to see their own suggestions for matches. If you're ever in the Cooperstown area, you can enjoy the bizarre experience of visiting Belgium and the Baseball Hall of Fame in a single afternoon.

STRONG GOLDEN ALES

Ardently imitated, but never quite equaled, **Duvel** (pronounced "DOO-fl") is the sole progenitor of the strong golden ales brewed today in Belgium. The Belgians might not recognize the style designation "strong golden ale," but they certainly all recognize Duvel, which has come to be regarded as one of the world's classic beers. It is produced by the family-owned Moortgat brewery of Breendonk. Taking the opposite tack from the abbey breweries, the Moortgats appealed to a lower authority and named this beer after the Flemish word for the devil. The beer is sly, seductive, powerful, and deceptive, so the name seems apt. This innocent-looking pale golden beer looks like a pilsner but is packing a hidden wallop at 8.5 percent. In Belgium, Duvel is always served in its own special tulip-shape glass, which is twice the size of the bottle. Pour a Duvel and you'll see why—the beer is bottle-conditioned and virtually erupts into the glass, raising a massive, cloudlike, fluffy white head. The nose is perfumy, showing hops, pear brandy, and citrus. In the mouth, the beer opens up, foaming like champagne. Soft, light-bodied, but expansive and flashy on the palate, it is smooth, dry, and full of spicy flavors backed by hay and a hint of tobacco. It signs off with a snap of hops and a spicy aftertaste warmed by alcohol. In Belgium it is often served ice-cold, an anomaly in a country where most serious beers are served very lightly chilled. Duvel just shrugs it off—it's snappy and refreshing when cold, fruitier and more profound when warmer.

The years have been kind to the Moortgats, and Duvel is now the best-selling specialty beer in Belgium. (Even in Belgium, pilsner sells best.) The brewery was founded in 1871, but it has been continually modernized and has an almost rakish modernist appearance. Until several years ago, it retained its own maltings in order to prepare the especially pale malts that allow Duvel to achieve its golden color despite its strength. The malt is still specially produced, but it is now made by an outside malting house. Originally, the brewery produced only dark ales, of which Duvel was one until it was reformulated in the late 1960s, when the brewery sought to compete with the onslaught of golden pilsners. In its cleanliness of malt character, there is a certain resemblance to pilsner, and it is these clean lines of flavor that distinguish Duvel and its imitators from heavier tripels. In the mid-1990s, Duvel's characteristic aromatics seemed to be fading, the pearlike notes replaced by a pilsnerish hop character. I voiced my disappointment to one of Moortgat's brewers, who conceded my point but said that the brewery hadn't pinpointed exactly what had changed. In a beer this subtle, every tiny difference is noticeable to devotees. Happily, in recent years Duvel seems to have regained its footing. The pears are back in evidence and have taken up residence with the newly refreshed hop character. Other beers in this style are still scrambling to catch up, but many of them are very fine beers in their own right, if perhaps not quite as beguiling as the beer that inspired them.

Belgian Strong Golden Ales and Food

Despite their strength, these beers are quite delicate and very clean in their flavors. They are brewed from specially produced extra-pale malts that are very lightly kilned. This leaves bready and toasty malt flavors at a minimum, allowing bitterness, high carbonation, and fruity aromatics to take over. These beers are great with hors d'oeuvres—the dry, effervescent fruitiness makes a terrific counterpoint to salty, fatty snacks. You can serve prosciutto next to smoked salmon without difficulty. Strong golden ales are efficient palate scrubbers and wonderfully thirst-quenching. When they are served as aperitifs, it's no wonder that many Belgians consider them better than champagne. No Duvel glasses on hand? Pour carefully, and you can serve it in flutes, where it looks so much *cooler* than champagne.

Once you move past hors d'oeuvres, Belgian strong golden ales really put their scrubbing bubbles to work. These beers can take on dishes that make most beverages wilt in abject fear. Take linguine al vongole, a simple Italian pasta with clam sauce. It's delicious, but it's screaming with nearly raw garlic. That's pretty much the whole dish—pasta, olive oil, garlic, clams, and parsley. If it's made properly, the garlic should set your tongue afire. The beer's clean hop bitterness greets the garlic cordially, then lifts the oils and floats them over your tongue, allowing the flavors of the olive oil and the clams to shine through. Afterward, your palate is refreshed rather than overwhelmed. This combination is really something to experience. White wines, imagining themselves native and capable, often get slapped into the next room by this dish, but the beer handles the unruly garlic with cool aplomb.

Speaking of garlic, bring on the pesto. This throws basil and parmesan into the mix, and the beer welcomes both. I once got home from work and discovered that all I had in the house for dinner was some frozen pesto sauce, frozen sausages (chicken, prosciutto, and leek), and dry linguine. I had been remiss in stocking my cellar, so all I had left was a few stray bottles of Duvel. Somewhat doubtfully, I defrosted everything and rustled up a meal. To my surprise, the Duvel was absolutely perfect with the pesto and excellent with the sausages. I've had that meal many times since, but on purpose.

At New York's Felidia Ristorante, a much fancier setting than my dining room, I've had Duvel with housemade ravioli filled with pear and fresh pecorino cheese then sautéed with aged pecorino and crushed black pepper. The beer's pear aromatics met those of the filling, and the cheese and black pepper expanded beautifully under the beer's influence. It was a great dish and a stunning match.

I've often seen Belgium's strong golden ales on the table in Indian restaurants in New York and Philadelphia. Again, deftness with strong flavors is the key here. Firm bitterness cuts through ghee (Indian clarified butter—you wondered why the food tastes go good?) and cream, while the explosive carbonation cleanses the palate. It matches some flavors and merely lifts others, but the beer's cleanliness of flavor is an asset, giving it a remarkable versatility. Herbal Thai preparations also make good matches, especially chicken with holy basil.

Clean flavors are also an asset with fish, and these beers will work with almost anything. Delicate fish, especially with a squeeze of lemon, will have their essential flavors accentuated, while strong, oily fish will have their oiliness scrubbed away. Grilled sardines coated in sea salt are great with these golden ales, as are fresh anchovies. The beer will handle considerable acidity, so you can try it with shrimp cocktail. Good cocktail sauce is sweet, acidic, and hot with horseradish sauce, so some scrubbing power is definitely in order—you do want to taste the shrimp, don't you? The same goes for oysters, with or without sauce. Drinking a beer that can reset your palate between oysters helps you enjoy each one individually. You'll especially appreciate this when you have a selection of oysters, each with its own texture and flavor. When you're done, the beer will leave your palate as fresh as sea air.

Notable Producers of Belgian Strong Golden Ales

RIVA The Riva brewing group, based in Dentergem in west Flanders, is noticeably ambitious and does a fine job brewing a wide range of styles. Of the breweries that have tried to emulate Moortgat's success with Duvel, perhaps Riva is the most obvious about it. Riva's version of the style is called **Lucifer** and comes in a large corked bottle with the eponymous devil lording it over the label. Lucifer has a translucent pale gold color and raises a pillowy white head. Pears lurk in the background of a fresh, yeasty aroma with a floral hop overlay. Expansive carbonation makes the beer bloom across the palate, where it shows a clean balance of restrained bitterness and malt sweetness. The overall impression is dry, light-bodied, and brisk, with a quick glimpse of pears in the center. The finish is dry and very clean. This is a very nice beer indeed, if lacking Duvel's trademark snappiness. Riva has given Lucifer its own personality—slightly toned down from that of its inspiration. This has advantages—Lucifer is excellent with even the most delicate fish dishes, but it can also handle relatively spicy Indian and Thai dishes. I've also enjoyed it with pasta in a carbonara sauce, where the beer's slight sweetness set off the gamy pancetta while the carbonation brightened and lifted the sauce.

VAN STEENBERGE The Van Steenberge brewery of Ertevelde in east Flanders is perhaps as ambitious as its rival Riva and just as prolific. It entered its third century in fine fettle, brewing a vast array of beers under its Bios label, the family name Van Steenberge, and a blizzard of licensees. Through it all, Van Steenberge has managed to keep the quality of its beers quite high. Given its ambitions, it was inevitable that it would brew a strong golden ale. It put its **Piraat** ("pirate") in the same distinctive bottle that Duvel uses, in case anyone was about to miss the point. The color is a bit deeper, though, pale orange rather than gold. It has a pleasant aroma of warm spices, hops, and kumquats. It turns into a fine mousse on the tongue, showing fruity sweetness first and then a drying bitterness. The overall impression is soft and refined. The finish is just off-dry, and there's a warming glow of alcohol and hops. At 10.5 percent, this is a quite strong version, and its strength shows, though elegantly. Piraat has enough heft to pair nicely with herbal rabbit dishes, roast chicken, terrines, and sausages.

HUYGHE There's been a brewery on the site of the Huyghe family brewery in Melle, near Ghent, for 350 years. The family has been brewing here for four generations, and when the fourth generation took over in 1985, the product range expanded greatly. It seems that the younger members of the family had a modern sense of humor, since they named one of their new beers **Delirium Tremens**. For quite some time, the authorities in the United States let it be known that they were not amused, and the beer was sold here as Mateen. They seem to have relented, and the Delirium Tremens label, complete with dancing pink elephants and lizards, now graces the stone-colored bottle. The beer is the same as ever, showing bright gold with an expansive white head and an aroma of oranges, limes, hops, and a touch of rum. It smells almost like a good margarita. On the palate, the beer expands, showing its hand all at once; firm hops coat the mouth as sweet, juicy, fruity malt bursts out of the center. The finish is fast, clean, and fruity with a twinge of drying acidity. It leaves behind pear flavors roaming through a warming glow. Despite the silly name, this beer shows considerable finesse in a bold, racy frame. At 9 percent, it's a bigger, flashier, more complex beer than Duvel, though it is less refreshing as a result. It has considerable cutting power, so put it up against grilled salmon, spicy grilled shrimp, chicken tikka masala, sausages, and pasta carbonara.

FRENCH BIÈRE DE GARDE

If the brew pub strikes you as a modern concept, consider the ubiquitous French brasserie. The word means "brewery" and is a holdover from the days when many French establishments brewed beer and served it with food. France is surely more famous for its wines, but it has an ancient traditional beer culture that has survived tenuously in the modern world. The vast majority of French beer is brewed in the international pilsner style, which is not particularly interesting—Kronenbourg tastes pretty much like Heineken. There's nothing noticeably French about it. Over the past several years, however, more than 100 small breweries have sprung up in France, almost all of them making beer that is distinctly French.

The indigenous French style is bière de garde ("beer for keeping"), which usually arrives stylishly dressed in champagne-like bottles. The area that produces these beers is quite small, focusing on the hop-growing lowland regions of French Flanders, Nord-Pas de Calais, and Picardy, near the channel ports and the Belgian border. Bières de garde were originally produced by farmers, who brewed them as winter gave way to the spring planting season. The beer was meant to last through the summer months until the weather was once again cool enough for brewing. In this, bières de garde served the same purpose as the saison beers of Belgium, but the flavor profile of bière de garde is quite different. The champagne bottles, sometimes with the full regalia of cork and wire hood, are not a modern conceit—the Champagne region is a mere fifty miles to the south, and commercial brewers of bière de garde have always used the same bottles as the winemakers. The farmers were usually less fussy, selling the beer by the cask or filling whatever container the customer cared to bring. These days, you'll see the same thing at many small French wineries, where customers fill their containers from a hose fitted with a gas-station nozzle.

Truly traditional bières de garde are top-fermenting ales, though some examples are produced with lager yeasts that were introduced in the early decades of the twentieth century. Where lager yeasts are used, a warm fermentation will sometimes be used to coax out some fruitiness. The indigenous ale yeasts for bière de garde seem to have a common ancestry, carrying a particular "house character" to all the beers fermented with them. Farmhouse breweries were ramshackle affairs that frequently burned down. When a farmer rebuilt his brewery, he'd go to a neighbor to borrow some yeast. Eventually, all the farmers in the area were using closely related yeast strains, producing similar flavors.

The barley malt, sometimes locally grown, is kilned to a light amber, resulting in beers with burnished gold to deep amber colors. The distinctive yeast shows itself in the aromatics, which are herbal and spicy, with an almost musty underpinning of damp earth, anise, and wood. Bitterness is restrained, allowing soft, biscuity malt to play through to the finish, which is sometimes fairly warming with alcohol. There's usually some gentle sweetness in the center of the palate. Bières de garde tend to be on the strong side, with most ranging from 6 percent to 8 percent. This would originally have given them the keeping power implied by their name and relied on by farmers and customers. A warm fermentation is usually followed by a long, cold maturation, which produces a round smoothness in the finished beer. The soft, herbal complexity of these beers is a perfect

Many wines have difficulty with France's funkier cheeses, but the native bières de garde match them beautifully.

accompaniment to dishes with a strong herbal component and amazing with the best of France's smelly cheeses.

Bières de Garde and Food

It should come as no surprise that France's great indigenous style of beer is terrific with food. The uniquely earthy and herbal flavors of traditional bières de garde are perfect matches for much of the classic French culinary repertoire. The *bouquet garni*, a tied bundle of thyme and bay with a varying mix of sage, rosemary, parsley, marjoram, and lovage, finds its way into many French dishes, releasing a flood of complex aromatics. Bière de garde plays the same tune, and when you combine the beer with these dishes, you have a true symphony of flavors.

Cassoulet, the hearty stew of white beans, duck, goose, garlic sausage, ham hocks, and herbs, is one of my favorite cold-weather dishes. Classic cassoulet takes days to make, but you can make a perfectly good one in a few hours, and there are few more pleasant ways to spend a rainy or snowy Sunday afternoon. Cassoulet is to Gascony what chili is to Texas—a high point of local gastronomy and an excuse for arguments. Everyone has his or her own version, and bière de garde is brilliant with each. It wields enough bitterness and carbonation to bust through those beans and go straight for the meat. The robust, biscuity malt is a fine match for the duck and sausages, while the beer's herbal flavors dance with the sprigs of thyme scattered through the dish. The combination is magical.

If you don't have all Sunday afternoon, you can cook some duck legs with thyme while you're watching a football game. Use the duck fat to brown some potatoes, and toss some rosemary in there with them. Bière de garde will complete the picture, a simple meal of beautiful harmonies. Sausages are another quick meal that's great with these beers—pick sausages that have some herbs in them, and you'll get a particularly stellar match.

You've only got half an hour? Try a frenched rack of lamb chops, covered in olive oil, cracked pepper, and rosemary, oven at 450 degrees Fahrenheit, about twenty minutes. You can't beat it—it's virtually foolproof, and it's so tasty you can serve it to your most esteemed guests. Bière de garde links up perfectly with the rosemary and can even withstand a brief run-in with mint jelly.

Every year, a few days before Thanksgiving, I get a call from my brother Roger. I know what he's looking for. "Zo—you are bringing zee French beer, oui?" he'll ask. "Mais bien sur!" I'll answer. "Le Thanksgiving sans le bière de garde—c'est impossible!" The French have yet to discover this food match, so let me be the one to tell you—bière de garde is brilliant with turkey. And not just with turkey—it is also brilliant with the turnips, the stuffing, the cranberry sauce, the potatoes, the whole darned thing. Bière de garde is *the* Thanksgiving beer. My sommelier friends rack their brains every year, trying to answer the constant nagging question everyone asks them—what wine is good with turkey? The answer, of course, is not wine but beer.

Why this one? Well, let's face it—the Butterball is a sideshow; modern turkeys don't really have much flavor. That's why you're staring at the stuffing and the gravy, scheming to get your rightful share. Both have strong herbal flavors, which anchor the match with the beer's herbal flavors. Then the caramelized malts meet the browned turkey skin, the biscuity malt flavors match the lightly nutty flavor of the meat, and the carbonation lifts everything, so you don't realize you're eating so much. (Can't help you there.) Even a perfectly cooked turkey is a little bit dry, and a poorly cooked turkey is like a mouthful of sawdust. A few bottles of bière de garde can save the day—the beer makes everything taste juicy. (If you're planning to get a moist turkey by frying the whole thing, perhaps you can use the beer to put out the flames when your house catches fire.) My mom cooks a perfect turkey, and she loves it with bière de garde. So will you.

If you have any room left, you can consider one more great match with your bière de garde—cheese. Serious cheese. I'm not talking Kraft Industrial Blocks here—it's fine with those, but I'm talking about France's most prized washed-rind cheeses. The smelly ones, like Livarot, Pavin, Munster, and Vacherin Mont d'Or. Bière de garde will match these cheeses far more sympathetically than wine does. The beer's complex aromatics of damp earth and anise echo the pungent flavors developed by the molds and bacteria that ferment the cheese to ripeness. The combination is unbeatable. If you love these cheeses—and I do—you absolutely must try this at home.

Notable Producers of Bière de Garde

BRASSERIE DUYCK It was the cork that first intrigued me. I was in a Parisian supermarket one day in 1984, and I saw something in the beer aisle in a champagne-style bottle, with a cork and wire hood. This I had to try. I bought a baguette and some cheese and headed out to the palace grounds at Versailles, where I parked myself on a bench under the chestnut trees. I popped the cork and began to shred my baguette—I suddenly felt invincibly French. I'd love to claim that I first tasted bière de garde with some fantastic Parisian meal, but in fact I swigged it out of a bottle on that park bench, where I paired it with La Vache Qui Rit, which I later learned was the French counterpart to Kraft slices. The flavor of the beer, **Jenlain**, grabbed my attention, and I was soon pairing it with better partners. Jenlain is brewed by the Duyck family. The Duycks started brewing commercially in 1922 on their farm in the village of Jenlain, southeast of Valenciennes.

Along with the Castelains, they were largely responsible for the repopularization of bière de garde, allowing dozens of craft breweries to flower in that region of northern France. Jenlain achieved a sort of cult status among students in Lille in the late 1970s, and the brewery shrewdly capitalized on its newfound popularity. Félix Duyck founded the brewery, which is now run by his son Robert and grandson Raymond. The family name is clearly Flemish, and the spicy Flemish brewing tradition shows in its beer.

Jenlain Original French Ale has a pale honey-amber color and a sweet, fruity, herbal nose featuring biscuits, apples, and fennel. Hops take a backseat on a soft, round, and juicy palate with an off-dry malt center full of earth, caramelized malt, and apple peels. The finish is long and semisweet. The classic bière de garde flavors of herbs and fruit make this beer terrific with a wide variety of dishes. It's just the ticket with a stuffed roasted chicken, stuffed pork loin, cassoulet, garlic Toulouse sausages, and smelly washed-rind cheeses like Livarot.

BRASSERIE CASTELAIN In Bénifontaine, near the Flemish border, the Delomel Brewery was built as part of a farm in 1926 and bought in 1966 by Roland Castelain. His son Yves has taken the brewery from a small village concern into a pioneering regional success. Nord-Pas de Calais is still hop-growing country, but at one time Bénifontaine was a mining village, and the brewery catered to men caked with coal dust at the end of the workday. The mines are gone, but until recently the image of the coal miner was recalled in the French label design for Ch'ti, the French name for the beer sold here as **Castelain**. The name is Picardy dialect for *c'est toi*, meaning "it's you," and is used to suggest the joie de vivre of the northern French. Yves Castelain's sister Annick also works for the brewery, and his son Bertrand has opened a brew pub in St.-Pol-sur-Ternoise.

For obvious reasons, the name Ch'ti doesn't survive translation, and the American label depicts an anonymous castle. Castelain it is, then, and the cork-finished bottle pours a deep golden beer that appears rather like a pilsner. The nose, however, says bière de garde—earthy hops, fennel, licorice, hay, lavender, and herbs. The beer may be from the north, but it smells like the air in Provence in summertime. Light bitterness and pinpoint carbonation open onto a clean, dryish, full-bodied malt palate showing a subtle and complex swirl of earthy, herbal flavors. The finish is long and shows some sweetness until the hops sign off with a snap. A beautiful piece of work—it's distinctive and flavorful. This beer is actually produced with a lager yeast at warm, ale-like temperatures to produce a traditional flavor profile. Castelain is the very best beer to match the Thanksgiving turkey and all the trimmings. It's also excellent with many other dishes, including cassoulet, sausages, roast pork, and spring lamb, especially with rosemary.

Yves Castelain uses a more traditional top-fermenting ale yeast to produce a beer called **St. Amand French Country Ale**, which is packaged in a large bottle with a Grolsch-style stopper seal. This beer has a deep amber color and a classic aroma of caramel, musty cellar, fertile earth, and anise. On the palate, it is very soft, round, and malty, showing plenty of caramel malt flavor on a full-bodied off-dry frame. It's softly herbal at its core, but, interestingly, it isn't as herbal as the golden Castelain. St. Amand is a fine choice for just about any roasted fowl, and also for duck breast, lamb, sausages, filet mignon with mushroom sauce, cassoulet, and roast suckling pig.

BRASSERIE ST. SYLVESTRE Outside the village of St. Sylvestre-Cappel, in the heart of the hop country of French Flanders between Dunkerque and Lille, there was once a Trappist monastery. Like all Trappist monasteries of its time, it brewed beer. The monastery has been lost to history, but the beer has not. In 1919, the Ricour family took over a brewery in St. Sylvestre-Cappel, and Remy Ricour started to make beers based on the old Trappist recipes. Ricour's son Pierre and his grandsons Serge and François continue in his tradition, brewing traditional Flanders ales in a jumble of farmhouse buildings, some of them dating back to the 1800s.

French Flanders is quite flat, so in the minds of local villagers, three small hills become mountains worthy of names—Mont de Cats, Mont Cassel, and Mont des Recollets surround St. Sylvestre-Cappel. **3 Monts Flanders Golden Ale** comes in a large bottle with a straight cork held in place by an unusual metal brace—once this is pried loose, you'll need a corkscrew. The beer has a full bright gold color and a tantalizing aroma of baking bread, candy sugar, herbs, green apples, pears, anise, and classic bière de garde musty cellar notes. On the palate, the beer opens up to a fine prickly mousse, sweet at first but quickly dried by moderate bitterness. It's soft, round and smooth, with biscuits in the center. The finish is light, mineraly, dry, and spirituous. Hops linger cleanly. At 8.5 percent, it's a bit on the strong side for bière de garde, and here the beer shows its Trappist influences—it's quite close to being a tripel. The anise and musty cellar notes, however, place it firmly on the French side of the border. I once served this at a luncheon at New York's Gramercy Tavern, where I paired it with a rabbit dish prepared with rosemary, olives, and garlic. It was a perfect accompaniment, the dark herbal, earthy flavors of the beer melding seamlessly with the olives and rosemary. Try it also with herbal Provençal preparations of monkfish and chicken, stuffed squid, cassoulet, sausages, and washed-rind stinky French cheeses like Livarot and Pavin.

Haute refers to top fermentation. The "three mountains" are more like hills, but in flat Flanders, people will take what they can get.

BRASSERIE LA CHOULETTE The rural French town of Hordain is in the industrialized mining region of Pas-de-Calais, south of Valenciennes. Brasserie La Choulette occupies a farmhouse building, dating from 1885, where Brasserie Bourgeois-Lecerf operated until Alain and Martine Dhaussy bought it in 1977. The name "La Choulette" refers to a ball used in an antiquated local game. The name is appropriate, as the Dhaussys brew quite traditional top-fermented beers that are aged for up to six weeks. The beers are lightly filtered, allowing some yeast to find its way into the bottles. The brewery has been quite successful, and its revivalist beers can now be found in many French supermarkets. It brews several interesting beers, but perhaps the most traditional is **La Choulette Ambrée**, which comes corked in a champagne-like bottle. The beer has a handsome glowing amber color and an earthy, fruity, honeyed herbal aroma featuring notes of basil and anise with caramel undertones. The palate is off-dry, round, and full-bodied, showing clean caramel malt flavors surrounded by a faint cellarlike mustiness. The center is voluptuous and smooth—hops play a supporting role for the sweet malts. The finish is long and somewhat drying, trailing off into a haylike grassiness. At nearly 8 percent, La Choulette Ambrée is muscular but graceful and full of traditional bière de garde flavors. It's perfect with funky washed-rind cheeses, cassoulet, sausages, stuffed pork loin, lamb chops, and stuffed roasted chicken, turkey, pheasant, or partridge.

8

THE Czech-German Lager Tradition

In Europe of the 1400s, no one knew what yeast was. Europeans knew only about as much as the Egyptians had known 2,000 years earlier—

that the magical foam from one batch of beer could be used to start the fermentation of another. They knew simply that the foam was special, and that their beer would not ferment properly without it. Nor did brewers anywhere else know what yeast was. The foam went by a number of names in different languages, from "barm" to "God-is-good" to "phlogisticated air." About this time, however, the Bavarians made a discovery. They had begun storing their beer in icy caves in the foothills of the Alps to keep it from spoiling during the summer, when the heat made brewing impossible. It was no surprise that cold preserved food—everyone knew that. The surprise was that the cold-fermented cave-aged beer was more stable than other beer, even when kept through the heat of the summer. Something about cold aging had given the beer a special keeping power, even when it warmed up. By 1420, a document of the Munich city council mentions cold fermentation.

Encouraged by this discovery, brewers started to build their own caves and cellars near the breweries. They cut huge blocks of ice from rivers and lakes during the winter and put them deep inside the beer cellars, keeping the cellars cool all summer long. They no longer just stored the beer in the caves; they also fermented it there. This practice became essential in 1553, when Duke Albrecht V of Bavaria, worried by declining beer quality, banned the brewing of beer during warm weather. His decree allowed beer to be brewed only from St. Michael's Day (September 29) to St. George's Day (April 23). Of course, it's good to be the king—members of the royal family were allowed to brew wheat beer

KLD 45
65-67
05,02

during the other months. But the only way commoners could sell beer during warm weather was to brew it during cold weather and then store it. Brewers expanded their cellars into vast underground fermentation and storage halls. The summer ban on brewing was rescinded in 1850, but by then Bavarian beer had changed. Gradually, yeasts that fermented at warm temperatures had disappeared and had been replaced by an entirely different sort of yeast. This new yeast liked the cold. Warm ale fermentations tended to be plagued by spoilage bacteria that loved the warm temperatures as much as the ale yeast did. At temperatures of 40 to 50 degrees Fahrenheit, bacteria struggled and died while the new yeast fermented and thrived. This had been the secret of the stability of Bavarian beer.

The new yeast had a few odd habits in addition to liking the cold. When it was finished fermenting, it didn't float on top of the beer the way the old yeasts did. Instead, it sank to the bottom of the barrel and stayed there, leaving the beer relatively clear. Brewers collected new yeast for brewing by scooping it from the bottom of barrels rather than skimming it from the top. Also, this yeast took its time fermenting—fermentations lasted a week or two rather than only a few days. When the fermentation was finished, the beer was still rather rough, with strong sulfurous aromas. After the beer was left to rest in the caves for a few months, though, the brewer's patience would be rewarded. The beer emerged delicious, clear, and incomparably smooth.

The Bavarians had no idea that their special new yeast would one day change brewing forever. The yeast was brought to Czech Bohemia in 1842 to ferment the new golden beer from Pilsen, launching a style that quickly swept the world. In 1873 the German engineer Carl von Linde, backed by Munich's Spaten brewery, completed the first working model of his "ammonia cold machine." This was the world's first artificial refrigeration in commercial use, and Spaten used it to cool the fermentation vessels in order to brew lager beer year-round. In 1883 Emil Hansen, a brewing scientist at the Carlsberg Brewery in Denmark, isolated a pure culture of the lager yeast procured from Spaten decades earlier. It is a separate species from ale yeast strains and was dubbed *Saccharomyces carlsbergensis* (it has since been given the surname *uvarum*). All true lagers are fermented with a strain of this yeast species, whereas all true ales are fermented by a strain of the species *Saccharomyces cerevisiae.*

In German, *Lagerung* means storage, and anyplace where things are stored, kept, or defended might be referred to as a *Lager*. Ales may be ready to drink within little more than a week after brewing, but lager beer must be stored to

OPPOSITE: Brewmaster Michael Braun draws a sample in the royal castle brewery at Schloss Kaltenberg.

allow its slow, cold fermentation to finish and its rough flavors and aromas to evolve away. Traditional lagers will be stored, or lagered, close to the freezing point for months, though these days several weeks is often considered sufficient. The result is a beer with an exceptional soft smoothness and straightforward but delicious flavors. Whereas ales often have complex fruity flavors developed in warm fermentation, lagers tend to stick to the facts—the flavors are of malt and hops in a clean, delicate, and often sophisticated interplay. Sometimes a haylike, hot-spring sulfury aroma will linger in the nose. Some brewers carbonate their beer by a method called *Krausening*, in which partially fermented wort is blended into maturing beer. The remaining sugars in the added wort then ferment out, and the resulting natural carbonation is trapped in the beer.

Lagers can be pale as golden pilsner, black as schwarzbier, light as helles, or warmingly strong as doppelbock. Some are sold unfiltered and called kellerbier, though these are rarely bottled. It is the use of lager yeasts and a cold fermentation followed by cold aging that distinguishes lagers from ales and gives lagers their uniquely smooth flavor profiles. Lagers are rarely flashy, but in the hands of a good brewer, this clean simplicity is a real strength.

German brewing, with a few notable exceptions such as weissbier and kölsch, is dominated by lagers. High quality and purity of flavor has been an obsession of German brewmasters for centuries. Concern over poor quality and the use of adulterating ingredients prompted King Wilhelm IV of Bavaria to enact the "Beer Purity Law" (*Reinheitsgebot*) in 1516. Under this law, only barley malt, hops, and water could be used to make beer. Yeast had yet to be discovered—amendments were added later to admit it, along with malted wheat for producing weissbier. The *Reinheitsgebot* later spread to the rest of Germany, and to this day all German beers destined for consumption within the country must adhere to it. One can argue that the *Reinheitsgebot* has strangled creativity by disallowing many interesting ingredients, but at the same time it is part of a conservative mind-set that has spared German beer drinkers the depredations visited on Americans since the end of Prohibition. It is rare to find a genuinely bad beer in Germany. For the Germans in general and the Bavarians in particular, good beer is an essential part of the fabric of life.

As far as the Germans are concerned, quality is more important than flash. When lagers pair up with food, the pleasures are more simple than profound, but that subtracts nothing from our enjoyment. The straightforward nature of lager beer gives it versatility and tact, making it a team player at the table.

Pilsner, the world's most popular style of beer, was invented in Czech Bohemia, perfected in Germany, and turned into flavorless mass-market fizz in America. Some version of pilsner is the only style that many people have ever seen or heard of. Many people who have recently become beer aficionados turn up their noses at the sight of it. So familiar, so yellow. What could it have to offer? The answer is plenty—if you get your hands on the real thing. Genuine pilsner is a thing of beauty—delicate, sharp, flavorful, aromatic, and appetizing. Beer snobs who disdain its bright, simple, linear flavors don't realize what they're missing. Alas, we are awash in ersatz mass-market "pilsner," the equivalent of the flavorless, blindingly white sliced sponges that masquerade as bread on our supermarket shelves. Let's have a look at real pilsner, shall we?

While most people think of pilsner as a German style, it actually has its origins in Bohemia, which is now part of the Czech Republic. In 1842, a Bavarian monk (historically, monks never seem to be far from beer) smuggled some bottom-fermenting lager yeast from Munich to the Bohemian town of Pilsen. He gave it to the Bavarian-born brewer at the Plzensky Prazdroj brewery, who had plans for Bavaria's special yeast. The brewer, Josef Grolle, had a trick up his sleeve. The British had learned to make pale malts, and he had traveled to Great Britain to learn the secret. Grolle had then developed a technique to make the malt paler still, to the point where the beer brewed from it could be truly golden in color.

Only a year before, the Spaten brewery had stunned and delighted the people of Munich with its light bronze Märzen Oktoberfest beer. Before then, all German beers had been dark and usually murky. That beer had been a sensation, but now Grolle took this refinement one crucial step further. Grolle's Pilsner Bier stopped people in their tracks. It had the color of burnished gold, and light sparkled through it as no one had ever seen before. The bottom-fermenting yeast, true to its promise, dropped to the bottom of the vessel after the cold fermentation was finished, leaving the beer clear and bright after its long aging. The sharp, clean bitterness and flowery aromatics of the region's native Saaz hops and the full breadiness of the Moravian barley malt were accentuated by the remarkably soft water of the brewery's wells. The high carbonation, developed by months of aging, formed a white pillowy head on top of the golden liquid. People were enraptured, and word of the new golden pilsner beer raced past the borders of Bohemia and swept throughout Europe.

Josef Grolle and his brewery, today known as Pilsner Urquell ("original

True pilsner retains a snappy bitterness that is particularly appetizing with seafood.

source") can take credit for the first pilsner beer, but the industrial revolution can take some credit for the rapid spread of its popularity. What was so special about the sparkling, golden beer from Pilsen? Until the 1840s, virtually all Europeans drank beer (and wine, for that matter) out of crockery steins, metal tankards, wooden mugs, or even leather jars. These drinking vessels were opaque, but that was fine, since the beer wasn't much to look at anyhow. Only the rich could afford glassware. Now, however, a new process of mechanized glassmaking brought the price of glassware within the means of the middle class, who, not surprisingly, took quickly to this former luxury item. Once the middle classes were sat down in their beer gardens with the sunshine sparkling through their golden, clear glasses of beer, they were hopelessly smitten. The new railroads brought the beer to Bavaria, Prussia, Vienna, and Berlin, where local brewers quickly discovered that they would be forced to brew similar beers or be left in the dust. The rest of Europe fell in love with pilsner beer as well, and within only a few years pilsner was being brewed in the United States by German and Czech immigrants.

The original Budweiser beer is still brewed in Cěské Budějovice (Budweis in German) in the Czech Republic. *Budweiser* originally meant beer from Budweis, just as *Pilsner* meant beer from Pilsen. Deferring to the sensitivities of the Czechs, most German breweries abbreviate Pilsner as simply *Pils*. The Bohemian roots of pilsner beer can be discerned in the names of the American National Bohemian (Natty Bo) beer and the Mexican beer Bohemia. Those beers, however, have strayed far from their roots. Genuine pilsners are all-malt beers, which means that they conform to the *Reinheitsgebot* and contain no rice, corn, wheat, or any grain other than malted barley. True pilsner is full yellow to deep gold in color and has a sharply snappy well-focused hop bitterness, a floral hop aroma, a soft bready malt center, and a very clean dry finish. A prickle of bitterness and the taste of barley linger. It is a beer of great finesse. Brewers sometimes refer to pilsner, with some trepidation, as "naked," meaning that there's nowhere for imperfect flavors to hide. Like all lagers, pilsner expresses very little fermentation character, except perhaps for a faint whiff of sulfur. The flavor and aroma are pure malt and hops, with little if any fruit. The alcohol content of pilsner is moderate, about 5 percent.

Even among the true pilsners there are regional variations. In southern Germany the Bavarian pilsners are round and full-bodied, while in northern Germany the preferred version is drier, racier, and more boldly hoppy. Bohemian pilsners tend to retain a deeper gold hue than their German counterparts, and they are slightly sweeter, sometimes featuring a full-bodied, almost buttery malt character. The classic Czech hop, the delicately flowery Saaz, virtually leaps from the glass, lending an alluring nose. American craft brewers, after years of studiously ignoring the pilsner style, have started to brew full-flavored all-malt pilsners that are worthy of their European roots. Some of these new American pilsners are truly world-class, and their freshness can give them an edge over imports.

Once off its home turf, though, the pilsner style tends to be less steady. An "international" pilsner style is brewed around the world, but its pedigree is less impressive than that of the original. These beers tend to be lighter in color and malt flavor and less bracingly hopped, both in bitterness and in aroma. Sometimes adjuncts—rice, corn, and other cheap grains excluded from German brewhouses—make their way into these beers, lightening them enough to achieve mass-market ambitions. Heineken (an all-malt beer), Belgium's Stella Artois, and Denmark's Carlsberg are well-known European examples of the international pilsner style. In Asia, examples include Sapporo, Asahi, Suntory, Kirin, Tsing-Tao, Singha, Kingfisher, and dozens of others. Some of these beers are acceptably clean and refreshing, the beer world's answer to the average $6 pinot grigio. There's not a lot of depth here, but they'll be OK in a pinch.

From there, it's a long, depressing slide to mass-market American pilsner, a style that includes the world's best-selling brands. Many of these beers are marvels of technology and quality control that, combined with successful mass marketing, have allowed big American brewers to make beer with almost no taste at all. This is not an easy feat—yeast likes to make flavors when it ferments wort. Technology worthy of a nuclear power installation is needed to prevent anything pleasant from happening. These beers are hollowed out by the heavy use of virtually flavorless corn and rice. Gone are the bready all-malt flavor, the sharp fragrant hops, and the smoothness achieved through months of aging. In their place, American mass-market pilsner presents a watery beer that is quickly produced out of a half-malt mash, with virtually no hops at all. Some big American brewers actually don't use hops but stoop to all manner of chemically altered hop extracts. The beer is then filtered to within an inch of its already pallid life.

The result is essentially alcoholic seltzer water with a thin head. It bears the same relationship to genuine pilsner that mass-market white bread does to a warm loaf of Italian ciabatta—that is to say, virtually none. Do you bake bread at home? Try to make a loaf of Wonder Bread. Just try. Believe me, you can't do it. No home baker can. You'd need a laboratory and millions of dollars of equipment to achieve such a remarkably bland creation. American mass-market beer is exactly the same thing. It's *undead.*

The Czech Budweiser Budvar, still brilliantly brewed in the original style, bears no resemblance to its ungrateful American nephew of the same name. While Czech Budweiser is known as the "beer of kings," the American version boastfully calls itself "The King of Beers." The problem is that the king isn't wearing any clothes. Most people who say "I don't like beer" are recalling their unhappy encounters with this sort of stuff. No wonder. It's like eating processed cheese spread out of a can and then deciding that you don't like cheese. Surely we all deserve better than that. For pennies more, you can have the real thing and enjoy the pleasures of one of the world's most versatile styles of beer. Genuine pilsner is truly mouthwatering, deeply satisfying, and incomparably refreshing. Don't settle for less.

Genuine Pilsner with Food

Pilsner is a study in purity, simplicity, and cleanliness of flavor. With food, its lack of fruity, spicy, roasty, or caramelized flavors turns out to be no hindrance; sometimes, characterful simplicity can be just what you want. Pilsner brings bracing, palate-cleansing bitterness, invigorating carbonation, malt sweetness, bready flavors, and bright floral aromatics to the table. With spicy dishes, its knifelike bitterness cuts right through the spices and finds the heart of the dish. The sweetness of the malt marries into the dish and helps cool the fire while the carbonation physically lifts the hot oils away from your palate. This talent is especially pleasant with many Thai and Vietnamese dishes, which often feature bright, spicy flavors in a complex interplay. When you're up against duck in a red coconut curry sauce, for example, you need a bright beer with enough guts to parry fat, chilies, and strong spices. Pilsner is up to the job, as long as the dish isn't too sweet. It's also a good choice with dishes that combine sweetness, sourness, and heat, such as Thai red snapper in tamarind sauce. If you're having Indian food, try to bypass the ubiquitous Indian beers and get your hands on a good German, Czech, or American craft-brewed pilsner. The Indian versions will do in a pinch, but they have neither the malt depth nor the hop snap you're looking for. The same goes for popular Jamaican dishes like jerk chicken and pork—put away the Red Stripe, which is basically just Caribbean Budweiser and doesn't do a thing for food.

Traditional Mexican food is rarely fiery, but the United States has taken a liking to salsa and hot sauce. Pilsner can deal with this blunt attack, cutting effortlessly through salsa, beans, cheese, jalapeños, and sour cream. In between bites, the beer refreshes and resets your palate, while the hop notes play with the cilantro and cumin. With more complex preparations, pilsner is content to play the straight man and let the food put on its own show. It can simply refresh the palate and then get out of the way, and sometimes that's exactly what you want.

Pilsner can handle almost any shellfish with aplomb. You'd think that the aggressive bitterness would obliterate the delicate flavors, but it doesn't. Pilsner's bite is quick, snappy, and short-lived—once it passes, delicate flavors just bloom on your palate. Fried calamari is terrific with pilsner, which scrubs the palate, leaving the squid's flavor intact. Crab, clams, shrimp, oysters, and lobster are accentuated, their flavors punched up by the opposing blast. Fish with similar textures and flavors can be successful matches, monkfish being a good example. The only exception to pilsner's affinity for shellfish is scallops, which really want more delicate treatment to bring out their best flavors. If the preparation is spicy, though, go for it. All strong fish will do just fine with pilsner. Salmon, whether grilled, baked, smoked, or poached, has enough texture and flavor to stand up to pilsner, and salmon is best when it has something to cut it. Arctic char does well here too, as do even stronger oily fish like sardines, mackerel, herring, and anchovies. Someday when you've got the grill fired up, slather some fresh sardines with olive oil and coarse sea salt and toss them on. When they're done, hold them up by the tail and just a touch with a knife or fork will filet them right onto your tongue. Drink your pilsner and smile.

Please don't even think of bringing wine anywhere near caviar. No, not even champagne, which finds itself tasting oddly fishy after an encounter with the precious roe. The Russians, of course, are partial to vodka with caviar, and they have a point, but I can't go there. (Perhaps the idea is that if you can afford the caviar in the first place, there probably isn't anything pressing that you have to do later.) Pilsner, the sharpest, driest one you can get your hands on, is absolutely perfect with caviar. Generally speaking, no great beer should ever be served ice-cold, but here's an exception—a bit of overchilling accentuates the snappiness of pilsner, and the caviar tastes that much better. A brunch of Russian blinis, some dressed with smoked salmon and others with a dollop of caviar and crème fraîche, and a nice cold glass of pilsner—it's so tasty you won't just feel great—you'll feel downright smug.

Ham in general and prosciutto in particular go well with pilsner, which cuts right through the fat and pulls the salt out of the meat. That allows the essential flavor of the ham to step out front. If you're just having an everyday ham and cheese sandwich, pilsner will be a very pleasant accompaniment. If you're having a croque monsieur, the classic French grilled Gruyère and ham sandwich, the combination is delicious. If you're having prosciutto or Serrano ham with melted Brie and sliced apples on ciabatta bread, it's outrageous. There really aren't any sausages that pilsner can't handle, and it's especially good with spicy sausages like chorizo, andouille, and merguez.

Because it is so versatile, pilsner can be a great choice for mixed hors d'oeuvres. There's little chance of an outright clash, even if the match with one of the snacks is less than perfect. The snappiness of pilsner virtually guarantees a certain amnesia on your palate—when the next hors d'oeuvre comes along, your tongue won't remember the previous one. That can be a great advantage when you've decided to set out some smoked salmon alongside the pâté, Buffalo chicken wings, and shrimp cocktail. Sharp, dry pilsner also makes a great aperitif, and it looks pretty cool in champagne glasses.

All this means that a good pilsner should be a candidate for permanent residence in your refrigerator. Pilsner can't do everything—it's not the best choice for very delicate fish or a beefy winter stew. But pilsner can do most things, and that makes it handy to have around. Don't wimp out, though—get the real thing, whether it's brewed in Europe or here in the United States. Real pilsner is an all-malt beer with a sharp, snappy hop bitterness. That's what makes it work. Defanged versions like Budweiser (the Wonder Bread of beers) or Heineken (the Pepperidge Farms white bread of beers) aren't going to do it. Any beer you can buy in your average gas station is probably going to miss the boat. Real pilsner will cost a little more than those beers, but if you weren't worth it, you wouldn't be reading this, would you?

Brewmaster Prince Luitpold of Bavaria enjoys a glass of his König Ludwig Dunkel. The Bavarian royal family has been brewing for centuries.

Castle Kaltenberg houses a sizable brewery. Prince Luitpold holds jousting tournaments on his grounds—every year more than 100,000 people come to see the spectacle and drink the castle-brewed beer. OPPOSITE: No trip to Munich would be complete without a visit to the famous Hofbrauhaus. This archetypal beer hall can seat more than 2,000 people.

HB
Samstagrunde
HB

Ayinger
BRÄU VON AYING
BIERSPEZIALITÄTEN
AYING

Franz Inselkammer's Ayinger beers are renowned for their bready malt character. Inselkammer himself cuts a princely figure. OPPOSITE: Ayinger Helles has a captivating golden shimmer. It's a perfect accompaniment to shellfish, but Bavarians also love it with pork.

GEGR·MDCCCIII
·AUGUSTINER-BRÆU-AUSSCHANK·

The ornate interior of Munich's Augustiner beer hall. Like many Bavarian breweries, Augustiner was founded by monks, but has long been secularized. **OPPOSITE:** The Hofbrauhaus is more famous, but Munich's beer aficionados flock to Augustiner's beer hall nearby.

TOP: These old enamel signs are part of Ayinger's impressive collection, which decorates the walls of the brewery's restaurant. **BOTTOM:** The classic tiled brewhouse at Kaltenberg Castle. **OPPOSITE:** A traditional look—the town of Aying has a storybook quality about it, and the Ayinger brewery weaves the same spell.

Aecht Schlenkerla Rauchbier
(ges gesch)
BAMBERG
SEIT 1678
MARZEN
e 0,5 l
SEIT 1678
Bambergs Spezialität
entsprechend gebrautes
Aecht Schlenkerla Rauchbier
(ges gesch)
MARZEN
BAMBERG

Should the advertising say "fire-malted"? This beechwood fire will dry Brauerei Heller-Trum's malt and suffuse it with smoke flavor. OPPOSITE: Lunchtime at Brauerei Heller-Trum in Bamberg. The Schlenkerla smoked beers are excellent with this onion stuffed with pork and capped with bacon.

Home sweet home—Brooklyn Brewery's brewhouse inhabits an 1860s building in the now-hip neighborhood of Williamsburg. The street outside has been renamed "Brewer's Row" in honor of Brooklyn's brewing heritage.

As pilsner beer marched triumphantly through Europe, America, and northern Germany in the late 1800s, the stubborn Bavarians held tight to their traditional dark brown lager, dunkel. Some Bavarian beers were paler, particularly the malty bronze märzenbier, but in Munich dark beer was still king. The Bavarians were the most conservative beer drinkers in Germany, and that's saying a lot. But eventually, even they began to waver, as the imported sparkling golden beer winked at them in the beer gardens. The brewers of Munich were frightened. In 1894, Munich's Spaten brewery released an answer to the foreign pilsner beer. It was called "helles," or simply "hell." Though it sounds like a ticket to perdition, *hell* means "pale" in German, and the beer was certainly that—a glowing straw-gold. Helles was a shade or two lighter than the Czech pilsners, but it emphasized malt character more than hops. The beer was considerably less bitter than pilsner and had less hop aroma as well. A well-developed bready flavor was its main highlight, and the people of Munich flocked to it. Traditional dark lagers were soon shoved aside. Many of the Munich brewers were incensed—brewing this new beer was tantamount to caving in to the Bohemians! The Association of Munich Breweries even considered banning the production of pale beers. It was too late, though—the Bavarian public had spoken, and the brewers had no choice but to listen. Within thirty years, even the breweries that had denounced the new helles as a foreign abomination were brewing it themselves. The dark dunkel beer was finally eclipsed in the 1950s as helles took the throne of Bavarian brewing.

Today, helles is brewed throughout Germany, but its true home is Bavaria, where it is still the everyday beer of the people. Helles accounts for the majority of the more than 50 gallons of beer per capita consumed yearly by the Bavarians. Its malty, balanced, easy-drinking character has earned it the sobriquet "liquid bread," and you'll often see it served for breakfast. Even at Munich's Oktoberfest, most of the beer served is the popular helles rather than the stronger Oktoberfest-Märzen beer style. At the Hofbrauhaus, helles fills the one-liter glass "mass" mugs that the barmaids in dirndls sling with such impressive aplomb. If a brewer wants to convey old-fashioned authenticity, his label may refer to "urtyp" or "urhell"—*ur* means "original." The name "edel-hell" attempts to confer nobility on the beer and its hops, while "spezial helles" implies that the beer has been brewed for an occasion or for the season.

The line between helles and pilsner is fuzzy. This is scarcely surprising, given their history. Helles, at about 4.5 percent, tends to be slightly less strong than pilsner. Despite this, helles beers are fairly full-bodied rather than thin.

In Germany, northern beers tend toward hoppiness, while southern beers tend toward maltiness. A northern helles and a Bavarian pilsner may be distinguishable only by the characteristically bready quality of the helles. Pilsner never did conquer Bavaria, which has always marched to its own oompah band. Helles is a style that is often overlooked elsewhere—pilsner, with its racy hop character, is a flashier beer, and it is pilsner that conquered the world. But hellesbier is indisputably pleasant, especially in Bavarian beer gardens and beer halls, where it is always magnificently fresh. Helles relies on balance and subtlety to work its charms. Many Bavarian brewers consider helles the crowning glory of German brewing, and the Bavarian public is certainly not arguing.

Helles with Food

Given the similarities between helles and pilsner, it will not surprise you that the food affinities are similar as well. The main difference between the two styles is in the level of hop bitterness and aroma. In helles, the balance is tilted toward the malt, which often shows a wonderful depth of flavor. When matching helles with food, we'll rely a bit less on the cutting power wielded by pilsner and look for more subtle pleasures. The malt flavors in helles have a deep yeasty freshness

The *Hof* in Hofbrauhaus is an old royal reference, but the brewery and its famous beer hall are now owned by the state of Bavaria.

If you go to Munich, you must at least have one beer at the world's most famous beer hall, the Hofbrauhaus. This was the old court brewery of the house of Wittelsbach, the dynasty that ruled Bavaria for nearly 800 years. Duke Wilhelm V built it in 1591 to produce the popular brown beers of the day, but within a few decades the Hofbrauhaus (which essentially means "royal brewery") was producing weissbier and bockbier. In order to ensure their success, the Wittelsbachs forbade anyone else in Bavaria to brew weissbier or bockbier for more than 200 years. Both beers were very popular, so the monopoly worked wonders for the royal coffers.

The Hofbrauhaus has operated continuously for more than 400 years and has never stopped serving, even as bombs fell during World War II. In the early years, it admitted only members of the aristocracy, but this changed in 1829, when for the first time ordinary people were allowed to enter. The building has been renovated many times, most recently in 1897, when the serving area was expanded to allow more than 4,000 people to be seated at one time, on three levels. The brewery moved out many years ago and is now a modern facility on the edge of town. Over the years, the Hofbrauhaus has had many famous visitors and some infamous ones. Lenin and his wife spent many happy evenings here in the early 1900s, and Hitler's Brown Shirts met here in the 1930s. The Hofbrauhaus has seen and survived it all.

I first visited the Hofbrauhaus in 1984, when I was making my poststudent grand tour of Europe. The building sits in a small square called Platzl, which looks like an elaborate movie set on a Hollywood back lot. The impression increases when you step inside the cavernous vaulted hall, which is populated by tourists, locals in their finest lederhosen, bustling barmaids carrying five steins in each hand like foamy battering rams, and, of course, the oompah band. It is the sort of spectacle that, like the Eiffel Tower, no pictures can ever quite prepare you for. Everyone crowds together at the rustic tables or, if the weather's nice, in the beautifully shaded courtyard garden, where the atmosphere is less frenzied. All the beer is from the Hofbrau Brewery, which—like the Hofbrauhaus—is now owned by the state of Bavaria. Somehow, it's impossible to imagine any segment of the American government owning such a place. Everything about the Hofbrauhaus, from its inhabitants to its excellent beer, is the very archetype of a Bavarian beer hall, or at least our image of one. Touristy? You bet—the nearby Augustiner beer hall will give you a somewhat more authentic experience. I might not want to spend the whole evening at the Hofbrauhaus, but I wouldn't miss it for the world.

that picks up nicely on similar flavors in bread. That makes helles particularly nice with sandwiches and pressed panini. As long as you don't go too heavy on the hot sauce, helles is strangely pleasant with falafel. I like mine with extra tahini, and there's something in the malt character of the beer that pairs up with the nutty chickpea and sesame flavors.

The mild hopping of this beer opens the door to the most delicate fish dishes; we need not fear that we'll overwhelm sole, plaice, flounder, or even turbot. A squeeze of lemon will accentuate the flavors in the fish and counterpoint the beer nicely. Helles has a fine relationship with shellfish, and here you can toss in the scallops, too. Crab or clams can climb onto a bed of linguini with some herbs, and this beer will do just fine. Helles can be very nice with sushi—delicate enough to leave the flavor and texture of the fish untrammeled, but tough enough to fend off occasional blasts of wasabi and pickled ginger. Trout in a delicate cream sauce is about the lightest meal you'll find in southern Germany, and helles is a very good local match. A bit of dill with that? Not a problem. Of course a sophisticated person like you would never stoop to eating fish sticks—but if you did, helles would fill the bill. Helles is a natural accompaniment to mild sausages, and the Bavarians particularly enjoy it with weisswurst and sweet mustard. Roast chicken and roast turkey will also appreciate the light touch, and the breadiness of the beer will link up nicely with the stuffing.

The patron saint of Bavarian restaurants is Miss Piggy. Most of the beer halls and beer gardens will be happy to serve you any entrée you like, as long as it's pork. You'd better be hungry, because they'll be bringing you plenty of it. The good news is that German pork is brilliant—it's much fuller flavored than most modern American pork. Sometimes you'll get a double dose of pig—roast pork with bacon, sauerkraut, and potato dumplings is a classic Bavarian dish. The malty sweetness of helles is a perfect foil for these dishes, playing into the sweetness of the meat while the carbonation and hops cut through everything else. I'm partial to stuffed pork loin or the Italian version, porchetta, and helles is a nice match with either. Helles is very pleasant with ham, cooked (but leave off the pineapple) or air-dried like Parma, Serrano, or Bayonne.

Pilsner is a bit sharp for most salads, but helles does fine with heftier salads, especially if they include cheese, ham, or bacon. You'll appreciate the light touch of helles at brunch, where it will really light up huevos rancheros or a Spanish omelette. Helles will also do nicely with eggs Benedict—it cuts right through the hollandaise sauce, finds the bacon, and sets it off, providing a counterpoint to the saltiness.

Notable Producers of Pilsner and Helles

PILSNER URQUELL If you travel to Prague, you'll see signs for it everywhere—Plzeňský Prazdroj, or **Pilsner Urquell**. In German, *Urquell* means "original source," and the claim is as true as it is stark. From this brewery in Czech Bohemia, the pilsner style and its descendents marched out to take over the world. The original pilsner has a full burnished antique gold color and a beautifully balanced, slightly spicy aroma of hops and baking bread. The bitterness is focused and powerful, driving a bone-dry palate through to a snappy finish, where soft malts emerge in the aftertaste. It's a marvelous beer—no wonder the brewers of Munich were terrified when it pounded on their doors in the 1840s. Only fifteen years ago, this beer was still fermented in open oak vats and matured in giant oak casks arranged in underground galleries tunneled through sandstone. The beer was fuller bodied then, with a faintly buttery character possibly derived from the oak, but more likely from a blend of lager yeasts then in use. For a while, the beer seemed to suffer a postcommunist hangover—it showed up in the United States old and listless, with little to recommend it. It's recovered wonderfully since then, as a result of modernized brewing techniques that have removed the romance of oak and underground aging but have restored freshness and an ability to travel. If you live in Prague, you probably miss the complex nuances of the old version, but if you live here, you'll welcome back an old friend. I first tasted Pilsner Urquell in Prague in 1984, and I was astonished. I still am. It's very robust and perfect for spicy Indian or Mexican dishes, where its cutting power will be appreciated. It's also particularly excellent with oily fish—grill some fresh sardines and go to town.

BUDWEISER BUDVAR-CZECHVAR Bohemia was once a separate kingdom, and the royal court brewery was in the town of České Budějovice, known in nearby Germany as Budweis. Just as beer from Pilsen was known as *Pilsner*, beer from Budweis was known as *Budweiser*. České Budějovice once had forty-four breweries, but now there are only two—Budweiser Burgerbrau and Budweiser Budvar. The success of the golden pilsner style was not lost on any brewer in the late 1800s, and that success inspired the American Anheuser-Busch brewery to name its beer Budweiser in the 1870s. The breweries of Budweis produced their own full-bodied golden beers based on the pilsner style, and Budweiser Budvar brewed more than 40,000 barrels in its first year of production in 1895. At first, the Czech and the American Budweisers coexisted peacefully, but eventually legal battles ensued. The Czech beer was barred from the United States, and the Anheuser-Busch product was sold in Europe as "Bud." After decades of legal threats and buyout offers, the Czech company surrendered to the onslaught of cash; it now offers its **Budweiser Budvar** in the United States under the humiliating name **Czechvar**. Anheuser-Busch's lawyers have done their job well, and there's no mention of Budweis, Budvar, or Bud-anything on the label.

The beer has a deep gold color and biscuity malt aroma with spicy Saaz hops floating overhead. The bitterness is broad and mouth-coating; it then lets go and allows sweet malt flavors to play through on a full-bodied but dry palate. Fresh baguettes linger in the aftertaste. This beer, not surprisingly, is everything that the insipid American Budweiser isn't. Czechvar is great with spicy food and seafood, but beefy enough to stand up to a thick burger. Will the real Budweiser please stand up?

SPATEN Spaten, founded in 1397, is Munich's oldest brewery. Gabriel Sedlmayr, brewmaster of the royal court of Bavaria, took over in 1807 and showed a flair for innovation. His son, Gabriel II, inherited his father's talent and launched Spaten into a leading position as one of the world's most advanced breweries. In the 1870s, Spaten became the first brewery in the world to use mechanical refrigeration. In 1894, the Sedlmayrs released Munich's first clear golden lager, Spaten Helles LagerBier. Other brewers in Munich wanted to put the genie back in the bottle and boycott the production of golden beer, but the Sedlmayrs would have none of it. Helles was here to stay.

Spaten Premium Lager has a pale gold color and a delicious aroma of bready malt and floral hops. There's a slight, pleasant whiff of hot-spring sulfur, a hallmark of lager fermentations. On the palate, sweet, bready malt is finely balanced with snappy hopping. Spaten seems to offer this beer as a bridge between its less assertive helles and its drier, sharper Pils. Regardless of nomenclature, this beer is full of lager character. It would be a fine place to start if you want to learn the difference between lagers and ales. A perfect beer to pair up with oysters, crab, lobster, and tapas.

JEVER Friesland is a region in the northwest of Germany, but—like Flanders—it contains parts of other countries, in this case Denmark and the Netherlands. Frisians have a distinct culture, and all southern Germans have at least a few Frisian jokes in their repertoire. The town of Jever, hard by the North Sea, couldn't care less about the jokes—no one's laughing at its brewery, of which it is intensely proud. The brewery is equally proud—the proper name, Friesches Brauhaus Zu Jever, flies the banner high. This was a small family-owned brewery until it was purchased in 1923 by the Bavaria–St. Pauli brewery of Hamburg, which later became part of an international conglomerate. Though the brewery has changed hands several times over the past century, Jever's distinctive beer hasn't wavered a bit. **Jever Original Friesland Pilsener** has a pale gold color and a magnificent resiny hop nose backed by notes of fresh bread. The bitterness is vivid and brilliantly snappy, bouncing off the palate like the crack of a whip. The beer is light-bodied, and malt is in the backseat, enjoying the ride out to a breathless dry finish. This is a great example of the north German pilsner style, bone-dry and razor-sharp. Serve it in champagne glasses as a mouthwatering aperitif, or chill it well and serve it with caviar or shellfish. It's also great with tapas; you can match it with almost anything except desserts, sweet dishes, or red meat. In fact, even then, a burger wouldn't be offended by it.

STAROPRAMEN Prague's favorite brewery was founded in 1869 and brewed great beer right through the dark days of communism. Staropramen doesn't refer to its beer as a pilsner—the Czechs regard that name as an appellation rather than a style description. So the beer is called simply **Staropramen**. It has a deep gold color and the bright spicy-floral aroma of the renowned Bohemian Saaz hop. It's medium-bodied but quite dry, with sharp bitterness supporting layers of bready malt. It finishes cleanly, leaving hops dancing on the tongue. This beer can be particularly good on draft, even outside the Czech Republic. In London, I once had a mind-blowing pint of Staropramen at the famous White Horse pub on Parson's Green. This was years ago, but I remember it vividly—the resiny hops just leapt out of the glass, and the malt character was profound. (I also remember it because it was one of the few pints of lager I've ever drunk in England.) You can serve this with all the usual suspects, but there's enough malt depth here to let the beer do a really great job with pork, Wiener schnitzel, and saltimbocca.

BITBURGER PRIVATBRAUEREI THEOBOLD SIMON The small Rhineland town of Bitburg is home to one of Germany's best-known breweries. It started off as a brew pub, founded by Johann Peter Wallenborn in 1817. Ludwig Simon married into the family in 1842, and his son Theobold embarked on an ambitious scheme of change and expansion. The brewery, founded before the lager revolution, originally brewed top-fermented altbier, but Theobold decided to switch to lager. Production of the now famous pilsner began in 1884. In the early 1900s, the brewery took advantage of new rail links from Bitburg and began to sell its beer

throughout Germany. The Simon family still runs the brewery, and today its old advertising slogan *Bitte ein Bit*—"a Bitburger, please"—is familiar to any German.

Bitburger Premium Pils has a bright pale gold color and a magnificent aroma of fresh bready malt and delicate, spicy floral hops, bound together by the slightest whiff of sulfur. It is a definitive lager aroma. The hop attack is sharp and fast, stunning the palate momentarily before the clean, soft malt pops out in the racy center. The finish is quick, clean, and very dry, leaving the palate humming with a bitter hop tang. Light, dashing, bready, and snappy, this is the archetypal north German pilsner. Well chilled, it makes a brilliant aperitif, especially when served in champagne glasses. It's a perfect accompaniment to caviar or oysters. At more moderate temperatures, it's a fine partner to robust fish, lobster, crab, and ham.

THE BROOKLYN BREWERY For a long time, my colleagues and I were beer snobs and tended to look down on pilsner. It seemed too ordinary for us to brew, and we were worried that our customers might feel we were selling out if we produced it. As we became more sophisticated beer drinkers over the years, we began to realize that genuine pilsner is a truly great style. It's also difficult to brew. As a beer with very simple, direct flavors, pilsner needs to be fresh to taste its best. We figured that we could brew the freshest pilsner around, so we got to work. I brought in malts, hops, and yeast from Germany and brewed **Brooklyn Pilsner** entirely from those German ingredients. They're not necessarily better than American ingredients, but they do taste different, and I wanted classic flavors. Brooklyn Pilsner has a crystalline full gold color and raises a fluffy white head. Spicy Bohemian Saaz and floral Bavarian Hallertauer hops waft overhead, along with the bready aroma of the malts. The palate opens up with a quick snap of bitterness, followed by dry, bready malt. The malt is juicy in the center and shows a brief flash of sweetness before moving into a fast, hoppy finish. Great ingredients, very cold fermentation, and long lagering times are the keys to our classic pilsner. Enjoy it with oily fish, fried fish, calamari, lobster, crab, shrimp, sushi, ham, hot dogs, and pizza. Or ice it and bring on the caviar.

Dortmunder Export

The industrial city of Dortmund, where the Dort River meets the mighty Ruhr, is home to its own distinct variant of pale lager. In the early 1800s this city was already renowned for its dark wheat beers, which it supplied to other towns in the area. Steel and coal made Dortmund a powerhouse, and Dortmunder beer fueled the workers who made its factories hum. When bottom-fermenting lager techniques were introduced in the 1840s, some brewers took them up. By the 1870s, Dortmund had developed its own adaptation of the pilsner style that had swept Europe. The Dortmund style is slightly darker than pilsner, a burnished honey-gold edging toward amber. It forsakes the effusive hop bitterness and aroma of pilsner, preferring a firm maltiness; a full-bodied, slightly sweet palate; and a clean, dry finish. In its strength, about 5.5 percent, it resembles märzen and Oktoberfest beers. The extra strength no doubt helped the beer survive the rigors of its journeys. Dortmunder beer became so popular throughout Germany and the rest of Europe that it became known simply as "export." On the strength of export, Dortmund became the biggest beer-producing city in Germany, and one of the biggest in the world.

World War II was unkind to Dortmund and left the city irrevocably altered. Dortmunder Export is still produced there, but the style has fallen on hard times. Miners and steelworkers are a thirsty lot, and as Dortmund's industrial base eroded, so did the market for the workers' favorite beer. The breweries have moved on to producing and promoting other styles, particularly the ubiquitous pilsner. For Dortmund's brewers the export style seems to be an afterthought, a reminder of another age. Brewers in other countries have fonder memories, and the style is still produced by American craft brewers, as well as breweries in Europe and even Japan.

Dortmunder Export with Food

In its affinities with food, Dortmunder export is similar enough to pilsner and helles that you can largely refer to those sections for food matches. You can think of Dortmunder export as pilsner's big brother—stronger, quieter, a bit less brash. Keep in mind that Dortmunder has a fuller malt character and that its bitterness is not as knifelike as that of pilsner. This gives it a bit more heft and makes it particularly nice with pork, burgers, seared venison, veal, and plain grilled steak. It will work wonderfully with veal or pork saltimbocca, the Italian dish of meat pounded flat and fried with prosciutto and sage leaves. Dortmunder is still bitter enough to deal with spicy food, but it also has a bit more sweetness than the pilsner; this gives it an advantage with Thai food, which almost always has some sweet elements. The same is true of many Indian dishes, which will appreciate a little bit of sweetness to counteract spicy preparations like vindaloo.

If you're having Tex-Mex, Dortmunder can handle almost anything: fajitas, chimichangas, burritos, and tacos will appreciate the beer's combination of brightness and sturdiness. It's even better than pilsner with pizzas. Like just about all German beers, Dortmunder export is terrific with wursts and ham. I find it especially good with a ham and Swiss sandwich on rye. And a bag of corn chips.

Notable Producers of Dortmunder Export

DORTMUNDER ACTIEN BRAUEREI The name sounds like a brewery on the move, but *actien* means "stock-issuing." The DAB brewery was founded in 1868 by the Fischer family, who took the company public only four years later. A series of mergers and acquisitions over the past two decades consolidated several brands under this one roof, all of them having brewed the Dortmunder export style in its heyday. In 1971, DAB started to brew pilsner, and other breweries were soon forced to follow suit. DAB's beers were once fairly popular in the United States, especially in areas with large immigrant populations from Germany. As those areas slowly dissolved, so did the American market for Dortmunder export beer, and it is now difficult to find. DAB's rival across town, the Dortmunder Union Brauerei (DUB), makes DUB Export but doesn't seem to export it, and it isn't even mentioned on the company's website. It is so rarely seen that there seemed little point in listing DUB here as a notable producer of the style.

OPPOSITE: Dortmund still brews its old export style. This poster depicts the beer's world travels.

Courtesy DAB.Brauerei.

DAB Original is a full golden beer with a fluffy white head and bready malt aroma with floral hops floating over it. The beer seems sweet at first, then finds firmness through the bready, emphatically "lagerish" medium-bodied center. The hops emerge in the end, to pull it in for a long drying finish showing a flash of hop flavor. This beer is a nice accompaniment to lobster, where the touch of sweetness will pick up on the lobster's sweet flavor. It's also nice with grilled shrimp, especially when the shrimp have been brined first with sugar and salt. Otherwise,

DAB
DORTMUNDER
ACTIEN-BRAUEREI

it's broadly versatile, especially with spicy foods, and perfectly nice with just about everything at the picnic table.

GREAT LAKES BREWING COMPANY Perhaps no brewery outside Dortmund has claimed the export style as enthusiastically as Cleveland's Great Lakes. It has won a number of awards for its version and is obviously proud—the gold medal from the Great American Beer Festival covers the label for its flagship **Great Lakes Dortmunder Gold**. The beer has a deep gold color pushing into orange and a pleasant aroma balanced between bready malt and floral hops. The hops leap in first, delivering a clean whack of sharp bitterness before fat, juicy, bready malt flavors jump into the driver's seat. The palate is medium-bodied, dry, and racy, and it slides out to a long, dry, hoppy finish. This is a robust, hoppy interpretation, a bit like a German pilsner on steroids. It's very tasty. The brash hop attack will handle steaks and burgers, and it's also very good with spicy Indian, Thai, and Mexican dishes.

All beer was once dark, and this was as true in Germany as anywhere else. The Bavarian brewers' practice of aging their beer in ice-filled caves eventually favored cold-fermenting yeast strains that were not truly "discovered" until the 1840s. Before the advent of modern malt kilning in the early 1800s, the use of lager yeasts would have made little difference to the flavor of the beer—it would have been smoky regardless. Once the flavors of the malt were smoke-free, though, things were different. While the British were producing fruity brown ales, the Bavarians and nearby Bohemians were producing cold-fermented dark lagers that eschewed fruit flavors. Instead, these beers showed a distinctive deep malt flavor, developed to great intensity by the intensive German style of mashing known as decoction. When the golden helles style of lager was introduced in 1894, dark lagers ruled the roost in Bavaria's beer halls. Helles was instantly popular, but dark lagers gave way to helles only in the 1950s and are still widely produced. They are known as dunkel or dunkles, meaning "dark."

Dunkels are typically a deep reddish-brown color, capped by an impressively sturdy tan head. As in all lagers, the flavors in dunkel are produced directly by the ingredients, and in this case some of the malts have been lightly roasted or stewed (or both), giving the beers caramel, toffee, coffee, chocolate, and even licorice notes. At about 5 percent, they are of average strength, but they can show considerable depth. A slightly sweet, nutty palate is common, and the best of them achieve complexity without being heavy or cloying. Hop aromas are muted, and the bitterness is just enough to balance out the malt. There can be little doubt that the Bavarians referred to this beer as "liquid bread" before the upstart golden hellesbier showed up to claim the title.

The region of Franconia in northern Bavaria is a particular stronghold of the dunkel style. Franconians are known for their staunch cultural conservatism, and although competing beer styles have been knocking on their door for a century, the Franconians have ignored the noise and stuck to their ways; dunkel is still quite popular in Kulmbach and Bamberg. Across the border in the Czech Republic, similar beers are known as *cerny pivo*, "dark beer." These tend to have more pronounced roasted flavors than the German versions. The Scandinavian countries and Poland can boast some credible examples as well. Dunkel was once a popular style in the United States, but eventually it gave way to Prohibition and the onslaught of mass-market pilsner. The "darkness" in the few remaining mass-market dark lagers is little more than food coloring, and the beers are rarely worthy of consideration.

Dunkels with Food

Dunkel is a terrific accompaniment to the sorts of dishes that warm the hearts of Bavarians. Typically there is some sweetness in pork dishes, often from an addition of fruit. A dash of acidity is common as well—sauerkraut and other pickled vegetables are popular. The slightly sweet, malty, caramely flavors of dunkel wrap around these foods like a warm blanket. The beer has enough sweetness to avoid being toughened by the fruit and to blunt the acidity of pickled dishes. Caramel flavors pick up on browned meats and pan juices. Venison, another great companion, may be served with a reduction sauce of sour cherries. Dunkel is a great choice for handling these sweet-and-sour combinations. It is easy to see that this beer and this food have had a long, happy relationship.

The German palate loves dumplings almost as much as it loves pork. In the north, you'll be served klosse, in Bavaria they'll bring on the knodel, and the Swabians are partial to little spätzle (or spaetzle). Some are made from potatoes, others from flour or a combination of both. The texture is usually slightly springy and gelatinous, as reminiscent of pasta as of potato. They sound stodgy, but once they've been flavored with cabbage, bacon, fruit, cheese, or wurst, they can be amazingly delicious. The dark malts in dunkel just melt into this sort of food. The same goes for liver, which the Germans also enjoy, either sautéed or in pâtés such as leberkäse.

Every region of Germany has its own wurst, or sausages. Bratwurst, blutwurst, liverwurst, rindwurst, weisswurst—all are great with dunkel. No need to stick to German sausages—this beer is just as nice with garlic Toulouse or sweet Italian sausages. Germany is famous for its excellent ham, and dunkel is a nice match, whether the ham is baked and served for dinner with potatoes or communing with mustard and cheese inside your sandwich at lunchtime. It's also a good partner for a Reuben sandwich or just about any sandwich containing bacon.

Of course, dunkel isn't only for German food. Dunkel is very pleasant with roasted or spit-roasted chicken, especially the more flavorful free-range chicken. A good hot oven or flame will give you some nice caramelization of the skin, which links up with the dark malts in the beer. Stuffing and gravy will seal the deal. Vegetables that give wine conniptions—brussels sprouts, for example—are no problem at all for dunkel, especially if they're sautéed. Dunkel is also good for handling robust fish in darker preparations—roasted monkfish with pancetta, for example. Cooked mushrooms will find a good partner in dunkel, which has enough earthiness of its own to meld with a mushroom strudel or porcini risotto.

The sweetness in dunkel lets it pair up well with a number of Chinese dishes, especially the ones we always swear we don't eat, like sweet-and-sour pork and sesame chicken. Dunkel can handle a little bit of heat if you want it spicy. This beer also works with darker-flavored Chinese dishes, such as beef in a black bean sauce or moo shu anything. Try it also with cold sesame noodles—the nutty flavors in the beer will find echoes in the sauce. Dunkel is also tasty with crispy duck.

Notable Producers of Dark Lager

SCHLOSSBRAUEREI KALTENBURG Somehow it seems especially humiliating to call up a prince in his castle and tell him that you're lost. However, I eventually decided that calling was better than keeping the prince waiting, so I pulled over and telephoned the castle. Schloss Kaltenberg, it turned out, is nearly hidden by trees on top of a hill outside the village of Geltendorf, about thirty miles west of Munich. The site held a monastery before Duke Rudolph of Bavaria built a castle here in the 1200s. The last 800 years or so have been rather tumultuous at Kaltenberg—the castle has been destroyed, changed hands, and rebuilt many times. The last rebuilding was in 1670, though the castle was remodeled into its present fairy-tale appearance in the mid-1800s. Members of the Wittelsbach family, which ruled Bavaria from 1180 to World War I, still occupy the household. The head of the family, Prinz Luitpold von Bayern (Luitpold, Prince of Bavaria), is still very much involved in state affairs, though largely in a diplomatic role. I asked the prince's young head brewer, Michael Braun, whether the family's name

was still Wittelsbach. He suddenly turned serious. "The family name is *von Bayern*, meaning *of Bavaria*. They have no other name—this is what it says in the prince's passport."

This sounded a bit much at first, but when I met Prince Luitpold, it began to make sense. The history of Bavaria and of Bavarian brewing flows through his household, and he is an expert on both. His forbears had a well-regarded brewery by 1260, wrote the Beer Purity Law (*Reinheitsgebot*) in 1516, founded the Hofbrauhaus in 1589, held the royal weissbier monopoly from 1570 until 1770, and started the Munich Oktoberfest with a royal wedding in 1810. At one time, says the prince, the royal household in Munich served meals to 500 people every day—not only the royal family but local clergy, hunters, and the workers on the estate. This financial burden was so heavy that meticulous records were kept starting in 1600, even noting who drank what and when. The prince, who has the original records, says that for more than 200 years the average daily beer consumption was about 2.2 liters per person. It is enough, he points out, "to make you really care about what you're drinking."

Prince Luitpold, who has a technical degree in brewing, clearly cares a lot. He took over the house brewery, which is within the castle walls, in 1976, when dark beers had fallen out of favor. The dunkel style has since made a comeback, partially as a result of the prince's brewing skill and marketing savvy. Schloss Kaltenberg makes only dark beers, though golden lagers and wheat beers are produced for it at another brewery nearby. The prince is an affable man, but he speaks tersely of other brewers, who he claims have tried to copy his beer, his labels, and even his lineage. Of course, people copied his family's beer for more than 800 years, so it is not surprising if they haven't stopped. The brewery now has about half of the market for dark beer in Bavaria, and the prince expects it to become the number one producer of dark beer in Germany before long. He introduces 100,000 people per year to his dunkel beer at elaborate jousting matches held every summer on the castle grounds. More than 200 people, mostly stuntmen, take part in vigorous "battle" in an arena holding 10,000 people. As far as the prince is concerned, not only does this make money for the household, but it's a brilliant marketing tool that no one else can match.

Prince Luitpold has very definite ideas about how a dunkel should taste, and these are reflected in his **König Ludwig Dunkel**, named after two of his ancestors who were kings of Bavaria. The beer has a pillowy head, a dark mahogany color, and a wonderfully deep malt aroma with a floral hop overlay. A lively effervescence and a quick snap of hops give way to a medium-bodied, rather dry malty palate showing complex light chocolate and caramel notes through the center. There is a brief glimpse of sweetness before the beer moves into a long drying finish, with coffee and chocolate in the aftertaste. The prince is adamant about malt flavors—his recipe seeks to avoid harsh malt tannins that lead to astringency. Unusually, he also dry-hops his beer, a technique usually associated with English (and now American) ales. The beer's dry but malty profile makes it very drinkable and gives it a great affinity for food. I enjoyed it immensely with an array of pork dishes at the castle's restaurant. It is also excellent with Mexican food, burgers, steaks, and sausages. As I left the restaurant, the prince gave me his business card. Embossed in gold, it shows the heraldic symbol of the state of Bavaria, topped with a crown, a symbol which only he is allowed to use. Sure enough, it reads "Luitpold, Prinz von Bayern." I probably have about a thousand business cards, but I have to admit that this is my favorite.

DINKELACKER-SCHWABEN BRÄU Carl Dinkelacker founded his brewery in Stuttgart in 1888 and was an innovator from the start. Technical innovations quickly found their way into his brewery, which was one of the first breweries in Germany to deliver beer by truck rather than by horse-drawn wagons. Several years ago, the Dinkelacker brewery merged with its rival Schwaben Bräu (also in Stuttgart) to form the current company. Some of Dinkelacker's beers are produced under license by the Spaten brewery in Munich, and **Dinkelacker Dark** is among them. It has a full mahogany color and a toffeeish nose with a hint of smoke. The bitterness is crisp, snappy, and clean, and the malts play out juicily through a medium-bodied center. The beer dashes out to a clean, dry finish. This beer is well structured, with a nice malt flavor throughout—a classic dunkel. It's great with barbecue, pork, steaks, and earthy Mexican dishes, especially those made with mushrooms or huitlacoche.

PRIVATBRAUEREI FRANZ INSELKAMMER The brewery is better known as Ayinger, but Franz Inselkammer is very much in evidence. The town of Aying is storybook pretty, and the Alps provide a gorgeous backdrop on clear days. Inselkammer is a traditional Bavarian gentleman—you won't see him wearing jeans. He looks just like the town—traditional, neat, and stylish, with a baronial air. The last time I visited him, my photographer, Denny, wanted his suit, while I fancied his beautiful loden coat. I'm probably half his age, but I doubt that I've ever looked as good as he does.

Ayinger's beers taste just the way Inselkammer looks—traditional, neat, and

Back to the source—a waitress serves beer in Ayinger's brewhouse restaurant.

stylish. **Ayinger Altbairisch Dunkel** is a classic of the style. (*Altbairisch* means "old Bavarian.") It has full carbonation and a radiant mahogany color, with a thick cap of tan foam. The aroma is malty and bready, with toffee notes and only a hint of smokiness. The palate is virtually racy, with crisp hopping stepping aside for juicy, flavorful malt on a medium-bodied frame. It zips right out to a dry malty finish, with plenty of fresh grain flavor in the aftertaste. It may seem contradictory, but here it is—a malty beer that's surprisingly refreshing. Serve it with the usual porky suspects, but don't forget burgers, steaks, and Mexican dishes featuring mushrooms or black beans.

DIXIE BREWING COMPANY Founded by German immigrants in 1907, Dixie Brewing remains a well-loved regional brewery in its native New Orleans. A century ago, New Orleans had ten breweries; only Dixie has survived to see the twenty-first century. It remains a somewhat hands-on affair, with some of the beer aged in old tanks made from Louisiana cypress wood. The brewery's principal product, called simply Dixie Beer, has strayed far from its German roots and has flavors only slightly better than the average mass-market beer. When this brewery decided to enter the modern world by producing a more flavorful beer, it reached back into its Germanic past and came up with a dunkelish dark lager. Though the label for **Dixie Blackened Voodoo** features a dark, forbidding swamp, the beer is rather inviting. It has a deep reddish-brown color and a candyish aroma of treacle and caramel with a hint of dark fruit. Any fear of sugary flavors turns out to be unfounded—light bitterness balances a dry, medium-bodied palate showing plenty of chocolate and caramel. The finish is quick and dry, with a slight astringency in the aftertaste. This is a version of the style well suited to the weather and food of New Orleans—a bit less malty than the German originals, but still full-flavored enough to stand up to robust food. Try it with burgers or barbecue, or stick to the theme and have it with blackened chicken or pork, dirty rice, and black-eyed peas.

LAKEFRONT BREWING COMPANY On the banks of the Milwaukee River, near downtown Milwaukee, the small Lakefront brewery turns out a wide range of flavorful ales and lagers. It opened in 1987 as a part-time venture between two brothers—Russell and Jim Klisch—and a third partner, and for years it brewed on a patchwork two-barrel system, with an output that would fill perhaps four kegs. In the late 1990s, Lakefront bought an old German brewhouse that had been mothballed in Pennsylvania and brought it to Milwaukee. It sits incongruously aloft inside an old brick factory building, looking vaguely like a ramshackle spaceship cobbled together by a mad scientist. Milwaukee was once home to dozens of breweries, and the Germanic beers they produced are recalled in **Lakefront Eastside Dark**, a beer with a deep reddish-brown color and a bready malt aroma adorned with rich chocolate notes. The bitterness is firm but balances very nicely against round, sweetish malts in a smooth, almost oily center. Soft chocolate and caramel lead into a long, dry, clean finish, with nuts and cocoa in the aftertaste. It's an excellent beer, and a real winner with grilled steaks, burgers, venison, Cajun blackened pork chops, and Mexican mole dishes.

Vienna, Märzen, and Oktoberfest Beers

In 1841 the influential Viennese brewer Anton Dreher released a new beer with a reddish, coppery color and a juicy malt character. He thought that the new beer was delicious, but he could have no idea that it was the start of a revolution in German brewing. The British were already producing paler malts, and now the new malting technology had helped Dreher create an amber malt. He used it to produce a beer far paler than the common smoky dark lagers of the time. The amber malt was stewed after the barley was sprouted. This converted some of the malt starches into sugars, which were then caramelized by a gentle roasting. (I've tasted some of this malt in mid-process, right out of a roasting drum at Bamberg's Weyermann maltings. It tasted wonderful, like sugary hot cereal.) Within a couple of years the Bohemians were taking things one step further with their new golden pilsners but Dreher's Vienna beer had charms all its own, and the Viennese loved it.

The success of Dreher's Vienna beer did not go unnoticed by Gabriel Sedlmayr at the Spaten brewery in Munich. He was soon using the new malt to produce a beer called *Märzen* ("March beer"). Before mechanical refrigeration made year-round brewing possible, stronger beer was made in the early spring and then laid down in ice-filled caves until the following harvest in September and October, when it would be greatly enjoyed at harvest festivals. Sedlmayr brewed his in March and then tapped it to be served at Munich's Oktoberfest in September. It emerged bronze and incomparably smooth, with a round, slightly sweet palate and a deep, toffeeish, almost spicy flavor and aroma. Märzen beer has an appetizing bitterness that serves to balance rather than challenge the malt underpinnings. At a strength of about 5.6 percent, it's a bit stronger than pilsner, but not as strong as bock beer. The balance between bready, malty, juicy sweetness and firm bitterness makes traditional märzen one of the most tantalizing of beers.

At one time märzen beer was inextricably linked to the Oktoberfest, and many beers still carry the label "Oktoberfest Märzen." These tend to be traditional. Over the years, though, changes in public taste and the internationalization of the Oktoberfest have led to a golden style of Oktoberfest beer that, while pleasant, lacks the caramelized malty depth of the original märzens. The label will often say just "Oktoberfest" or "Festbier." This style is essentially a slightly stronger version of helles. True märzens are usually copper-colored, so a beer with a golden color is unlikely to have been brewed in the original style. A close look may be needed to avoid confusion, since the terms are used almost interchangeably. Even Sedlmayr's Spaten brewery now produces a golden Oktoberfest beer, though thankfully it still makes the original märzen as well.

Anton Dreher left Vienna and went on to work in Budapest and then Trieste, where a brand of beer still carries his name. Later he ran a brewery in Michelob, Bohemia, the town from which the American giant Anheuser-Busch derived the name of its less bowdlerized products. Regarding the popularity of Dreher's beer, a brewers' publication wrote in 1878:

> *We find Dreher's beer-shops in Trieste, where they number twenty-five; in Pola, Fiume, Monica, Istria, and Dalmatia; in Greece, Egypt, Palestine, Asia Turkey, India and even in China and Japan. The credit of introducing beer into many a foreign land is due to Dreher and he has much reason to be proud of his establishment.*

The Vienna style is scarcely ever brewed in its native city anymore, but its offspring are still to be found not only in Germany but in Scandinavia and the New World as well. Beers based on the Vienna lager style were popular in the United States before Prohibition. This style of brewing is enjoying a popular revival in the form of beers such as my brewery's flagship Brooklyn Lager and the Boston-based Samuel Adams. Interestingly, the progeny of the Vienna style are to be found in Mexico as well. Dos Equis, Negra Modelo, Leon Negro, and the very tasty Christmas beer Noche Buena are all brewed broadly in this style, though none of them approaches the malty depths of the original. The Hapsburg dynasty of Austria ruled Mexico for three years before people grew tired of the hapless Emperor Maximilian and sent him back to Vienna in a coffin. They liked the beer, though, so they kept it, along with a lasting predilection for the polka rhythms that still run through Mexican music. Now that's multiculturalism.

Vienna and Oktoberfest-Märzen with Food

The caramel, bread, and malt flavors of märzenbier give it many of the same food affinities as dunkel, but a firmer hop underpinning lends it more firepower at the table. Märzen can stand up to a charbroiled steak; the hops cut through fat while the juicy malt mingles with the steak juices. It will take on most sauces, though A.1. sauce is too acidic to make a happy match. (You shouldn't be putting A.1. sauce on a decent steak anyway.) Märzen will do just fine with Stilton or béarnaise sauce. Venison will work nicely too—once again, we'll want to go easy on the sauce, especially the sort of fruit sauce it's sometimes served with. Naturally, märzen is terrific with pork, almost regardless of how it's prepared. Any Bavarian beer that doesn't match with pork has no future at all.

If you've ever been to the Oktoberfest, you've seen massive grills turning out truckloads of pork, whole chickens, and fish for the masses. Crude, perhaps, but pretty tasty too. The malt flavors in märzen just love everything about grilled meats. I imagine that you probably need a one-liter mug to accompany a whole chicken. There's no need to leave out your veggies, though the Germans often do. Grilled vegetables on a skewer develop sweet flavors that work well with märzen's deep malt character. Peppers, zucchini, onions—just about whatever you like. The

Courtesy Spaten North America.

Oktoberfest beer is traditionally tapped from wooden kegs. Spaten's malty Ur-Märzen is now available year-round.

only exception is the tomato, which develops sweetness on the grill but doesn't relinquish its sharp acidity. Besides, the tomato is a fruit, so that's cheating.

Märzen beer will happily meet the tomato on a different turf, especially one including cheese. American pizzas feature a sweet tomato sauce, its acidity already conveniently blunted by sugar. The beer sweeps in to match its own bready flavor to that of the crust, the malt sweetness matches that of the sauce, and the carbonation and hops slice through the cheese. Märzen will deftly handle all the usual toppings, but don't even think about the pineapple.

As long as you don't pile on a ludicrous tower of toppings, märzen will be great with your burger. Lots of cheese, bacon, and onions are fine—tons of ketchup, mustard, and pickles might want something hoppier (the American version of amber lager comes to the rescue here). The same sort of principle applies to barbecue—märzen will be great with slow-cooked dry-rub barbecue, but if you're reaching for the sauce, I'd pick a different beer. Märzen is terrific with ham, even if the ham is glazed, honeyed, or peppered. Baked ham with homemade macaroni and cheese will absolutely light up—you'll forget that any other beverage even exists when you taste this combination.

Sausages are an obvious match, and märzen will be happy with all but the very spiciest of them. You might want to step up to some of the terrific specialty sausages available these days. I'm partial to the offerings of D'Artagnan, Trois Petits Cochons, and Bruce Aidells, but you might have your own local specialty house or, better yet, a butcher who makes his own. The Bavarians eat their wursts with a type of mustard (*Senf*) that is mild and sweet. If you can find it, it's great stuff, especially with this beer. Choucroute—the classic Alsatian dish of cabbage, smoked meats, and sausages—is also an excellent match for märzen.

Märzen is not an obvious match for seafood, but it actually works just fine with battered fried fish and mildly spiced crab cakes. It also makes a fine partner for smoked trout, especially with a cream sauce.

Notable Producers of Vienna, Oktoberfest, and Märzen

PAULANER-SALVATOR-THOMASBRÄU Every year, Paulaner's brewmaster dresses in an ermine robe and joins his fellow brewmasters of Munich to stride across the Theresienwiese for the opening ceremonies of the Oktoberfest. It is quite a sight to behold. At the time of the first Oktoberfest, the Paulaner brewery was on the outskirts of town. Now the city of Munich has grown around it, and the brewery has run out of room to expand. So it has expanded down into the ground; in a stunning feat of engineering, some of the brewery's fermenting halls basically float on the water table underneath the brewery. It seems fitting that Paulaner, who did pioneering work in refrigeration and steam power in the 1800s, should look to technology to solve its more modern problems today.

If times have changed, at least the beer retains a great deal of character. **Paulaner Oktoberfest Märzen** has an attractive pale amber color and a distinctively German toffeeish malt aroma. Light bitterness quickly drops back behind a dry, round palate showing lightly malty, bready flavors and a hint of caramel. The finish is dry, crisp, and bready. At one time, this would have been a seasonal beer, but it is now available year-round. It's very versatile and will be equally at home with a roast chicken, a ham and Swiss sandwich, or pork-filled tamales.

SPATEN-FRANZISKANER-BRÄU No brewery is more closely associated with the history of Vienna-märzen beer than Spaten. Gabriel and Josef Sedlmayr worked with Anton Dreyer, the originator of the style, in the mid-1800s. Josef Sedlmayr premiered his version at the Oktoberfest of 1871 to adoring crowds. The Sedlmayr family still owns a sizable part of the company, and Spaten's märzenbier would probably be instantly recognizable to anyone who had tasted the original in 1871. In German, the prefix *ur* means "original," and Spaten has every right to append it to the name of **Spaten Oktoberfest Ur-Märzen**. The beer has a full honey color, a big pillowy head, and a wonderfully malty aroma with just a whiff of hops. Bitterness is light and stands aside to reveal a slightly sweet palate full of juicy

In 1810, in Munich, Prince Ludwig of Bavaria married Princess Theresia. The marriage took place at the same time as traditional harvest festivals, so it was decided that Munich should have a real blowout of a party that year to celebrate the royal wedding. The people of Munich enjoyed themselves so much that the party became enshrined as today's Oktoberfest celebration, which is held every year on Munich's Theresienwiese ("Theresia's meadow"). The two-week celebration opens with the brewmasters of Munich's six major breweries swanning onto the field in ermine robes. (I've always loved that bit.) Then, at noon, the mayor of Munich ceremonially taps the first keg. This "keg" is a traditional wooden barrel, and the tap is driven in with a mallet. If it's done correctly, the deed is achieved in a single stroke, but if not, everyone standing nearby is showered with beer. Failing to tap a barrel properly in front of all of Munich can be detrimental to a political career. In a four-man mayoral race in Munich in 1959, all the contenders met for a beer-tapping competition. Three of them botched the job, but Hans Jochen Vogel sank the tap with a single blow. Having publicly humiliated the other hopefuls, Vogel became mayor in 1960 and went on to a long political career.

malt flavor. This beer is round and soft through the center and dries into a long, bready finish. The malt flavors on display are strikingly delicious. Bring on the soft corn tacos, pork chops, roast suckling pig, turkey with gravy, and Wiener schnitzel.

THE BROOKLYN BREWERY In the middle to late 1800s, Brooklyn's beer gardens held an Oktoberfest every autumn. When we decided to brew our own Oktoberfest beer, we felt we were bringing an old Brooklyn tradition back to life. From the beginning, I knew that malt flavors were the key to brewing a classic märzenbier. So when it came time to brew our seasonal **Brooklyn Oktoberfest**, I imported Munich malts and Perle hops from Germany. The beer has a light amber color and a toffeeish bready malt aroma. The bitterness is quick and soft, standing aside for the round, slightly sweet, juicy malts that play through the center. It dries into the finish, leaving an impression of baking bread. It's very smooth, thanks to traditionally cold fermentations and months of aging. When I drink it, I can almost hear an oompah band, but I'm thankful that the impression vanishes when the pork roast arrives. This beer is great with any pork dish but also finds happy partners in roast chicken and turkey, cold cuts, sandwiches, burgers, and burritos.

SNAKE RIVER BREWING COMPANY Snake River is a classic American microbrewery. It started as a brew pub in Jackson Hole, Wyoming, and as its full-flavored beers became popular, it started bottling them. For now, the beers are distributed only in Wyoming and a few other Western and Midwestern states. **Snake River "Vienna Style" Lager** has a full honey color and an impressively rocky, sustained head. The aroma is bready with just a hint of hops and fruit. The palate is dry and round, with wonderfully juicy malts showing a flash of sweetness before bolting through the middle and out to a drying finish. Fresh grain flavors roam through the aftertaste. This beer is a very tasty interpretation from a great little producer, and it has won many awards. Try it with fried chicken, ham sandwiches, lightly loaded burgers, tacos, and pork chops.

Bock and Doppelbock

The art of brewing has always been a matter of intense civic pride in Europe, and particularly in Germany. Just as the Bohemian town of Pilsen lent its name to the world's most popular beer style, so the Hanseatic city of Einbeck is distantly recalled in the name of its native strong *bockbier*. By the middle of the fourteenth century, Einbeck's brewing prowess was well-known throughout Europe. The trading routes of the Hanseatic League flowed with Einbecker beer, which swept into Russia, Sweden, Denmark, the Low Countries, France, England, and eventually even the Mediterranean and the rest of the Holy Roman Empire.

The Bavarians were jealous. They had yet to establish their own name as great brewers, but they had plenty of opportunity to taste the beer from the north, known as *Ainpock* or *Oanbock* beer in the Bavarian dialect. Eventually the name was shortened to simply bock, and both the name and the beer were on the lips of the entire Bavarian nobility. For the Bavarian brewers to be bested on their own turf wasn't only costly, it was downright embarrassing. In 1540 Duke Ludwig X of Bavaria imported a northern brewmaster to Munich to re-create the famous northern bock beer and thus end Bavaria's humiliation. Over the years, the Munich brewers became increasingly successful, and the quality of their beer began to approach that of the north. When the Reformation and the Counter-Reformation split the Protestant north from the Catholic south, the Bavarian brewers were almost prepared to go it alone. There was just one more thing needed to complete their success. In 1612, Duke Maximilian I persuaded the chief brewmaster of Einbeck to come to Munich. The duke then detained him there and set him to work brewing authentic bock beer. By 1614, Munich's royal brewery, the Hofbrauhaus, was producing bock beer for the public, which instantly fell in love with it. Bavaria's beery ascendancy had begun.

It sounds like the plot of the next Bond film. Why all the fuss? Power and finesse, a combination the Bavarians found impossible to resist. Bock beers are strong and malty, with a smoothness developed over months of cold aging. Moderate bitterness serves to balance out a slightly sweet full-bodied palate packed with caramelish, toasty, bready flavors. The malt is the star here, and there's plenty of it, delivering a strength of 6 to 7 percent. These beers carry the weight gracefully and the palate dries out in the finish. Most bock beers are deep copper to brown in color, but paler versions have recently gained popularity. Hellesbocks are deep gold in color (hence their nickname blondebocks). Maibocks are generally light amber and served in springtime. These versions retain a similar strength, and the best of them also retain their deep malty flavors, while being somewhat lighter in body than darker examples. Before Prohibition, virtually all American lager breweries produced bock beers. Some produced it year-round; others reserved it as a much-awaited springtime specialty. These days, very few German bocks of standard strength are available in the United States, but American craft brewers have made some credible versions.

The German word *Bock* also refers to a billy goat, and brewers have made the goat the mascot of bock beer. (There's an intriguing tension in this, given that the beer originated with monks and that the goat has often been portrayed as satanic.) The goat, often dashingly dressed, is seen on various bockbier labels, drinking, cavorting, and behaving in a festively goatish way. And well he might, especially if he's enjoying the stronger version of bock called doppelbock. While bock beer originally came from northern Germany, Munich can lay claim to doppelbock. In German, Munich is München, or "place of the monks." Monastic brewing was common in Europe at one time, and the Trappists, Franciscans, and Paulists all brewed, supposedly more for sustenance than pleasure. The followers of St. Francis of Paula, known as the Paulaners, fasted twice annually. During the forty days of Lent leading up to Easter and the four weeks of Advent preceding Christmas, they were allowed no solid food. The monks brewed an especially sustaining beer, rich with nutrients, to be consumed during their fasts. While the hard-hearted might find the term vaguely blasphemous today, it is not surprising that the monks took to calling this "Holy Father" beer. It was first released to the public in 1780, and, impressed with its heftiness, people called it doppelbock, or double bock. When Franz Zacherl purchased the Paulaner brewery in the early 1800s, he named the strong Lenten beer Salvator, or "savior."

The name doppelbock is a bit fanciful—the beer doesn't literally have twice the goods of the original—but it's not hard to see why people were impressed. These beers have a strength of more than 7 percent, hidden behind a veil of smooth malt flavor. A glass of doppelbock smells just like a loaf of dark bread, fresh out of the oven. The aroma follows through onto a silky palate supported by just enough hop bitterness to keep the sweet malt from becoming cloying. Doppelbocks range in color from a deep garnet to nearly black, though truly roasty malt flavors are rare. They are beers to warm the soul in the dark days of winter or ward off an early spring chill. Because of their early connection to Lent, doppelbocks have become associated with the coming of springtime. Even though they are now produced year-round, many breweries release a special version in the early spring.

The beer brewed by the Paulaners became so famous that when the brewery was secularized, the company was officially named Paulaner Salvator. The monk still appears on the label, but not in the brewhouse. The secularized Paulaner brewery makes Salvator to this day, but it no longer has the field to itself. Soon after Salvator became famous, other breweries started to produce their own versions and began tacking the suffix "-ator" to their brand names. Today we can grace our palates with Celebrator, Maximator, Optimator, Magistrator, Kulminator, Triumphator, and Bajuvator, among others. Occasionally, brewers take things even further, producing lagers with a strength exceeding 10 percent.

These are often aged for nearly a year before bottling and emerge with an astonishing smoothness. They are brilliant with cheese or desserts.

Eisbock

Brewing lore abounds with dubious tales of beer styles discovered through fortuitous accident, but the story of eisbock is almost certainly true. As anyone who has ever put a beer in the freezer and forgotten it can attest, beer does freeze if the temperature is cold enough. A Bavarian tavern keeper learned this the hard way—he left a cask of strong bock beer outside, and by the time he went to retrieve it, it had partially frozen. It was the only beer he had left, so he had little choice but to serve it anyway. As it turned out, the resulting beer was particularly strong and delicious—the patrons thought he was a genius! The beer had essentially been distilled; some of the water had frozen, leaving the alcohol and the rest of the beer intact.

A new type of beer had been discovered, and it was called eisbock, no doubt a play on the German eiswein, which is produced from grapes that have frozen on the vine. Eisbock is warming and spirituous, making a wonderful digestif. It is now a specialty of the Kulmbacher Reichelbrau brewery, though the occasional American craft brewer has a go at the style. Eisbock also has the dubious distinction of being the apparent inspiration for the pallid "ice beers" made in Japan, Canada, and the United States by mass-market brewers. You can ignore these "ice beers," which are little more than an excuse to send sparkling ice shards flying fetchingly across your television screen during commercial breaks. They taste exactly the same as other mass-produced suds.

Bock Beers with Food

No beer has a truer, purer, more concentrated flavor of barley malt than bock beer, especially the stronger doppelbock style. It is a strikingly luscious flavor that can wrap silkily around food and melt right in. The bitterness is just high enough to allow the malt access to the essential flavors of a dish, while the malt's sweetness can handle a moderate amount of sugar in accompanying sauces. It is this balance that makes doppelbock unbeatable with game.

In doppelbock, venison meets its closest partner. The slightly burnt high caramel flavor of the malt latches onto the flavor of the meat and doesn't let go. Malt sweetness matches classic fruit sauces like sour cherry, and the intensity of malt flavor can handle dark, tacky reduction sauces. The flavor of the beer then becomes one with the flavor of the venison, and the match is perfect. It's amazing—the affinity is so complete that you'd think the deer spent its whole life eating nothing but malt. If you're partial to venison, you absolutely owe it to yourself to try it with doppelbock. Speaking of furry game, have you ever had moose? Doppelbock is the beer to handle its deeply gamy flavor.

Other dark-meat game fares almost as well. Duck and goose are very good matches, especially if served with fruit sauces. Squab and wood pigeon, with their almost chocolaty meat, find doppelbock an elegant accompaniment. These birds may seem a bit small to stuff, but it's worth taking the trouble, especially when you are pairing them with the beer, which links up with the bread in the stuffing. Wild boar is another strongly flavored game that pairs well with doppelbock. At Felidia Ristorante in New York, I've had Ayinger's Celebrator doppelbock to accompany pappardelle with wild boar, porcini mushrooms, and carrots. It was a wonderful match, and the beer was as good with the mushrooms as it was with the boar. Cooked carrots tend to be sweet, so the beer's sweetness helped there, too. Sweeter doppelbocks are also fine matches for sautéed foie gras and sweetbreads.

Pork, of course, is excellent with doppelbock. Roast suckling pig is an absolutely spectacular match—when the malt flavor hits that crackling skin, magical things happen. If you don't happen to have a rotisserie spit for roasting your own pigs, try a stuffed pork loin with sautéed apples and potato dumplings. The beer will be great with all the elements of the dish: lusciously juicy with the pork, familiar and friendly with the stuffing, sweet and silky with the apples. And doppelbock loves potatoes, which echo the starchy biscuit flavors of the grain. Potato dumplings, mashed potatoes, roasted potatoes, baked potatoes, home fries—doppelbock is great with all of them. Sausages, whether they are German bratwursts, Italian sweet sausage, or French garlic Toulouse, will find doppelbock a very good partner. The only exceptions are very hot sausages such as real Louisiana andouille, for which a brighter beer might be preferable.

Ham, bringing salt to the palate, will find a nice contrast with doppelbock's sweetness. Boiled ham and baked ham are fine matches, and air-dried hams like prosciutto di Parma are even better. For a brilliant hors d'oeuvre, try wrapping some thin-sliced prosciutto around chunks of aged Gruyère cheese. If you serve it with doppelbock, watch out—your guests may want you to forget about dinner and just serve this all evening. If the ham is in a sandwich, doppelbock is very tasty indeed, but if you want to avoid something as strong as doppelbock, you might want to go with plain bockbier or maibock if you can find it.

Malt sweetness gives doppelbock a special ability to handle dishes with sweet elements. Many Italian raviolis are stuffed with sweet root vegetables or squashes. Pumpkin ravioli with walnut sauce is one of my favorite examples; goat cheese and beet ravioli is another. Doppelbock is terrific with these, and it can also handle the sweet side dishes that are often served with meat. Sweet potatoes, turnips, and parsnips can all be somewhat sugary, and doppelbock is able to match them without tasting thin or overly dry. You can also use doppelbock to match sweet elements in salads. The Italian brewery Moretti makes an excellent doppelbock called Doppio Malto, which I've paired with a salad featuring fresh figs, walnuts, and sweet Gorgonzola. It is an absolutely delicious combination.

You wouldn't necessarily think that doppelbock would be a great choice with Mexican food, but it is. We tend to think of Mexican cuisine as being full of bright flavors—lime, cilantro, and chilies. That's only partially true—what about all those earthy beans? Then there are the mushrooms; the pungent adobo, mole, and pipian sauces; and lots of vegetable flavors like epazote, prickly pear, and stewed chilies. Roasted and smoked chilies bring other dimensions to many Mexican dishes. Doppelbock works wonders with these, and the malt sweetness helps the beer stand up to fiery spices. The malt flavors remain intact and meld with earthy flavors in the food. Here in New York, the traditional Mexican restaurant La Palapa serves a puerco en pipían (pork tenderloin in pumpkin-seed sauce) that I frequently dream about. The malt character of the Salvator doppelbock was a wonderful match for the smokiness of the sauce and the nutty flavors of the pumpkin seeds. The match was surprising and brilliant. We're talking more about traditional Mexican food than we are about Tex-Mex, but many of the same principles still apply to Tex-Mex. Mexican beers are much thinner these days, but the original Vienna-style lagers brought to Mexico by its Austrian rulers had the same flavors as doppelbock, just a bit less concentrated. It's not hard to see why these beers became quite popular.

And let's not forget about dessert. Stronger, sweeter bockbiers can be very nice with custards, especially the classic caramel flan or crème brûlée.

Notable Producers of Bock Beer

PAULANER-SALVATOR-THOMASBRAU The original "Holy Father" beer was once associated with Lent but is now available year-round. The secularized Paulaner brewery still maintains the tradition of ceremonially tapping a wooden barrel of Paulaner Salvator a few weeks before Easter, to begin the early springtime Starkbierfest, or "strong beer season." **Paulaner Salvator** has a dark amber color, a thick cap of tan foam, and a toffeeish deep malt aroma with spicy hints of dark rum, treacle, and honey. Rich sweet malt is up front on the palate before measured bitterness steps forward to balance it out. The body is fat, round, smooth, and silky, and the finish is short and semisweet. This beer begs for braised pork belly or roast suckling pig. The sweet malt melts into slow-cooked pork, creating a

Spaten's Optimator retains enough malt sweetness to provide a fine match for a classic crème brûlée.

match so perfect and pleasurable that I've sometimes felt almost guilty for enjoying it so much. That match is almost obvious, but I've found Salvator to be multitalented. When I went to taste beer with traditional Mexican dishes, Salvator was the unexpected star of the show, using its deep malt flavors to latch onto nutty flavors in the dishes. The sweetness also doused fires started by robust chilies. Salvator is a great partner for nutty cheeses—try it with harder cow's milk cheeses, especially aged Swiss Gruyère.

AYINGER When you walk with Franz Inselkammer through the picturesque village of Aying, it quickly becomes clear that although he has no royal title, Inselkammer is considered a prince. A strikingly handsome grandfather of regal bearing, he is greeted warmly by everyone he passes. Aying is in the foothills of the Alps, only ten miles or so from Munich, but it seems a different world entirely. Six generations of the Inselkammer family have lived in Aying since 1804, first as farmers, then as brewers, starting in 1878. When, several years ago, Inselkammer's eldest son told him that he wanted to continue the family business, the father was delighted and built a beautiful new brewery in lush fields at the edge of the village. The new brewery contains a restaurant, where diners can enjoy excellently prepared Bavarian specialties while sitting virtually amid the large brewing vessels. From the best tables, there's a panoramic view of the Alps in the distance. Ayinger also owns a charming guesthouse and a restaurant in the village.

Outside Germany, the brewery has been made famous by its doppelbock, **Ayinger Celebrator**, a very dark, virtually black beer with a rich pillowy tan head. Each bottle has, hanging rakishly off the neck, a little plastic billy goat, the unofficial mascot of doppelbock. The aroma shows plenty of malt, along with coffee and chocolate notes. They all come together in a well-structured, full-bodied malty palate featuring a harmonious balance between sweet, chocolaty, toffeeish malt and a drying bitterness that propels the beer into a long finish. Bready coffee and chocolate flavors waft through the aftertaste, recalling *pain chocolat*. Celebrator is an excellent partner for the gamy flavors of venison, duck, goose, and wild boar. It's also terrific with stuffed pork loin and good ham.

SPATEN Though it now strikes me as loitering or even delinquency, my brother Roger and I used to make a pastime of sitting on stoops on St. Mark's Place in Manhattan, watching the world go by. In the early 1980s, the street was like a carnival, the wild and woolly bridge between the straitlaced world of New York University and the dark, punky East Village. It made for terrific theater, and it wouldn't have been the same without some good beer.

Among our beers of choice was **Spaten Optimator,** one of the first truly great beers I ever drank. Surprisingly, it was widely available in delis even back in those days. Optimator probably originally lured us with its enthusiastic name and its boldly heraldic-looking label featuring the "Doppelspaten," two white spades on a red shield. The name Spaten and the symbol of the spade recall the name of Georg Spät, who became owner of the brewery in 1622. The label was cool, but it was the flavor of the beer that retained our loyalty. Spaten Optimator has a deep russet-brown color and a light toffee aroma with a fleeting hop note. Sweet caramel and toffee dominate the flavor profile, with hops providing good balance on a full-bodied frame. The beer turns lean in the long finish. Chocolate and caramel linger. You can almost imagine fasting monks living on this beer—there's plenty of residual sugar and the description "liquid bread" seems particularly appropriate. It's excellent with roast suckling pig, stuffed pork loin, venison, and sausages. It's also great with pumpkin ravioli, especially with walnut sauce. The East Village's thrilling punk-rock days are far behind it—now it's full of trendy restaurants where you can enjoy your Optimator without loitering on someone's stoop.

SCHLOSSBRAUEREI EGGENBERG *Schloss* means "castle," though in this case it refers to a great house in the town of Eggenberg, between Linz and Salzberg, Austria. Austria is no longer known for its beer, though it has an illustrious brewing tradition. This small "castle" brewery keeps the flag flying with a roster of robust beers. When the German Feldschlossen brewery bought the Swiss Hurlimann brewery in 1996, one of the world's most notable beers soon found itself homeless. Hurlimann was the brewer of **Samichlaus**, the strongest lager in the world at 14 percent. It brewed Samichlaus, which means "Santa Claus," once a year on December 6, St. Nicholas Day. The beer was then aged for a full year and not released until the following December 6. Feldschlossen decided that it had no interest in brewing this famous but tiny specialty, and to the dismay of beer connoisseurs the world over, it ceased production of Samichlaus. Schloss Eggenberg, no doubt recognizing a good opportunity, picked up the rights to brew the beer and reintroduced it.

The label is unfortunately silly, with its vulgar proclamation "Der stärkste Bier der Welt—Guinness Book of World Records." That record has long since been surpassed, and the beer has far more important things to recommend it. Samichlaus is a very pretty ruby red color and raises a head that quickly collapses to a ring around the glass. The malt aroma is amazingly intense and almost meaty, with notes of toffee, baking bread, tawny port, and nuts. The palate is round, smooth, syrupy, and sweet, with juicy acidity and perfectly tuned hopping that reins it in for a long, clean finish. Honey flavors linger on the palate. Samichlaus is probably better than ever, and absolutely stunning. Pair it with sautéed foie gras or foie gras terrine, magret of duck, ice cream, crème brûlée, or chocolate desserts. Or have a flavor riot with cheese, anything from sweet fresh goat cheeses to Stilton or other salty blues, or nutty, fruity aged Gruyère. It's also a spectacular digestif all by itself, or with a cigar. Enjoy it like vintage port or a fine single malt, neither of which has anything on Samichlaus.

OPPOSITE: Given the name, one might expect a donkey, but it's pronounced "orse" instead. No horses either, though—a goat, the traditional symbol of bockbier, frolicks on Aass Bock's label.

EINBECKER BRAUHAUS "Ohne Einbeck gäb's kein Bockbier," reads a placard outside Einbeck's last brewery: "Without Einbeck, there would be no bock beer." True enough. The Einbecker Brauhaus is the sole inheritor of the Hanseatic brewing tradition that led to Einbeck's nickname, "the beer city." A Städische Brauerei, or state brewery, was built here in 1794, consolidating private brewing rights into a publicly owned entity. In 1854, the brewery offered its first

AASS BREWERY NORWAYS
AASS
Aass
Established
1834

BOCK BEER
PREMIUM NORWEGIAN
AASS BRYGGERI, DRAMMEN, NORWAY.

beer in bottles, and the same distinctive low-shouldered bottle is used today. In 1880, the state sold shares in the brewery, which was finally incorporated in 1967. Today, Einbecker Brauhaus is owned by the large German brewing group Brau und Brunnen, who also own Dortmunder Union Brauerei, among many others.

Einbecker produces two bockbiers. Einbecker Ur-Bock Dunkel isn't very dunkel—it has a bright, full amber color and a spicy malt aroma lifted by notes of floral hops. Concentrated toffeeish malt flavors make the first impression, but momentary sweetness is quickly pulled into line by broad, sturdy bitterness. The palate dries as it reaches the juicy, malty center, then slides out to an almost flinty dry finish. An appetizing bitterness remains. Firm and well structured, the beer carries its 6.5 percent with a confident hoppy swagger. Let it sink its teeth into roast pork loin, fried chicken, barbecue, and mushroom quesadillas.

Einbecker Mai-Ur-Bock is a traditional springtime beer with a pale orange color, a fluffy off-white head, and a honeyed, toffeeish malt aroma. Round, soft malts emerge first, quickly followed by brisk bitterness to balance out the malt sweetness. The center is spicy, toffeeish, and juicy; and the beer maintains a refreshing balance into a long, dry, malty, hoppy finish. This is a delicious beer in which hops and malt vie for dominance on the palate. At one time, the robust hopping would have enhanced this beer's ability to travel. The interplay between the malt and hops makes it an interesting drink and a great food beer. It has both cutting power and malt depth, making it a great selection for roast suckling pig, steaks, burgers, and barbecue. Einbeckers also enjoy it with fried fish.

AASS BRYGGERI Founded in 1834, the Aass Brewery is the oldest in Norway. Stop tittering—the name is pronounced "orse" and means "summit" in Norse. The brewery is in Drammen, on the banks of the Drammen River about twenty-five miles south of Oslo. Poul Lauritz Aass bought the brewery in 1860, and today it is run by the fourth generation of his descendents. Long before I knew what malt was, I loved the malt flavors of **Aass Bock**. On the unique pink-and-black label, a billy goat helps himself to a frothing stein of beer. The beer has a deep garnet-red color and an amazing malt aroma. It smells like a bowl of hot cereal, or, actually, like the mash at a brewery. The palate is round, luscious, and smooth, with light waves of malt, chocolate, licorice, and toffee caressing the tongue through the juicy off-dry center. The finish is long, malty, and clean. This beer is lagered for six months before bottling, and you can taste it. Aass Bock is a gorgeous world classic that is scarcely matched in Germany. It's very versatile, and a perfect choice for roast suckling pig, roast pork loin, puerco en pipían, venison, and a full range of game dishes.

AUGUSTINERBRÄU WAGNER The German name for Munich is München, which means "the place of the monks," and this concept is depicted in the town symbol, a hooded monk with his arms outstretched. The Franciscans gave rise to Spaten, the Paulists founded Paulaner, but the Augustinians were there first. They laid the foundations for their monastery in 1298, within steps of the famous Frauenkirche. By 1328, they had a brewhouse. The brewery was secularized in 1803 and for a short time was owned by the state, until Anton and Therese Wagner bought it in 1829. The stately Augustiner beer hall now stands where the brewery once stood, and the present brewery was built nearby in 1885, over the old cellars. Many people in Munich consider Augustiner the city's finest brewery and often refer to Augustiner beers as suitable for connoisseurs. All the Augustiner beers have a wonderful depth of malt character, none more so than the doppelbock, **Augustiner Maximator**. It has a very pretty garnet-brown color and a wonderfully deep aroma of toffee, caramel, and burnt raisins, with a hint of smoke. Luscious sweet malts softly caress the tongue as light bitterness rises to balance the sweetness. In the center there is a flavor of dark raisin bread, straight out of a hot oven. The finish is long, off-dry, and raisiny, leaving a lingering impression of grain. It is not hard to imagine monks living on this beer for weeks during their Lenten fasts. Maximator is a beautiful beer, sweet, rich, and uncompromisingly traditional. Wrap it lovingly around roast suckling pig, pork loin, venison, boar or venison sausages, short ribs, Gorgonzola dolce, or panna cotta.

Although all beers were once dark, few have ever been truly black. Some stouts can make a reasonable claim, at least until a bright light shows up their reddish highlights. The Thuringian town of Bad Kostritz in the former East Germany is home to a beer so black that it is simply called *Schwarzbier*, or "black beer." **Kostritzer Schwarzbier** bears some resemblance to Irish stout in that it combines snappy bitterness with dry, coffeeish roast flavors on a light to medium-bodied frame.

Locked into the time capsule that was East Germany, the Kostritzer Schwarzbierbrauerei emerged into Europe after the cold war with this old style intact, when it had apparently long since died out elsewhere. How the brewery managed this is difficult to say. Other breweries did what had been previously unthinkable—reacting to a lack of hard currency, they disregarded the *Reinheitsgebot* and started adding corn to their beers, as Americans had done decades earlier. Lacking the technology of the American mass-market brewers, most East German breweries made ghastly products. One blustery afternoon in 1986 I wandered into a bar in East Berlin and ordered a beer called Bären. It was the worst beer I've ever had on German soil, thin and soapy. After the wall fell, the Bitburger brewery purchased and refitted Kostritzer, bringing it into the modern age while brewing a classic old style almost lost to history.

The Japanese brewers Sapporo and Asahi make very similar beers, probably inspired by the black beers of Thuringia. Most older Asian breweries were originally started by German monasteries, and it is likely that the monastic breweries brought this style of beer to Japan with them. (German monasteries once dotted the globe, and this probably also explains why India brews only lagers, despite centuries of English influence.) Recently, American craft brewers have taken note of this obscure beer style and started to produce their own schwarzbiers. The Thuringians would no doubt be amused to know that many more schwarzbiers are now being brewed in the United States than in Germany. Perhaps because this beer style packs plenty of flavor into a beer that is light in alcohol, at about 3.5 percent, it is a favorite with brewers in states where the alcohol content of beer remains restricted. The pub brewers of Utah, for example, make some spectacular schwarzbiers.

Schwarzbier with Food

Even though schwarzbier is a lager, the roasted malts drive its flavor, giving it a strong resemblance to Irish stout. However, schwarzbier is never served with the sort of creamy nitrogenated head that Irish stouts are famous for, and its higher carbonation gives it an extra zing on the palate. This is a great beer for a grilled steak, especially if you get a nice char on the exterior. The same goes for burgers, and the beer will withstand the usual toppings. Bitter chocolate flavors will make schwarzbier a nice partner for traditional Mexican mole sauces, which are austere and complex rather than sweet.

As it turns out, black beer is very tasty with blackened food. Schwarzbier is brilliant with Cajun blackened chicken and pork chops. My favorite versions of these dishes are fairly spicy, and this beer is robust enough to handle the fire. The beer's affinity with the pan-blackening technique seems obvious, but it can be surprising how profound the match can be. Let's not forget the side dishes—schwarzbier can handle black-eyed peas, dirty rice, and even okra. Jambalaya, the Cajun version of the Spanish rice dish paella, can be spicy and full of everything from crayfish to andouille sausage to chicken. Schwarzbier's clean roast flavors can cut through it all and help to meld the disparate flavors on the palate.

Sausages are an easy choice, and schwarzbier will be nice with any of them, especially if they're grilled. Ham will be a good match as well. This beer is great with sandwiches at lunchtime; using dark bread will enhance the match even further. Dark bread brings pastrami and corned beef to mind; they would also be fine partners for schwarzbier.

Notable Producers of Schwarzbier

EINBECKER BRAUHAUS This brewery is best known for its bockbier, and somewhat less widely for its sharp, dry, aromatic pilsner. Strangely, the brewery's website makes no mention of **Einbecker Schwarzbier**, which has recently made its way into the United States. It has a very deep russet-brown color and an aroma of toffeeish malt, caramel, and chocolate. On the palate, it's medium-bodied, soft, and round, with balancing light hopping, the roast contributing a nice juicy acidity in the center. The finish is quick, clean, and dry, with light coffee and chocolate flavors lingering. The roast is used here more for structure than for big flavors, leaving caramelized malts to do the heavy lifting. This beer is wonderful with Cajun and earthy Mexican dishes, and it makes a great accompaniment to baked ham with homemade macaroni and cheese.

KULMBACHER The Franconian town of Kulmbach has been known for its beer for more than 650 years. A brewing monastery was established here in 1349, and over the centuries the monks gained a widespread reputation for tasty dark beers. The beers of Kulmbach tend to be darker than those of its one-time rival, Munich, occupying an idiosyncratic space between the standard dunkel style and the black schwarzbier style. The Kulmbacher brewery's Mönchshof label recalls the monks who first brewed here, and the brewery reserves the Mönchshof label for its most traditional beers. **Kulmbacher Mönchshof Klöster-Schwarzbier** has a dark reddish-brown color, a flamboyantly rocky head, and an aroma of toffee, caramel, and milk chocolate. The palate is smooth, dry, and silky, with voluptuous chocolaty malts and brisk hopping in admirable balance. The flavors are linear—the beer finishes just as it opened, dry and smooth. Hops and coffee emerge in the aftertaste. Even though it's not quite black, this is an elegant interpretation of the style, racy and very drinkable. Enjoy it with steaks, roast beef, venison, pork loin, sausages, baked ham, and Mexican dishes featuring black beans.

9

New Traditions American Craft Brewing

In 1876, there were 2,700 breweries in the United States. Many of them were small, serving a restaurant, a neighborhood, a city, or a region.

None of their beers were nationally distributed. American breweries produced a wide variety of styles—pale ale, Vienna lager, pilsner, weissbier, brown ale, porter, stock ale, steam beer, and more. American brewing was a culture as varied and vibrant as the culture of America itself, invigorated by immigrants and the beer and food traditions they brought with them.

One hundred years later, it was all gone. There were only forty breweries left in the United States, a country of more than 240 million people. What was worse, almost all forty breweries made essentially the same product. Worse still, that product was flavorless. Whether it was Pabst (still the biggest-selling brand in 1976), Budweiser, Miller, or Coors—who could really tell the difference? The brewmasters themselves had a tough time telling their own beers apart from those of their rivals in blind taste tests. Their customers were loyal to the name on a bottle or can, but inside the package there was nothing to be loyal to. A peek into a supermarket or deli beer cooler would have revealed Budweiser, Miller, perhaps Coors, maybe a taste-alike regional brand, American Lowenbrau (brewed by Miller in a German disguise), and possibly a few stale bottles of Bass Ale. The mass-market brands have changed little since then. Bartenders tell me that when they run out of a mass-market brand on draft, they just hook up another mass-market brand to the same tap without bothering to change the handle. No one ever notices.

To be fair, these beers did fit the times. American food culture as a whole had become bland and commodified. In supermarkets, entire shelves were given over to different brands of plain white bread, many of them from subsidiaries of the same companies. "Whole wheat" bread was white bread with a handful of bran and plenty of food coloring. Coffee came in dissolvable crystals, vegetables came in frozen blocks, and ketchup was king. Cheese? From what I remember, there were

BROOKLYN
BREWERY

Courtesy Brooklyn Brewery.

three varieties—American cheese slices (individually wrapped for your satisfaction), yellow cheddar blocks, and shredded mozzarella. Perhaps if you lived in an Italian neighborhood you could find ricotta, when you were lucky. If you had spent some time in Europe eating and living with great food and drink, American culinary life was, to put it bluntly, hellish.

By the mid-1970s, a revolt was under way in California. People who had been to Europe had seen how wonderful food could be, and they resolved to bring that lost sensibility back to Americans. Alice Waters opened Chez Panisse in Berkeley, basing her restaurant on French techniques and great local sustainably grown produce. Winemakers in the Napa and Sonoma valleys started to set aside their gallon jugs and create serious wines, wines meant for food. Hidebound notions of beer as a bland, simple drink for the masses didn't convince people who'd been to England, Germany, or Belgium. They'd enjoyed malty English bitters at pubs, spritzy clovey weissbiers in Germany's sunny beer gardens, and Trappist ales at canalside cafés in Belgium. They were not about to drink the flavorless fizz being pitched to them by the big brewers.

Jack McAuliffe certainly knew better. He'd served with the U.S. Navy in Britain and was impressed by the pale ales and bitters he'd gotten used to enjoying. When he got back to the United States in 1976, there was nothing on the shelves with enough flavor for him. He solved the problem by establishing America's first new post-Prohibition microbrewery in Sonoma, northern California, in the middle of the wine country. The name of the brewery, New Albion, recalled his British inspiration, and he started to produce tiny batches of British-style ales. Although these beers were terrific, McAuliffe was ahead of his time—his brewery lasted for only six years. But it inspired dozens of others, including the current Mendocino Brewing Company, a successor to New Albion. A cultural change was happening, sparked by a new awareness of flavor.

The rising tide lifted old boats as well. The Anchor Brewery of San Francisco had survived the end of the nineteenth century, but it was on its last legs when Fritz Maytag, a scion of the washing-machine empire, bought it in 1965. Amazingly, Maytag revived the brewery on the merits of steam beer, a relic style made famous during the gold rush in California. Now things were going his way, and he started to revive other traditional styles as well. His beers inspired other brewers, and a chain reaction was set off.

Restaurant-breweries were once common in the United States, but Prohibition had killed them off. Now, new brew pubs (or brewpubs) started popping up everywhere. This concept was based on David Bruce's chain of revolutionary "Bruce's Breweries" in England. Brew pubs started making revivalist ales with great depth

OPPOSITE: A brewery grows in Brooklyn. Once home to forty-eight breweries, Brooklyn has a proud past and a bright future in traditional brewing.

A collection at the Brooklyn Brewery of beer bottles from nineteenth-century New York.

of flavor. Small stand-alone breweries producing less than 15,000 barrels were described by a new term—"microbreweries." The craft brewing movement began in California's wine country, moved into the hop-growing regions of the Pacific Northwest, and then spread to the East Coast. Jim Koch, an advertising and marketing man with several brewers in his family tree, founded the Boston Beer Company and launched its flagship beer, Samuel Adams Boston Lager. Brooklyn, New York, long stripped of the forty-eight breweries it had boasted at the end of the nineteenth century, saw the birth of the traditionalist Brooklyn Brewery, founded by the journalist Steve Hindy and the banker Tom Potter. The message was clear—flavorful beer was back, and it was proudly American. Using a shrewd mix of media savvy and guerrilla marketing, Jim Koch and his Samuel Adams Boston Lager brought the flavor of real beer to millions of Americans who'd had no idea what they'd been missing. As small breweries became regional enterprises, the term "microbrewery" started to lose its meaning—some of these breweries were no longer "micro." But they were still brewing terrific beer, and the term "craft brewery" was coined to describe a producer creating traditional beers with traditional ingredients by traditional methods. In other words, real beer. Once someone started to drink real beer, there was no turning back.

As I write this, it's a brand-new world. There are once again more than 1,000 breweries in the United States. My local deli in Brooklyn carries more than 100 brands of beer, five brands of real maple syrup, ten different honeys, twelve vinegars, four olive oils, and a boatload of spices. Around the corner is a charcuterie worthy of Paris, with dozens of cheeses, six different hams, and rotisseried chickens dripping their juices onto a bed of golden potatoes. There is ice cream from Spain in flavors like "Grand Marnier and Chocolate." In *Brooklyn*. We've finally arrived.

Craft-brewed American beers are meant for this new world of flavor. They are inspired by European beer styles, but they tend to be bolder, louder, and flashier, just like many Americans. The watchword for American craft beer is *more*. More hops, more malt, more caramel flavors, more roast flavors, more aroma, and sometimes more alcohol. Some of these beers have become new styles unto themselves and have spawned their own imitators. These new American styles taste different from their European predecessors and work differently with foods. That is why they are worth looking at separately. The heady mix of a newly vibrant food culture, the wide availability of imported classic beers, and the emergence of excellent American craft brewing have made the United States the most exciting place in the world to enjoy the juice of the barley.

American Pale Ale, Amber Ale, and India Pale Ale

As American craft brewing started to flower in California in the late 1970s and early 1980s, the pioneering brewers found that they had a few problems. One problem, not surprisingly, was money. The brewers didn't have much capital to spend, and each brewery needed to establish a reasonable cash flow as soon as possible or be doomed to failure. Although the country's most popular beers were lagers, a need for economy pointed to ales. Lagers require serious refrigeration for their cold fermentation and maturation. Long aging means lower production from a finite number of tanks. Few new breweries could afford this, so ales it was. That suited the brewers fine—the wonderful ales in England had inspired many of them to brew in the first place. But this led to the second problem—ingredients. English malt and hops taste completely different from American malt and hops. English ingredients could be imported, but England was more than 6,000 miles from the West Coast, and the shipping would be ruinously expensive.

Then it started to occur to the brewers that there was no need to make a mirror image of British beers: the United States had its own malt and its own hops. The brewers looked for the best ingredients America had to offer. American and Canadian barley malts tend to be clean and lightly flavored, without a lot of deep biscuity flavors. They're good malts, but they don't have the kind of distinctive personality that sets the best German and English malts apart. Hops, however, are a different matter.

German and British brewers had long disdained American hops, finding their bitterness sharp and their aromatics too wild. The new American brewers found these hops alluring and based their beers on them. The new experimental Cascade hop growing in the Yakima Valley in Washington state was just what they were looking for. The Cascade was bred by crossing England's earthily aromatic Fuggle variety with a wild American hop. The result was a robust plant producing hop flowers with almost twice the aromatic compounds contained in the English variety, and it had personality in spades. The Cascade is a fine bittering hop, but the aroma is what makes it special. Cascade hops burst with a grapefruity citrus aroma, backed by notes of black currant and pine needles. The aroma is superbright, not unlike that of the finest Sauvignon blancs. The Cascade, together with its cousin the Chinook and the boldly resinous Centennial, became the basis for a style of American pale ale pioneered by California brewers.

American pale ales are deep gold to copper in color and highly aromatic, with a dry, medium-bodied palate supported by relatively light malt flavors. They have snappy bitterness up front and then give way to some fruitiness and malt flavor in the center, leading to a dry, clean finish. Sierra Nevada Pale Ale is the classic version of this style, and it may be the most copied beer in the United States. Anyone who brews pale ale in the United States defines his or her product against this beer in one way or another. If an American brewer tells you he's never tasted it, he's probably lying.

Darker versions of American pale ale are sometimes referred to as amber ales, or, even more vaguely, just "amber." To some extent, "amber ale" is a catchall term and is therefore difficult to pin down. You can expect these beers to be copper-colored and to show more caramel malt flavor than paler beers. They are sometimes fuller-bodied and can be fairly fruity. Almost all will show some citrusy American hop character. Whether amber ale is a separate style is an argument far too esoteric for our pursuit. No matter how many angels can dance on the cap of the bottle, if the word "amber" appears on the label, expect more caramel malt flavor and perhaps a bit more fruit.

The IPA style was repopularized by the revivalist brewer Bert Grant in the 1980s. Grant, originally a brewing scientist and an expert on hops, set up his brewery in Yakima, Washington, and started to put the nearby hop fields to good use. He produced a relatively light-bodied but scorching IPA—its searing bitterness practically blew the socks off anyone who dared to drink it. Bert Grant was an iconoclast, and if you told him his beer was too hoppy, he would blithely tell you that he had brewed it for his own satisfaction, not yours. A similar attitude is still popular among some western brewers of IPA, symbolized most notably by the Stone Brewing Company's amazingly severe (and popular) Arrogant Bastard IPA.

American India pale ale has become a style unto inself. There are few British examples left of the original style, but dozens of IPAs are now brewed in the United States, and IPA is one of the most popular styles among craft brewers. The best IPAs retain a brashly resinous dry-hop bouquet and a knifelike bitterness opening up to a solid malt center that supports the hops through to a dry finish. These ales can be unbalanced, but pleasantly so. Anyone can throw tons of hops into a kettle, though, and coarser versions, while interesting, are to be avoided by all but the most devoted "hopheads." Great versions are endlessly appetizing and have hop aromatics that are just waiting to get busy with your food.

American Pale Ales, Amber Ales, and India Pale Ales with Food

A few years ago, American food culture crossed a threshold, though most of us barely noticed. For the first time, ketchup, king of American condiments, was outsold by salsa. Americans are eating spicier foods than they ever ate before, and much of the influence is coming from Mexico. Mexican food is quite regional—you will not find the Tex-Mex burrito in the Yucatán, for example. There are common elements, however—chilies, citrus, cumin, cilantro, and other bright flavors, sometimes married to the darker flavors of mushrooms, corn, nuts, and smoke.

American pale ales revel in these flavors, and their bright, citric aromatics provide perfect matches for a wide range of Mexican food. Cascade, Chinook, and Centennial hops taste of lime and cilantro. The robust bitterness of American pale ale will cut through cheese and then lift the fire of chilies off your palate while the hop flavors dance with the spices. These beers are lively and vivacious. The comedian Steve Martin once said that it's hard to play a sad tune on a banjo. True enough, and I feel that a great American pale ale tastes the way a banjo sounds—with vibrant, clear, happy notes. These beers are great with spicy seafood preparations, especially shrimp. What else? Tacos, quesadillas, tamales, chimichangas, chiles relleno, tostadas, chilaquiles, panuchos, enchiladas, fajitas, huevos rancheros—the list is endless. All these foods are virtually foolproof with American pale ales.

Mexican food culture is strong in California, and it's hard for me to resist the notion that the early development of this young beer style was somehow tied to its affinity for Mexican cuisine. Of course, the dishes I've mentioned are only a tiny corner of the vast world of Mexican cooking. I can tell you, though, that I've read entire Mexican cookbooks and not seen a single dish that wouldn't be great with a fresh pint of a great American pale ale.

For similar reasons, Thai and Vietnamese dishes are very good matches as well. Thai food is famous for its balance of sweet, sour, salty, and spicy elements, and the hop character of American pale ales dovetails with each. The beer does a beautiful job of picking up on lime, galangal, and tamarind flavors. One of my favorite Thai dishes is a whole snapper, fried until crispy and then topped with a tangy, fiery tamarind-based sauce. The snappiness of the pale ale stands up to the sauce and helps define the flavor of the fish. It's a great combination. The exuberant American hops also provide a nice counterpoint to the darker flavors in Thai food such as tofu, coconut, peanuts, and fish sauce. With Vietnamese food, we add other elements such as black pepper and mint leaves, and the beer works beautifully with these too.

Something about cilantro, spices, and chilies just begs for the piney, limey aromatics of American Cascade hops. American pale ales sometimes use them in profusion.

India pale ales were originally brewed in England to be sold to British colonists and soldiers in Calcutta. I've always found it interesting that the English no longer seem to see Indian food as ethnic—as far as they're concerned, it's as English as steak and kidney pie. Even in the early 1800s, fragrant, hoppy India

pale ales must have been the perfect foil for the local food in Calcutta. Today, American IPA is probably better still when it comes to dealing with spices. Indian cuisine is stunningly complex, but the vast majority of dishes are terrific with these beers. Most Indian cooking is based on an elegant interplay of fragrant herbs and spices. American hop aromatics insinuate themselves into this interplay, and great harmonies can result. With cream- or yogurt-based sauces, the cutting power of the hops and the lifting power of carbonation help refresh the palate. These beers can also go toe-to-toe with jerk and Cajun spicing, where you'll want plenty of cutting and lifting power.

American pale ales are great with spicy, complex food flavors, but this doesn't mean that their abilities end there. These are great beers for everyday drinking—they are very versatile and will work perfectly with a ham and cheese on rye. They're great for burgers—you can pile on whatever toppings you want, and these beers will just slice right through them. Tomatoes, ketchup, raw onions, pickles—nothing's going to be a problem here. Fried or grilled chicken is a very good partner as well, making a great combination on a hot summer day.

Strong, oily fish, especially salmon, will appreciate the hoppy character of this beer style. I love to grill salmon steaks with olive oil and coarsely cracked black pepper, and American pale ales make a great accompaniment. American pale ales are also a great match for crab cakes, especially spicy ones.

Notable Producers of American Pale, Amber, and India Pale Ales

SIERRA NEVADA BREWING COMPANY These days, some people use the term "California pale ale" to denote a golden beer with snappy bitterness and a big aroma of citric Cascade hops. The designation is generally expanded to include the rest of America, but there can be no doubt that northern California was the origin of the style and the Sierra Nevada Brewing Company the fount. In 1981, the homebrewers Ken Grossman and Paul Camusi started making beer in Chico, California, using a mishmash of vessels cobbled together out of old dairy tankage. When they outgrew these vessels, they bought a copper brewhouse from Germany that lasted them more than a decade. When this brewhouse was finally stretched to the breaking point, Sierra Nevada stepped up to the big time, with state-of-the-art equipment in a shiny new modern brewhouse. A fanatical dedication to quality has brought this brewery from its birth in a shed to its current status as one of the top-selling craft breweries in America. Size and success have not dimmed its vision.

All of Sierra Nevada's beers are quite good, but this brewery is best known for its flagship **Sierra Nevada Pale Ale**, an American original. The ale is deep orange-gold in color, with a signature aroma of Cascade hops—grapefruit, lime, pine needles, and black currant. The bitterness is broad but moderate, supporting a round, dry, lightly fruity palate with gentle carbonation and bready grain flavors. The finish is very dry, and hop bitterness lingers. This beer is bottle-conditioned and contains a fine dusting of yeast, which settles to the bottom of the bottle. The draft beer is filtered. As soon as I taste Sierra Nevada Pale Ale, I instantly start thinking of Mexican and Cal-Mex food—quesadillas, burritos, pork tacos, fish tacos, shrimp dishes, and just about anything containing lime juice, chilies, and cilantro. It goes well with Thai, Vietnamese, and Indian food too. A very versatile beer—one to have in your fridge every day.

FULL SAIL BREWING COMPANY Full Sail's slogan is "Beer you can believe in." Its employees put their money where their mouths were when they bought the company several years ago. Since then, they've continued to brew an excellent and popular range of ales in their beautifully situated brewery in Hood River, Oregon. **Full Sail Pale Ale** has a pleasant orange color and a fantastic citric aroma of fresh American hops. The bitterness is focused and clean, giving way to a lightly fruity, biscuity malt center and a dry mineral finish. This is a highly versatile beer of considerable finesse. It's particularly good with Mexican food. **Full Sail IPA** has almost the same color as the pale ale but is somewhat stronger. The nose is brightly hoppy but surprisingly muted compared with the pale ale. The hops make themselves clear on the palate with a broad drying attack supported by a sturdy malt center. Bitterness lingers in the dry finish. There's plenty of cutting power here—this is a beer that can take on anything from a grilled steak covered in cracked black pepper to spicy Thai food. A big addition of caramel malts give **Full Sail Amber** a mahogany color and some caramel in the aroma. The caramel sweetness shows through on the palate, but this is still very much a northwestern beer, and the hopping is robust. The center is nice and juicy, and the finish is clean and dry. This is a muscular beer, big enough to take on barbecue, steaks, and loaded-up burgers.

ANDERSON VALLEY BREWING Boonville, California, is home to a peculiar dialect called "Boontling," developed in the nineteenth century to allow the locals to speak their minds without being understood by outsiders. It is also apparently home to a prodigious marijuana crop, which may explain the paranoia. The Anderson Valley brewery names its products in Boontling, but these beers are bright and fearless.

Poleeko Gold Pale Ale is deep gold in color with a gorgeous American hop aroma of pine needles and freshly sliced grapefruit. The bitterness is sharp, broad, and clean, leading the beer in a light-footed dance across the palate. A touch of fruity malt holds up the center before the whole affair vanishes in a quick burst of hops at the dry finish. Absolutely delicious, and a fine partner to spicy seafood dishes and almost any Mexican, Thai, or Vietnamese dish.

Hop Ottin' IPA goes for a deeper full amber color. The nose is a citrusy, piney hop bomb—if you want to know what American hops smell like, here's your answer. The palate follows through on the promise, with a knifelike bitterness held barely in check by biscuity malt. The finish is bone-dry, and the hops linger. Try this beer with grilled salmon and shrimp, Indian vindaloos, Jamaican jerk chicken, or Cajun blackened chicken.

The hop aromatics are a little more restrained in **Boont Amber Ale**, which shows some nice reddish highlights in the glass. Fruit and caramel sneak into the aroma and nestle up to the hops. True to form, the palate remains bracing and dry, with a bit of caramel flavor in the middle. This will work with the same dishes as the other two beers, but the caramel will help this partner pork chops, roast beef, and fried chicken.

REDHOOK ALE BREWERY Founded in 1982 as the Independent Ale Brewery in Seattle, Redhook has grown to be one of the country's largest producers of craft-brewed beers. In the mid-1990s, Anheuser-Busch (the brewer of Budweiser) bought a stake in Redhook, allowing the company to build a new brewery in Merrimack, New Hampshire, and gain nationwide sales. The beers are cleaner tasting than they once were, though some people have complained that they've lost character. Apparently worried that the word "bitter" would put off potential customers, Redhook renamed their popular Ballard Bitter and called it **Redhook IPA** (in the Pacific Northwest, even grandmothers know what IPA is). Redhook IPA has a full gold color and aromatics of zesty citrus fruit. The bitterness is relatively light, but the palate is very dry, with a pilsner-like breadiness in the center. The beer makes a quick impression, then exits drily. It is less aromatic than some IPAs but still characterful. This would be very refreshing on a hot summer day and would make a fine partner for grilled sardines, salmon, and shrimp.

GOOSE ISLAND BEER COMPANY The father-and-son team of John and Gregg Hall have quietly built the Goose Island Beer Company from a well-regarded Chicago brew pub into a very successful regional brewery. Their flagship product is **Honkers Ale**, a pale amber beer with a pleasant aroma of tea biscuits and fruity hops. The palate is soft and round, with a gentle bitterness supporting a dry, biscuity malt center. The finish is clean and crisp. This beer is as much British as

American and seems to have a foot firmly in each camp. It's a nice everyday beer for pairing with fried chicken, pork chops, barbecue, roast beef, and cold cuts.

Goose Island India Pale Ale is perhaps only slightly paler than Honkers, but it has an entirely different character—orangey hop aroma leaps out of the glass. The bitterness is broad and bracing, but the beer is held together firmly by a solid backbone of malt—some grain flavors and a touch of sweetness show through. The finish is dry and snappy. A great beer to have with spicy shrimp, crab cakes, enchiladas, tamales, quesadillas, Indian food prepared with Goan spices, and robust Panang and Massamun Thai curries.

VICTORY BREWING COMPANY According to the label, a mythical creature called a "hop devil" once lurked in the imagination of farmers. I think it's more likely that the hop devil lurks in the minds of these skillful brewers in Downington, Pennsylvania. **Victory Hop Devil Ale** is a copper-colored beer with a bright lemongrass aroma. The bitterness is sharp, focused, and crackling but allows some malt to show through on a bone-dry palate. The finish is clean and snappy—the hops hang around to see who's up for a rematch. I certainly am. This beer just begs for Thai food; there's a big cilantro note in the nose that can't wait to meet the chilies. Bold Mexican dishes, especially fajitas, will do just as well.

RUSSIAN RIVER BREWING The Russian River area of Sonoma County is better known for its wines than its beers. In Sonoma County, appreciation for wine grew into beer connoisseurship over the course of the past two decades. Most Sonomans seem to be aficionados of both the grain and the grape. This small California brewery isn't just in wine country, it was originally owned by the winemaker Korbel, widely known as a producer of ersatz "champagne." **Russian River India Pale Ale** is a slightly hazy pumpkin orange beer with a hop aroma so intense that it reminds me of my own brewery's hop storage room. The beer's carbonation is quite low—it looks innocuous enough. The devastating hop attack dissolves any illusion of innocence—the bitterness is scorching. But it's also flavorful and somehow oddly compelling. This beer clearly revels in being completely unbalanced. Anyone can throw lots of hops into the kettle and fermenting tanks, but it takes real skill to develop, retain, and deliver this much hop flavor. If you're a true hop lover, here's your beer. Try it with quesadillas and cheese enchiladas—the cheese will blunt the blast of hops. This would also be a tasty match for a pizza paved over with good pepperoni. The young brewmaster Vinnie Cilurzo is clearly itching for a fight, so bring it on. In 2002, Cilurzo bought

Courtesy Victory Brewing Company.

Many American brewers have made a deal with the "hop devil" to render their beers wonderfully aromatic. Pennsylvania's Victory Brewing Company gives him a starring role.

the Russian River brand from Korbel and moved to a thirty-barrel brewhouse twelve miles away in Santa Rosa. He plans to expand his distribution outside northern California.

BRIDGEPORT BREWING COMPANY Portland, Oregon, is very much a beer city, and its residents are steadfastly loyal to their local breweries. The fine regional brewery BridgePort Brewing earns that loyalty with flavorful, well-balanced beers. Most of its beers are rooted firmly in the British tradition, but **BridgePort India Pale Ale** marks a departure from the malty house character. The beer is bottle-conditioned, deep gold with a big, bright hop aroma of oranges, limes, and kumquats. The bitterness is broad and mouth-coating, married to a refreshing twinge of acidity. The center of this beer is all pale malt, a support structure for the hop castle built on top of it. The beer sails through to a long, dry finish. There are some nice fresh "Grape-Nut" grain flavors in the aftertaste. This beer would be fine with Thai, Mexican, and Indian food. Somehow, though, something about this beer makes me think of bacon and cheddar omelettes, grilled cheese sandwiches, or cheddar cheeseburgers. Why cheddar? I think it's that bit of acidity—the beer seems to want something sharp. You'll have fun obliging it.

THE BROOKLYN BREWERY In 1994, we had a great success with our winter holiday beer, Brooklyn Black Chocolate Stout. The next year we decided that we should produce a special beer for summer—but what should it be? Perhaps something light would have been a logical idea, but brewers are not always logical people. We had hops on our minds, and we decided to indulge ourselves. The veteran British brewer David Bruce had recently given me a magnificent old book, *The Theory and Practice of Brewing Illustrated*, by William Tizzard, printed in 1842. In the chapter "East India Pale Ale," Tizzard describes the development and brewing of the original India pale ales in fascinating detail. I was captivated and decided to base our next beer on the original IPA style. IPAs were quite strong, of course; but since it was surely sunny and hot in India, I reasoned, our beer would be just the thing to help you through a steamy New York summer. Our other beers had been brewed with American malts, but I wanted biscuity British malts for this one. With Tizzard's descriptions buzzing in my head, I headed off to the kettles to brew the first batch of **Brooklyn East India Pale Ale**, a pale amber beer with a fruity, earthy, lemongrass aroma featuring the prized East Kent Golding hops mentioned in the old book. Snappy bitterness strikes first on the flinty, dry palate; and then biscuity, juicy malts flood into the center, developing some orangey fruit. The malts hold the hops at bay until the mineraly finish, when the beer signs off with a quick, citrusy snap.

I like to think that George Hodgson, the eighteenth-century originator of India pale ale, would be pleased. Like the original IPAs, Brooklyn East India Pale Ale is robust, a hefty 7 percent. A summer beer? Well, it is very refreshing, and it was so popular that it soon became our third year-round beer. I'm particularly fond of it with Thai, Malaysian, Vietnamese, Mexican, and, of course, Indian food. The beer is robust enough to stand up to strong flavors, and its citrusy flavors mingle wonderfully with those in the dishes. At the restaurant Panang in New York, it's a big favorite with duck in red coconut curry sauce. In my brewery's neighborhood in Williamsburg, Brooklyn, I enjoy it with authentically bright, fresh pad thai and pungently spicy chicken with Thai holy basil. After dinner, I love the way its snappy hoppiness perfectly mirrors good aged cheddars, especially Grafton Village from Vermont and Lincolnshire Poacher from England.

In our East India Pale Ale, the malt stands firm, but the hops are king. In our **Brooklyn Ale**, the malts get their close-up. And not just any malts. We use the old heirloom Maris Otter variety, which is grown on limited acreage in England and Scotland. Maris Otter is loved for the depth of its flavor and aroma. Like many foods, barleys have been bred over the years for high yields and resistance to bad weather and pests. Flavors that are muted in these newer barleys are fully retained in Maris Otter malts. Ours are "floor malted" by hand in Scotland, and to these we add some Belgian aromatic malts and caramelized "crystal" malts from East Anglia, England. When we start the mash in the morning, the whole building quickly fills with the distinctively bready aroma of these malts. The resulting beer has a full amber color and the same bready, hot cereal aroma exuded by the mash, accented by marmalade notes and light citrusy hops. The hops announce themselves with a quick snap on the palate, but malt quickly takes over, driving dry, fruity, biscuity flavors through the juicy center. The finish is quick and drying with a refreshing mineral tang. Flavors of fresh bread linger in the aftertaste. That bready flavor ties in brilliantly with stuffing, and I love this beer with stuffed roasted chicken, pheasant, turkey, and pork loin. Nice caramel flavors give it an affinity for venison, steaks, and burgers, and it's a real star with breaded veal. At lunchtime, it's a great sandwich beer, and after dinner it makes a very good accompaniment to Stilton or Gorgonzola dolce.

ANCHOR BREWING COMPANY Anchor is so well-known for its steam beer that many people are under the impression the brewery is called "Anchor Steam." As fond as I am of that beer, I am much fonder of the brewery's groundbreaking **Anchor Liberty Ale**. In 1975, Fritz Maytag set out to brew a distinctively American beer to commemorate the 200th anniversary of Paul Revere's ride to warn American revolutionaries of an impending British attack. Ironically, it was robust British beers such as Timothy Taylor's Landlord and Young's Special London Ale that provided the inspiration. The beer used the newly developed (and already endangered) Cascade hop variety in abundance, and it turned out to be so popular that Anchor made it a permanent part of the roster in 1983. Anchor Liberty Ale has a light honey color with a slight haze, the result of heavy dry-hopping in the maturation tanks. The dry-hopping creates a nose that is absolutely magnificent, a towering monument to hops. It smells like a roomful of fresh Cascade hop cones—pine needles, limes, oranges, and grapefruit leap out of the glass. The hop attack is brisk and direct, coating the tongue in finely tuned bitterness before biscuity malts peek through the dry center along with a burst of fruit. The finish is long, dry, juicy, and resinous. Fresh malt roams deliciously through the aftertaste. I've always loved this beer. It's a wonderfully pure expression of American brashness and creativity, played out with malt and hops. It's unbalanced and likes being unbalanced. Anchor Liberty Ale is especially good with spicy American and Thai food. When those citric Cascade hops latch onto cumin, lime juice, and cilantro, they don't let go. It's a riot of flavor.

Once American craft brewers had finished supercharging the British pale ale and making it their own, they soon turned their attention to brown ale. Northern British brown ales, exemplified by the ubiquitous Newcastle Brown Ale, are light-bodied and thirst-quenching, with little if any roasted character. Southern English brown ales are mild and sweet, with some pleasant nuttiness standing in for the roast. Pleasant, yes, but not bold enough for the Americans. "We can rebuild this beer," said the Americans. "Faster. Brasher. Roastier. Stronger."

Bill Moeller, the retired and reformed mass-market brewer who preceded me as Brooklyn Brewery's brewmaster, led the charge. Moeller introduced Brooklyn Brown Ale as a holiday beer in the winter of 1989–1990. It was powerfully flavored and dry-hopped, like nothing anyone had tasted before. It became so popular that Brooklyn Brewery decided to retain it as the second beer in the lineup. Others quickly followed, and before long a new style of brown ale was on the move.

American brown ales stake out a previously unoccupied spot in the range of flavors between pale ales and porters. The roast, which had been somewhat neglected by the British, comes forward in these beers and becomes a real player on the palate. It is not dominant, though—it usually plays out as a mellow chocolate flavor rather than a sharper coffee character. Caramelized malts are also used more heavily, lending body, sweetness, and caramel flavors. These beers are often darker than most British brown ales, but not as dark as porters or stouts—a deep russet-brown is the preferred color. Finally, American hops are brought into play, lending these beers robust bitterness and brightly citric aromatics. These beers are sometimes dry-hopped to bring out a distinctively fresh hop character. This combination of flavors and aromas would be fairly unrecognizable to the average British beer drinker. Then again, the British have little exposure to barbecue or Cajun food, which American brown ales are uniquely equipped to handle.

American Brown Ales with Food

American brown ales have a unique combination of bright hop character and dark roast flavors wrapped around a full-bodied malt center. A rack of barbecued pork ribs has a bright, tangy sauce or dry-rub character balanced against dark smoky flavors wrapped around a full-bodied pork center. See any affinities here? American brown ales are uniquely talented with barbecue. Barbecue is a big word in this country, and it shouldn't be used lightly. There are many types of barbecue, and I don't want to set off a war between South Carolina and Texas. No need for fighting—American brown ale works with all barbecue styles.

Everyone agrees on one thing about barbecue: true barbecue doesn't involve putting the meat directly over a flame—that's grilling. True barbecue uses indirect heat and smoke to cook the meat slowly, preferably for many hours. Over the hours of cooking, the smoke infuses the meat, which becomes fork-tender. The results can be miraculous. American brown ale uses robust bitterness to cut through the fat, bright citric hop aromatics to echo the tangy sauce, and sweet malt flavors to meld with the meat. The roast flavors in the beer pick up on the smoke flavors in the meat, and the harmony is complete. Carbonation lifts away the strong flavors, and you're ready to start again. These two American originals are perfect for each other.

If you're planning to slather barbecue sauce over a rack of ribs and cook them to perfection over a bed of hot coals, that's not barbecue, it's grilling—at least according to the barbecue guys. I never argue with the barbecue guys. Whatever you want to call it, all of us cook this way, or at least we want to. The average backyard cookout is a grill fest. Grilling caramelizes, smokes, and chars the exterior of the meat—those flavors are the whole point of grilling (aside from looking supercool in your apron while deftly wielding a long fork and tongs). Very similar flavors are at work in American brown ale, so it's a natural partner to these foods. Vegetables react to grilling much as meat does—they acquire char and smoke flavors, they become sweeter, and their natural flavors concentrate. The beer will work well here, too.

Of course, we need vegetables, and I love them, but right now I'm thinking about steak. My favorite steak preparation is very simple. A good thick (an inch or more) rib eye or shell steak, with olive oil, coarsely ground black pepper, and sea salt rubbed liberally over the surface. Then into a very hot broiler. When the surface of the steak is dark brown with blackish edges, I turn it over with a pair of tongs and cook the other side until it's medium brown. It turns out medium-rare and juicy. The same preparation works wonders on the outdoor grill. Of course, I've got Brooklyn Brown Ale in my fridge, and it's the perfect partner for this steak. All the flavors seem to line up. I particularly love the way the hops in the beer pick up the black pepper on the steak and run with it. Another good partner is venison, which is usually served medium-rare with a good char. The beer will be happy to work with most sauces, as long as they're not too sweet.

American brown ales are probably a bit muscular for hot sliced roast beef (stick with the British version here), but they're excellent with cold roast beef and roast beef sandwiches. The same is true of cold pork or lamb, whether in sandwiches or on their own. When the meat cools, the fat solidifies and the flavors concentrate—you need a bit more heft to work with the leftovers. If you're putting together a sandwich, the beer can easily handle onions, tomatoes, cheese, and horseradish sauce.

Many Mexican dishes, especially those using nuts and roasted or smoked chilies, will work beautifully with American brown ales. Puerco en pipian—pork tenderloin in a pumpkin-seed sauce—makes an excellent match. Traditional Mexican cooking includes many rich, complex meat stews, and American brown ales are a great accompaniment for most of them. Almonds are often used, and the beer's malt flavors pick up on them beautifully. The bright American hop character finds harmonies with cumin, lime or orange juice, and chilies.

Notable Producers of American Brown Ale

THE BROOKLYN BREWERY By 1990, the popularity of the three-year-old Brooklyn Brewery was rising on local people's admiration for its only beer, Brooklyn Lager. The founders, Steve Hindy and Tom Potter, were thinking about expanding their lineup and decided to stick a toe in the water by brewing a special beer for the holidays. Steve frequently brewed a strong, hoppy brown ale at home, and he brought his recipe to brewmaster Bill Moeller, who adapted it to create the original **Brooklyn Brown Ale**. Packed with caramel and roast flavors, it was an instant success, and the brewery soon added it to the permanent portfolio. Brooklyn Brown Ale is the progenitor of the American brown ale style, stronger and roastier than its English ancestors. I've changed the recipe a bit over the years, adding some English and Belgian malts for greater depth, but the overall character of the beer remains the same. Brooklyn Brown Ale has a deep mahogany brown color and an aroma that combines caramel with chocolate and fruit and a citrusy display of hops. The bitterness is snappy up front but drops back to reveal a full-bodied, dry malty palate delivering waves of caramel and light chocolate flavors. Some malt sweetness shows through in the juicy center before the beer dries into the long finish. Warm, nutty flavors glow in the aftertaste. Brooklyn Brown Ale is full-flavored and slightly strong but retains an easy drinkability that has made it one of the most popular dark beers in the Northeast. It's particularly good with steaks, burgers, and barbecue, where it can put its caramel flavors to work with the caramelized flavors in the meat. The robust hopping gives it the cutting power to deal with toppings and sauces—I have to admit a weakness for melting Stilton on a rib steak. This beer is also very good with venison, ham, and roasted pork, which enjoy the depth of malt character. After dinner, Brooklyn Brown Ale is a perfect accompaniment to well-aged, fruity-nutty cheddar, Gouda, and Gruyère.

SMUTTYNOSE BREWING COMPANY New Hampshire's leading craft brewer was founded in Portsmouth in 1993, using the facilities of the failed Frank Jones

Brewing Company. The Smuttynose Brewery, which is named after a nearby island, sold its first beer in 1994 and has grown considerably since then. The brewery has a deft hand with both roasted malts and amusing designs for labels. "Olive" strikes a regal Wegman-like pose on the label of **Smuttynose Old Brown Dog Ale**, which has a nice russet-brown color and a fruity-spicy aroma displaying hops, caramel, and chocolate. The palate is soft and round, with moderate bitterness balancing juicy caramel sweetness. The finish is long and dry, leaving behind tingling bitterness and coffeeish roast flavors. This beer has a nice structure and plenty of flavor to match grilled meats, especially a good juicy steak. It would also be excellent with ribs and grilled sausages.

ABITA BREWING COMPANY The south was generally slow to discover craft-brewed beer, but there are some notable exceptions. Abita Brewing Company was founded by Jim Patton and Rush Cummings in 1986, in the early days of microbrewing. The brewery is in the small town of Abita Springs, Louisiana, about thirty miles north of New Orleans. The location was chosen partly for its excellent spring water, which the brewery draws from deep wells. Abita has a brew pub on one side of town and a full-scale production brewery on the other side, and the latter is being modernized with state-of-the art equipment from Germany.

Abita Turbodog has a very deep brown color and an aroma of toffee, prunes, raisins, and chocolate. A winy, dry, full-bodied palate features dark fruit and caramel balanced by a moderate bitterness. The finish is very long and dry, with roast and caramel leading the way. What is a "Turbodog"? I don't know, but it likes meat. This beer is excellent with steaks (especially flavorful hanger steaks), grilled meats, venison, chili con carne, and, naturally, Cajun blackened chicken and pork chops.

GOOSE ISLAND BREWING COMPANY From Chicago's well-loved regional brewery comes **Goose Island Hex Nut Brown Ale**, a deep brown beer with a big fluffy head and an enticing aroma of hops, chocolate, and coffee. Tingly hops quickly stand aside for a round, fruity, slightly sweet malt center packed with caramel and light cocoa flavors. This beer dries out in the finish with a twinge of juicy acidity. A very tasty, well-balanced beer that would be great with genuine "low and slow" barbecue, grilled meats, roast suckling pig, sausages, steaks, and earthy Mexican dishes, especially those with mole sauce.

DOGFISH HEAD BREWING COMPANY I'm not sure what the cultural reasons are, but most of the country's madly creative brewers seem to be in the West. Sam

Calagione of Dogfish Head, located in sleepy Rehobeth, Delaware, is a notable exception. He has made beer from grapes, raisins, and bread and has brewed a stout that topped out at a strength of more than 20 percent. Even his more commercial beers aren't exactly restrained. **Dogfish Head Indian Brown Ale** has a concentrated brown color and an outrageously fruity hop aroma, with notes of rum, caramel, and port. Round, juicy, caramelized malts caress the tongue before hops coat the mouth, grabbing your attention. The hops and malt tussle their way into a long, hoppy finish, leaving the palate tingling. Both the heavy hopping and the hefty strength—7.2 percent—explain the name of the beer. This is a sort of brown ale interpretation of the IPA style, brewed with brown sugar and American hops. It's a crazy mix, but it works. It's perfect for barbecue, and it certainly won't be afraid of any sauce. It's also great for seriously piled-on burgers and big sharp cheeses.

American-Style Wheat Beer

In the late 1800s and early 1900s, German immigrants streamed into the United States, and it was not long until they occupied most of the brewhouses in the country. Suddeutches weissbier, the hazy, fruity wheat beer of Bavaria, came to be widely brewed in the United States. Dozens of breweries produced wheat beer, particularly in the Germanic areas of Pennsylvania and the Midwest. Many of these were very light, spritzy beers, even lighter than today's German weissbiers. Few if any of these American-brewed wheat beers survived Prohibition—most brewers went straight into brewing lager and never looked back.

When American microbrewers looked to Europe for styles they could follow, weissbier seemed a reasonable choice. It was very light on the palate, and many brewers wanted a lighter style they could make without sacrificing their credibility as serious brewers. What could be more serious than a beer that was hazy with yeast? It's ironic that as some of these brewers started to make their own wheat beers, the unique Bavarian yeast strain was the first thing they left behind. It is the special yeast that gives the Bavarian beers their aromatics of bananas, cloves, and bubble gum. In the early days of American microbrewing, most brewers weren't thrilled with the idea of carrying more than one yeast strain in the brewhouse—the chance of cross-contamination was considered too great. Besides, German wheat beer was an acquired taste. So instead of traditional yeast-produced fruitiness, these brewers went for a more neutral flavor, produced by their house ale yeasts and a heavier hand with the hops.

American wheat beers are often unfiltered and quite hazy, sometimes to the point of being nearly opaque. The brewers eschew the clove and banana flavors imparted by German yeasts and the spices favored by Belgian brewers. These beers tend to be light, bright, and zippy on the palate with a slight wheat tartness enlivened by high carbonation. Suspended yeast and protein provide some body and sometimes a faint earthiness. Hop bitterness is often higher than that of their European counterparts, and citric American hop aromatics are common.

Confusingly, some brewers refer to these beers as "hefeweizens." They ought not to—customers could be forgiven for expecting traditional German flavors. A mention on the label of a German or "Weihenstephan" yeast strain will alert you to a Germanic version, as will any mention of cloves or bananas. In the Pacific Northwest, the Americanized version reigns supreme, led by the Widmer Brewery, which probably originated the style. I'll be frank—I don't find American wheat beer nearly as interesting as the German and Belgian versions. It is often served with slices of lemon, and you're not going to hear any argument from me. To be fair, though, perhaps not every moment calls for profundity. The best of these beers still have far more to offer than the mass-market beers they have displaced in the affections of many beer drinkers in the Pacific Northwest.

American-Style Wheat Beers with Food

American wheat beers are uncomplicated, bright, and refreshing, great for summer foods. While they lack the fruit flavors of the German originals, they retain the slightly tangy quality imparted by wheat. This makes them easy partners for salads, where they can handle anything from the delicate flavors of cucumbers and bean sprouts to the stronger character of spinach and endive. More robust salads enhanced by cheese, meat, or fish will work fine, so these beers are a nice choice to accompany a chef's salad. The mild acidity lent by the wheat will parry vinaigrettes, and the beer is neutral enough to go along with fruit-flavored vinaigrettes.

With very mild fish, this neutrality translates into subtlety and tact. Sole, turbot, halibut, and John Dory can be served poached or steamed, and this beer will step in to refresh the palate and then step aside, leaving the flavor of the fish heightened rather than trammeled. Even if the fish is not so delicate, these slightly citrusy beers can be a good foil for the flavors of the seafood. The slice of lemon becomes perfectly appropriate here, providing extra acidity and citrus character.

All wheat beers are great for brunch, and the American version is no exception. It's especially nice with cheese omelettes, particularly goat cheese omelettes. American wheat beers often wield more bitterness than their European counterparts, and this makes them better with spicy brunch dishes like omelettes made with andouille or chorizo sausages, or huevos rancheros. Despite being light and brisk, they can use their high carbonation and fine acidity to slice through bacon, sausages, and just about anything else you're likely to have with your eggs. You can toss in an orange slice to brighten things further if you like.

Notable Producers of American-Style Wheat Beer

WIDMER BROTHERS Kurt and Rob Widmer are pioneers of American craft brewing. They opened their doors in 1985, offering a hoppy, dark Düsseldorf-style altbier to the people of Portland, Oregon. These days, the Widmers' altbier is harder to find, but their wheat beer is ubiquitous. The Widmers themselves have become a regional power, and they recently built a large state-of-the-art brewhouse to take them into the twenty-first century. An alliance with Anheuser-Busch has aided the spread of their flagship **Widmer Hefeweizen**, the modern progenitor of the American style of wheat beer. Now I'm going to mouth off about one of my big pet peeves—this beer is *not* a hefeweizen. The name is confusing at best. Hefeweizens taste of cloves, bananas, bubble gum, and smoke—yeast-given qualities that this beer does not have.

Instead, this hazy orange beer shows aromatics of malt, bread, and citrusy, piney American hops. The hops assert themselves immediately, slipping down the sides of the tongue. The palate is mercilessly dry, with cracker-like wheat flavors in the center. Hops dominate in the long, mineraly finish. A minute or two later, a ghostly aftertaste of fresh malt and wheat emerges. This is an archetypal northwestern wheat beer—you can tell that it comes from hop country. It's often served with a slice of lemon, and the brewery encourages the practice, which gives the beer a citric lilt. It leaves me wanting some fat for the beer to sink its hoppy teeth into—I suddenly crave a grilled cheese sandwich. Even better, you can add some ham and make a croque monsieur. It's also nice with northwestern salmon, spicy seafood dishes, eggy brunches with bacon and sausages, and really piled-on chef's salads.

ODELL'S Doug Odell, who has the look and manner of a genial farmer, brews fine, straightforward English-style beers in his growing facility on the outskirts of Fort Collins, Colorado. He, his wife, Wynne, and his sister Corkie established Colorado's second modern microbrewery in 1989. They installed the brewery in an old grain elevator, and for years they produced only draft beer. Bottles followed later, and the Odells built a larger modern facility. Their wheat beer is a departure from English flavors.

Odell's Easy Street Wheat has a full hazy gold color and a big wheaty aroma enlivened by a whiff of grapefruit. Hops combine with a light, thirst-quenching acidity to balance the beer's off-dry core, which is beautifully light, wheaty, and orangey, leading into a quick, clean finish. There's an expansive flavor of grain in the aftertaste. This beer is a wonderfully balanced and self-assured display of grain flavors, with everything in harmony. It's very versatile, but especially terrific with chef's salads, grilled shrimp, crab cakes, and fish. Lemons? You don't need them.

NORTH COAST BREWING This microbrewery in Mendocino County produces hoppy, distinctively California-style beers under several names, including the amusing Acme label. Its **Blue Star Wheat Beer** has a hazy gold color and an American hop aroma full of tangerines and grapefruit. Crisp bitterness ushers in a light-bodied, very dry, mineraly center dominated by citrusy hop flavors. The finish is clean and dry. There's plenty of hop character here, hung on a very light, refreshing frame. This makes it a nice aperitif and a good beer to serve with grilled seafood, especially calamari, octopus, sardines, and salmon. Try it also with earthy hams: the snappy hops will pull the salt out of the meat, exposing its essential flavors.

As microbrewing got under way in the early to mid-1980s, brewers who had previously considered only ale turned their attention to lagers. Pilsner, they thought, was too pedestrian, too yellow. (Many later repented of this heresy as they discovered the charms of genuine pilsner.) To them, pilsner didn't seem distinctive enough—perhaps a deeper color would suggest a heartier beer? An amber beer would certainly appear more robust, and caramelized or roasted malts would allow the brewer to pack more flavor in. Many brewers loved the wonderful Oktoberfest beers they'd had in Germany, but the bready, aromatic German malts were unavailable in the United States in those days. American brewers had clean-flavored neutral malts, very aromatic hops, and a surfeit of creativity—they'd have to work with those.

A new style of beer started to emerge. First, Jim Koch's Samuel Adams Boston Lager hit the market, and although he sometimes referred to it as a pilsner, it clearly had Viennese leanings. The light bronze color was deeper than that of the darkest Czech pilsner—surely a dash of colored malts had found its way into the mash. In 1987 Steve Hindy and Tom Potter tapped the veteran brewmaster Bill

Moeller and launched the Brooklyn Brewery's flagship product, Brooklyn Lager. For inspiration, Moeller looked to Vienna-style beers brewed in New York before Prohibition. The color was a full copper, a hue that Anton Dreher would have recognized. He would not, however, have recognized the flavor, which was far bolder than anything he had ever produced. In place of Dreher's special bready Vienna malt, this beer was brewed with a healthy addition of caramel malts, giving it a deep color and juicy caramel flavor. The beer was also faintly fruity, the result of fermentation at relatively warm temperatures with a lager yeast strain. The bitterness matched that of many German pilsners—positively snappy. The hops were a blend of the piney, grapefruity American Cascade and the more demure floral "noble" hops of Germany. If that weren't enough, the beer was also dry-hopped, a technique previously limited to ales. The resulting beer was a uniquely American hybrid, with the smoothness of a lager and some of the aromatic qualities of an ale.

These early beers have since evolved, but all show their roots clearly. Amber lagers are now a popular style in American craft brewing, and while they all can trace their lineage back to Vienna, each has taken a different route from those beginnings. The style, as such, hasn't really developed its own name, so brewers have taken to calling it, rather boringly, American amber lager. I hate to admit it, but I haven't thought of anything better myself. We simply call our version "Brooklyn Lager." What American amber lagers have in common is bright hop aromatics, usually showing some citric American varietals; bronze to copper coloring developed by caramelized malts; and robust bitterness supporting light caramel flavors on a medium-bodied palate. The best of them will display nice malt juiciness in the center and a quick, clean finish. American amber lagers are very versatile—great beers to have in the refrigerator all the time.

American Amber Lagers with Food

While European pilsners are quite versatile, they lack the caramel flavors that give American amber lager some of its food affinities. A little bit of caramel and a touch of malt sweetness can do wonders for the versatility of a beer. The sweetness gives the beer a way to grab on to the sugar in the tomato sauce on a pizza, while the snappy bitterness cuts through the cheese and the caramel flavors find an echo in the browned crust. The match is excellent—I've never found a better style to have with a good pizza. Does the pizza have sausages on it? Better still—sausage has sweetness and caramelized flavors, too. Pepperoni? Bring on the hops—they'll deal with the spices, while the carbonation lifts hot oils. Mushrooms, onions, garlic—no worries; the beer will still be perfect.

Peter Luger Steak House in Brooklyn, founded in 1887, is one of the oldest restaurants in New York City, and home to the best steak in the United States. I can hear the protests already, the accusations of chauvinism—but these will be coming only from people who haven't eaten at Peter Luger. I was once skeptical myself. I am now a convert. Come to scoff and you shall remain to pray.

Peter Luger does, of course, have a wine list. Approach it at your peril—the wines are pretty pedestrian. No one ever complains, though. Brooklyn Lager is on draft, and our amber lager is a perfect accompaniment to the steak. Who needs wine? Peter Luger's broiler operates at 2,000 degrees Fahrenheit, so hot that the surface of the meat caramelizes instantly, leaving the center juicy and red. (I once saw a waiter carrying a medium-rare steak out to a table—the steak still had a jet of pale blue flame leaping out of the bone.) When the snappy hops cut through the butter (the steak is swimming in it) and the caramel malts meet the steak, you will forget that wine even exists. Peter Luger was a German immigrant, and the restaurant has the plain air of a simple German *Gasthof* or beer hall. I think that the waiters and the management, who are nothing if not opinionated, are vaguely offended by the idea of people drinking wine with their world-class porterhouse. They've been serving steaks here for 125 years, and they have reason to feel they know best. Wine with steak? Peter Luger's doesn't think so.

When I roast a chicken, I rub it down in half-and-half before I sprinkle on salt, pepper, and herbs. Why the half-and-half? The natural milk sugar will caramelize, giving me a browner, tastier skin. This is where the chicken's flavor is concentrated, and I want to make the most of it. Amber lagers have enough caramel flavor to link up with caramel flavors in roasted meats and poultry. The beer is light and snappy enough to remain refreshing, though. That makes it a good choice for barbecue and cookouts, especially if you can go a little easy on the sauce. On a hot day in front of the grill, amber lager will work with grilled sausages, chicken, burgers, hot dogs, pork chops, and even corn on the cob. It is also a great choice for fried chicken, where a good crunchy surface is particularly prized.

Amber lagers usually have bright hop aromatics and enough heft to handle spices, so they're good with Cajun and Caribbean food, as well as Thai, Indian, and Szechwan Chinese dishes. I've enjoyed these lagers with spicy empanadas and crab cakes, too. They also do well with spicy Middle Eastern food such as falafel or merguez sausages.

Seafood isn't this beer's strongest suit—amber lager will overwhelm delicate fish. But amber lagers can work with stronger oilier fish, battered fried fish, and fried calamari, and with shrimp. It's a great sandwich beer, and it has a particular affinity for salty cured meats such as ham, prosciutto, and pastrami. Its versatility makes it a great choice to bring to parties and dinners. It'll go with almost any dish your host might serve, and most of the other guests will probably enjoy it. If your host isn't serving any decent beer, you, at least, will have a good beer to drink.

Notable Producers of American Amber Lager

THE BROOKLYN BREWERY As the nineteenth century gave way to the twentieth, Brooklyn's brewers were on top of the world. There were forty-eight breweries in Brooklyn, and they produced one out of every ten barrels of beer brewed in the United States. There was even a street in Bushwick that everyone called Brewer's Row, where major breweries were stacked on top of one another for many blocks. This was the heyday of brewing in Brooklyn, which had started in the 1840s. Unfortunately, it wasn't to last much longer. Prohibition, followed by the Great Depression, put most of Brooklyn's great brewers out of business. After World War II, consolidation and rising property prices claimed those that had survived. Brooklyn's last brewery, F & M Schaefer, shut down in 1976.

Eight years later, in 1984, Steve Hindy, a correspondent for Associated Press, returned from a six-year stint in the Middle East and settled in Brooklyn, in Park Slope. While he was in the Middle East, Steve had been bombed, shot at, and even

Days of beer and roses—the Brooklyn Brewery started small. Tom Potter, Steve Hindy, and the Brooklyn Brewery crew in 1988.

Courtesy Brooklyn Brewery.

kidnapped. He looked forward to a quieter life in Brooklyn. Steve was a great reporter, but he had also picked up some interesting new skills overseas. Working in Islamic countries where alcoholic beverages were forbidden, many correspondents and diplomats became clandestine brewers. Steve and his colleagues brewed in their kitchens in Saudi Arabia and Kuwait, swapping recipes along with their war stories. By the time Steve landed in Brooklyn, he was a dedicated homebrewer, and his downstairs neighbor Tom Potter frequently brewed with him. Tom had a good job as a lending officer at a major bank, but he hung up his suits to join Steve in founding the Brooklyn Brewery in 1987.

Tom and Steve wanted to bring great beer back to New York City and restore Brooklyn's proud brewing heritage. They had one problem—they had scarcely any money, and a new brewery could cost millions of dollars. They decided that they had little choice but to brew their beer outside Brooklyn. Tom and Steve visited the century-old F. X. Matt Brewery in Utica, New York, and contracted to brew their new beer there. They commissioned a fourth-generation German-American brewmaster, William M. Moeller, to develop a recipe for **Brooklyn Lager**. Moeller's grandfather had brewed beer in Brooklyn and had willed his brewing logs to his sons. Moeller developed the original recipe for Brooklyn Lager from these old Brooklyn recipes, adding a few twists of his own. The world-renowned designer Milton Glaser, best known for his "I❤NY" logo, designed Brooklyn Brewery's logo and packaging.

Steve Hindy now likes to joke that being bombed and shot at in the Middle East was good training for starting a brewing company. Fortune and glory were in short supply in the early years. One of the first batches of Brooklyn Lager was hand-labeled in the basement of Tom and Steve's brownstone apartment building. Beer distributors weren't interested in flavor—they were interested in money. Steve, Tom, and their partners ended up selling their beer by hand, door-to-door. Other small brewers were having the same problem in New York City, so Brooklyn Brewery started to distribute a vast array of excellent foreign and domestic beers along with its own.

By 1994, Brooklyn Lager and Brooklyn Brown Ale were becoming popular, and the partners itched to have their own brewery. Steve recruited me from the Manhattan Brewing Company, a brew pub across the river in SoHo. Steve was quite persuasive—now that I think of it, I seem to remember him mentioning that I would have my own boat docked a couple of blocks away on the river. I'll have to talk to him about that.

Over the years, I've made very few changes to Brooklyn Lager. Like the Vienna lagers it's based on, it has a light amber color, but the flowery, piney hop aromatics give it away as an American original. Robust hops are snappy up front on the palate but quickly give way to a dry, smooth, rounded, juicy malt center full of biscuit and caramel flavors. Some malt sweetness shows through before the beer goes out in a dry, biscuity flourish. Some hop flavors linger on, developed by the English technique of dry-hopping, steeping the beer with fresh hops.

Brooklyn Lager has a marvelous versatility and is at home with pizza, burgers, Mexican food, roasted chicken, barbecue, fried fish, pork, and Chinese food. The full caramel flavors in the beer link up with those in the food, while the robust hopping provides some cutting power to deal with strong flavors. In Japan, people have been enjoying it with sushi for years, and in England, people find it a fine accompaniment to classic fish and chips.

Brooklyn Lager remains our flagship beer, and I'm glad to say that it's growing fast. I may get my boat after all.

THE BOSTON BEER COMPANY The Koch family, who emigrated from Germany in the 1800s, produced six generations of brewers, and the last has been the most influential. The Koch brewery, in St. Louis, was quite successful until it was eventually eclipsed by a larger neighbor a few blocks away—Anheuser-Busch. When Jim Koch told his father, who had left the declining brewing industry three decades earlier, that he wanted to be a brewer, his father was not amused. Jim had a degree in management from Harvard and was using it to good effect; why go into a dead business like brewing? He went ahead anyway, and the first bottles of Samuel Adams Boston Lager hit the streets in April 1985. The beer was made under contract at the old Pittsburgh Brewing Company, which had plenty of excess capacity. The Samuel Adams brand combined solid flavor with ruthlessly aggressive marketing tactics to produce meteoric growth for the company, which eventually started to make beer in various breweries around the country. The Boston Beer Company is now the largest craft brewer in the country, producing more than a million barrels per year. It has a tiny showcase brewery in Boston, and several years ago it bought the large Hudepohl-Schoenling brewery in Cincinnati, which now handles a considerable portion of its production.

Samuel Adams Boston Lager has a pale amber color and a fresh, bready malt aroma with a spicy floral hop overlay. The palate is soft and rounded with restrained broad hopping moving alongside dry biscuity malts in the center. The hops step forward as the beer dries into a clean finish. This beer has no bells, whistles, or fanfare, yet it possesses full flavor with the kind of easy, gentle, rounded drinkability found in a good merlot. Its softness makes it quite versatile, a good beer for parties and picnics. This beer represents a turning point—it was the first craft-brewed American beer to become ubiquitous. For many Americans, it has been the first real beer they have ever tried. Try it with roasted chicken, cold cuts, fried chicken, and lightly loaded burgers.

As American settlers and gold rushers poured into California in the mid-1800s, ramshackle breweries popped up almost instantly. Beer was considered a staple in those days, and no one could contemplate life without it. A brewery could therefore be a profitable business, but supplies and sophisticated equipment were hard to come by. Lager yeasts had become widely available by then, but the German-style cold fermentation and lagering were impossible in California's warm climate. It would be years before the first refrigeration units were used in American breweries. Ice was considered so valuable that it was sometimes delivered by sea, all the way from Boston, by way of Cape Horn. It cost a fortune and showed up infrequently.

Brewers got around this problem by using the lager yeast to ferment their beer in very shallow vessels, room-sized pans only a couple of feet deep. The shallow vessels allowed heat to dissipate; this prevented the fermentation from overheating, which could lead to spoilage or off flavors. After a rapid fermentation, the beer was put into barrels; after a short settling period, it was hurried off to market. The fermentation wasn't quite finished, though, and considerable pressure built up in the barrels. The barrels for steam beer were made specially with double-thick staves, so that they could withstand a pressure of fifty to sixty pounds per square inch, about three times the carbonation of a modern keg of beer. Tapping such a beer was perilous. A contemporary account says:

> *To draw steam beer from the half-barrels requires some skill and experience and is best accomplished in the following manner: the faucet key should be held firmly and raised slightly upward without turning the same, to release the exceedingly high pressure.*

One hesitates to think of what happened when you did this incorrectly. When a barrel of this beer was tapped, the "exceedingly high pressure" let loose a mighty hiss, leading to the name "steam beer."

Dozens of breweries produced steam beer, and it was considered superior to the ales available in what was then called the Far West. Steam beers were brewed entirely from malted barley and were pale and clear, with a clean flavor and sharp bitterness. Production centered on San Francisco. However, as refrigeration established itself in the brewing industry, many western brewers eventually converted their plants to lager production, which was easier and more reliable. By the end of the nineteenth century, there were few steam beer breweries left.

In 1965, Fritz Maytag bought and saved San Francisco's Anchor Brewery, the last of the steam beer breweries in California. Anchor Steam Beer is still produced by the original method and is considered a true American classic. The modern generation of American craft brewers took to brewing steam beer; many of them first tried their hand at it while they were still amateurs. Like the brewers of the gold rush in the 1850s, the homebrewer rarely has access to refrigeration for fermentation and is forced to ferment lagers at ale-like temperatures. This is a technique that gives a beer a touch of ale-like fruitiness, though modern practice calls for a cold maturation period that results in a very smooth flavor profile. Most brewers prefer to stick to pale malts, with perhaps a dash of caramel malt, producing a beer with a deep gold color. Bitterness is sharp and clean, and the palate is dry, medium-bodied, and brisk—the beer should show at least a touch of the high carbonation that gave the style its name. While Anchor no longer produces the only steam beer in the country, it is fair to say that our perception of the style is based on Anchor Steam Beer, the last steam brewery standing before the dawn of craft brewing.

In his zeal to protect the brand name Anchor Steam Beer, Fritz Maytag has rather actively "discouraged" other American brewers from using the term "steam beer," which is the correct name for the style. Not wanting to incur the well-financed wrath of the respected veteran brewer, everyone else has refrained from using that name. As a result, you'll have a hard time ferreting out steam beers other than Anchor. This being the case, I won't devote a separate section to food matches for steam beer, but I will note some good matches under my comments on Anchor Steam Beer.

Courtesy Anchor Brewing Company.

Notable Producer of Steam Beer

ANCHOR BREWING COMPANY It's one of the handsomest bottles around, with its short, low-shouldered design and horizontal oval label. **Anchor Steam Beer** has an orange-amber color and a lightly fruity aroma with minty hop notes. The hop attack is fast, mouth-coating, and brash, but it quickly fades to let loose a bone-dry juicy malt palate full of bready fresh grain flavors. The finish is quick and scouringly dry, with hop bitterness lingering. The aftertaste, which takes a few minutes to emerge, is wonderfully bready. Anchor Steam has remained true to itself over the years and is still admirably sharp and appetizing. It has the cutting power to take on big charbroiled steaks and lamb chops, but it can also blast through a burrito and cozy up to shrimp quesadillas.

The indigenous American steam beer was once a popular style in California and beyond. San Francisco's Anchor Brewery, the sole survivor of those days, has flourished as a modern innovator.

American Porters and Stouts

You would be hard-pressed to find an American craft brewer who isn't in love with stout. The love affair started early for me. All of sixteen and proudly sporting a feathery mustache, I sauntered into the hidden inner sanctum of Chumley's, a former speakeasy in New York's West Village. My best friend, Larry, had brought me there to try Guinness Stout, which he proclaimed the best thing he'd ever tasted. This was going to be the first beer I'd had since I'd spit my uncle Bill's Miller Genuine High Life onto his lawn at age thirteen. I wasn't exactly looking forward to my next encounter with beer. But Larry was right—the stuff was delicious. As I drained my very first pint of real beer, I never suspected that a decade later I'd be brewing my own version, using a homebrewing kit bought for me by—Larry.

Many people are surprised to hear that famous Irish stouts such as Guinness, Murphy's, and Beamish are actually rather light beers. The imposing black appearance and the creamy tan head give an impression of heaviness, but the strength of these beers rarely tops 4.5 percent, making them lighter than many mass-market beers.

This was not always the case. Many stouts of the late 1880s and early 1890s were very strong—7 percent would have been fairly average. The current light style seems to be a relatively recent invention, the heavier versions having withered away during the world wars. American craft brewers are reviving a more robust type of stout, the sort of beer that a Dubliner of James Joyce's day might well recognize. Stout seems to have a way of sticking in the mind—most brewers seem to remember their first pint, and it retains an element of personal mythology. I almost feel that when American brewers approach stout, they seek to re-create the impact that their first pint of stout had on them.

Certainly many American stouts are high-impact beers. The range of flavor is wide—from somewhat sweet to very dry. Strengths range from 5 percent to 11 percent. Some stouts follow Irish and English styles, but others have a depth of hop and roast character not found in their European counterparts. Those are the ones we're looking at here. Citrusy American hop aromas may leap out of the glass, blended with coffee and cocoa aromas. Bitterness is often quite high and is married to an espresso-like bite from the heavy use of roasted grains. The bite will then be followed by waves of coffee, caramel, and chocolate flavors, supported by a full-bodied malt center. A clean finish leads the way out as hops linger. Hungry yet? Many of these stouts are virtual meals in themselves, but if you've got dishes with big flavors, American stouts can be brilliant companions.

The line between stout and its antecedent, porter, is fuzzy. Many American breweries produce both styles. When they do, the porter is invariably the lighter of the two, with a less assertive roast character. Porters rarely show a real bite in the roast; brewers rely on the caramel and roasted grains for a more subtle harmony. Bitterness is often snappy, and the overall impression is usually fairly dry. Porters have their own particular food affinities, based on chocolate and caramel flavors. Some porters are bold enough to be considered stouts by other brewers. Like American brewers, porters are highly individualistic, so you'll have to check out a few to see which appeal to you most.

American Porters and Stouts with Food

Although American porters and stouts are quite varied in their intensity, they do have some important things in common at the table. Roasted malt flavors will give almost any of these beers the ability to partner a charbroiled steak—the roasted flavors will pick up on the char. There's a reason why one of the finest cuts of steak is called a "porterhouse"—beer has always been the traditional accompaniment for the great American steak.

Look for solid porters and medium-bodied stouts to pair up with your porterhouse, strip steak, or shell steak. For tender but less flavorful cuts such as filet mignon, look for a stout with a little sweetness—oatmeal stouts are almost always a good choice. Filet mignon is often served with a sauce, and the beer will pair up with any sauce, from a simple stock reduction to béarnaise to a rich Stilton sauce. For hanger steak, which is a bit tougher but full of flavor, you can go for a more assertive beer—Anchor Porter or Sierra Nevada Stout, for example. If you're not sure how roasty or assertive a particular beer is, check out the label. There's often a description of the flavor that can guide you. Otherwise, just buy it and check it out. A bottle will rarely cost more than two dollars, and you can chalk that up to research.

Porters and stouts are an excellent choice with barbecue, whether it's the traditional "low and slow" variety or the popular backyard grill fest. Porters are great with burgers and are big enough to stand up to all the fixings. Both porters and stouts can take on ribs. A big American stout will match the char on the meat while dealing with pungent, spicy barbecue sauces. If you're doing your barbecue "low and slow," go for porters, which are are great with pulled pork. The caramel and roasted malts provide a perfect match for the smoky meat, and the beer won't be pushed around by the sauce. You might not think you'd want a dark beer at a summer barbecue, but even if it's a hot day, the hoppy character of these beers keeps them surprisingly refreshing.

There's an interesting tension between roasted malts and cured meats. Somehow, the dryness of the roast flavor seems to draw out salt, allowing the flavor of the meat to shine. Sweetness and fruitiness provide a contrast to salty meats, and that can be enjoyable as well. Ham goes particularly well with porters and stouts. Milder cooked hams are best with porters and lighter stouts, while air-dried hams such as prosciutto, Serrano, and Bayonne can take on heavier stouts. For ham sandwiches, porter is your best bet—stout will work fine, but a heavy one could be a bit overwhelming. No doubt I'm going out on a limb here, but I find that wine is an utter failure with ham. I've tasted dozens of supposed matches and remained unconvinced, even by some very nice off-dry whites. Even if you don't pick the perfect porter or stout to accompany your ham, you may well find the match far better than what any wine can hope to achieve. Pastrami, "turkey ham," and other cured meats are fine partners as well.

American porters and stouts are great with Mexican and Cajun dishes, which are often full of their own roasty flavors. Bright, assertive American hops commune with spices and citrus, while slicing through cheese and beans. Black beans, refried beans, and black-eyed peas all have earthy flavors that work perfectly with roasted malts. Porters and stouts are great with jambalaya and dirty rice, and you really need to have a good porter to bust through your gumbo. Roasted and smoked chilies will latch onto the beer's roast flavors.

Mole negro, the traditional Mexican sauce made with chocolate, is an obvious and delicious match with porters and stouts. American versions of these styles have the bitterness, fruitiness, and heft to handle heavy spicing.

American-style porters and stouts are sometimes less deft than their Irish counterparts when it comes to seafood. American roast character tends to be bigger and broader—more coffee flavor than espresso-like snap. But drier American porters and stouts can still be excellent with some seafood, particularly oysters. With more delicate oysters, go for porter. More assertive oysters can pair up with stouts. Porters and stouts are also great with shrimp, which develops powerfully smoky flavors when grilled or stir-fried over very high heat.

That big American roast character turns into a real asset with desserts—the affinity with chocolate desserts can be astonishing. The beer doesn't have to be sweet. Look for beers with deep chocolate and coffee flavors and pair them with chocolate tarts, chocolate cakes, chocolate anything. You don't have to stick to chocolate, though—these beers are terrific with fruit desserts as well. On your palate, they work just like chocolate or coffee, both great combinations with fruit. With a fruit tart, for example, a strong stout can be just like a cold espresso, providing a brilliant contrast to the fruit flavors while cleansing your palate for the next bite. No dessert wine can do this—sauternes, Banyuls, and ports all turn flabby and lifeless up against fruit desserts. Strong stouts are also brilliant with vanilla ice cream. Need I say why? When I worked for Manhattan Brewing Company, the pioneering brew pub in SoHo, we combined our chocolaty stout with vanilla ice cream to make a delicious "stout float." It was absolutely sinful—the perfect adult dessert.

Notable Producers of American Porter and Stout

SMUTTYNOSE BREWING COMPANY Smuttynose's labels are almost as well admired as its beers, and the label for **Smuttynose Robust Porter** is certainly interesting; a circus strong man holds a wooden barrel in one arm and an alarming-looking woman in the other. I'm not sure whether the beer will give you similar abilities (or whether you'd want them), but it is certainly robust and quite opaque. Hops lend notes of lemon and orange rind to a nose dominated by dark chocolate. The hops dive in first on the palate, sharp and sturdy, mingling with the roasted malts. When they reach the center, some slight sweetness blooms and the beer becomes round and silky. The roast character, midway between French roast and espresso, drives the beer into a lean, dry, hoppy finish. I'd consider this a stout myself, but I'm not about to argue with the fellow on the label. It's a very well-crafted beer that will be happy with oysters, prosciutto, spareribs, ham, and vanilla ice cream.

MAGIC HAT BREWING COMPANY Magic Hat, based in Burlington, Vermont, has had a meteoric rise since its founders—Alan Newman and the brewmaster Bob Johnson—launched it several years ago. This brewery's good beer and highly imaginative graphics have captured the imagination of Vermonters, and the beers are now found throughout the Northeast. Johnson is just as excited about great food as he is about beer, and this shows in the structure of his ales, which are excellent with food.

Magic Hat Heart of Darkness is a deep black beer with a fluffy tan head and a nose full of chocolate and butterscotch. The palate is light, fruity, dry, and flinty, with restrained bitterness and delicate roast keeping everything juicy right through the center. It leaps nimbly into a clean, dry finish. This is a fresh, racy beer brewed in the finest Irish stout tradition. You could easily stick with it for an entire evening. If you're having it with lunch or dinner, go for oysters, grilled shrimp, ham, steaks, Cajun blackened dishes, or anything with black beans.

ANCHOR BREWING COMPANY Anchor, a pioneer of craft brewing, is best known for its steam beer; but although this is a very pleasant beer, I've never felt it to be Anchor's best product. Anchor started brewing porter in 1974, when the style had virtually died out in the United States. **Anchor Porter** was a spearhead of the American craft brewing movement, and it's still a winner. It has a full black color and a complex nose of French chocolate, espresso, licorice, leather, and hard candy. The flavors are robust right out of the gate, rounded and slightly sweet, with moderate bitterness balancing. Caramel, coffee, and chocolate ride confidently through the middle, leading out to a long, off-dry finish. Many brewers would certainly consider this a stout, but in 1974 it was presumably necessary to distinguish this beer from Guinness. I won't quibble. This is a great partner for Mexican mole dishes, grilled meats, serious ham, and chocolate or fruit desserts.

ANDERSON VALLEY BREWING COMPANY The folks at Anderson Valley are fond of Boontling, a local dialect developed in the 1800s to thwart snooping by outsiders. In this dialect, a nearby redwood forest takes on a different name, and the brewery has named a beer after it. **Anderson Valley Barney Flats Oatmeal Stout** is appropriately black and has an awesome nose of fresh piney hops and dark coffee. On the palate, it is equally impressive—round, soft, and silky, the pillowy head cushioning the slightly sweet beer as it greets your tongue. Hop bitterness is perfectly integrated with the roast in the juicy, chocolaty center. The beer glides into a long, drying finish with hops lingering. A brilliant creation, full-bodied and malty, even slightly oily, a signature of oats. It deftly shows some sweetness without cloying in the slightest. This is hard to beat with Mexican mole dishes, and it works equally well with ice cream or chocolate or fruit desserts.

SIERRA NEVADA BREWING COMPANY Sierra Nevada's flagship pale ale is so famous that it tends to obscure some of the brewery's other beers, including two nicely roasty ones.

Sierra Nevada Porter is deep russet brown with a nice fluffy head. There's a soft aroma of chocolate and coffee, with piney, citric American hops drifting overhead. The hops hit the palate clean and sharp, and the roast rows in right behind it. The flavor is flintily dry and lightly espresso-like, with a hint of caramel bereft of its sweetness. It flies straight through to a hard mineral finish. This is a no-nonsense rendition of the porter style, and it's distinctly American. The hops are in the driver's seat; and the roast, though not intense, is very direct. This beer is very versatile and makes a great accompaniment to a wide array of Mexican dishes, where it can put its roasty dark flavors to work alongside its brightly citric hop character. Try it also with burgers, sausages, and ham.

Sierra Nevada Stout has a full black color and a very pleasant nose of hops, coffee, and fresh grain. The palate is brisk, angular, and dry, with bitterness and roast gripping the sides of the tongue as caramel malts cruise up the center. The finish is very clean and flintily dry, and coffee and chocolate waft through the aftertaste. Also very versatile, this beer will be as comfortable with oysters as with ribs, burritos, fajitas, and burgers.

KALAMAZOO BREWING COMPANY Among his fellow brewers, Larry Bell is best-known for two things. The first is his artistic eccentricity, especially his flair for throwing outlandish and memorable parties. The second is his range of inimitably flavorful stouts; at any given time, four or five may be on offer. Larry Bell opened Kalamazoo Brewing Company in 1983, the very early days of the American microbrewing movement. Based in Kalamazoo, Michigan, it is the oldest craft brewery east of Boulder, Colorado. Its first beers were brewed in a 15-gallon soup kettle. It now has four separate brewing systems, all operating simultaneously to produce a mad swirl of flavorful beers.

Bell's Kalamazoo Stout is a completely opaque beer with a voluminous, rocky beige head. The nose is amazing, an enticing blend of chocolate and coffee ice creams. The beer smells sweet, but the attack is dry, with sharp bitterness joining an espresso-like roast to drive the full-bodied malts through the center. Dark chocolate, coffee, and caramel intertwine in the long bitter finish and drift across the palate for minutes afterward. This beer has a strength of 6.5 percent but seems to carry even more flavor than that strength might imply. It's beautifully put together, with a complex, towering roast structure. Enjoy it with strong briny oysters, salty well-aged hams, fruit pies and tarts, chocolate desserts, and of course chocolate and coffee ice cream.

If Kalamazoo Stout is opaque, **Bell's Expedition Stout** seems to actually absorb light, mopping it up like a black hole in space. It pours like motor oil and raises a magnificent sustained brown head with a consistency of lightly whipped cream. The aroma is heady, combining dark coffee, caramel, and dark chocolate with orangey fruit and bright hops. The palate is sweet, rounded, syrupy, and powerful, with roasted malts and caramel striking first before deep hop bitterness falls in behind it. The center is thick, chewy, and juicy, a maelstrom of coffee, chocolate, hops, and fruit. Think of melting a very good chocolate truffle in a small cup of strong espresso, and you'll start to get the idea. The finish is bittersweet and endless. This is a breathtaking beer that is a dessert in itself. Only the most flavorful fruit tarts, chocolates, or very concentrated chocolate desserts could stand up to it, but the right combination will be magnificent. If you've got cigars, it's time to break out the Cubans.

ROGUE BREWING COMPANY Jack Joyce, a former advertising executive for Nike, built his popular brewery in Newport, Oregon, with a freewheeling attitude of independence, quality, and experimentation. His promotional savvy captured people's imagination, and brewmaster John Maier's beers have kept customers fiercely loyal. Joyce and Maier built their first brew pub in Ashland in 1987 and named it after a beautiful local river. The microbrewery is in Newport, a couple of hours south of Portland.

Rogue Mocha Porter is fairly black, though a glint of red occasionally escapes the glass. It has an orangey aroma of fresh hops with a milk chocolate underlay. The beer is medium-bodied and surprisingly soft, and the hopping seems gentle at first. Caramel malt flavors allow a slight impression of sweetness. Then the hops circle back and assert themselves in concert with the roast, rising up and overtaking the malt flavors. The bitterness is intriguing—high and thin rather than broad. It drives the flavors into a bone-dry, hoppy finish. This is a sneaky beer with very interesting flavor development. Put a good char on some burgers or a steak, or send it in against some very flavorful hams or sausages.

Rogue Shakespeare Stout is completely black and has a thoroughly western nose of coffee, chocolate, and American hops. The whole flavor profile shows itself at once—broad, robust bitterness combines with espresso-like roast to grip the tongue, and there's a quick burst of fruit and refreshing acidity. The whole affair then dives into a clean, racy finish. Flinty hops and coffeeish roast are left to wander the palate. Flashy, sharp, and delicious, this beer is great with briny oysters and mussels. Also, try it with burgers, ribs, blackened chicken, black bean burritos, chocolate desserts, ice cream, and fruit tarts.

VICTORY BREWING COMPANY This brewery in Downington, Pennsylvania, produces a very nice range of flavorful beers, and its stout is no exception. **Victory Storm King Imperial Stout** is very black—even the head has a full brown color, like the cream on a good espresso. In the nose, battalions of espresso beans and licorice sticks lie in wait under an aromatic blanket of fruity, piney hops. The attack is swift; the tongue is momentarily stunned by the thickness of the beer, which waits a few seconds before revealing a profoundly deep bitterness. This is gamely opposed by waves of heavily roasted malts, showing espresso and serious chocolate. The storm rolls over, but it's not done yet—the aftertaste echoes espresso, hops, and licorice for ages. Brash, complex, and beautifully structured, this beer is relatively light on its feet considering its strength of 9.1 percent. It will show best with serious deep chocolate desserts, fruit tarts, cheesecake, vanilla ice cream, and Stilton cheese.

GREAT LAKES BREWING COMPANY Brothers Patrick and Daniel Conway founded their microbrewery and pub in Cleveland, Ohio, in 1988. The neighborhood they chose had once been home to many breweries, but its industrial base had been sapped over the years. The Conways installed the brewery in a century-old Victorian building, and today their impressive new brewhouse incorporates parts of buildings once occupied by the Schlather Brewing Company. Along the way to building a great brewery, they have also helped revitalize their neighborhood, which is now dotted with good restaurants and bars, including their own. They are best known for their award-winning Dortmunder Gold, but I'm even more impressed by their porter.

Great Lakes Edmund Fitzgerald Porter is very dark brown with red highlights and raises an impressively sturdy tan head. The aroma reminds me of opening a box of good chocolates, though there's an orangey hop note there as well. Hop bitterness and roast flavor enter together in lockstep, broadly gripping the tongue. Some malt sweetness peeks through on a full-bodied palate, with hops and roasted grains dominating, leading through to a mineraly dry finish. This porter is dry, hoppy, and quite roasty—you could even call it aggressive if it weren't so extraordinarily balanced and smooth. This impressive finesse has won many awards. Reward yourself with oysters, grilled shrimp, aged ham, burgers, charbroiled steaks, sausages, barbecue, Cajun dishes, and chocolate desserts.

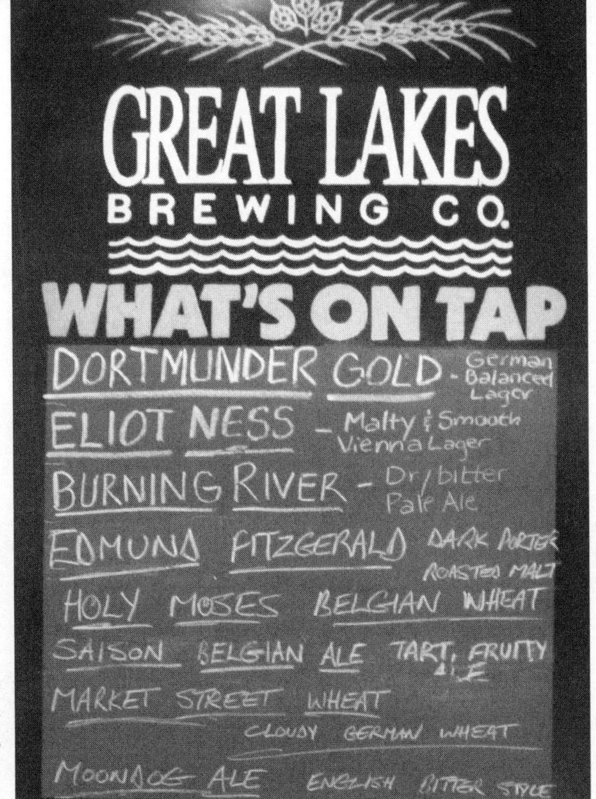

Courtesy Great Lakes Brewing Company.

American craft brewers are inspired by all of Europe's traditional brewing styles. The Great Lakes brewery in Cleveland, Ohio, offers Belgian, German, and English styles.

DESCHUTES BREWERY The town of Bend, Oregon, was named for a kink in the scenic Deschutes River, and restaurateur Gary Fish named his brewery after the river when he opened its doors in 1988. Food and drink ran in Gary Fish's blood; he'd worked in the restaurant industry for twelve years, and his father had spent many years in the wine industry in California. He saw a growing market for flavorful beer and decided to build a brew pub. It wasn't long before demand started to build for his beers elsewhere, and Deschutes began a slow, deliberate ascent from brew pub to microbrewery to a regional powerhouse producing more than 100,000 barrels a year. The devotion to quality has never wavered, and brewmaster Bill Pengelly produces a roster of popular full-flavored beers.

Deschutes is an unusual brewery in that roasted beers actually lead its lineup. Its flagship **Deschutes Black Butte Porter** is named after a local mountain. This porter is deep brown and has a complex aroma of hops, dark fruit, licorice, and coffee, with a hint of mint. The palate is soft, and bitterness is restrained as caramel and gentle coffee and chocolate flavors play through the middle, showing a flash of malt sweetness. It glides into a chalky dry finish, though it leaves a fruity impression, as if it had been sweeter. Versatile and immediately likable, this beer will be great with roast suckling pig, pork chops, cassoulet, burgers, ham, and barbecue, if you go light on the sauce.

Deschutes Obsidian Stout is a whole different animal. Impenetrably black, it

Courtesy The Matt Brewing Company.

The Matt family piloted their brewery through rough waters and emerged as respected craft brewers.

exudes a powerful aroma of espresso, oranges, and melons. Sweetness makes the first impression, followed by juicy waves of chocolate, espresso, caramel, and fruit flavors in a round, soft, full-bodied frame. Hop bitterness holds everything together and leads it out to an off-dry coffeeish finish. This is a scrumptious beer that packs plenty of flavor, and at 6.7 percent carries its strength with considerable grace. It's great with barbecue, ham, and burgers, and it will really shine with chocolate desserts, fruit tarts, cheesecake, and ice cream.

MATT BREWING COMPANY The grand train station in Utica, New York, designed by the firm that designed Manhattan's Grand Central Station, is a testament to the city's former status as a major textile center. Brand names still refer to "Utica" sheets, but they are now made in Malaysia. This area of central New York, at the edge of the Adirondack Mountains, was once dense with breweries. Only one has survived into the modern age. A full-fledged regional brewery, the Matt Brewery was once famous for Utica Club, a standard post-Prohibition mass-market beer. Despite the striking giant neon sign glowing its name from the roof of the handsome brewhouse building, Utica Club has fallen out of fashion and is rarely seen outside the local area. Frances Xavier Matt, known as F. X., inherited the brewery built by his German grandfather in the 1850s, and he devoted his life to its survival. His single-minded tenacity saw the brewery through difficult years, and he had the vision to join the craft brewing movement, first through contract production and then through the Saranac line of beers. F. X. Matt opened his kettles to two entrepreneurs—Steve Hindy and Tom Potter—in 1987, when they came to him looking to produce their first beer, Brooklyn Lager. The Matt Brewery still produces beer under contract for several firms, including the Brooklyn Brewery, though we now brew in Brooklyn as well. The Matt Brewery's own Saranac brand, named for a nearby lake, features full-flavored, well-balanced beers brewed for easy drinkability. The popularity of these beers helped restore the brewery to health. By the time F. X. died a few years ago, he was a respected town father and a legend among brewers. His brother Nicolas and son Frederick now handle the business, which is entirely family-owned.

There is something wonderfully traditional yet utterly American about **Saranac Black & Tan**. The brewery doesn't call it a porter, but it falls firmly within that style. The beer is a blend, just as the original porters were. In this instance, an Irish-style stout is blended with a German-style amber lager. By the late 1800s, many American porters were brewed with lager yeasts, so this beer manages to combine the history of English, German, and American porter. Black & Tan has a deep reddish-brown color and a pleasant aroma of hay, hops, earth, dark fruit, and chocolate. The bitterness is crisp but pulls its punch to allow coffeeish roast to show through in the dry, medium-bodied, juicy center. There are some nice caramel notes before it glides out to a long, dry finish, flashing a burst of pruny fruit on the way out. Fresh malt flavors linger. This beer is very nice with steaks, burgers, ham and Swiss sandwiches, baked ham, barbecue, and Cajun blackened pork chops.

THE BROOKLYN BREWERY While Brooklyn Lager is my brewery's flagship, our imperial stout may well be our most famous beer. In 1994 I was the brewmaster of the Manhattan Brewing Company. Steve Hindy, president of the Brooklyn Brewery, was thinking about luring me across the river to build a new brewery. Steve and I were already friends, so before I'd even made up my mind, we embarked on a project to produce a new beer for the Brooklyn Brewery. Steve said that he wanted a new beer for the winter holidays, one that would make a dramatic statement with its bold flavor. "Once people taste it," he said, "I don't want them ever to forget it." Steve decided that this beer should be a strong stout, and he coined the name **Brooklyn Black Chocolate Stout** to describe the flavor he wanted. Within several days, I had written a recipe and brewed a seven-barrel batch at Manhattan Brewing Company. A few weeks later, I brought the beer to a meeting at Brooklyn Brewery. We originally thought we might actually add chocolate to the beer, but it turned out to be unnecessary—the blend of roasted malts gave the beer the flavor Steve and I had been looking for. The beer had basically been my résumé; I was hired. A few months later, we produced the first batch of Brooklyn Black Chocolate Stout. At first, we were worried that there might not be an audience for a very strong stout. That worry didn't last long—the beer sold out within two weeks. It was gone so fast that we forgot to hold on to any, and we had to go to shops to buy some for ourselves. To this day, people ask about it wherever we go, and it has won many awards.

Brooklyn Black Chocolate Stout is indeed quite black and raises a firm tan head. The aroma is deeply chocolaty, with strong coffee notes and fruity, winy notes reminiscent of the best Belgian or French dark chocolates. Sharp bitterness, accentuated by the roast, strikes first, but it is quickly joined by off-dry juicy malts, sending waves of intense chocolate and coffee flavor across the soft, rounded, full-bodied palate. Fruit and licorice join the chocolate and espresso in the center, before the beer dives into a long, drying, winy finish. Chocolate lingers in the aftertaste, along with a hoppy tang. We do three mashes for every batch of Black Chocolate Stout. The "first runnings," the concentrated wort extracted from the mash before it is rinsed with water, are taken from each mash, and then the mash is discarded, still loaded with plenty of sugars. (Every year,

Wine cannot match well with chocolate, but strong stouts do so beautifully.

some cows get very lucky when this stuff shows up in their feed.) This leaves us with an undiluted wort, which is fermented into a beer with a strength of nearly 9 percent. It's aged for more than two months before it leaves the brewery. Many people like to age it in their own cellars, feeling that it improves over time. As it ages, it becomes leaner and smoother, developing notes of sherry and port. Brooklyn Black Chocolate Stout is the ultimate dessert beer and makes a fine match for fruit tarts, ice creams, soufflés, chocolate desserts, and actual chocolates. You can have it as a dessert unto itself, or with your favorite cigar. If you've got a Cohiba Esplendido in your humidor, here's its partner.

American Fruit Beers

Many Americans first encounter Belgian brewing in the form of kriek (fermented with cherries) or framboise (fermented with raspberries). Both are usually though not always based on tart lambic beers or acidic Flemish brown ales. American breweries rarely produce these tart styles, yet many are in love with the idea of producing beer with fruit. And there's the rub.

American fruit beers fall into two basic categories. Brewers seduced by the "dark side" of fruit will succumb to the ease of "natural" extracts. These are oils and essences that largely carry some of the aroma of the original fruit—but they have very little true flavor. A fad for fruit beers rippled through the craft brewing community a few years ago, and an unfortunately large number of brewers decided to flavor their beers with extracts. These beers taste like a caricature of Belgian lambics, and they have little to recommend them. Most of them faded quickly from the market, but there are still some lurking out there, ready to pounce on the unsuspecting. If a label says something along the lines of "Ale with Natural Fruit Flavors," move on. The dark side leads to disappointment.

Brewers entranced by the "light side" of fruit will be inspired by the Belgians to do things the hard way, and their beers can ultimately provide a real reward at the table. These beers will be refermented with whole fruit, or at least with fruit purees. The base beer is often an American-style wheat beer, chosen for its light body, low bitterness, and slightly tart edge. Other breweries add fruit to golden ales. Fruit or puree is usually introduced into the fermenting or conditioning vessel after the main fermentation has finished. The yeast will attack the fruit sugars, starting a refermentation during which the flavors of the fruit will suffuse into the beer, completely transforming it.

The results are as varied as the imaginations of the brewers. Some are bone-dry while others are quite sweet. A wheat beer may be given a light blush of cherry or raspberry flavor and take on a rosy glow. A golden ale may spend months consuming huge amounts of fruit, becoming a beer with great fruit depth and intensity. Some brewers, inspired by their favorite Belgian beers, will introduce fruit to a special lambic-like beer they've created by using a collection of wild yeasts and souring bacterial strains. While true lambic is produced only in Belgium, some of these American fruit beers are very interesting, and a few are spectacular. The best of them display a depth surpassing that of most Belgian versions. Fruit is very expensive, and the breweries producing these beers tend to be small and fiercely dedicated to their art.

The Belgians haven't stuck to the traditional cherries and raspberries, and neither have the Americans. While judging at the Great American Beer Festival, I've had dozens of beers made with all sorts of fruit. Bananas, oranges, strawberries, damson fruit, grapes, raisins, cranberries, plums, passion fruit, mangoes, and black currants have all ended up married to beer, with varying degrees of success. Some have been dismissed ruefully, while others have induced smiles of surprised delight. If you'd told me that I'd enjoy a beer brewed with oranges, I wouldn't have believed you, but it was really delicious. When serious brewers really pull the stops out, they can create some wonderful fruit beers, and the food affinities can be unparalleled.

American Fruit Beers with Food

The obvious place for American fruit beers is with dessert, but we shouldn't ignore the possibilities earlier in the meal. Many of these beers will make excellent aperitifs, especially when served in a champagne glass or a small wineglass. They look really appealing, and the beer will certainly start conversations. If you're going to serve a fruit beer as an aperitif, you want it to be dry—we'll save the sweet versions for later. Off-dry fruit beers can be a very refreshing choice for brunch, taking a role more frequently occupied by a kir royale or a mimosa. Choose a beer with zippy acidity, just a hint of sweetness, and not too much fruit intensity, and it will work nicely with the majority of brunch dishes.

These beers can also be an excellent choice for salads. Raspberry vinaigrettes are very popular, and a well-made raspberry beer can dovetail perfectly. Raspberry flavors seem to have a particular affinity for balsamic vinegar, and raspberry beers take well to balsamic-based salad dressings. If a salad is dressed with goat cheese, you'll have an even better match, since goat cheese and fruit are great partners.

Semisweet fruit beers are surprisingly versatile with a range of savory dishes. Keep an open mind, and you can have a lot of fun here. Any meat that is sometimes served with a fruit-based sauce may match beautifully with a fruit beer. Here you can try beers that show considerable fruit intensity while keeping the sugar in balance. Venison and wild boar, which take well to sour cherries, will also enjoy an encounter with a well-made cherry beer. Duck and goose go very well with a wide variety of fruit beers—beers brewed with oranges, cherries, peaches, or mangoes will be the most successful. If this seems outlandish to you, think of Chinese "duck sauce" on crispy duck, and you'll get the idea. In this case, you can allow a fair amount of sweetness, since duck goes well with sweet fruit. Duck is often served with a fruit compote, and a fruit beer can take a similar role. Indian dishes are frequently served with fruit-based chutneys, some of them quite spicy. I've found that peach beers can work particularly well here, and the sweetness of the beer helps quench fiery spicing. Raitas, the tasty yogurt relishes that help put out the fire of Indian cuisine, can also link up deliciously with fruit beers. Pork is friendly to fruit—I almost always serve pork with sautéed apples. Fruit beers can make a lively accompaniment to pork chops or stuffed pork loin. If there's some fruit in the stuffing, all the better. In Mexican cuisine, pineapple and chilies are often added to pork, with brilliant results. Oranges and raisins are also used, both with pork and with chicken. Orange-, mango-, and peach-based beers are your best bet here. Finding such matches requires some creativity, but that's at least half of the fun. Wait for a creative mood to strike you, and then go for it. You may not hit a home run every time, but you'll enjoy yourself, which is the entire point of eating well.

Sweet fruit beers, or course, are great for desserts. As I mentioned in the section on fruit lambics, sommeliers should be ashamed of themselves for selling us the idea that dessert wines go with dessert. By and large, this idea is a fallacy that should be dismissed once and for all. Sauternes and chocolate? Please—on what planet is that a nice match? What are these people thinking? The Hungarian Tokajs, German trockenbeerenausleses, French Banyuls, ports, Madeiras, Italian picolits—yes, I've had them all, and they're very tasty. Just not with dessert, thank you.

American fruit beers, on the other hand, are brilliant matches for chocolate and dairy-based desserts. Cherry or raspberry beer with chocolate mud cake, mango beer with vanilla ice cream, peach beer with panna cotta, blueberry beer with crème brûlée—the possibilities are endless. There's only one pitfall here—beware matching fruit beers with fruit desserts. It sounds like a good idea, but the fruit flavors can meld too well, canceling each other out. Not a disaster by any means, but not brilliant either. (Stout is your best choice for fruit desserts.) Other than that, it's hard to go wrong. If you can't decide which beer to serve, why not serve more than one? I once served a rich Belgian chocolate ice cream with three fruit beers—cherry, raspberry, and peach—each in its own champagne glass. They glowed pink, red, and orange, with strings of bubbles streaming up to the pastel-colored foam. The guests gasped when they came to the table, then sighed with delight as they tasted the beers with the ice cream. Sauternes? Oh, please.

Notable Producer of American Fruit Beer

NEW GLARUS BREWING COMPANY Daniel and Deborah Carey are archetypal American craft brewers; they have an Irish name, Irish fortitude, German expertise, and Belgian creative flair. In the town of New Glarus, Wisconsin, they run one of the finest breweries in the United States. Deborah Carey founded the brewery in 1993, raising the start-up money as a gift for Dan, who worked as a production supervisor for Anheuser-Busch. Dan Carey had a considerable technical background, having studied brewing at the University of California–Davis and apprenticed in Bavaria. He put that background to work, brewing traditional German-style beers in a twenty-barrel kettle. Dan did the brewing, and Deborah ran the business. By 1998, they'd outgrown their equipment, so they went to Germany and came home with a gorgeous 100-barrel brewhouse. All their beers are beautifully made, but they've become most famous for their fruit beers. Inspired by Belgian lambic brewers, they ferment whole fruit in wheat-based beers that are aged in oak vats. There are many other brewers making good fruit beers in the United States, but the beers from New Glarus are singular and have won many awards.

As befits a beer with more than a pound of fruit in every bottle, **New Glarus Wisconsin Belgian Red** comes in a wine bottle, its neck dipped in red wax. Poured into a glass, the beer is quite a sight, with an intense red color reminiscent of a Beaujolais. The pink head gives it away as a beer. The nose is equally intense—cherry pie and almonds with an underlay of baking bread. The palate is startling—fat, round, sweet, and sour, with a powerful flavor of thoroughly American cherries in the juicy, fruity center. The cherries remain in full control through the long sweet finish, which signs off with an acidic tang. Malt asserts itself in the bready aftertaste. It's a breathtaking flavor experience, on the border between beer and wine. The whole cherries are of the Montmorency variety and are grown locally in Door County. New Glarus Wisconsin Belgian Red is wonderful with chocolate desserts, vanilla ice cream, cheesecake, and panna cotta. You can serve it as a dessert by itself or, if you're feeling adventurous, serve it with sautéed foie gras or roasted honey-glazed duck. You can also use it to make a sauce for duck or venison.

New Glarus Raspberry Tart comes in a similar bottle and pours deep red with a big lavender head. The aroma is packed with raspberries, with bready malts lurking underneath. Fruit acidity strikes first, followed by a flood of intense raspberry flavor. Fruity sweetness emerges in the center before the beer sails out to a long sweet-and-sour finish. Afterward, the palate feels oddly refreshed, as if by a thunderstorm of flavors. This beer is another tour de force, aged in oak vats, where it undergoes some spontaneous fermentation by wild yeasts. You can serve it as a sorbet-like palate cleanser or serve it by itself as dessert, well chilled, in a champagne glass. If it's sharing the stage after the main course, serve it with sweet cheeses such as mascarpone, teleme, or stracchino, or with intense chocolate desserts, ice cream, panna cotta, or cheesecake.

American Barley Wines

Barley wines are big beers to start with, and you'd think that they couldn't get any bigger. But this is America we're talking about—everything can get bigger, and it usually does. American craft brewers love barley wine. Is it the power, the macho swagger of a beer with a massive right hook? Is it the finesse that can be achieved with precious aging time? Is it the chance to pack as much flavor and aroma as possible into one beer? You guessed it—all of the above. Many breweries make barley wine only once a year, and it's a special day when they do. Brewers' preparations border on the

Big, bright, and powerful—Anchor's pioneering Old Foghorn barley wine.

mystical—a favorite shirt, special music in the brewhouse, the phones unplugged. They will spend the day pushing the brewhouse to its limits, squeezing out the most concentrated wort they can create, then boiling it for hours to concentrate it further. Then they'll try to coax their best friend, the yeast, to run a marathon and create a work of art.

Very strong American beers were rare before the rise of American craft brewing. Barley wines, which are voluptuously strong ales ranging from 8.5 percent to 14 percent, were originally brewed for the English aristocracy—perhaps the lack of an American aristocracy explains the fact that we missed the boat until recently. Even in the early days of microbrewing, most brewers were having a hard enough time producing their regular beers, never mind something as difficult and complex as barley wine. Barley wines must be aged for at least a few months, and many are aged for years before they're truly ready. Aging beer is expensive. The brewer who wants to produce barley wine must have both money and patience.

The best English barley wines can age for decades, but most American barley wines live fast and die young. American barley wines are excellent beers, but most of them are at their best for only five years or so. (There are exceptions—Rogue's Old Crustacean is a good example.) They make up for this by being drinkable at a much earlier age than many English barley wines, which usually need at least a few years to become really good. Sierra Nevada's Bigfoot, for example, is brilliant when it leaves the brewery and ages to a superior smoothness for a year or two. After that, its youthful hop character will fade, and the beer will still be nice, but past its prime. In this, it truly mirrors the wines it was originally meant to imitate—Barbera's youthful vibrancy lasts only a few years, while Barolo grows out of a tough, astringent youth into glorious old age. We're an impatient people; Americans don't like to wait. Perhaps we should enjoy the youthful vibrancy of the American barley wines and leave the pleasures of age to the English ones.

American Barley Wines with Food

Hoppy American barley wines have only one reliable food partner, and that's cheese. This is not to say that there aren't other possibilities—sweeter versions can match a wide range of desserts. But fruit beers and strong stouts are going to be better with desserts, so why not play to barley wine's strengths? American barley wines deploy a full peacock display of flavor and power—if pure ego could be distilled into a beer, this would be it. Wimpy cheeses need not apply.

American cheese makers are pretty bold themselves, and they make some excellent cheeses to match our barley wines. A few breweries, perhaps following the lead of Belgian monasteries, make both beer and cheese. As if owning one of America's pioneering breweries were not enough, Fritz Maytag also produces the famous Maytag Blue cheese at his dairy in Iowa. This cheese is stingingly sharp and very creamy, an excellent interpretation of the classic Danish blues. It is an excellent match to Anchor Old Foghorn.

Many barley wines show considerable residual sugar, balancing sweetness against hop bitterness. Sweeter beers can be a fine match for big blue cheeses. There are many great American blue cheeses—Bingham Hill of Colorado makes a blockbuster Rustic Blue, Great Hill Dairy of Massachusetts produces Great Hill Blue, and Point Reyes Farmstead makes Original Blue. Each of these is funky and Stiltonish when young, ripening to show a Roquefort-like "burn" on the tongue. American barley wines are big enough to tangle with these cheeses, wrapping malt sweetness around the bold mold, lifting the fat with carbonation, and then exploding on your palate. Stepping away from America for a moment, you'll also enjoy these beers with Stilton and Gorgonzola.

Sweeter barley wines can also match aged goat cheeses. In New York, Coach Farm makes a fine, austere Aged Pyramide with a beautiful cakey paste. It's incredibly rich, but a nice hoppy barley wine cuts it like a knife, then dissolves it on your tongue. Don't faint—you'll spill your beer.

Notable Producers of American Barley Wine

SIERRA NEVADA BREWING COMPANY In the Pacific Northwest, beer lovers wait patiently in the depths of winter for a glimpse of the elusive **Sierra Nevada Bigfoot**. It appears in February, and it's worth the wait. Bigfoot has a deep amber color and a gorgeous resiny nose of fresh American hops. The hop attack is fast, bright, and brash, coating the palate with crackling bitterness. Fruity malt struggles to peek through at the center but is finally overrun by the hop train, which roars out to a long bittersweet finish. The hops hang around to party long after the beer is gone. After its release Bigfoot will improve for a year or two, but at a relatively modest 9.6 percent it's not really built for the long haul. After a year, the scorching bitterness will have mellowed a bit, allowing some nice malt character to shine through. If you love hops, this beer has an odd drinkability—it's often served by the pint, and I've been a victim more than once. If you're feeling adventurous, try Bigfoot with quesadillas; its piney hop character is great with snappy Mexican food. Otherwise, go for a big, fruity aged farmhouse cheddar.

THE BROOKLYN BREWERY Most American brewers love to make barley wines, and I'm certainly not immune to the siren song of the challenge. We first brewed our barley wine in 1997 and decided to call it "Monster." Call me childish, but I've always wanted a beer called Monster. We put Bach's Toccata and Fugue in D Minor and Carl Orff's *Carmina Burana* on the stereo system and got to work. The mash was so large that it threatened to leap out of the mashing vessel, and the entire building filled up with the powerful aroma of English Maris Otter malt. We had a ball. We've brewed **Brooklyn Monster Ale** every year since, as a winter seasonal. It has a deep amber color and a bready malt aroma with an overlay of hops and orange marmalade. The hops crackle up front on the palate and then give way to a soft, round, medium-bodied off-dry center full of malt, fruit, and caramel flavors. The beer dries into a long, spirituous finish. I recently attended a tasting of Brooklyn Monster Ale at the Blind Tiger, the premier beer bar in New York City. The tasting was called "the Five-Headed Monster," since it featured all five years that the beer had been released. I found it fascinating to see how the beer aged—very nicely, so far. Enjoy Monster Ale with strong blue cheeses, aged Gruyère or Gouda, or a smooth medium-bodied cigar.

ANCHOR BREWING COMPANY San Francisco's Anchor Brewing Company, first in so many things, introduced its barley wine in 1975. The owner, Fritz Maytag, was inspired by beers he'd sampled in England and restored the barley wine style to these shores. **Anchor Old Foghorn** was the first modern American barley wine, and it has lost none of its character over the years. It comes in a 7-ounce "nip" bottle, the customer's first clue that this is a sipping beer. The color is a pretty mahogany, and the nose is packed with resiny, citric hops and bubblegummy fruit. Malt sweetness makes the first impression, but bitterness quickly steps in and the palate dries. The juicy, bubblegum fruit character occupies the round, medium-body center, along with some nice caramel flavors. The finish is short and hoppy, with deliciously bready grain flavors lingering in the aftertaste. This beer shows less malt concentration than classic English barley wines, relying instead on massive fruit and a very full-flavored hop presence. The end result is reminiscent of a great bourbon. Try it with aged Gruyère, boerenkaas, Parmigiano Reggiano, or the famous Maytag Blue, made on the family's farm in Iowa. It's also excellent with cigars, and the nip bottle fits a good robusto perfectly.

ROGUE ALE BREWERY Oregon's Rogue Brewery has always done things its own way. Its approach to the barley wine style is a good example of the "extreme brewing" that has become popular among craft brewers on the West Coast. **Rogue Old Crustacean** looks innocent enough in its little 7-ounce bottle. It even has a twist-off cap. The beer has a burnished mahogany color and a wonderful aroma of concentrated fruity malt with a minty, resiny hop overlay. The beer opens up round, sweet, and fruity, but then comes the sucker punch. Broad, massive bitterness comes out of nowhere and completely takes over, driving the beer into a long, dry, bitter finish. Hops linger menacingly, as if daring you to try another sip. This is quite possibly the bitterest beer I've ever tasted. The bottle I'm tasting is three years old, but it's still pretty tough stuff; even at 10.5 percent, the hops still overwhelm the malt. I once ran into the brewmaster John Maier and apologized for a magazine article in which I described young bottles of Old Crustacean as tasting "like turpentine." To my surprise and relief, he laughed. "Oh, no, you can't drink it when it's young," he said. "It needs at least a few years." The bottle says that the beer is best when aged for one year. Unless you're a committed hophead, I'd wait five years. Old Crustacean has a lot going on, and the hops eventually mellow, bringing a pleasant balance. The Pacific Northwest is hophead country, and this beer is revered by many of its denizens. Try it with Stilton or another big, buttery blue cheese.

10

UNIQUE SPECIALTIES

TRY AS I MIGHT, NOT ALL BEER STYLES FIT NEATLY INTO BROAD CATEGORIES. A FEW DISTINCTIVE STYLES HAVE FLOWN BELOW THE RADAR OF HISTORICAL TRENDS AND EMERGED INTO THE TWENTY-FIRST CENTURY AS INTERESTING—AND TASTY—LOCAL ANOMALIES.

ALTBIER

When lager brewing set out to conquer the world in the mid-1800s, not everyone got with the program. Though Germany was the center of the lager revolution, the cities of Düsseldorf, Münster, and Hanover retain a tradition of top-fermenting ale in the form of altbier. *Alt*, "old," is an adjective that Germans tend to use wistfully. No doubt its application to this style of beer at one time signified defiance in the face of change; some brewers continued to make the "old beer" from the days before lagers. Düsseldorf was once a great mining city, and it is not hard to imagine mine workers standing by their beer. Altbier is similar to ales found in Belgium and England, but the German style has its own unmistakable personality.

Düsseldorfer altbier has a color ranging from deep bronze to russet brown and a firm tan head. Its aromatics are faintly fruity, with biscuity underpinnings and pleasant hop notes. On the palate, only a hint of fruit gives it away as an ale—the flavors are very clean and round, with a medium-bodied malty center supported by a refreshingly sharp whack of hop bitterness. The finish is dry and clipped short. The beers are fermented warm but are matured at relatively cold temperatures for up to several weeks; this practice takes off the rough edges and produces a beer that is smooth despite its distinctive hoppiness. Altbiers are brisk and relatively light, usually reaching a strength just short of 5 percent.

Just as helles is the everyday beer of the Bavarians, Düsseldorfers tend to stick to their altbier. It is usually served in a short, cylindrical glass holding a

When cold-fermented lagers crashed the gate in the 1800s, some towns erected barricades. *Altbier* means "old beer," and this warm-fermented style is still a specialty in Düsseldorf, Germany. It's great with pork.

third of a liter. Some taverns dispense the beer directly from the barrel to the glass. If you ever find yourself in Düsseldorf, you should take the opportunity to visit the city's four brew pubs, particularly the famous Zum Uerige, whose altbier is prized for its hop character. The others—Zum Schlüssel, Im Fuchschen, and Ferdinand Schumacher—produce very fine examples as well. The hoppiness of altbier cuts through the heaviness of the local food, which tends to center on various parts of the pig. Should your meal lean in a different direction, you'll find that the snappiness of altbier works with a wide variety of dishes.

Altbier with Food

The combination of hop bitterness, full malt flavor, and restrained fruitiness makes altbier wonderfully versatile with food. The caramelized malt flavors will latch onto similar flavors in roasted chicken, grilled tuna, and many other foods. The hops give the beer the cutting power to handle sauces and gravies with aplomb. In Düsseldorf, tastes tend to run toward pork, including pork liver. Here too the beer works exceedingly well, and though I usually stick to plain old pork, good preparations of pig's feet make a fine accompaniment. In New York, Mario Batali's Lupa turns out an excellent version, as does Kerry Heffernan at 11

Madison Park. These are refined versions, terrific with altbier. The version you'll find in Germany tends to be more rustic.

Altbiers are very good with all manner of sausages, and most are robust enough to handle a loaded-up burger. I also enjoy these beers with cassoulet—the beer is malty and spicy enough to match the flavors nicely, and the hops slice through the density of the beans. Altbier is also snappy enough to handle burritos, quesadillas, and even pizza. Also, try it with full-flavored fatty fish—grilled salmon steaks are nice—and spicy crab cakes.

Notable Producers of Altbier

PRIVATBRAUEREI FRANKENHEIM The Frankenheim family still owns the large brewery founded by Heidrich Frankenheim in 1857. **Frankenheim Alt** has a full amber color and an impressively fluffy head. The aroma is malty with a note of light, raisiny fruit. Snappy, crisp hops step in first, followed by racy caramelized malts on a medium-bodied dry frame. The finish is brisk, hoppy, and short. This is an intriguingly hoppy beer that could almost pass for an American amber ale by a particularly judicious brewer. The forward use of hops and the restraint of the fruit and caramel give this beer great drinkability. You could serve it with traditional pork dishes, but it really seems to want a steak to sink its teeth into.

GROLSCH BIERBROUWERIJ When the name Grolsch is mentioned, the green swing-top bottle comes to mind. Grolsch has been using that bottle since 1897, and the beer inside is a European-style pilsner, which is ubiquitous. To look at Grolsch's website, you wouldn't even know that this brewer produces a top-fermented altbier, **Grolsch Amber Ale**. It is usually found in a clear bottle with a normal crown cap. It has a deep amber color, and the nose is softly malty, showing some caramel but little hop or fruit. The palate is superbly balanced, with light hopping bouncing off juicy, lightly fruity, caramelized malts on a dry, medium-bodied frame. The finish is short, dry, and very clean. This beer is pleasant with grilled chicken sausages, bratwurst, roast beef, pork chops, and breaded veal. It's tasty but not terribly robust, so try to resist piling too much onto that burger.

ALASKAN BREWING COMPANY Juneau, Alaska, was originally a mining town. Once gold was discovered in 1881, breweries started to pop up in the area. To those of us in the lower forty-eight, Alaska sounds like an inhospitable place for breweries, but during its gold rush it was home to nearly fifty. By the end of Prohibition, they were all gone. In 1986, the homebrewer and chemical engineer Geoff Larson and his wife, Marcy, opened the first brewery in Alaska since the

1920s. Larson based his first recipe on a beer that a German immigrant had brewed for local residents around 1900. From the information he could gather, it seemed that this old beer had been brewed in the German altbier style, so after several trials he selected a top-fermenting altbier yeast strain and brewed **Alaskan Amber**. It has an attractive bright amber color and an appetizing aroma of fresh malt with a light bubblegum note in the background. Crisp hopping opens up the medium-bodied palate, quickly followed by superbly juicy malts, developing light caramel and fruit flavors in a rounded center. The finish is long, dry, and clean and leaves the tongue almost strangely refreshed.

As it turns out, brewing in Alaska isn't easy, and Geoff and Marcy Larson have dealt with situations that would have had many brewers booking the first flight out of Juneau. In fact, the Larsons have flourished, falling in love with the beauty of Alaska and its local food, especially the salmon. Geoff Larson has become an expert salmon smoker, and I've enjoyed the fruits of his labor on many occasions. He even smokes malts in the Bamberg tradition and uses them in his much-imitated smoked porter. His Alaskan Amber is a delicious beer with subtle but instantaneous charms. One is tempted to drain the glass quickly. Instead, slow down and enjoy Alaskan Amber with steaks, burgers, roast chicken, sausages, crab cakes, and, of course, Alaskan king salmon.

In Germany, ye shall know a man by the beer he drinks, and this is especially true in Cologne. In German, the city is called Köln, and anything from Köln might be called Kölsch. The city has had a brewers' guild since 1254. The local Kölsch beer is revered and is as heavily protected as a baby snail darter in an American stream. No beer made outside Cologne and its designated suburbs may be referred to as Kölsch. The shape, size, and decoration of the little cylindrical glasses in which Kölsch is served are codified in law. Kölsch is an *appellation très controlée*.

Why the fuss? What are the brewers of Cologne afraid of? The big, bad wolf—pilsner. Like altbier, Kölsch is a top-fermented ale, a throwback to the days before lagers took over the Germanic world. Cologne, far closer to Brussels than to Munich, has always had close links to the Low Countries, and these links extend to the local beer culture. When pilsner finally came knocking on Cologne's door between the world wars, Cologne refused to answer. Instead, it held on to top-fermentation, lightened the color of the beer, and sued any outsider who dared to brew a beer called Kölsch. It worked. Cologne and its surroundings support about twenty breweries, all of them making Kölsch beer. It is doubtful that any other major city in the world can boast such a large number of breweries.

For all the effort, you'd think that the beer would be something wonderfully distinctive, but Cologne's brewers have settled for a style that offers simple pleasures. A typical Kölsch is a very pale top-fermenting beer brewed from pilsner malt and up to 15 percent malted wheat. The aromatics are a light mélange of hops, malt, and fruit. Bitterness is restrained, but the palate is light-bodied and bone-dry, with a soft malt flavor in the center giving way to a drying, slightly acidic finish. Smoothness is conferred by one to two months of cold conditioning. Fresh Kölsch is very delicate but oddly satisfying. Confusingly, the locals sometimes refer to the beer as *Wiesse*, local dialect for "white," especially if the beer is unfiltered. If you ask for *Wiesse*, you'll get a hazy Kölsch, not a Bavarian weissbier. Kölsch beers are very drinkable and refreshing, and since they have a strength of about 5 percent, they are beers one can stick with for the evening.

If you're in a tavern in Cologne, this may take some effort. The designated tall, cylindrical Kölsch glass holds only about six ounces of beer. By the time you manage to get one from the waiter, who slings circular trays of full glasses in an impressive if frightening manner, you'd better start thinking about how you're going to get your next one. If you become frustrated, you may decide to ask for something else, but there isn't anything else—in many cases, Kölsch is all the

You'd better order more than one—those traditional little glasses of Kölsch don't tend to last very long.

tavern sells. In such taverns, the tap, once opened, rarely closes. Few Kölsches are widely exported, but some do find their way to the United States, and several American craft brewers produce their own versions. These brewers want to produce a very light-tasting beer while preserving their own credibility, and Kölsch fills the bill. No doubt Cologne would call for their extradition.

Kölsch with Food

Kölsch beer approaches its food affinities with more diplomacy than flash. It's a lawn mower beer with flavor, and this fact alone means that it deserves a place in most refrigerators, especially in summertime. It's terrific with salads—it's light enough not to overwhelm tasty greens and will play along with hard-boiled egg, ham, cheese, or whatever else you want to toss on top. Sharp vinaigrettes won't disturb it much, so don't worry about the dressing. Delicate fish will scarcely find a better partner. Kölsch has light fruity flavors to work with citrus-based preparations, and enough bready malt flavor to echo mushrooms, especially porcinis or morels. You can even steam turbot or John Dory without fear that the beer is going to upstage the fish. It's a pleasant accompaniment to lobster, clams, shrimp, and crab too, unless the preparations are outrageously spicy. Even then, it will cool the fire nicely.

Kölsch is a team player at brunch, rowing along happily with omelettes, smoked salmon, and eggs Benedict. It's also very nice with a croque monsieur, the grilled ham and Swiss sandwich so popular in bistros in Paris, New York, and elsewhere.

In Cologne, people enjoy Kölsch with just about everything, including a wide array of pork dishes. I find maltier beers more satisfying with pork, but, frankly, there's nothing wrong with grilled pork chops and a nice cold glass of Kölsch. Kölsch doesn't step on your food's toes, so relax and go with the flow.

Notable Producers of Kölsch

PRIVATBRAUEREI HEINRICH REISSDORF The Reissdorfs were a family of farmers in the Rhineland who planted and managed land on behalf of the church. When political upheaval and disastrous weather forced them off the land, they moved to Cologne, where Heinrich Reissdorf became a tailor. He was quite a good tailor, and he made enough money to start a small brewery in 1894, when he was fifty-five years old. He built the company steadily until his death in 1901, and then his wife, Gertrude, ran it for another seven years until her death in 1908. Heinrich had five sons, so the family legacy was ensured. In 1936, Reissdorf became the first brewery to put Kölsch beer in bottles. The brewery was almost completely destroyed in World War II, but the family rebuilt it quickly. It remains completely family-owned.

Reissdorf Kölsch has a bright gold color and a lovely soft, malty aroma with oranges and hops wafting alongside. The palate is light, soft, and round, with crisp bitterness, gentle carbonation, and some fruity sweetness showing in the middle. From there it drops into a lengthy finish featuring a tiny lilt of refreshing acidity. It's a very nice rendition—light, simple, fresh, and satisfying. It's perfect for delicate fish, a far gentler partner than even a light Kabinett Riesling. If you're having turbot, especially in an earthy preparation, this will be an excellent choice. It's also great with salads and brunch dishes.

KÜPPERS The largest producer of Kölsch is Küpper's, which has a brewery on the Rhine and a taphouse on Alteburger Strasse in Cologne. Gustav Kupper founded the brewery in the 1800s, and this Kölsch is one of the few that can be found outside Germany. **Küppers Kölsch** is an excellent example of the style. It has a pale gold color and a beautiful aroma of floral hops with a nice bready malt underlay. The bitterness is crisp and light, and the beer is lightly fruity and sweet in the center but dries into the quick finish. It's soft, well rounded, and refreshing. It's not the best choice with the usual assortment of German pork dishes, but it finds a welcoming home with delicate fish, shellfish, and salads.

Most brewers were delighted when clean-tasting coke-dried malt became available in the mid-1700s, but some people never gave up on malts dried over wood fires. Just as Scotland's whisky producers have retained peat-smoked malts, citing their unique flavor contributions, several breweries in the Franconia region of Germany have done the same. The local style of smoked beer, called rauchbier (*Rauch* means "smoke"), remains particularly popular in the town of Bamberg. Bamberg is an old brewing center where monastic breweries once held sway over both body and soul. These days, it still has nine breweries to serve its 70,000 people, and there are ninety more breweries within an hour's drive. Clearly body and soul are still willing.

Two breweries in Bamberg, Heller-Trum and Spezial, brew the local specialty. Beech wood is gathered from the surrounding forests and used to fuel the smokehouses in which the malt is dried. The resulting beers are light to dark brown, with a quietly intense smokiness backed by malt in the nose. Malty smoke dominates the palate, which also sometimes finds fruity notes, and the beers finish dry. These beers are assertive and unique, and even most Germans find them odd. They are also entirely fascinating and surprisingly delicious, and they have inspired brewers in the United States and elsewhere in Europe. If you keep an open mind, you will soon see that there are many foods for which these beers can provide uniquely perfect companions.

Smoked Beers with Food

At an elaborate dinner hosted by the maltsters Thomas and Sabine Weyermann of Bamberg, I looked at the menu and innocently asked whether there were any chicken dishes. I'd been in Germany for several days, and I'd had pork with every meal. My hosts looked at each other, then at me, clearly somewhat confused. "No . . ." said Thomas. "We don't really eat . . . chickens." He looked at me as if I'd scooted down out of the hills of rural Tennessee and inquired into the availability of fried squirrels. The pork was delicious.

Smoke and pork are a natural combination, most brilliantly expressed in this country by classic barbecue. Smoked beers are an obvious choice, but you have no idea how tasty this beer is until you've had it with barbecue. The beer is like the last critical instrument in a symphony orchestra, tying together every element of the food. Ham and bacon, whether they're smoked or not, work wonderfully with smoked beers. I'm especially fond of fresh bacon or braised pork belly. At Gramercy Tavern in New York, chef Tom Colicchio serves it very simply, with the cube-shaped block of meat capped with sinfully browned fat. It's fork tender and floats on a bed of tiny green lentils. Taste it with smoked beer, and the room simply disappears, leaving just you, the beer, and the dish. It's that good.

Smoked fish and smoked meats are also obvious partners for this beer, and it works as perfectly as you'd imagine. Smoked salmon with a bit of cream cheese and dill on dark bread makes a great lunch, and the smoked beer makes everything complete. If that sounds like too much smoke flavor, believe me, it isn't.

Once you get over the initial shock of the flavor of smoked beer, you may find the strangest thing happening. Suddenly, almost everything seems to go with smoked beer. I'm not kidding. I've had smoked beer with Chinese food, and the beer picked up on the smoky flavor of black bean sauces and mushrooms. I've had it with Thai food, and it worked wonderfully with the caramel flavors developed in the wok. It's very nice with grilled fish and shrimp. It's a natural with just about any sausage you can imagine. It's terrific with burgers and steaks, bringing the flavors of an open-fire grill to dishes made in your own kitchen. Yes, it's even good with roasted chicken.

I've had this beer with Mexican food, which is full of smoky flavors such as smoked chilies and beans. When we tasted Schlenkerla Rauchbier with the Mexican food at La Palapa in New York, my friend Jim, an editor at *Gourmet*, initially turned up his nose. "I've never really liked smoked beers," he said. Three minutes later, having tasted the beer with puerco en pipian (pork tenderloin in a toasted pumpkin-seed sauce), he had completely changed his mind. We went through a raft of dishes, and we were both stunned by the beer's versatility. By the end of the meal, I was starting to contemplate buying a case of this stuff. It may be a stretch, but I almost think that we must have an instinctive prehistoric memory of the days when much of our food came into direct contact with fire. There's something about smoky flavors that is deeply satisfying, something that is not easy to explain logically. I decided to stop trying to explain it. I bought a case of Schlenkerla.

Notable Producers of Smoked Beer

BRAUEREI HELLER-TRUM *Schlenkerla* is old Bamberg dialect for someone who walks with a strange, stooped gait. Apparently such a man once owned Bamberg's Schlenkerla tavern, which was founded as a brew pub in 1678. The Heller family once owned the pub before it passed into the Trum family five generations ago. Young Matthias Trum is now learning the brewer's art. The pub remains in the town center—a handsome half-timbered building where a very good version of the hearty local cuisine is served. When the brewery needed to expand, it moved into a nearby hilly neighborhood that has since become smartly residential. The brewery is a good neighbor that hardly stands out from the other buildings. Inside the gate of the brewery, under a half shed, split stacks of beech wood sit neatly crosshatched. In the basement, small malting boxes are used to germinate barley, while old screws turn slowly through the grain to keep it separated. Several underground hallways lead to an iron door in a wall, and brewmaster Martin Knab swings it open to reveal a wood fire. As he tosses in a five-foot beech-wood log, it bursts instantly into flames. Above the firebox sits the smokehouse, where smoky air dries green malt laid out on a mesh. I held my breath as I walked in, and the moist smoke fell over me like a blanket, whirling silently through the grain. As I emerged, Matthias looked worried. "You know you'll have to have your jacket cleaned now," he said. "All my clothes smell like smoke." This smoke was somehow wonderfully inviting and reminded me of childhood campfires.

The brewery's principal beer is called **Aecht Schlenkerla Rauchbier Märzen**. It's quite a mouthful; *aecht* is an old spelling of the German word meaning "genuine," and the beer is actually a smoked märzen—hence the rest of the name. The beer has a deep brown color and a fine rocky head. The aroma stops you in your tracks; it's powerfully smoky, bringing to mind barbecue sauce, a smoky fire, bratwurst, and beef jerky. More childhood memories, this time of Slim Jims (thankfully long forgotten), come flooding back. On the palate, the smoke temporarily relents and the märzen shows itself, as sweet, round, juicy caramelized malts play through the center, gamely opposed by robust hops. The finish is short and dry, with a smoky flourish that lingers. This beer seems odd, even bizarre at first. Given a chance, it becomes deliciously compelling, and finally, with food, it comes to seem like a necessity. Paired with roast suckling pig, pork loin, braised ham hocks, or barbecued ribs, it's unbelievable. With Mexican food, it is a revelation, deftly enhancing everything—burritos, puerco en pipian, duck in mole negro sauce. It's wonderful with steaks, making them taste as if they've been cooked over beech-wood fires themselves.

Along a very similar line, the brewery also produces a smoked bock beer, with an even more intense smoke profile, balanced against fat, robust malts. A departure is represented by an incredible hybrid—a smoked wheat beer. **Aecht Schlenkerla Rauchbier Weizen** has a full brown color and is hazy with yeast. The aroma is wonderful, less barbecue-like than the märzen or bock, and more like an evocative whiff of smoke from a fireplace. The wheat, which makes up half the recipe, isn't smoked, so the weizen ends up with a less smoky profile than the other beers. On the palate, the bitterness is very light, and the traditional wheat beer yeast shows itself in a sweet burst of banana and bubble gum. The middle is spritzy and juicy, and the finish is long, fruity, and smoky. I think this beer is fabulous. It's great with almost any pork dish you can think of and every Mexican dish I've ever tasted it with. It's also great with Chinese dishes. And naturally, a better match with smoked salmon is hard to imagine.

CHRISTIAN MERZ BRAUEREI SPEZIAL Brauerei Spezial was founded in 1536 as a brew pub and remains one today. It's an old-fashioned inn, serving simple food and offering simple rooms. The brewery still does its own malting over beechwood fires. **Spezial Rauchbier** has a light honey-amber color and a pleasant aroma of smoke and toffeeish malt. The smoke character is immediately evident, but it is subdued compared with the beers produced by Schlenkerla. The bitterness is quite restrained and sweet; candyish malt breaks through to the center. Juicy malts remain in control right through into the drying finish. Smoke then reasserts itself, drifting through the aftertaste. This is a more delicate interpretation of the rauchbier style, and it is well suited to being drunk on its own. It's great with Chinese food in particular, and it also works well with Thai and Vietnamese dishes, especially those with some sweetness.

ALASKAN BREWING COMPANY When Geoff Larson moved to Juneau, he fell in love with all things Alaskan, especially the local cuisine. Across the road from the

brewery, the Taku fish smokery turns out spectacularly tasty hot-smoked salmon. One day Larson had the idea of asking the smokery to smoke some malts over an alderwood fire for him. Soon he had created a new style of beer, one that has since been much imitated but never equaled. **Alaskan Smoked Porter** is completely opaque—not even direct sunlight can punch through. The magnificent aroma starts the fun with a complex tapestry of coffee, dark chocolate, smoke, and bubble gum. The palate delivers what the nose promises, with an appetizing whack of hops up front leading into a rich, fat center packed with sweet, juicy malts. As the sweetness drops away, the roast emerges—dry, coffeeish, chocolaty, and gorgeously structured. The smoke rises behind it, and the whole show rides out to a drying, snappy finish. Coffee, hops, and smoke all linger together in the aftertaste. This is a tour de force, and quite deserving of its numerous awards. At a gala dinner for the World Beer Cup Awards at the Jerome Hotel in Aspen, I served this beer with chef Todd Slosberg's venison in a sour cherry sauce. The combination was stunning, as the beer went confidently where no wine could have gone. Alaskan Smoked Porter is also perfect with barbecue, steaks, sausages, and smoked salmon.

They wouldn't have it any other way—regulars enjoy a quiet afternoon of newspapers and rauchbier at Bamberg's Schlenkerla.

CHIMAY
VAPEUR
Reissdorf
Kölsch
Einbecker
Ur-Bock
DE KONINCK

PART THREE: The Last Word

Glassware, Temperature, Storage, and Service

Part of the fun of eating and drinking well is the accompanying ceremony. I don't mean the stilted stuffiness of overly serious French restaurants, but I do mean the heavy silverware, nice plates, and graceful glassware. Temperature, glassware, and service are at least as important for beer as they are for wine. It's not just a matter of manners—when you serve beer incorrectly, you risk taking all the flavor and fun out of it.

Imagine that you are in a fine restaurant, anticipating a brilliant meal. You order a bottle of good red wine. It's a bit expensive, but, hey—you're worth it. Now imagine that the waiter brings you a stubby little jam jar and unceremoniously pours ice-cold red wine from it into your glass. May I assume that you would be stunned, and perhaps somewhat miffed? That's about how I feel when a waiter pours an overchilled Trappist ale into a glass better suited for orange juice. In Belgium, where every brewery has its own specialized glassware, this would never happen. But you're not in Belgium, you don't have an entire cabinet full of special beer glasses, and the temperature of your fridge is set at 40 degrees Fahrenheit. So how do you get the best out of your beer at home?

PREVIOUS PAGE: Pour it as though you mean it—good glassware enhances your enjoyment of flavorful beers.

First of all, relax. Beer is supposed to be fun, and your glassware should help you get the most enjoyment out of it. Even though some labels have amusingly stern grapics admonishing you to serve the beer only in a particular glass, the fact is that you probably already have what you need. Let's take a good look at glassware.

What do we want out of a glass? Well, to begin with, we'd like to be able to see the beer and admire its color, so I always prefer a clear, clean glass. If you have a dishwasher that tends to leave a residue, it's best to rinse your beer glassware thoroughly, since trace amounts of oils or soaps will quickly kill the head on a beer,

Courtesy Chimay.

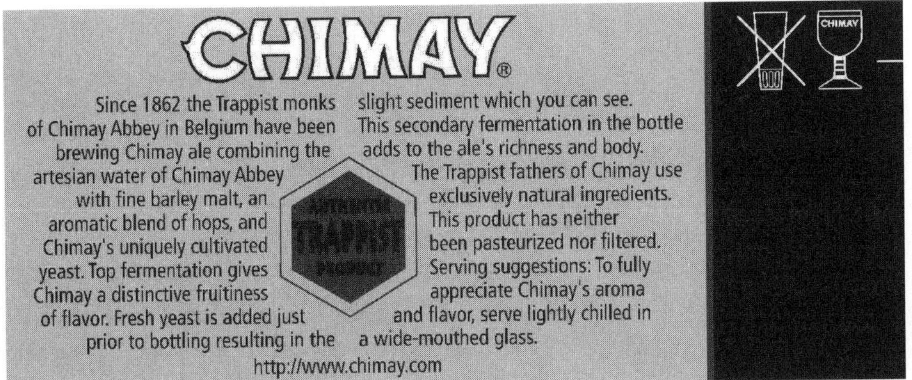

Chimay implies that pouring its complex Trappist ales into a mere tumbler would be sinful.

leaving it looking forlorn and unappetizing. Brewers refer to squeaky-clean glassware as "beer-clean," and we tend to be rather serious about it. We worked hard to get that nice fluffy head on your beer, and we'd like it to stay there, thank you very much. For most styles of beer, the head is an important part of the appearance and texture.

Next, we'd like to enjoy the beer's aromas. The best glasses in this regard are rounded, allowing you to swirl the beer a bit, releasing the aromatics as some of the beer evaporates from the sides of the glass. Is this starting to sound familiar? Most wineglasses fit this description, as do brandy snifters, and for the same reasons. Wineglasses are designed to help you get the best out of your wine. Almost any stemmed wineglass will do the same for beer. Holding the glass by the stem prevents the glass from getting grubby while you're eating, and also prevents your beer from warming up too quickly. You can serve aperitif beers such as pilsner, Belgian strong golden ales, tripels, and wheat beers in glasses designed for white wine, where they look quite elegant. These beers also look terrific in champagne flutes. For darker beers, I tend to prefer something a bit heftier, such as a glass for red wine. You can cup your hand under the bowls of these glasses if you want to warm up beer that's a bit too cold. You don't have to use wineglasses; many good glassmakers now produce suitably shaped goblets, which are widely available at department stores and housewares stores.

Of course, the best thing is to get your hands on a few nice beer glasses. Traditional beer glasses are not necessarily designed for tasting per se; rather, they are designed to emphasize or accentuate some particular attribute of the beer style they are meant for. For example, the typical Bavarian weissbier glass is about ten inches (twenty-five centimeters) tall, with a broad heavy foot, a low cinched waist, and a graceful flare up to the lip. The reason for this design is the high carbonation and voluminous fluffy head that weissbier is known for. The glass is designed to hold a good three inches of foam, and in Bavaria, pouring weissbier is an art. You'll quickly get the hang of it: pour the beer slowly down the side of the glass until it's two-thirds full, then turn the glass upright and slowly bring the head up above the rim of the glass. A properly poured glass of weissbier is a striking sight, especially in a beer garden when the sun is shining through it.

Belgian wheat beer is usually served in a chunky faceted glass tumbler that shows off the beer's hazy pale gold color and invites a deep draft on warm days. The British largely go for the classic pint glass for serving ales of relatively modest strength. British pint glasses hold nearly 20 ounces, but these are for drinking rather than tasting, and they suggest the old-fashioned proletarian appeal of the pub. In Bavarian beer halls, the stein-shaped glassware for lager beers is also large, but most German breweries produce nice stemware for other venues. Pilsner glasses tend to be tall and slender, to show off the beer's clarity and golden color. In this they bear a passing resemblance to champagne flutes. For darker beers, short-footed goblets are usually preferred. These seem to imply both elegance and sturdiness.

One of my least favorite glasses is the straight-sided American "shaker pint," a 16-ounce tumbler that was originally used to shake mixed drinks. Many American craft brewers produce it, but this is largely because bars prefer it for its sturdiness. It doesn't hold a head well, nor does it concentrate the bold aromatics of American craft-brewed beers. It's ubiquitous, though, so it's hard to avoid. It doesn't do the beer any favors, but it won't ruin the beer either. Still, I never drink out of such a tumbler at home.

The Belgians are particularly enamored of their beer glassware. A bar or restaurant that carries only two or three different wineglasses may carry more than a dozen beer glasses. Many Belgian brewers produce tulip-shaped stemware that concentrates aromatics and also helps hold a nice cap of foam on the beer. The huge short-footed tulip that announces the Belgian strong golden ale Duvel is a classic. The glass is twice the size of a bottle of Duvel—the rest of the room is reserved for the huge pillowy head. The tulip glass comes in a variety of shapes and sizes, usually with the brewery's logo printed on the side.

The Trappist and abbey brewers produce some of the nicest glasses. The usual shape is a chalice-like goblet, which is both beautiful and evocative. When you drink from these goblets, it's hard to escape the feeling that you've found the Holy Grail. A nicely poured chalice of Chimay, Orval, or Westmalle is almost too handsome to resist, and I have to admit that I don't usually try very hard. If you have a good beer shop near you, it may well have some brewery glassware for sale. Many American craft breweries make some fine glassware, too. At Brooklyn

Brewery, we make standard American pint glasses, traditional weissbier glasses, stein-shaped Oktoberfest glasses, chunky witbier glasses, and snifters for enjoying our imperial stout and barley wine. We occasionally brew a batch of Brooklyn Abbey Ale—can a chalice be far behind?

Here's a piece of advice, one that probably pegs me as a real New Yorker. If you order a nice bottle of beer in a restaurant, and the server gets ready to pour it into some little juice glass, politely stop him and ask for a wineglass meant for white wine. Assert yourself—you're the one paying for the beer, and you have a right to have it served well. You'll enjoy your beer far better, believe me.

If you're having a barbecue or a picnic, the last thing you need is to be worrying about your nice glassware. It would take the patience of a monk to forgive someone who'd just smashed your beautiful Trappist chalice. We're chilling out here, and worry about glasses isn't conducive to relaxation. Swigging out of the bottle is for rank amateurs: the beer warms up quickly; you can't enjoy the head or aroma; the beer will be overly gassy; and besides, you wouldn't chug wine out of a bottle, would you? There's a happy middle ground here—plastic. This will sound like heresy to some serious beer lovers, but the fact is that really decent plastic glasses are available these days. I'm talking not about Dixie cups but about solid plastic stemware. Big chains such as Crate and Barrel, Pottery Barn, and Williams-Sonoma stock handsome, thick plastic stemware, and some of it is quite nice and inexpensive. Much of it looks just like glass, has no plastic aroma, has a broad sturdy base, and can be put through the dishwasher. What's not to like? I wouldn't use plastic at the dinner table, but it does a great job outdoors when I don't want to bring out my good glasses.

Temperature

With beer, just as with wine, temperature has a major effect on flavor. Cold temperatures enhance dryness, bitterness, carbonation, and refreshment but lower your perception of flavor, aroma, and body. Conversely, warmer temperatures enhance body, aromatics, sweetness, acidity, and flavor. What we're looking for, then, is a happy balance, and that balance falls in different temperature ranges for different styles of beer. Americans tend to drink red wine too warm, white wine too cold, and beer virtually frozen. Serving beer ice-cold is prudent if you want to stun your taste buds into accepting a can of mass-market beer, but terrible if you'd like to taste what you're drinking.

What's the right temperature for your beer? The honest answer is "It depends"; but here are some simple guidelines. Most lagers do well at cool temperatures,

between 40 and 48 degrees Fahrenheit. Your refrigerator is probably set at 40 degrees, and while that's on the cold side, it's fine for pilsner and helles, especially in warm weather. Lagers don't usually have fruity flavors or aromatics to express, so there's less need to let the beer warm up in order to release them. Lager flavors are clean and straightforward, and a chill suits them. Darker styles of lager such as dunkel and doppelbock have plenty of deep malt flavor, though, so they'll prefer the upper end of that temperature range. Many Bavarian bars have beer-warming trays; patrons who prefer their beer warmer can sink their glasses into warm water to remove the chill. There's no need for such drastic measures at home; taking the beer out of the refrigerator ten or fifteen minutes before you plan to serve it will usually do the trick.

Ales develop fruity flavors and aromas during their warm fermentations. The more complex or subtle these flavors are, the warmer you might wish to serve the beer. Bavarians serve weissbier at about 50 degrees Fahrenheit, but a few degrees cooler won't hurt, and will make the beer more refreshing. Similarly, Belgian witbier is best at about 45 degrees, but pouring it a little colder is certainly no crime. Traditional British ales taste their best at 52 to 60 degrees, which we'll refer to as "cellar temperature." These temperatures are not warm; they are slightly cool, but not cold. If you serve British ales cold, you'll miss all the subtle flavors and aromatics they are prized for.

Most Belgian ales also taste best in this temperature range. Generally speaking, paler beers, such as tripels, will express themselves best at the lower end, around 52 degrees, while darker beers will flourish at slightly warmer temperatures. If your beer is in the refrigerator, take it out at least half an hour before you plan to serve it. If it's warm, half an hour or less in the refrigerator will probably cool it sufficiently.

Again, the most important thing is to relax and enjoy your beer. If you feel it's too warm, stick it in the freezer for a few minutes; if it's too cold, you can wrap your hands around the bottle or glass to warm it up. Erring on the cold side is best, since the beer can always warm up in your glass. There's little basis for the myth that beer shouldn't be quickly chilled, or that sudden temperature fluctuations will ruin it. That said, if you've got some nice beer, you should do your best to store it properly.

Unless you have a beer that is meant to age, it is always best to store beer in a cold, dark, dry place. In other words, in your refrigerator. If your refrigerator won't hold your entire supply, choose the coolest place in your house or apartment and store the beer there in a box. Heat damages beer by bringing on premature aging and staleness—most beers are at their best when they leave the brewery, and you'll want to keep them fresh. Light damages beer by reacting with hop components to form "skunky" aromatic compounds. Brown glass bottles help protect beer from the ultraviolet rays that do the damage, but green glass affords little protection. Clear glass is even worse—good beer in clear glass bottles should always be stored in complete darkness.

Some American mass-market brewers do use clear glass bottles. They avoid the "skunking" problem by avoiding hops altogether; instead, they use chemically altered hop extracts that won't react with light. How very appetizing. Somehow, this reminds me of Dracula, and the idea that you can't see him in a mirror. The undead have many tricks at their disposal, so beware.

If you want to age a fine strong ale, you should seek to store it at cellar temperatures. About 55 degrees Fahrenheit is perfect, but few of us have any place in our homes that remains at such a temperature year-round. The refrigerator is the wrong place to age your beer—the cold will prevent the maturation that you're looking for. So you'll just have to do the best you can. Keep the bottles upright in the coolest, darkest place in your home. Unlike great wine, great beer is usually inexpensive, so you can afford to experiment. Just don't forget to taste a bottle every once in a while—that *is* why you bought the beer, isn't it?

A few quick words about service. Now that you have your good, squeaky-clean glassware and the beer is at the right temperature, you're ready to pour. Generally speaking, the glass should be tilted first, and the beer should be poured gently down the side of the glass. This preserves the carbonation and prevents foaming over. Pour down the side, and when the glass is about two-thirds full, turn the glass upright and pour the rest into the center to raise the head to the lip of the glass. For most beers, a head "two fingers" high is perfect. When you drink the beer, some of the foam goes down with it, contributing to a creamier texture. And a beer with a fluffy head looks better, too, doesn't it?

If you're planning to host a beer dinner, as I do frequently, there's one simple rule that will help you best enjoy the beers. That rule is to serve the beers in order of *impact on the palate*. If this sounds like an esoteric idea, let's think about it. If we were to serve a delicate fish after a charbroiled steak, wouldn't that seem strange? We tend to arrange our meals so that lighter dishes come before heavier ones. The same should be true of our beers. If you serve a light Belgian witbier after a powerful imperial stout, the witbier will taste very thin. So try to start with lighter-bodied, less bitter beers and work your way up to heavier ones. You might serve the light witbier with a salad; a snappy pilsner with the salmon; a fruity, chocolaty American brown ale with the short ribs; and an espresso-like imperial stout with the chocolate tart. Then, perhaps, a small glass of barley wine with the cheese course?

The same principle especially applies to a beer tasting, where there's no food to interact with the beer on the palate. The correct order helps give each beer its star turn and lets it show its best at the table. Sometimes, figuring out the best order is tricky. Do the best you can, and remember afterward what worked well and perhaps not as well. You can also taste the beers side by side before the dinner or tasting to help determine the order. That would be an expensive proposition with good wine, but beer is an affordable luxury, so we can relax and open a few bottles. Never forget to have fun. *Bon appétit!*

Beer with Food: A Reference Chart

Let me be plain here—this table is *not* the definitive word on matching beer with food. If it were, there would have been little point in writing a whole book on the subject. Instead, this is a crib sheet meant to give you some quick suggestions. If you're on your way out the door, and you have to decide what beer to buy to match your dinner, I hope this will help you out. I haven't listed every food known to man, nor have I listed every style of beer that might match a dish, but these beers will tend to match nicely with these foods.

Aioli Belgian strong golden ale and saison

Almonds, salted British or American brown or pale ale

Anchovies, salted Well-chilled north German pilsner

Apple pie Imperial stout, strong Baltic porter, cream stout

Asparagus Belgian tripel

Au gratin potatoes Doppelbock, dunkel, Oktoberfest märzen

Avocado (as salad or guacamole) American pale ale and IPA

Bacon

With eggs at brunch Bavarian weissbier or Belgian witbier

With other savory dishes Belgian dubbels, German rauchbiers and doppelbocks

Bananas (fried, or with dessert) Weissbock, imperial stout

Bass (grilled) Weissbier, witbier, north German pilsner

Beans Doppelbock, bière de garde, British and American brown ale

Beef

Roast British bitter and pale ale, German altbier

Braised, short ribs, cheeks Belgian dubbel and strong dark Trappist and abbey ales

Beets Weissbier, witbier, sweeter abbey ales and doppelbocks

Biriyani Weissbier, weissbock, Belgian strong golden ale, saison

Bison (steak) American brown ale, porter

Blinis (with fish or caviar) Very well chilled Czech or German pilsner

Bouillabaisse Tripel, bière de garde, Belgian strong golden ale

Brandade (bacala) Weissbier, sharp pilsner, Belgian strong golden ale

Brownies Imperial stout, Baltic strong porter

Burgers American brown ale, pale ale and IPA, schwarzbier, altbier, American amber lager

Burritos American pale and brown ale, altbier, smoked beers

Caesar salad Weissbier, witbier, American wheat beer, Kölsch

Cajun American pale and brown ale, schwarzbier, dunkel, saison

Calamari (fried) Pilsner, helles, Kölsch, American amber lager, American pale ale, saison

Calf's liver Strong dark Trappist and abbey ales

Carbonnade flamande Dubbel, strong dark Trappist or abbey ale, doppelbock, stronger Flanders brown ales, old ale

Caribbean Pilsner, American pale ale, saison, Irish or foreign-style stout

Carpaccio Weissbock, British pale ale or bitter

Cassoulet Bière de garde, dubbel, doppelbock

Caviar Very well chilled north German pilsner

Ceviche Gueuze, Flanders red and brown ales, Berliner weisse

Charcuterie Bière de garde, Belgian pale ale, dubbel, Oktoberfest märzen

Cheese (See page 58.)

Cheesecake Sweet fruit beer, Baltic strong porter, imperial stout, American stout

Chicken Depends on the dish, but these suggestions are good if it's by itself.

Roasted Bière de garde, dunkel, bock, British bitter and pale ale, British brown ale, Oktoberfest märzen, dubbel, American amber ale, Belgian pale ale

Fried American amber lager, American brown ale, altbier

Barbecued American amber and brown ales, American amber lager, porter, smoked beers

Tandoori American pale ale, saison, Belgian strong golden ale

Chili, con carne or Texas-style American pale ale, brown ale and IPA, Irish stout, smoked beers

Chili relleno American pale ale or IPA, smoked beer, doppelbock, Irish stout

Chinese (broadly speaking) Weissbier, weissbock, smoked beers, dunkel, Belgian strong golden ales

Chocolate Sweeter fruit beers, imperial stout, stronger American stout, Baltic strong porter

Chorizo American pale ale and IPA, saison, or if flavoring a delicate dish, Belgian strong golden ale

Choucroute Belgian pale ale, Oktoberfest märzen, bière de garde, dunkel, doppelbock, weissbock

Chowder Weissbier, witbier, helles, Kölsch, pilsner

Chutneys Strong saison, strong Flanders red or brown ale

Clams Pilsner, Belgian strong golden ale, helles, Kölsch

Cod (fried) British bitter or pale ale, pilsner, American amber ale

Coq au vin Bière de garde, dubbel

Corn on the cob Helles, Kölsch, Dortmunder, weissbier

Couscous Witbier, weissbier, helles, American pale ale, Belgian strong golden ale

Crab Witbier, weissbier, helles, pilsner, Irish stout, saison

Crème brûlée Old ale, barley wine, stronger doppelbocks, Baltic strong porter, American stout, imperial stout, sweet framboise and kriek

Croque monsieur Helles, Dortmunder, Kölsch, altbier, witbier, weissbier, Oktoberfest märzen

Crudités Bière de garde, dunkel, weissbier, tripel

Dim sum Weissbier, helles, American wheat beer, Kölsch

Duck

Roasted Dubbel, strong dark Trappist or abbey ales, doppelbock, weissbock, bière de garde

Honey-glazed or with fruit sauce Off-dry framboise, kriek, and other fruit beers; sweeter doppelbocks; strong dark Trappist or abbey ales; cream stouts; Baltic porters

Crispy-spicy Pilsner, saison, American pale ale and IPA

Confit Bière de garde, dubbel, doppelbock, drier fruit beers

Eel (smoked) Weissbier, smoked beers

Eggs Weissbier, witbier, American wheat beer, helles, Kölsch

Empanadas American pale ale and IPA, saison, pilsner

Enchiladas (in general) American pale ale and IPA, doppelbock, Oktoberfest märzen, smoked beers, Irish stout

Fajitas American pale ale, brown ale, and IPA; American amber lager; saison; Irish stout

Falafel Saison, American IPA, pilsner, Dortmunder

Fish cakes Weissbier, witbier, helles, Dortmunder, Kölsch, gueuze

Foie gras Sweet doppelbocks, sweet barley wines, off-dry strong dark Trappist or abbey ale, off-dry framboise and kriek, stronger Flanders red and brown ales, strong Scotch ales

Fondue (cheese) Bière de garde, dunkel, Oktoberfest märzen, hellesbock

Fruit tarts Imperial stout, cream stout, American stout, strong Baltic porter

Game Bière de garde, dubbel, strong dark Trappist or abbey ale, doppelbock, strong Scotch ale

Goose Dubbel, strong dark Trappist or abbey ales, doppelbock, weissbock, strong Baltic porter

Goulash Spiced beers, dunkel, doppelbock, strong dark Trappist or abbey ale, English brown ale, Baltic porter

Guacamole American pale ale and IPA, American amber lager

Gumbo American pale ale, brown ale, and IPA; American amber lager; Dortmunder; weissbock

Haddock (smoked) Weissbier, smoked beer

Haggis Strong Scotch ale, smoked beer

Halibut Witbier, weissbier, Kölsch, helles, American wheat beer

Ham

Baked Irish stout, pilsner, Dortmunder, hellesbock, Oktoberfest märzen, tripel, Belgian strong golden ale, English brown ale

Aged (prosciutto, Serrano, Bayonne) Irish stout, schwarzbier, porter, hellesbock, doppelbock, Dortmunder, weissbock

Herring (pickled) Pilsner, Flemish red and brown ale, gueuze, Berliner weisse

Hummus Weissbier, Oktoberfest märzen, Belgian pale ale, dunkel, bockbier, English brown ale

Ice cream Imperial stout, American stout, cream stout, strong Baltic porter, sweet fruit beers

Indian

Mild dishes Weissbier, witbier, helles, Kölsch, Belgian strong golden ale, pilsner, British pale ale

Spicy dishes Saison, pilsner, Dortmunder, hellesbock, American IPA

Jambalaya American pale ale and IPA, American amber lager, saison, pilsner, Irish stout, schwarzbier

John Dory Kölsch, witbier, helles

Kebabs (meat) British and American brown ales, American amber ales and lagers, strong bitter (ESB), Irish stout, schwarzbier, smokedbeers

Kidneys Dubbels, Scotch ales, strong dark Trappist and abbey ales

Kippers Smoked beers, well chilled pilsner

Lamb

Roasted Dubbels, Scotch ales, strong dark Trappist and Abbey ales, old ales, bière de garde

Grilled British and American brown ales, American amber lager, schwarzbier, Irish stout

Langoustines Weissbier, witbier, pilsner, helles, Belgian strong golden ale

Lasagna American amber lager, Belgian pale ale

Lemon tart American stout, imperial stout, strong Baltic porter, Berliner weisse (with lemon syrup)

Lentils Oktoberfest märzen, doppelbock, English brown ale, dunkel

Lobster Weissbier, witbier, pilsner, helles, Irish stout

Macaroni and cheese British bitter and pale ale, dunkel, altbier, Oktoberfest märzen

Mackerel Pilsner, American IPA, gueuze

Meatloaf British bitter, brown ale, and pale ale; porter; dunkel; Oktoberfest märzen; altbier

Melon Weissbier, framboise, kriek, Berliner weisse (with syrup)

Merguez sausage Saison, American pale ale and IPA, Dortmunder

Monkfish Weissbier, dunkel, bockbier, British bitters and brown ales, dubbels

Moroccan (in general) Weissbier, saison, American pale ale and IPA, Dortmunder, helles, Belgian strong golden ale

Mushrooms Doppelbock, dunkel, dubbel, British brown ales, Scotch ales

Mussels Witbier, weissbier, saison, gueuze, pilsner

Nachos American pale ale and IPA, American amber lager, Oktoberfest märzen, Irish stout

Nuts British brown ale, dubbels, doppelbock

Octopus Tripel, Belgian strong golden ale, weissbier, witbier

Olives Tripel, dubbel, bière de garde

Omelettes Weissbier, witbier, American wheat beer

Onion tart Bière de garde, Oktoberfest märzen, dunkel, American amber lager

Osso buco Strong dark Trappist and abbey ales, dubbels, doppelbocks, Scotch ales

Ostrich Bière de garde, tripel, Dortmunder, hellesbock

Oxtail British and American brown ales, dubbels, strong dark Trappist or abbey ales, doppelbocks, Scotch ales, old ales, light barley wines

Oysters Irish stout, pilsner, helles, Kölsch, gueuze, Flanders red ale

Paella Belgian strong golden ale, bière de garde, Dortmunder, hellesbock, bitter

Panna cotta Imperial stout, American stout, oatmeal stout, fruit beers, strong Scotch ales, Baltic strong porter

Partridge Bière de garde, dubbel, strong dark Trappist or abbey ales, old ales

Pasta

- **Cheese/cream—Alfredo, carbonara** Tripel, bière de garde, doppelbock
- **Seafood** Weissbier, Kölsch, helles
- **Meat sauce** American amber lager, Belgian pale ale
- **Pesto** Tripel, Belgian strong golden ale

Pâté Bière de garde, dubbel, strong dark Trappist and abbey ales, old ale, British or American brown ale

Peanut sauce (Satay, Thai) American pale ale and IPA, American amber lager, American brown ale, saison

Peas Weissbier, witbier

Pecan pie Imperial stout, American stout, cream stout, strong Baltic porter

Pheasant Bière de garde, dubbel, strong dark Trappist or abbey ales, old ale, strong British bitter (ESB)

Pizza American amber lager, American pale and amber ale, Oktoberfest märzen

Pork (roasted) Dunkel, dubbel, doppelbock, altbier, Oktoberfest märzen, bière de garde

Prosciuttto (see Ham)

Pumpkin pie Spiced ale, cream stout, imperial stout, oatmeal stout, strong Baltic porter

Quail Bière de garde, tripel, Belgian pale ale, best bitter

Quiche Weissbier, witbier, helles, Kölsch, American wheat beer

Rabbit Bière de garde, tripel, Belgian pale ale, strong British bitter (ESB)

Raspberries (tarts or with cream) Imperial stout, cream stout, American stout, strong Baltic porter

Ratatouille Bière de garde, tripel, Belgian strong golden ale, dubbel

Rillettes (duck or goose) Bière de garde, tripel, Belgian pale ale, dubbel, doppelbock, Oktoberfest märzen

Risotto Belgian strong golden ale, tripel, bière de garde

Salads Weissbier, witbier, American wheat beer, Kölsch, or with strong blue cheese, doppelbock

Salami Pilsner, Dortmunder, Belgian strong golden ale, tripel, saison, Irish stout

Salmon Weissbier, witbier, American wheat beer, saison, pilsner, American IPA

Salsa American pale ale and IPA, saison, pilsner, American amber lager, Oktoberfest märzen

Sardines Well-chilled dry north German pilsner, saison, gueuze, Flanders red ale

Sausages Almost all beers work well with sausages, but particularly Belgian pale ale, bitter, Oktoberfest märzen, dunkel, altbier, bière de garde, saison

Scallops If seared, then British brown ale or porter, Baltic porter, doppelbock. If spicy, then weissbier, witbier, helles, Kölsch

Sea urchin Tripel, Belgian strong golden ale, weissbock

Shepherd's pie Bitter, British brown ale, porter, Irish stout, dunkel

Shrimp Pilsner, weissbier, witbier, helles, saison, Belgian strong golden ale, American pale ale, Irish stout

Skate Witbier, weissbier, helles, Kölsch, Belgian strong golden ale

Smoked salmon Pilsner, Dortmunder, saison, weissbier, witbier, smoked beers, gueuze

Snails Pilsner, saison, Belgian strong golden ale, tripel

Snapper Saison, pilsner, helles, American wheat beer, witbier

Sole Witbier, Kölsch

Soufflè American stout and porter, cream stout, imperial stout, Baltic porter, sweeter fruit beers

Spinach (with cheese/eggs) Weissbier, witbier, Kölsch

Squid (grilled, stuffed, salads) Weissbier, witbier, Belgian strong golden ale

Steak American amber lager, American brown ale, altbier, porter, dubbel

Steak tartare Tripel, strong dark Trappist or abbey ale

Strawberries (tarts or with cream) Imperial stout, cream stout, American stout, strong Baltic porter

Sushi Weissbier, witbier, Kölsch

Sweetbreads Dunkel, doppelbock, English brown ale, Belgian pale ale

Swordfish Saison, American pale ale, tripel, weissbock, American amber lager

Tapas Weissbier, witbier, American wheat beer, pilsner, helles, Kölsch

Tarte Tatin Baltic strong porter, imperial stout, cream stout

Tempura (vegetables or seafood) Weissbier, witbier, Kölsch

Terrines Dubbel, strong dark Trappist and abbey ale, bière de garde, English or American brown ale, off-dry fruit lambic

Thai food (in general) Weissbier, saison, American pale ale and IPA, American amber lager, altbier

Tiramisu Sweet fruit beer, cream stout, strong Baltic porter

Tongue Bitter, British brown ale, dunkel

Trout Weissbier, weissbock, or if smoked, smoked beer

Truffles Bière de garde, doppelbock, strong dark Trappist and abbey ales

Tuna

Tuna salad or tartare Witbier or weissbier

Otherwise Saison, American pale ale

Turbot Weissbier, witbier, Kölsch

Turkey Bière de garde, dunkel, dubbel, Oktoberfest märzen, American amber lager

Veal Dunkel, hellesbock, Belgian strong golden ale, weissbock, saison

Venison Doppelbock, dunkel, old ale, British and American brown ale and porter, strong dark Trappist and abbey ale, strong Scotch ale, smoked beer

Vichyssoise Weissbier, doppelbock

Vietnamese (in general) Weissbier, saison, pilsner, American pale ale and IPA

Walnuts Doppelbock, dunkel, English brown ale

Wild boar Doppelbock, dunkel, porter, strong dark Trappist and abbey ale, strong Scotch ale, smoked beer

Index

Page numbers set in italics indicate an illustration reference